UNDERSTANDING GROUP BEHAVIOR

Small Group Processes and Interpersonal Relations

Volume 2

UNDERSTANDING GROUP BEHAVIOR

Small Group Processes and Interpersonal Relations

Volume 2

Erich H. Witte
University of Hamburg, Germany

James H. Davis
University of Illinois, Urbana–Champaign

LEA

LAWRENCE ERLBAUM ASSOCIATES, PUBLISHERS
1996   Mahwah, New Jersey

Lawrence Erlbaum Associates, Inc., Publishers
10 Industrial Avenue
Mahwah, New Jersey 07430

Library of Congress Cataloging-in-Publication Data

Understanding group behavior / [edited by] Erich H. Witte, James H.
Davis.
      p.   cm.
   Based on papers presented at a conference held at the University
of Hamburg, Nov. 1992.
   Includes bibliographical references and index.
   Contents: v. 1. Consensual action by small groups — v. 2. Small
group processes and interpersonal relations.
   ISBN 0-8058-1639-9 (v. 1 : cloth : alk. paper). — ISBN
0-8058-1640-2 (v. 1 : pbk. : alk. paper). — ISBN 0-8058-1641-0 (v.
2 : cloth : alk. paper). — ISBN 0-8058-1642-9 (v. 2 : pbk. : alk. paper).
   1. Small groups—Congresses. 2. Decision-making, Group—
Congresses. 3. Interpersonal relations—Congresses. I. Witte,
Erich H., 1946–   . II. Davis, James H., 1932–   .
HM.133.U526 1996
302.3′4—dc20   96-12707
                                                          CIP

Books published by Lawrence Erlbaum Associates are printed on acid-free paper,
and their bindings are chosen for strength and durability.

Printed in the United States of America
10 9 8 7 6 5 4 3 2 1

CONTENTS

Preface   **vii**

PART I: INTRODUCTION

Small-Group Research and the Crisis of Social Psychology:
An Introduction   **1**
Erich H. Witte

PART II: GROUP STRUCTURE AND COMPOSITION

1   Creating the Ideal Group: Composition Effects
at Work   **11**
Richard L. Moreland, John M. Levine, and Melissa L. Wingert

2   Social Compensation and the Köhler Effect:
Toward a Theoretical Explanation of Motivation
Gains in Group Productivity   **37**
Wolfgang Stroebe, Michael Diehl, and Georgios Abakoumkin

3   Status Congruence in Small Groups   **67**
Henk A. M. Wilke

4   Leadership: Micro–Macro Links   93
Jorge Correia Jesuino

5   Effective Teamwork—A Theoretical Model and a
Test in the Field   127
Wolfgang Scholl

6   Toward a Theory of the Acting Group   147
Mario von Cranach

**PART III: INTERPERSONAL INFLUENCE, CONFLICT,
AND RESOLUTION**

7   The Conflict Elaboration Theory of Social Influence   191
Juan Antonio Pérez and Gabriel Mugny

8   Information Seeking Among Individuals and Groups
and Possible Consequences for Decision Making in
Business and Politics   211
Dieter Frey, Stefan Schulz-Hardt, and Dagmar Stahlberg

9   Social Identity, Self-Categorization, and the Small Group   227
Michael A. Hogg

10   A Behavioral Interaction Model: Toward an Integrative
Theoretical Framework for Studying Intra- and
Intergroup Dynamics   255
Jacob M. Rabbie and Hein F. M. Lodewijkx

11   Similarities Among Various Conceptual Positions
and Theoretical Points of View   295
Erich H. Witte

Author Index   303

Subject Index   315

PREFACE

The project that was to become the two volumes, *Understanding Group Behavior*, began about 15 years ago with a book by one of us (Witte, 1979) on behavior in group situations. This book took the rather idealistic position that researchers studying small groups should emphasize empirical work because there already was an abundant literature, documenting many phenomena and "effects": The conformity effect; Ringelmann effect; obedience effect; minimal group paradigm effect; social inhibition/facilitation effect; bystander effect; and many more. What was lacking was sufficient theory and conceptual work that would improve our understanding of group behavior. Subsequently, empirical research continued to outpace theoretical work, albeit perhaps with some amelioration of the unfavorable empirical/theoretical ratio. This continuation motivated a proposal (Witte, 1991) to the Deutsche Forschungsgemeinschaft (DFg) for an international conference on theoretical and conceptual issues in small group research. Upon the funding of this proposal, the Hamburg conference was arranged for November 1992. The general idea was to bring together from all over the world those scholars who were emphasizing theory construction and conceptual problems in small group behavior. With an accent on synthesizing approaches and ideas, subsequent discussions and exchanges resulted in the chapters that form these two volumes. In short, these volumes constitute a theoretical platform for the explanation and prediction of group behavior—and to some extent address applied problems as well.

The special emphasis of Volume 2 is on the theoretical basis of interpersonal processes, and their consequences, within and between groups, and less on consensual action itself, the primary emphasis in Volume 1. Thus, Volume 2 contains theoretical conceptions that are relevant to the structure, systems, and conflicts within groups, and consequently have particular implications for improving group functioning. Although none of these contributions report direct studies of such actual assemblies as aircrews, surgical teams, or juries (groups that are notoriously difficult to study directly), conceptual work of this sort greatly aids application by enabling simulations and by suggesting what phenomena to assess most usefully when rare observations are actually possible.

Erich H. Witte
James H. Davis

INTRODUCTION

SMALL-GROUP RESEARCH AND THE CRISIS OF SOCIAL PSYCHOLOGY: AN INTRODUCTION

Erich H. Witte
University of Hamburg, Hamburg

During the 1970s a discussion about the crisis in social psychology in general (House, 1977) and about small groups in particular (Steiner, 1974) took place. Both discussions have much in common, although at first glance, they started with different foci: The general discussion concentrated on the unintegrated three "faces" of social psychology, whereas the specific view on small groups was concerned with historical waves and cultural influences. Thus, the general discussion was concentrated on internal scientific causes of the crisis, and the specific discussion was seen as externally caused by pragmatic, cultural, and other reasons from outside of our science. In my opinion, both kinds of causes converge in small-group research, making this area a focal point of the crisis in social psychology. The crisis still exists in the sense that small groups have not been the center of social psychology for a long time. What, then, is the central research area of social psychology? And what is social psychology? The answer to the last question is also an answer to the first question about the central research area, because there are different social psychologies. Furthermore, small-group research itself has been fragmented into the different social psychologies so that its publication rate appears reduced; this, however, seems to be an erroneous idea (Fisch, Daniel, & Beck, 1991). Small-group research has been segmented into different parts that do not notice each other. And, in each single part, small-group research no longer plays a dominant role, as there are many other interesting research areas. There seems to be no decrease in small-group research, rather an increase in other areas, giving the appearance of a reduction in each segment (see, for the psychological small-group research, Moreland, Hogg, & Hains, 1994).

I

What is necessary is to identify the segments not on an empirical base, but rather as grounded on fundamental methodological approaches necessary for the study of social psychological phenomena in general and small-group processes in particular. What can be learned from this discussion is that each segment alone is insufficient and therefore needs the other approaches for a valid explanation of social processes. The question is not one of paradigm change but of paradigm enrichment. Thus, the consequence must be the insight that the different paradigms or better disciplinary matrices (Kuhn, 1978) have to be combined into a more complex strategy for developing and testing theories in the area of small groups as a means to better understanding group behavior. A methodological argument for integration, developed later, is an internal scientific reason against the more or less rational variation of following the fashion. Such a discussion might be conducive to a reintegration of segmental small-group research, overcoming what has been called the crisis of social psychology and thus the crisis of small-group research.

FOUR DIFFERENT APPROACHES
OF SMALL-GROUP RESEARCH
AND THEIR DISCIPLINARY MATRICES

The beginning of the crisis in explaining social behavior in general and small groups in particular lay in the perception of other disciplines that were also engaged in research on small groups. At best, four such disciplines (not three as House, 1977, proposed) can be identified.

Psychological small-group research, as the first discipline, is dominated by the experimental method and research of ad hoc groups. Its basic model of human beings is a machine model (Herzog, 1984). The main research interest (Habermas, 1968) is functional. The dominant research method is the experiment. A theory or hypothesis is seen as true if experimental manipulation leads to the predicted effect. This might be called the operationism criterion of truth. The basic pattern of explanation is the combination of a sufficient condition with an observed effect. The classical statistical method is the analysis of variance. The ontological premise assumes that human beings function like complex machines according to fixed laws under special conditions. This partial methodology has been called "scientistic" (Witte, 1987, 1994a). In my view, this kind of disciplinary matrix is not wrong, only one-sided.

Next, there is sociological small-group research. Its main research interests deal with socialization, rules, roles, and conformity. The dominant model of the human being is a victim model, which sees people as products of social circumstances. The usual statistical methods are correlational, for example, the adoption of a new antibiotic among physicians with rate of change per time unit and percentage of adopters (Witte, 1994b). The criterion of truth is consensual, which means that lawful behavior by the great majority of people can be described by a curve or a correlation. The pattern of explanation is based on necessary and not sufficient conditions as in an experiment. The research interest is emancipatory, because of the central idea of unmasking "a wrong consciousness." This partial methodology has been called ideology critique (Witte, 1987, 1994a). This disciplinary matrix is likewise not wrong, but one-sided.

The third approach of small-group research shares positions with symbolic interactionism or cultural anthropology. The main idea is that an individual develops idiosyncratic cognitive structures through contact with unknown group situations or general unknown cultures. Also each small group develops to some extent its own culture. The main method is participatory observation or introspection. Reality is a product of individual consciousness (Harré, 1989). The model of the human being is that of a creative constructor. The contents of research are everyday understanding and subjective theories as individual products. But what truth concerning individual products is yielded by a form of introspection? The only criterion is a measure of consistency over different expressions. The research interest is communicative, meaning that the understanding of individual cognitive structure through communication lies at the center of this kind of research. The partial methodology is called hermeneutics. Once again, this disciplinary matrix is not wrong, but one-sided.

The fourth approach of small-group research is the applied version, especially stressed by Lewin. The main function of applied small-group research is the resolution of conflicts, the reduction of biases, and the increase of productivity. Such social conditions are idiographic: The aim is founded on specific circumstances, people with idiosycratic motivation, and a particular aim to be reached. The model of the human being might be called a pupil model, as the people involved are seen as able to learn from social psychological theories and results. The empirical methods come from the area of evaluation procedures. The criterion of truth derives from observed effects. The pattern of explanation is the inversion of a teleological explanation (von Wright, 1974). This partial methodology has been called action research. Finally, this fourth disciplinary matrix is not wrong, but one-sided.

All four approaches have different models of the human being, different research interests, different patterns of explanation, different strategies of empirical research, different areas of content, and different criteria of truth. They are thus different partial methodologies, or what are sometimes called disciplinary matrices. Thus, small-group research conducted according to different approaches only leads to a kind of unsatisfaction with the research done, because the researcher in each segment feels the one-sidedness of his approach without taking the next step of combining different approaches. The main reason for this, in my opinion, is that the systematic relationships between the different approaches are not explained more deeply. Without this methodological discussion showing a systematic bias, everybody can go on as before because the paradigm changes are irrational and unpredictable—they simply occur.

One interesting area of content is research on minority influences and innovation. There is a psychological approach employing experiments, with major reviews deploring the static explanation and the absence of field research (Maass & Clark, 1984). But the fact is that many studies and theories in sociology have precisely this content (Witte, 1994b). Both approaches or disciplinary matrices are unintegrated, although it is felt, in this case, that the psychological approach is one-sided. However, each approach is one-sided and must be reintegrated. There are not only historical changes, but formal methodological reasons for doing this.

INTEGRATION OF THE FOUR DIFFERENT
CRITERIA OF TRUTH

The crucial aspect of the four disciplinary matrices is their criterion of truth and the possibility of an integrated criterion. At first, it is necessary to show their independence and then the possibility of integration. Because truth and its various criteria is the general aim of science, theories are evaluated in terms of these criteria, and science is theory construction. If it is possible to show that the criteria of truth are independent, then the reconstruction of small-group reality by different theories developed according to the four partial methodologies would describe four separate sections of reality without connection. The result is that theories and their empirical proof in terms of all four partial methodologies are required in order to develop an explanation and understanding of small-group phenomena.

To understand these four criteria of truth better, I would like to give some simple logical descriptions and an example.

The operationism criterion of truth is formulated by an implication, because it is a sufficient condition:

$$A(x) : f(x) \rightarrow g(x). \tag{1}$$

Example: For all groups $A(x)$ the following is true: If they are in a condition of groupthink then the quality of the group decision is inferior.

Under this partial methodology, called scientistic, all experimental studies are subsumed. Such an implication is wrong, if $g(x)$ has not been observed, but $f(x)$ is given. From this logical basis, problems arise with the experimental method (Harré, 1989; Moscovici, 1989), because nobody other than the experimenter usually knows whether $f(x)$ is given. Sometimes some questions concerning the effectiveness of the experimental manipulation arise, but there is never a validation study comparable with the validation of a test. Usually, all believe in the face validity of the experimental condition. However, if the existence of $f(x)$ has not been proved, the occurence of $g(x)$ as an observed effect is no longer a corroboration. In particular, there is some discussion in the area of groupthink whether the group shows high or low cohesion during the time of the decision.

The consensus criterion of truth has been identified as a necessary condition, which means that a result was observed and the specific antecedent conditions had preceded necessarily if the theory is correct:

$$A(x) : f(x) \leftarrow g(x). \tag{2}$$

For example, for all groups the following is true: If a fiasco, caused by a group decision, has been observed, then the symptoms of groupthink were present.

The third criterion of truth is a consistency criterion used to accept individual "thinking-aloud protocols" or other introspections as true. The following proof, a conjunction, is needed:

$$E(x) : f(1,x) \wedge \ldots f(n,x) . \wedge . g(1,x) \wedge \ldots g(n,x). \tag{3}$$

For example, there is a person (x) and for this person the following is true: This person feels the syptoms of groupthink $f(i,x)$ and this person will show the reactions of groupthink $g(i,x)$.

Under these circumstances the person (x) is consistent with the theory of groupthink, which is an individual corroboration of this theory.

The last criterion, a practical criterion of truth, is very seldom used as a test of a theory. For the most part, knowledge of the practitioner is ignored as a proof of theories. Applied social psychology seems to be a one-sided communication: The theoretician knows the right way and practitioners use theories to reach their goals. But what a theoretician needs to do is use the knowledge of practitioners more systematically for proving theories, for their experience sometimes helps to establish the limits of the theories. Most of the time practical aims $[Z(x)]$ require a combination of theories $[f,h,q, \ldots]$ for their realization. Such combinations, however, are never used in the other strategies, but are important for the explanation of complex social reality, which is never so simple that a single theory is able to explain it. Such a practical criterion might be formulated as:

$$E\{Z(x)\} : f(x) \wedge h(x) \wedge q(x) \ldots \rightarrow Z(x). \tag{4}$$

For example, the aim is to find a high-quality group decision in a specific committee of a specific content. For that reason the organizer has to determine the heterogeneity of the member, the number, the interaction process by a group technique, the avoidance of groupthink symptoms, and so on. This is an idiographic condition and application is always a very specific endeavor—not a tautological transformation of theories into modes of acting. A detailed evaluation of the processes will help in learning more about the theories, their limitations, and their combination (action research).

If the four criteria of truth yield the main evaluation of theories examined, discussion of the value of a theory proved by a single partial methodology will be endless when representatives of different approaches try to find an agreement: The criteria of validation are independent and one-sided, as the special issue of the *European Journal of Social Psychology* (Vol. 19) demonstrated (Rijsman & Stroebe, 1989).

However, if there is only a specific truth dependent on a partial methodology, how is it possible to talk about the truth of a theory? A coherence criterion of truth should be used (Rescher, 1973), which involves the "addition" of the four criteria as their basis. The aim of research should be to use the four different partial methodologies to evaluate theories, remaining conscious of the fact that no partial methodology is better than the other. Thus, the unintegrated disciplinary matrices of small-group research look like a crisis created by external reasons in the sense of Steiner (1974), but this crisis is based on internal scientific reasons and only capable of being resolved by a more complex approach.

THE INTEGRATION OF THE DISCIPLINARY MATRICES

Discussions about epistemological problems often occur in the form of a dichotomous demarcation, for example, the social and the individual, idiographic versus nomothetic, theory or practice, correlational or experimental, and so on. This discussion of dichotomous categories was extended by Karl Bühler (1927) when he talked about social sciences, natural sciences, and humanities. However, a more careful study of Aristotle could lead to the assumption that there are *four* different causes to be studied in the sciences (Kuhn, 1978): *causa efficiens, causa materialis, causa formalis, causa finalis*. These four *causae* are connected with the partial methodologies described here as: scientistic, ideology critique, hermeneutics, action research. Thus the given differentiation is as old as the philosophy of science. These four different kinds of causal explanation combined with ontological, epistemological, scientific aspects and related to the content form a disciplinary matrix characterized by *two* dimensions: (a) the way data are obtained—interpretation of natural processes versus active experimental manipulation, and (b) the extension of the generalization of the data—idiographic versus nomothetic.

From Table 1 it follows that the aim should not be a simple paradigmatic change, rather a paradigmatic enrichment in the sense of the four partial methodologies. This is a consequence of the independent criteria of truth, which means that each partial methodology can corroborate a theory without the corroboration by another partial methodology. The theory of truth is much less

TABLE I.1
Integration of the Four Disciplinary Matrices

Extension of the Generalization	Kind to Get the Data	
	Interpretation	Change
Idiographic	1. creative constructor model 2. internal conditions 3. hermeneutics 4. communicative 5. consistency criterion of truth	1. pupil model 2. resolving social conflicts 3. action research 4. evolutionary 5. praxis-criterion of truth
Nomothetic	1. victim-model 2. socialization 3. ideology-critique 4. emancipatory 5. consensus-criterion of truth	1. machine-model 2. experimental small groups 3. scientistic 4. functional 5. operationism-criterion of truth

Note. The numbers: 1 = model of men, 2 = center of research, 3 = partial-methodology, 4 = interest of knowledge, 5 = criterion of truth.

simple than usually assumed, independent of what has been called the significance test controversy, although the significance test is our central instrument to find out the truth.

CONCLUSION

There is a crisis in small-group research, but, because this crisis does not depend on external causes, there will be no uprise of research in the future. The crisis is caused by independent, segmented approaches or disciplinary matrices that ignore the other approaches but nevertheless feel that each needs a supplement through other kinds of small-group research. The systematic relationship among these four approaches leads to the conclusion that the now divergent publications and research traditions in different disciplines have to be reintegrated to resolve the crisis. Small-group research is multidisciplinary, and the old times of group dynamics as a new research content have been passed forever (see also Davis, chapter 1, Vol. 1, of this book). In the future, an intensive cooperation between different disciplines is necessary due to methodological fundamentals, and not because of historical or cultural "waves" in the past. The core of such cooperation is, however, theories that organize this joint endeavor (Moreland et al., 1994).

In this sense, the two volumes are in the center of small-group research overcoming the crisis.

REFERENCES

Bühler, K. (1927). *Die Krise der Psychologie* [The crisis of psychology]. Jena, Germany: Fischer.

Fisch, R., Daniel, H.-D., & Beck, D. (1991). Kleingruppenforschung—Forschungsschwerpunkte und Forschungstrends [Small-group research—Central research areas and trends]. *Gruppendynamik, 22,* 237–261.

Habermas, J. (1968). *Technik und Wissenschaft als Ideologie* [Technics and science as ideology]. Frankfurt, Germany: Suhrkamp.

Harré, R. (1989). Metaphysics and methodology: Some prescriptions for social psychological research. *European Journal of Social Psychology, 19,* 439–453.

Herzog, W. (1984). *Modell und Theorie in der Psychologie* [Model and theory in psychology]. Göttingen, Germany: Hogrefe.

House, J. S. (1977). The three faces of social psychology. *Sociometry, 40,* 161–177.

Kuhn, T. S. (1978). *Die Entstehung des Neuen* [The genesis of the new]. Frankfurt, Germany: Suhrkamp.

Maass, A., & Clark, R. D. (1984). Hidden impact of minorities: Fifteen years of minority influence research. *Psychological Bulletin, 95,* 428–450.

Moreland, R. L., Hogg, M. A., & Hains, S. C. (1994). Back to the future: Socialpsychological research on groups. *Journal of Experimental Social Psychology, 30,* 527–555.

Moscovici, S. (1989). Preconditions for explanation in social psychology. *European Journal of Social Psychology, 19,* 407–430.

Rescher, N. (1973). *The coherence theory of truth.* Oxford, England: Clarendon.

Rijsman, J., & Stroebe, W. (Eds.). (1989). Controversies in the social explanation of psychological behavior [Special Issue]. *European Journal of Social Psychology, 19.*

Steiner, I. D. (1974). Whatever happened to the group in social psychology? *Journal of Experimental Social Psychology, 10,* 94–108.

von Wright, G. H. (1974). *Erklären und Verstehen* [Explanation and understanding]. Frankfurt, Germany: Athenäum.

Witte, E. H. (1987). Die Idee einer einheitlichen Wissenschaftslehre für die Sozialpsychologie [The idea of a united methodology for social psychology]. *Zeitschrift für Sozialpsychologie, 18,* 76–87.

Witte, E. H. (1994a). *Lehrbuch Sozialpsychologie* [Textbook social psychology]. Weinheim, Germany: Psychologie Verlags Union.

Witte, E. H. (1994b). Minority influences and innovations: The search for an integrated explanation of psychological and sociological models. In S. Moscovici, A. Mucchi-Faina, & A. Maass (Eds.), *Minority influence* (pp. 67–93). Chicago: Nelson-Hall.

GROUP STRUCTURE
AND COMPOSITION

1

CREATING THE IDEAL GROUP: COMPOSITION EFFECTS AT WORK

Richard L. Moreland
John M. Levine
Melissa L. Wingert
University of Pittsburgh

In a recent review of social psychological research on small groups, Moreland, Hogg, and Hains (1994) found considerable variability in the popularity of major topic areas. Many researchers study conflict among group members, group performance, and intergroup relations, but group composition, group structure, and the ecology of groups are neglected. This imbalance is unfortunate, because the latter topic areas are both interesting and important. For example, experiences in a group often depend on the number and types of people who are group members. Yet few researchers study group composition, and no general theory guides their work. Progress toward understanding group composition phenomena has thus been slow and sporadic.

In an effort to stimulate interest in group composition, Moreland and Levine (1992) offered an integrative review of relevant theory and research. They categorized work in this area along three major dimensions. First, different characteristics of group members can be studied. Some researchers study the size of a group, noting the simple presence or absence of members, whereas other researchers study the kinds of people who belong to the group, focusing on their demographic characteristics (e.g., sex or race), abilities (e.g., intelligence or expertise), opinions (e.g., beliefs or values), or personalities (e.g., traits or needs). Second, the characteristics of group members can be measured in several ways. Researchers who prefer measures of central tendency assess the proportion of group members who possess a characteristic or the mean level of that characteristic within the group. Researchers who prefer measures of variability assess the variance of a characteristic within a group, or simply classify groups as heterogeneous or homogeneous for that characteristic. Special configurations of characteristics among group members also interest some researchers (e.g., Kanter, 1977; Schutz, 1958; Zajonc, 1976). Finally, several analytical perspectives can be taken toward the composition of a group. Some researchers regard group composition as a *consequence* or outcome that needs to be explained. Other researchers regard group composition as a *context* that moderates or shapes various behavioral phenomena. But most researchers regard group composition as a *cause* that can influence many other aspects of group life, including group structure, dynamics, and performance.

This last perspective, which traces other important aspects of groups back to their composition, is especially exciting because it has so many practical implications. If composition effects were better understood, then they could be used to create the ideal group. Managers, for example, could improve work groups through procedures designed to produce the optimal blend of employee characteristics (Bass, 1980; Driskell, Hogan, & Salas, 1987; Heslin, 1964; Jackson, 1992; Morgan & Lassiter, 1992). Such procedures might include hiring new workers or firing old ones, training current workers, or engaging the services of adjunct workers, such as temporary employees or consultants. Much advice has indeed been offered about managing the composition of work groups (see Belbin, 1981; Dumaine, 1994; Larson & LaFasto, 1989; Parker, 1990). But such advice is seldom based on any clear theory or strong research, so it can be misleading and even harmful. The purpose of this chapter is to analyze more carefully three practical questions that often arise regarding group composition. These questions are (a) What is the best group size?; (b) How valuable is diversity?; and (c) Will any special chemistry occur? While considering each question, we try to contrast the popular wisdom with the available research evidence. Then, in a final section of the chapter, we describe briefly a general theory of group composition effects that may clarify these and other questions.

WHAT IS THE BEST GROUP SIZE?

Advice about the best sizes for various types of groups is readily available from many sources. Katzenbach and Smith (1993), for example, suggested that work teams should contain a dozen members, whereas Scharf (1989) suggested that seven was the best size for such groups. Parker (1994) suggested that cross-functional teams should contain four to six members, and Nasser (1988) suggested that six to eight members was the best size for marketing focus groups. These and other suggestions are often difficult to evaluate, because they are based on personal experiences rather than research evidence. Because one manager's personal experiences may not be generalizable to other settings, a more scientific approach would be helpful. But what kind of research should be done?

There are at least three paradigms that might provide useful information about the best group size. First, observations of social interaction in public places can reveal how often natural groups of different sizes occur. The assumption underlying such research is that people avoid groups that are too small or too large. Several studies of this sort (e.g., Bakeman & Beck, 1974; Burgess, 1984; Desportes & Lemaine, 1988; James, 1951) have been performed, and the results are remarkably consistent. The average group is quite small, containing just two or three people, and few groups contain more than five or six people. Another popular paradigm involves creating artificial groups of different sizes and then noting which groups experience the fewest problems (e.g., Bray, Kerr, & Atkin, 1978; O'Dell, 1968; Slater, 1958). Slater, for example, varied the size of small discussion groups and found that people complained least about groups containing five members. Finally, some researchers (e.g., Carron, Widmeyer, & Brawley, 1989; Cini, Moreland, & Levine, 1993) simply ask people to describe the ideal sizes for various types of groups. Many people say they prefer groups containing about a dozen members (cf. Buys & Larson, 1979; McPherson, 1983), but such preferences can vary widely, even when only one type of group is considered.

This brief summary suggests that there is no simple way to determine the best size for a group. A better approach to this issue might be to study some of the correlates of group size. Considerable research on group size has been performed and several reviews of that work are available (e.g. Hare, 1981; Latané, 1981; Shaw, 1981; Thomas & Fink, 1963). The evidence suggests that large and small groups differ in many important ways. Some of these differences favor larger groups, whereas others favor smaller groups.

Larger groups enjoy several advantages. For example, such groups often perform better because they have access to more resources, including time, energy, money, and expertise (see Dennis & Valacich, 1993; Grofman, Owen, & Feld, 1983; Haleblian & Finkelstein, 1993; Hill, 1982; Wegner, 1987). These resources not only allow larger groups to set and achieve more ambitious goals, but also provide more "slack" if environmental conditions worsen. Another advantage of larger groups is that they tend to be more diverse. Diversity can be a mixed blessing, as we shall see later, but it does allow such benefits as role differentiation, tolerance, and synergy to occur (Bond & Keys, 1993; N. Miller & Davidson-Podgorny, 1987). Finally, larger groups often seem more legitimate, perhaps because they are connected more broadly to surrounding social networks. Legitimacy inhibits outsiders from interfering in a group's affairs and may even encourage them to support the group in various ways (Singh & Lumsden, 1990).

Unfortunately, larger groups also suffer several disadvantages. For example, such groups often experience coordination problems that can interfere with their performance (Diehl & Stroebe, 1987; Latané, Williams, & Harkins, 1979; McGrath & Rotchford, 1983; Stasser & Taylor, 1991). These problems include confusion about task assignments, miscommunications, scheduling difficulties, and so on. The performance of larger groups can also be harmed by motivation losses associated with social loafing, free riding, and efforts to avoid exploitation (Albanese & Van Fleet, 1985; Karau & Williams, 1993; Shepperd, 1993). There is more conflict among the members of larger groups (Hare, 1952; O'Dell, 1968), who are less likely to cooperate with one another (Brewer & Kramer, 1986; Hamburger, Guyer, & Fox, 1975). Other forms of misbehavior, such as cheating or stealing (Diener, Fraser, Beaman, & Kelem, 1976; Erffmeyer, 1984), absenteeism (Baumgartel & Sobol, 1959; Durand, 1985), and failing to help people in need (Latané & Nida, 1981; Mann, 1981), are also more common in larger groups. Finally, levels of participation are lower and more variable in larger groups (Bales, Strodtbeck, Mills, & Roseborough, 1951; Bass & Norton, 1951; Patterson & Schaeffer, 1977), and membership in such groups is less satisfying (Carron, 1990; Mullen, Symons, Hu, & Salas, 1989).

Research of this sort is helpful, because it reveals what can happen in larger groups. But once again, there seems to be no simple way to determine the best group size. Larger groups have both advantages and disadvantages, but how should these be evaluated? If the size of a group were doubled, then would the benefits associated with access to greater resources outweigh the risks associated with coordination problems and motivation losses? And if the overall performance of the group indeed improved, then would that benefit outweigh the risk of dissatisfaction among group members? Issues such as these are rarely studied by researchers, who usually focus on just one outcome of group size. It is also worth noting that both the advantages and disadvantages of larger groups can vary in strength from one situation to another, reflecting the influence of various moderator variables. For example, the performance advantages of larger groups are stronger when their members are more capable (Yetton & Bottger, 1983), and the motivation losses suffered by such groups are weaker when their members are more committed (Hardy & Latané, 1988). Process losses are stronger when tasks require more coordination among group members (Steiner, 1972), and motivation losses are stronger when tasks are less interesting (Brickner, Harkins, & Ostrom, 1986; Zaccaro, 1984). And the advantages of diversity are stronger when disjunctive rather than conjunctive tasks are performed (Frank & Anderson, 1971; Steiner, 1966). Finally, the size of a group may be less important than its staffing level, which depends on the group's goals (Schoggen, 1989). Even a large group can be understaffed if its goals are ambitious, and mild levels of understaffing can be helpful. For example, understaffing can improve the motivation, satisfaction, and participation levels of group members (Wicker, Kirmeyer, Hanson, & Alexander, 1976).

These factors make the best size for a group even less clear, but their moderating influence also suggests that the effects of group size could be controlled, at least in principle. So, rather than worrying about the best group size, it might be wiser to work at maximizing the advantages, and minimizing the disadvantages, of whatever size a group has reached (cf. Guzzo, Jette, & Katzell, 1985). For example, training programs that improve the abilities of group members (Swezey & Salas, 1992) could strengthen the performance advantages of larger groups. Planning (Weingart, 1992), process consultation (Harbour, 1993), or restructuring (Fry & Slocum, 1984; Mullen et al., 1989) could weaken coordination problems in larger groups, whereas team building (Newman, Edwards, & Raju, 1989; Vogt & Griffith, 1988), task redesign (Williams, Harkins, & Latané, 1981), or goal setting (Weldon & Weingart, 1993) could weaken their motivation losses. Restructuring larger groups could also weaken interpersonal conflicts by regulating members' behavior in various ways (Kerr, 1995; Messick & Brewer, 1983; Yamagishi, 1992). Of course, some of these tactics may be impractical in particular situations, and even when such tactics are used, they may be implemented poorly or have unexpected consequences. For example, restructuring larger groups can weaken coordination problems and interpersonal conflicts, but it may also limit the freedom of group members, which can strengthen their feelings of dissatisfaction.

Few researchers have studied these tactics. Most studies of group size are conducted in laboratories, where strangers are randomly assigned to artificial groups that perform simple tasks (selected by researchers) for limited periods of time. This sort of research probably exaggerates the disadvantages of larger groups, because it ignores self-selection processes and restricts or eliminates many of the tactics that larger groups can use to cope with their problems. Cini et al. (1993), for example, asked the leaders from many groups on a college campus to describe how they responded to problems associated with group size. The answers revealed a wide variety of tactics. Some of those tactics focused directly on changing group size, whereas others involved managing its effects. For example, when campus groups became too small, they not only recruited more prospective members, but also reorganized themselves in more efficient ways, sought help from other groups or authorities, and adopted less ambitious goals. And when such groups became too large, they not only recruited fewer and better prospective members, but also worked at building greater commitment, punished deviance more harshly, reorganized themselves in more complex ways, and adopted more ambitious goals.

Clearly, groups are far from helpless when problems arise regarding their size. But more must be learned about what tactics groups use to cope with such problems, how particular tactics are chosen, and when those tactics are likely to succeed. To study these and related issues, more ambitious research will be needed. Longitudinal field studies, in which natural groups are observed over long periods of time, would be especially valuable. Such research might yield more satisfying answers to questions about the best group size.

HOW VALUABLE IS DIVERSITY?

Another question often asked about group composition effects involves diversity. Group members can vary in many ways, from demographic characteristics to abilities to opinions to personalities. How does diversity influence a group?

Are heterogeneous groups better than homogeneous ones, and if so, then how much and what type of diversity is best? Once again, advice about these matters is available from many sources. Most of that advice advocates diversity, which is portrayed as a valuable asset for work groups (see Caudron, 1994; Federico, 1994; J. P. Fernandez, 1993; Nahavandi & Aranda, 1994). Some of this enthusiasm reflects recent social trends. Moral and legal pressures have weakened the barriers around many groups, allowing people who were previously excluded (because of their race/sex/age, physical/mental handicaps, or lifestyles) to become group members. These trends are viewed favorably by most observers, especially those with liberal political orientations. But many claims on behalf of diversity are apolitical, focusing on group performance. Several observers have noted that the nature of work is changing—tasks are becoming more complex and changing more rapidly than ever before. Under these conditions, diversity could be an important asset, providing groups with the flexibility they need to succeed. Diversity can also promote innovation in groups, as traditional work procedures are challenged by new members or modified to accommodate their strengths and weaknesses. Finally, diversity within a work group can improve its relations with various outsiders, such as customers, investors, or regulators, who are likely to be diverse themselves.

Is diversity really so valuable? A scientific approach to this issue again seems preferable to relying on advice from practitioners. Fortunately, much research on diversity has been performed, and several reviews of that work are available (e.g., Haythorn, 1968; Jackson, 1992; Maznevski, 1994; Nemeth & Staw, 1989; Shaw, 1981; Ziller, 1972). The evidence suggests that diversity, like size, has many important effects on groups. Some of these effects are helpful, but others are harmful. The overall impact of diversity on a particular group thus can be difficult to predict.

The main benefit of diversity is that it can improve a group's performance. Wood (1987), for example, reviewed research on the sex composition of groups and found that heterogeneous groups tended to outperform homogeneous groups (male or female) on a variety of tasks. Bantel and Jackson (1989) used archival data to examine the ability composition (functional expertise) of top-management teams in banks and found that heterogeneous teams were more willing to adopt technical or administrative innovations in banking practices (see also Bantel, 1993; Wiersema & Bantel, 1992). In several experiments on minority influence, Nemeth and her colleagues (see Nemeth, 1992, for a review) manipulated the opinion composition of groups and found evidence of more thoughtful and creative decision making by heterogeneous groups. Finally, the personality composition of groups was studied by Hoffman and his colleagues (Hoffman, 1959; Hoffman & Maier, 1961), who compared problem solving by groups whose members had similar or dissimilar personality profiles (across a variety of traits). Heterogeneous groups proposed better quality solutions than did homogeneous groups.

The main risk of diversity is that it can produce conflict among group members. As a result, the group's cohesion may be weakened, and some members may be tempted to depart. Haythorn, Couch, Haefner, Langham, and Carter (1956), for example, observed problem-solving groups whose members had similar or different levels of authoritarianism. There was greater conflict and worse morale in more heterogeneous groups. Terborg, Castore, and DeNinno (1976) studied surveying teams whose members were similar or dissimilar in their abilities and/or attitudes. When the attitudes of team members were heterogeneous rather than homogeneous, group cohesion was lower. O'Reilly, Caldwell, and Barnett (1989) surveyed the members of work groups in convenience stores and found that as heterogeneity in job tenure increased, levels of social integration in these groups fell, which caused their turnover rates to rise. Many other researchers (e.g., Jackson et al., 1991; McCain, O'Reilly, & Pfeffer, 1983) have also observed higher turnover rates in more heterogeneous groups. The people who leave such groups are often those who differ most from other members (but see Tsui, Egan, & O'Reilly, 1992), so their departure helps to produce group homogeneity.

The benefits and risks of diversity are not entirely independent, because conflict among members can affect a group's performance. Moderate levels of conflict are often helpful—rivalries can motivate group members to work harder, arguments can lead group members to think about problems in more complex ways, and challenges can reveal which group members are really best at particular tasks. But higher levels of conflict are often harmful, diverting so much time and energy from work that group performance suffers. An intriguing study by Ancona and Caldwell (1992) illustrated the delicate balance among these effects. The performance of product development teams from several high-technology corporations was compared to their levels of diversity in functional expertise and job tenure. Measures of team members' work behavior were also obtained and examined as possible mediators of any group composition effects. The overall effect of diversity on performance was negative, yet diversity often affected work behavior in positive ways. For example, as functional diversity increased, team members communicated more often with other groups within their corporations, and this behavior helped them develop more innovative products. And as tenure diversity increased, team members spent more time clarifying their goals and setting priorities. Both of these behaviors also led to the development of more innovative products. Why was the overall effect of diversity on team performance negative, despite these positive changes in work behaviors? Apparently the conflict associated with diversity made it harder for team members to actually work together. For example, the members of such groups often overspent their budgets and failed to meet important deadlines.

To complicate matters further, many factors can moderate the effects of diversity on either group performance or conflict among group members. The effects of diversity on group performance, for example, may depend on what task is performed. If the task is relatively simple, requiring just one ability, then diversity can be helpful or harmful, depending on the level of that ability among group members. A homogeneous group of high-ability members should outperform a heterogeneous group, which should outperform a homogeneous group of low-ability members (e.g., DeBiasio, 1986; Laughlin, 1978). But if the task is relatively complex, requiring many abilities, then heterogeneous groups should outperform homogeneous groups, whose members may lack some of the necessary abilities. Tasks also vary in their coordination requirements (Steiner, 1972). Unitary tasks require group members to work closely with one another, whereas divisible tasks can be separated into activities that group members perform independently. Diversity should have more positive effects when groups perform divisible tasks, because conflicts among group members are less likely to arise when they are not working together. Finally, success at some tasks requires convergent thinking, or the ability to focus on important aspects of the task without being distracted, whereas success at other tasks requires divergent thinking, or the ability to consider many aspects of the task without focusing too narrowly on any one of them. When convergent thinking is required, homogeneous groups should outperform heterogeneous groups (if group members focus on important aspects of the task), but heterogeneous groups should outperform homogeneous groups when divergent thinking is required (Nemeth, 1992).

The effects of diversity on conflict among group members can also be moderated by several factors. Diversity can take many forms, and the amount of conflict that occurs may depend on which member characteristics are involved and how they are distributed within a group. For example, racial diversity may be more likely than sexual diversity to create conflict, whereas aesthetic diversity may be less likely to create conflict than either political or religious diversity. Regarding the distribution of member characteristics, Kanter (1977) argued that groups containing token members are especially likely to experience conflict, because the presence of a token focuses attention on the differences rather than the similarities among group members. And Schutz (1958) found that heterogeneity in the needs of group members for inclusion, affection, and control could actually reduce conflict (and improve performance) if those needs were distributed in ways that led to interpersonal compatibility. Another moderating factor is *how* a group becomes diverse. Conflict is less likely when a group chooses to admit a wider variety of members, rather than being forced to admit them. Research on affirmative action programs, for example, shows that White men often become resentful when jobs are set aside for people from various minority groups (Galen, 1994; Heilman, Block, & Lucas, 1992). This resentment can increase tensions within the work groups where such persons are assigned. Finally, conflict can also take many forms, some of which may actually be helpful rather than harmful (see Jehn, 1992; Kirchmeyer & Cohen, 1992). Jehn, for example, identified three distinct forms of conflict in work groups. Content conflict focuses on task performance, emotional conflict focuses on the relationships among group members, and administrative conflict focuses on group structure.

Emotional conflict is always harmful, but both content and administrative conflict can be helpful under some circumstances.

The influence of these (and other) moderating factors reveals just how complex the effects of diversity on groups can be. These factors also suggest, however, that it may be possible to control those effects in ways that strengthen the benefits of diversity and/or weaken its risks. Once again, much advice is available on how to "manage" diversity effectively (e.g., Epting, Glover, & Boyd, 1994; Hodson, 1993; Lundy, 1992; Rice, 1994). This advice falls into two general categories. One category involves tactics designed to control the conflict among group members that diversity often creates. Some of these tactics focus on limiting the amount of conflict that occurs. For example, special training programs can be developed to educate workers about their similarities and differences, or to encourage greater tolerance for diversity, or to improve social skills (Hollister, Day, & Jesaitis, 1993). And team-building activities can be used to build cohesion and trust among group members. Other tactics focus on conflict resolution. For example, special training programs in negotiation or intervention can be developed (Ancona & Caldwell, 1992). It may also be possible for leaders to improve the communication among group members (Maznevski, 1994), or redirect conflicts so that they focus more on task issues, and less on emotional or administrative issues.

Another category of advice for managing diversity effectively involves tactics designed to simulate diversity in a group without actually changing its composition. When such tactics are successful, they improve group performance without creating serious conflicts among group members. Some of these tactics involve changes in group structure. For example, the role of "devil's advocate" can be assigned to a regular group member, who is charged with evaluating and perhaps criticizing aspects of the group that are normally taken for granted (Cosier, Dalton, & Taylor, 1991). Changes in the group's decision-making norms can also be helpful. Requiring consensus rather than a simple majority, for example, can produce more thorough and thoughtful discussions of whatever issues a group faces (C. E. Miller, 1989). Group members can also be encouraged to criticize proposals, avoid premature consensus, reconsider decisions, and show more tolerance for dissent (Janis, 1972). Other tactics involve the use of adjunct group members. Process consultants, for example, can evaluate the group and offer suggestions for improving its operation, whereas temporary workers can provide skills and knowledge that regular members of the group lack.

Research on these and other tactics is clearly needed to test their feasibility and effectiveness. But another sort of research may be just as important. Until recently, most diversity research was done in laboratories, where (once again) strangers were randomly assigned to artificial groups that performed simple tasks for limited periods of time. Under these conditions, the ability of groups to manage diversity may be constrained. For example, natural groups are often rather homogeneous (see George, 1990; Jackson et al., 1991; Jones, 1974; Katz,

1981; Maccoby, 1990; Magaro & Ashbrook, 1985; McPherson & Smith-Lovin, 1986). Diversity levels in some laboratory groups may thus be abnormally high, creating problems that are especially difficult to solve. Natural groups can also manage diversity through various socialization processes (Levine & Moreland, 1994; Moreland & Levine, 1982; Schneider, 1987; see also Jackson et al., 1991). For example, when the effects of diversity become problematic, group norms about the kinds of people who can become or remain members may change, excluding people who are too dissimilar. And harsher socialization and resocialization practices may be adopted, forcing newcomers and marginal members (respectively) to change in ways that make them more similar. Laboratory groups rarely admit new members or eject old ones, and their techniques for controlling deviance are seldom very harsh. The low levels of commitment within these groups, whose members never really choose to work together, may also limit the effectiveness of whatever influence techniques are used. Given these constraints, laboratory groups may simply endure diversity, rather than trying to manage it.

Laboratory groups face another important constraint in managing the effects of diversity, one involving time. As time passes, a group may learn, in its own unique way, how to profit from diversity among its members. Little learning of this sort can occur in laboratory groups, whose lives are generally quite short. But natural groups, which live much longer, could learn a great deal about managing diversity. Watson, Kumar, and Michaelsen (1993), for example, manipulated the cultural diversity of student groups in a college management course. For many weeks, the interaction process in these groups, and their performance of various tasks, were measured. Homogeneous groups displayed better process and performance early in the study, but their superiority diminished as time passed. By the end of the study, heterogeneous groups were comparable to homogeneous groups and might have surpassed them eventually, if given more time. Students in heterogeneous groups apparently learned how to cope with diversity, but that learning required considerable time and experience.

This study demonstrates again the potential value of longitudinal field studies for investigating group composition effects. Groups may have many methods for managing diversity, but laboratory research on artificial groups seems unlikely to reveal much about them. Several important questions remain unanswered. For example, *why* do established groups cope more effectively with diversity? Is it because they are more familiar with the knowledge and skills available from their members? Or perhaps such groups are more cohesive, so that conflicts among their members occur less often or seem less threatening. And just how does diversity shape group socialization processes? Which characteristics are groups likely to evaluate in their members, and are specific changes in group norms about who can belong, or in the harshness of group socialization/resocialization practices, linked to particular characteristics? Once again, the answers to such questions will require more ambitious research.

WILL ANY SPECIAL CHEMISTRY OCCUR?

Finally, people who create groups often wonder whether any special "chemistry" will occur among group members. Advice about this issue is scarce, but can be found in commentaries about several kinds of groups, including quality circles in industry (Ferrini-Mundy, Gaudard, Shore, & Van Osdol, 1990), musical groups (Duffy & McAdams, 1991), and sports teams (Fimrite, 1991). The nature of chemistry in groups is never clearly specified, perhaps because its cachet depends on remaining somewhat mysterious. But there is at least implicit agreement among observers that chemistry is rare, valuable, and difficult to manage. Can a group's chemistry be managed at all? Some observers suggest that chemistry is a natural product of group development, so that management efforts are unnecessary and perhaps unwise, whereas other observers believe that chemistry can be nurtured through insightful staffing choices or charismatic leadership styles (Bass, 1985).

Scientific research on these and other issues involving group chemistry requires some clarification of that concept. What exactly happens when such chemistry occurs? The answer may lie in a closer analysis of the transformation process that converts individual into group characteristics. That process could be guided by several combinatorial rules (cf. Shiflett, 1979). One option is that individual characteristics combine in an *additive* manner. According to the additive rule, the effects of individual members on a group are independent. This rule implies that a person will affect every group that he or she joins in about the same way. The additive rule reflects a rather mechanistic view of groups, whose components can be separated and studied in isolation. Another option, however, is that individual characteristics combine in an *interactive* manner. According to the interactive rule, the effects of individual members on a group are (to some degree) interdependent. This rule implies that a person will affect every group that he or she joins differently, depending on who else belongs. The interactive rule reflects a more organismic view of groups, whose components must be studied together because they cannot operate alone. When the interactive rule is operating, the transformation of individual into group characteristics becomes more complex and difficult to understand or predict. We suspect that interactive composition effects produce the special chemistry that seems to occur in some groups.

There is abundant evidence for the operation of the additive rule in group composition effects. When the average level of some individual characteristic within a group is used to predict a related aspect of the group's structure, dynamics, or performance, a strong linear relationship is usually found. Jones (1974), for example, examined archival data on the abilities of players in various team sports, such as football, baseball, and basketball, and then used that information to predict the performance of the teams on which those athletes played. In every sport that he studied, team performance was related strongly and positively to players' ability levels. Hogan, Raza, and Driskell (1988) measured a variety of personality traits in students who were later assigned to groups that performed several tasks. On the basis of earlier theorizing (Driskell et al., 1987), specific linkages between personality and performance at the group level were predicted, and these predictions were largely confirmed. Performance on a technical task, for example, was better for groups whose members were more prudent, whereas groups whose members were more sociable performed better on a persuasion task. Many other examples of additive composition effects could be cited (e.g., Bray & Noble, 1978; Comrey, 1953; J. C. Fernandez, 1992; Gill, 1979; Laughlin, 1978); reviews of such work can be found in Bass (1980), Shaw (1981), Hill (1982), and Stasser, Kerr, and Davis (1989).

Evidence for the operation of the interactive rule in group composition effects is more rare. This may reflect the fact that interactive composition effects are less easy to detect. A relatively simple detection method involves searching for nonlinear relationships between individual and group characteristics. For example, if a group performs much better or worse than it should, given the average level of ability among its members, then perhaps some special chemistry (good or bad) is responsible. Despite its simplicity, this method is seldom used, perhaps because many researchers fail to test for departures from linearity in their data. And even when nonlinear relationships are discovered, their interpretation can be problematic. Michaelsen, Watson, and Black (1989), for example, compared the examination scores of student groups in a college management course to the scores (from earlier, practice examinations) of their average and best members. Group examination scores were much higher than the scores of their best members, a finding that was interpreted as evidence of interactive composition effects. However, this interpretation was later challenged by Tindale and Larson (1992a), and the ensuing debate (Michaelsen, Watson, Schwartzkopf, & Black, 1992; Tindale & Larson, 1992b) raised several important issues. One such issue was whether a nonlinear relationship between individual and group characteristics proves that interactive composition effects have occurred, or whether such a relationship could arise in other ways.

There are other, more complex methods for detecting interactive composition effects, but they require special kinds of data that are more difficult to acquire and/or analyze. As a result, these methods are used even less often, but when they are used, clearer and more convincing findings can be obtained. One such method involves assessing some individual characteristic within a large sample and then using the results to divide subjects into a limited number of categories. Subjects in the same category are regarded as equivalent to one another. Sampling from each category, researchers can then create groups representing all possible category combinations. Some characteristic of these groups can then be measured and related back to their composition using standard statistical techniques. This method was used by Tziner and Eden (1985), who studied the field performance of Israeli tank crews. The soldiers in those crews were first classified as either high or low in ability and in motivation. Three-man crews representing all possible combinations of ability and motivation levels were then created and observed. The results revealed strong additive composition effects for both ability and motivation—crews whose members were more capable or more motivated performed better. But interactive composition effects were also observed, at least for ability. When all the soldiers in a crew were high in ability, its performance was surprisingly good, and when all the soldiers in a crew were low in ability, its performance was surprisingly poor. In at least some of the crews, the effects of individual abilities on group performance were thus interdependent.

Another complex method for detecting interactive composition effects involves rotating people across groups. After assessing some individual characteristic within a sample, subjects are randomly assigned to groups. Some characteristic of those groups is then measured, but afterward a reassignment occurs, changing who belongs to which group. Several rotational schemes are possible; the most challenging scheme requires every possible configuration of subjects to occur at least once. This method was used by Rosenberg, Erlick, and Berkowitz (1955), who studied the performance of three-person laboratory groups on a manual task requiring considerable coordination among group members. A significant portion of the variance in group performance was related to particular configurations of individual members, providing evidence of interactive composition effects. These effects occurred, oddly, at the triadic but not the dyadic levels. That is, the effects of each person or his group's performance were shaped by *both* of the other people in the group, rather than by just one of them. More recently, Kenny and his colleagues (see Kenny & Hallmark, 1992; Kenny, Hallmark, Sullivan, & Kashy, 1993; Kenny & Zaccaro, 1983; Zaccaro, Foti, & Kenny, 1991) have developed clever statistical techniques for analyzing data from rotational designs and applied those techniques to both new and old data on leadership effectiveness. A central issue in that topic area is whether a leader's impact on group performance varies from one group to another. Early theories, which emphasized the personal qualities of leaders, suggested that additive composition effects should occur—a leader should affect each new group in about the same way. But later theories, which emphasized situational factors, suggested that interactive composition effects should occur—a leader should affect each new group differently, depending on who else belongs. Across several studies, Kenny and his colleagues found strong evidence of additive composition effects, especially for the personality trait of self-monitoring. However, interactive composition effects for some other leader characteristics were also found.

Evidence for the operation of the interactive rule in group composition effects may also require researchers to study different types of groups. In a nominal group, whose members never interact, no special chemistry among group members is likely to occur. Only additive composition effects will emerge in such a group. As we noted earlier, most research on group composition involves laboratory groups, containing strangers who are assigned to perform simple tasks for brief periods of time. Although the members of such groups do interact with one another, their interaction is often constrained in ways that may limit the depth of any relationships that develop. Laboratory groups thus may be closer to nominal groups than they are to natural groups, which are much more involving. Perhaps this is why there is so much more evidence of additive rather than interactive composition effects in previous research. Interactive composition effects may only emerge (or emerge more strongly) in groups whose members care about one another, because they have worked together for long periods of time on complex (and freely chosen) tasks with important consequences. This argument, which has several advocates (e.g., Michaelsen et al., 1989; Moreland & Levine, 1992; Tziner & Eden, 1985), has at least some support. When interactive composition effects are observed by researchers, they often occur in natural rather than laboratory groups. And there is some evidence that additive composition effects are weaker, or interactive composition effects stronger, in groups performing tasks with greater coordination requirements (see Comrey, 1953; Jones, 1974; O'Brien & Owens, 1969). The most direct support, however, comes from a longitudinal study by Watson, Michaelsen, and Sharp (1991) of student groups in a graduate course on organizational behavior. The members of each group participated in many activities together over a period of several months. On three occasions, each group's score on a course examination was compared to the scores of its individual members (from earlier, practice examinations), and measures of "synergy" were computed. These measures, which assessed the degree to which each group outperformed its best member, were interpreted as evidence of interactive composition effects. Synergy levels rose as time passed, suggesting that group development was an important factor in the occurrence of interactive composition effects.

Although these results are encouraging, understanding the special chemistry that can occur among group members will require more than simply demonstrating the existence of interactive composition effects and identifying when they are likely to happen. Other, more complex issues must be explored as well. For example, what is the underlying structure of these effects? Does each member of a group affect all the others in about the same way, or can that influence vary across different cliques within the group (Duchon, Green, & Taber, 1986) or even across different individuals? Another intriguing issue involves the strength and direction of interactive composition effects. When one member shapes the effects of another on a group, either enhancement (strengthening) or suppression (weakening) could occur. A creative person, for example, could serve as a catalyst to stimulute greater creativity in other group members. Or a competent person might allow other group members to indulge in free riding, devoting less effort to some task. Both of these examples involve changes in the strength of interactive composition effects, but directional changes could occur as well. For example, groups whose members are more motivated usually perform better, but when motivation levels rise too far, they can actually interfere with group performance. A group member who persuades others to adopt unrealistic performance goals, or who creates various kinds of performance anxieties, could produce such a reversal. Finally, the source of interactive composition effects deserves some consideration. When such effects occur, are they usually caused by just one or two group members, or does each person affect all the others? And when several people are responsible for producing interactive composition effects, does the structure, strength, and direction of those effects vary from one person to another?

A GENERAL MODEL OF GROUP COMPOSITION EFFECTS

Too little is known about group composition effects to provide much guidance for creating the ideal group. Practical advice is available from many sources, but such advice is often vague or simplistic and may be misleading. Scientific research on group composition effects can also be found, but that work often takes place in unrealistic laboratory settings that constrain the kinds of effects that occur and the efforts groups make to manage those effects. There is a clear need for more field research on group composition effects, especially longitudinal studies of natural groups. But changes in research methods are not enough—better theories about group composition effects are also needed. Few theorists have analyzed group composition very broadly. There is a general tendency to focus on just one characteristic of group members, such as their abilities or opinions or needs, ignoring all the others. As a result, not much theoretical integration of analogous work on different characteristics has occurred. This lack of integration is unfortunate, because researchers studying different characteristics have made important discoveries and acquired valuable insights about group composition effects. These discoveries and insights should be shared. We believe that it is now possible to develop a general model of those effects that both describes and explains how group composition influences other important aspects of group life. A preliminary model of this sort is shown in Fig. 1.1.

People possess many individual characteristics that could affect a group. A general model of group composition effects should help to identify which characteristics are most important. We assume that individual characteristics become important insofar as they are salient to group members. One variable that can influence the salience of a characteristic is how easily it can be assessed. Some characteristics, such as the mere presence of group members or their demographic characteristics, are simple and obvious. But other characteristics, such as abilities, opinions, or personality traits, are more subtle and less apparent, because they must be inferred from the behavior of group members. This suggests two general hypotheses:

H1: Individual characteristics that are easier to assess will produce stronger group composition effects.

H2: Composition effects involving characteristics that are more difficult to assess are unlikely to occur in newly formed groups.

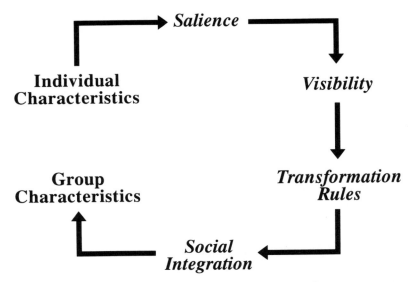

FIG. 1.1. A general model of group composition effects.

Another variable that can influence the salience of an individual characteristic is its distribution within the group. Several theorists, especially Mullen (1983, 1987, 1991), have argued that a characteristic attracts more attention from group members as its variance increases. For example, sex becomes an increasingly salient characteristic as the proportions of males and females in a group diverge (Kanter, 1977; McGuire, McGuire, & Winton, 1979). This suggests another general hypothesis:

H3: Composition effects will be stronger in groups that are more heterogeneous.

Of course, an individual characteristic could become salient even in a homogeneous group, if that group were embedded in an organizational context containing quite different types of people (Ridgeway, 1988). Finally, an individual characteristic can become salient to group members because it seems relevant to their outcomes or lends meaning to their experiences (Oakes, 1987). When will a characteristic seem relevant or meaningful? The answer depends partly on situational factors, which direct attention to specific individual characteristics, and partly on the prior beliefs about which characteristics are most relevant in a given situation (cf. Lockheed, 1985). This suggests yet another general hypothesis:

H4: When situations are more highly structured and/or more group members share a common perspective, a narrower range of composition effects will occur and those effects will be more powerful.

Once an individual characteristic becomes salient, group composition effects involving that characteristic will occur. Every person in the group possesses some level of that characteristic and thus can contribute to those effects. Many researchers assume that every individual is equally important in this regard, but that assumption is clearly unrealistic. A general model of group composition effects should identify which individuals will be most important. A useful concept here is visibility (Marwell, 1963), or the extent to which someone's characteristics are noticed by other group members. Several variables could affect visibility in a group. For example, people who participate more often in group activities should have more impact on the group, because their characteristics are more visible to other members. Another potentially important variable is a person's status within a group. Schein (1983), for example, claimed that many groups take on the characteristics of their founders, and several studies suggest that leaders have more impact than followers on their groups (see Haythorn, 1968). Seniority may also increase a person's importance, because someone who has been in a group longer is more familiar to its members (Moreland & Levine, 1989). Finally, situational factors can also determine an individual's impact on a group. When groups work on disjunctive or conjunctive tasks, for example, their performance depends primarily on the ability of their best or worst members, respectively (Steiner, 1972). And on discretionary tasks, information about the relative abilities of group members can be used to develop schemes for weighting their contributions in optimal ways (Libby, Trotman, & Zimmer, 1987). Relationships with outsiders could also make some group members more visible, if those relationships seem important for the group's success (Ancona & Caldwell, 1988). All of this suggests two further general hypotheses, namely:

H5: Group members seldom contribute equally to composition effects.

H6: The strength of a person's contribution depends on such variables as participation in group activities, social status, and any situational factors associated with visibility in the group.

There is a final theoretical problem that a general model of composition effects should solve: How do individual characteristics combine to affect a group's structure, dynamics, or performance? As we noted earlier, the most common composition effects are additive in nature, but interactive composition effects have also been observed. When are the additive and interactive transformation rules likely to operate? We believe that a group's level of social integration is the key variable. Moreland (1987) described social integration in terms of the environmental, behavioral, affective, and cognitive bonds that bind group members to one another. The more its members think, feel, and act like a group, rather than a collection of individuals, the more integrated a group becomes. Additive composition effects require little or no social integration, and can occur even in nominal groups. But interactive composition effects require higher levels of social integration for their occurrence. This suggests two final general hypotheses:

H7: Additive composition effects are more likely to occur than interactive composition effects.

H8: Interactive composition effects will occur primarily in natural groups and/or groups with higher levels of social integration.

Our model seems promising, in the sense that it transcends different individual characteristics, fits the available research evidence well, and suggests some interesting new hypotheses about group composition effects. Nevertheless, much work will be needed to evaluate the model and develop it in ways that broaden and deepen its predictions. We hope that this chapter, in conjunction with our earlier paper (Moreland & Levine, 1992), will motivate researchers to join us in that work.

REFERENCES

Albanese, R., & Van Fleet, D. D. (1985). Rational behavior in groups: The free-riding tendency. *Academy of Management Review, 10,* 244–255.

Ancona, D. G., & Caldwell, D. F. (1988). Beyond task and maintenance: Defining external functions in groups. *Group and Organizational Studies, 13,* 468–494.

Ancona, D. G., & Caldwell, D. F. (1992). Demography and design: Predictors of new product team performance. *Organization Science, 3,* 321–341.

Bakeman, R., & Beck, S. (1974). The size of informal groups in public. *Environment and Behavior, 6,* 378–388.

Bales, R. F., Strodtbeck, F. L., Mills, T. M., & Roseborough, M. E. (1951). Channels of communication in small groups. *American Sociological Review, 16,* 461–468.

Bantel, K. A. (1993). Comprehensiveness of strategic planning: The importance of heterogeneity of a top team. *Psychological Reports, 73,* 35–49.

Bantel, K. A., & Jackson, S. E. (1989). Top management and innovations in banking: Does the composition of the top team make a difference? *Strategic Management Journal, 10,* 107–124.

Bass, B. M. (1980). Team productivity and individual member competence. *Small Group Behavior, 11,* 431–504.

Bass, B. M. (1985). Leadership: Good, better, best. *Organizational Dynamics, 13,* 26–40.

Bass, B. M., & Norton, F. T. M. (1951). Group size and leaderless discussion. *Journal of Applied Psychology, 35,* 397–400.

Baumgartel, H., & Sobol, R. (1959). Background and organizational factors in absenteeism. *Personnel Psychology, 12,* 431–443.

Belbin, R. M. (1981). *Management teams: Why they succeed or fail.* New York: Wiley.

Bond, M. A., & Keys, C. B. (1993). Empowerment, diversity, and collaboration: Promoting synergy on community boards. *American Journal of Community Psychology, 21,* 37–57.

Bray, R. M., Kerr, N. L., & Atkin, R. S. (1978). Effects of group size, problem difficulty, and sex on group performance and member reactions. *Journal of Personality and Social Psychology, 36,* 1224–1240.

Bray, R. M., & Noble, A. M. (1978). Authoriarianism and decisions of mock juries: Evidence of jury bias and group polarization. *Journal of Personality and Social Psychology, 36,* 1424–1430.

Brewer, M. B., & Kramer, R. M. (1986). Choice behavior in social dilemmas: Effects of social identity, group size, and decision framing. *Journal of Personality and Social Psychology, 50,* 543–547.

Brickner, M. A., Harkins, S. G., & Ostrom, T. M. (1986). Effects of personal involvement: Thought-provoking implications for social loafing. *Journal of Personality and Social Psychology, 51,* 763–769.

Burgess, J. W. (1984). Do humans show a "species-typical" group size? Age, sex, and environmental differences in the size and composition of naturally-occurring casual groups. *Ethology and Sociobiology, 5,* 51–57.

Buys, C. J., & Larson, K. L. (1979). Human sympathy groups. *Psychological Reports, 45,* 547–553.

Carron, A. V. (1990). Group size in sport and physical activity: Social psychological and performance consequences. *International Journal of Sport Psychology, 21,* 286–304.

Carron, A. V., Widmeyer, W. N., & Brawley, L. R. (1989). Perceptions of ideal group size in sport teams. *Perceptual and Motor Skills, 69,* 1368–1370.

Caudron, S. (1994). Diversity ignites effective work teams. *Personnel Journal, 73,* 54–63.

Cini, M. A., Moreland, R. L., & Levine, J. M. (1993). Group staffing levels and responses to prospective and new group members. *Journal of Personality and Social Psychology, 65,* 723–734.

Comrey, A. L. (1953). Group performance on a manual dexterity task. *Journal of Applied Psychology, 37,* 207–210.

Cosier, R. A., Dalton, D. F., & Taylor, L. A. (1991). Positive effects of cognitive conflict and employee voice. *Employee Responsibilities and Rights Journal, 4,* 7–11.

DeBiasio, A. R. (1986). Problem solving in triads composed of varying numbers of field-dependent and field-independent subjects. *Journal of Personality and Social Psychology, 51,* 749–754.

Dennis, A. R., & Valacich, J. S. (1993). Computer brainstorms: More heads are better than one. *Journal of Applied Psychology, 78,* 531–537.

Desportes, J. P., & Lemaine, J. M. (1988). The sizes of human groups: An analysis of their distributions. In D. Canter, J. C. Jesuino, L. Soczka, & G. M. Stephenson (Eds.), *Environmental social psychology* (pp. 57–65). Dordrecht, Netherlands: Kluwer Academic Publishers.

Diehl, M., & Stroebe, W. (1987). Productivity loss in brainstorming groups: Toward the solution of a riddle. *Journal of Personality and Social Psychology, 53,* 497–509.

Diener, E., Fraser, S. C., Beaman, A. L., & Kelem, R. T. (1976). Effects of deindividuation variables on stealing among Halloween trick-or-treaters. *Journal of Personality and Social Psychology, 33,* 178–183.

Driskell, J. E., Hogan, R., & Salas, E. (1987). Personality and group performance. In C. Hendrick (Ed.), *Group processes and intergroup relations* (pp. 91–112). Newbury Park, CA: Sage.

Duchon, D., Green, S. G., & Taber, T. D. (1986). Vertical dyad linkage: A longitudinal assessment of antecedents, measures, and consequences. *Journal of Applied Psychology, 71,* 56–60.

Duffy, T., & McAdams, J. (1991). Black acts return to a live sound. *Billboard, 103,* 1, 71.

Dumaine, B. (1994). The trouble with teams. *Fortune, 130*(5), 86–92.

Durand, V. M. (1985). Employee absenteeism: A selective review of antecedents and consequences. *Journal of Organizational Behavior Management, 7,* 135–167.

Epting, L. A., Glover, S. H., & Boyd, S. D. (1994). Managing diversity. *Health Care Supervisor, 12,* 73–83.

Erffmeyer, E. S. (1984). Rule violation on the golf course. *Perceptual and Motor Skills, 59,* 591–596.

Federico, R. F. (1994). Multiculturalism makes good business sense. *Compensation and Benefits Management, 10,* 32–37.

Fernandez, J. C. (1992). Soldier quality and job performance in team tasks. *Social Science Quarterly, 73,* 254–265.

Fernandez, J. P. (1993). *The diversity advantage.* New York: Lexington.

Ferrini-Mundy, J., Gaudard, M., Shore, S. D., & Van Osdol, D. (1990). How quality is taught can be as important as what is taught. *Quality Progress, 23,* 56–59.

Fimrite, R. (1991). A chemical reaction. *Sports Illustrated, 75,* 66.

Frank, F., & Anderson, L. R. (1971). Effects of task and group size upon group productivity and member satisfaction. *Sociometry, 34,* 135–149.

Fry, L. W., & Slocum, J. W. (1984). Technology, structure, and workgroup effectiveness. *Academy of Management Journal, 27,* 221–246.

Galen, M. (1994, January 31). White, male, and worried. *Business Week,* pp. 50–55.

George, J. M. (1990). Personality, affect, and behavior in groups. *Journal of Applied Psychology, 75,* 107–116.

Gill, D. L. (1979). The prediction of group motor performance from individual member abilities. *Journal of Motor Behavior, 11,* 113–122.

Grofman, B., Owen, G., & Feld, S. L. (1983). Thirteen theorems in search of the truth. *Theory and Decision, 15,* 261–278.

Guzzo, R. A., Jette, R. D., & Katzell, R. A. (1985). The effects of psychologically based interventions on worker productivity: A meta-analysis. *Personnel Psychology, 38,* 275–292.

Haleblian, J., & Finkelstein, S. (1993). Top management team size, CEO dominance, and firm performance: The moderating roles of environmental turbulence and discretion. *Academy of Management Journal, 36,* 844–863.

Hamburger, H., Guyer, M., & Fox, J. (1975). Group size and cooperation. *Journal of Conflict Resolution, 19,* 503–531.

Harbour, J. L. (1993). Increasing efficiency: A process-oriented approach. *Performance Improvement Quarterly, 6,* 92–114.

Hardy, C. J., & Latané, B. (1988). Social loafing in cheerleaders: Effects of team membership and competition. *Journal of Sport and Exercise Psychology, 10,* 109–114.

Hare, A. P. (1952). Interaction and consensus in different sized groups. *American Sociological Review, 17,* 261–267.

Hare, A. P. (1981). Group size. *American Behavioral Scientist, 24,* 695–708.

Haythorn, W. W. (1968). The composition of groups: A review of the literature. *Acta Psychologica, 28,* 97–128.

Haythorn, W. W., Couch, A., Haefner, D., Langham, P., & Carter, L. (1956). The effects of varying combinations of authoritarian and equalitarian leaders and followers. *Journal of Abnormal and Social Psychology, 53,* 210–219.

Heilman, M. E., Block, C. J., & Lucas, J. A. (1992). Presumed incompetent? Stigmatization and affirmative action. *Journal of Applied Psychology, 77,* 536–544.

Heslin, R. (1964). Predicting group task effectiveness from member characteristics. *Psychological Bulletin, 62,* 248–256.

Hill, G. W. (1982). Group versus individual performance: Are N + 1 heads better than one? *Psychological Bulletin, 91,* 517–539.

Hodson, D. (1993). Managing an increasingly diverse work force. *Manufacturing Systems, 11,* 56–58.

Hoffman, L. R. (1959). Homogeneity of member personality and its effect on group problem-solving. *Journal of Abnormal and Social Psychology, 58,* 27–32.

Hoffman, L. R., & Maier, J. R. F. (1961). Quality and acceptance of problem solutions by members of homogeneous and heterogeneous groups. *Journal of Abnormal and Social Psychology, 62,* 401–407.

Hogan, R., Raza, S., & Driskell, J. E. (1988). Personality, team performance, and organizational context. In P. Whitney & R. B. Ochsman (Eds.), *Psychology and productivity* (pp. 93–103). New York: Plenum.

Hollister, L. A., Day, N. E., & Jesaitis, P. T. (1993). Diversity programs: Key to competitiveness, or just another fad? *Organization Development Journal, 11,* 49–59.

Jackson, S. E. (1992). Team composition in organizational settings: Issues in managing an increasingly diverse workforce. In S. Worchel, W. Wood, & J. Simpson (Eds.), *Group process and productivity* (pp. 138–173). Newbury Park, CA: Sage.

Jackson, S. E., Brett, J. F., Sessa, V. I., Cooper, D. M., Julin, J. A., & Peyronnin, K. (1991). Some differences make a difference: Individual dissimilarity and group heterogeneity as correlates of recruitment, promotions, and turnover. *Journal of Applied Psychology, 76,* 675–689.

James, J. (1951). A preliminary study of the size determinant in small group interaction. *American Sociological Review, 16,* 474–477.

Janis, I. L. (1972). *Groupthink: Psychological studies of policy decisions and fiascoes* (2nd ed.). Boston: Houghton Mifflin.

Jehn, K. A. (1992). The impact of intragroup conflict on effectiveness: A multimethod examination of the benefits and detriments of conflict (Doctoral dissertation, Northwestern University, 1992). *Dissertation Abstracts International, 53,* 2005.

Jones, M. B. (1974). Regressing group on individual effectiveness. *Organizational Behavior and Human Performance, 11,* 426–451.

Kanter, R. M. (1977). Some effects of proportions on group life: Skewed sex ratios and responses to token women. *American Journal of Sociology, 82,* 465–490.

Karau, S. J., & Williams, K. D. (1993). Social loafing: A meta-analytic review and theoretical integration. *Journal of Personality and Social Psychology, 65,* 681–706.

Katz, A. H. (1981). Self-help and mutual aid: An emerging social movement. *Annual Review of Sociology, 7,* 129–155.

Katzenbach, J. R., & Smith, D. K. (1993). *The wisdom of teams: Creating the high-performance organization.* Boston: Harvard Business School Press.

Kenny, D. A., & Hallmark, B. W. (1992). Rotation designs in leadership research. *Leadership Quarterly, 3,* 25–41.

Kenny, D. A., Hallmark, B. W., Sullivan, P., & Kashy, D. A. (1993). The analysis of designs in which individuals are in more than one group. *British Journal of Social Psychology, 32,* 173–190.

Kenny, D. A., & Zaccaro, S. (1983). An estimate of variance due to traits in leadership. *Journal of Applied Psychology, 68,* 678–685.

Kerr, N. (1995). Norms in social dilemmas. In D. Schroeder (Ed.), *Social dilemmas: Perspectives on individuals and groups* (pp. 31–47). Westport, CT: Praeger.

Kirchmeyer, C., & Cohen, A. (1992). Multicultural groups: Their performance and reactions with constructive conflict. *Group and Organization Management, 17,* 153–170.

Larson, C. E., & LaFasto, F. M. J. (1989). *Teamwork: What must go right, what can go wrong.* Newbury Park, CA: Sage.

Latané, B. (1981). The psychology of social impact. *American Psychologist, 36,* 343–356.

Latané, B., & Nida, S. (1981). Ten years of research on group size and helping. *Psychological Bulletin, 89,* 308–324.

Latané, B., Williams, K., & Harkins, S. (1979). Many hands make light the work: The causes and consequences of social loafing. *Journal of Personality and Social Psychology, 37,* 822–832.

Laughlin, P. R. (1978). Ability and group problem solving. *Journal of Research and Development in Education, 12,* 114–120.

Levine, J. M., & Moreland, R. L. (1994). Group socialization: Theory and research. In W. Stroebe & M. Hewstone (Eds.), *European review of social psychology* (Vol. 5, pp. 305–336). Chichester, England: Wiley.

Libby, R., Trotman, K. T., & Zimmer, I. (1987). Member variation, recognition of expertise, and group performance. *Journal of Applied Psychology, 72,* 81–87.

Lockheed, M. E. (1985). Sex and social influence: A meta-analysis guided by theory. In J. Berger & M. Zelditch (Eds.), *Status, rewards, and influence: How expectancies organize behavior* (pp. 406–429). San Francisco: Jossey-Bass.

Lundy, J. L. (1992). *Teams: How to develop peak performance teams for world-class results.* Chicago: Dartnell.

Maccoby, E. E. (1990). Gender and relationships: A developmental account. *American Psychologist, 45,* 513–520.

Magaro, P. A., & Ashbrook, R. M. (1985). The personality of societal groups. *Journal of Personality and Social Psychology, 48,* 1479–1489.

Mann, L. (1981). The baiting crowd in episodes of threatened suicide. *Journal of Personality and Social Psychology, 41,* 703–709.

Marwell, G. (1963). Visibility in small groups. *Journal of Social Psychology, 61,* 311–325.

Maznevski, M. L. (1994). Understanding our differences: Performance in decision-making groups with diverse members. *Human Relations, 47,* 531–552.

McCain, B. R., O'Reilly, C. A., & Pfeffer, J. (1983). The effects of departmental demography on turnover. *Academy of Management Journal, 26,* 626–641.

McGrath, J. E., & Rotchford, N. (1983). Time and behavior in organizations. In L. L. Cummings & B. M. Staw (Eds.), *Research in organizational behavior* (Vol. 5, pp. 57–101). Greenwich, CT: JAI.

McGuire, W. J., McGuire, C. V., & Winton, W. (1979). Effect of household sex composition on the salience of one's gender in the spontaneous self-concept. *Journal of Experimental Social Psychology, 15,* 77–90.

McPherson, J. M. (1983). The size of voluntary associations. *Social Forces, 61,* 1044–1064.

McPherson, J. M., & Smith-Lovin, L. (1986). Sex segregation in voluntary associations. *American Sociological Review, 51,* 61–79.

Messick, D. M., & Brewer, M. B. (1983). Solving social dilemmas: A review. In L. Wheeler & P. Shaver (Eds.), *Review of personality and social psychology* (Vol. 4, pp. 11–44). Beverly Hills, CA: Sage.

Michaelsen, L. K., Watson, W. E., & Black, R. H. (1989). A realistic test of individual vs. group consensus decision making. *Journal of Applied Psychology, 74,* 834–839.

Michaelsen, L. K., Watson, W. E., Schwartzkopf, A., & Black, R. H. (1992). Group decision making: How you frame the question determines what you find. *Journal of Applied Psychology, 77,* 106–108.

Miller, C. E. (1989). The social psychological effects of group decision rules. In P. Paulus (Ed.), *Psychology of group influence* (pp. 327–355). Hillsdale, NJ: Lawrence Erlbaum Associates.

Miller, N., & Davidson-Podgorny, G. (1987). Theoretical models of intergroup relations and the use of cooperative teams as an intervention for desegregated settings. In C. Hendrick (Ed.), *Group processes and intergroup relations* (pp. 41–67). Newbury Park, CA: Sage.

Moreland, R. L. (1987). The formation of small groups. In C. Hendrick (Ed.), *Group processes* (pp. 80–110). Newbury Park, CA: Sage.

Moreland, R. L., Hogg, M. A., & Hains, S. (1994). Back to the future: Social psychological research on groups. *Journal of Experimental Social Psychology, 30,* 527–555.

Moreland, R. L., & Levine, J. M. (1982). Socialization in small groups: Temporal changes in individual–group relations. In L. Berkowitz (Ed.), *Advances in experimental social psychology* (Vol. 15, pp. 137–192). New York: Academic Press.

Moreland, R. L., & Levine, J. M. (1989). Newcomers and oldtimers in small groups. In P. Paulus (Ed.), *Psychology of group influence* (pp. 143–231). Hillsdale, NJ: Lawrence Erlbaum Associates.

Moreland, R. L., & Levine, J. M. (1992). The composition of small groups. In E. J. Lawler, B. Markovsky, C. Ridgeway, & H. A. Walker (Eds.), *Advances in group processes* (Vol. 9, pp. 237–280). Greenwich, CT: JAI.

Morgan, B. B., & Lassiter, D. L. (1992). Team composition and staffing. In R. W. Swezey & E. Salas (Eds.), *Teams: Their training and performance* (pp. 75–100). Norwood, NJ: Ablex.

Mullen, B. (1983). Operationalizing the effect of the group on the individual: A self-attention perspective. *Journal of Experimental Social Psychology, 19,* 295–332.

Mullen, B. (1987). Self-attention theory: The effects of group composition on the individual. In B. Mullen & G. R. Goethals (Eds.), *Theories of group behavior* (pp. 125–146). New York: Springer-Verlag.

Mullen, B. (1991). Group composition, salience, and cognitive representations: The phenomenology of being in a group. *Journal of Experimental Social Psychology, 27,* 297–323.

Mullen, B., Symons, C., Hu, L., & Salas, E. (1989). Group size, leadership behavior, and subordinate satisfaction. *Journal of General Psychology, 116,* 155–169.

Nahavandi, A., & Aranda, E. (1994). Restructuring teams for the re-engineered organization. *Academy of Management Executive, 8,* 58–68.

Nasser, D. L. (1988). How to run a focus group. *Public Relations Journal, 44,* 33–34.

Nemeth, C. J. (1992). Minority dissent as a stimulant to group performance. In S. Worchel, W. Wood, & J. A. Simpson (Eds.), *Group process and productivity* (pp. 95–111). Newbury Park, CA: Sage.

Nemeth, C. J., & Staw, B. M. (1989). The tradeoffs of social control and innovation in groups and organizations. In L. Berkowitz (Ed.), *Advances in experimental social psychology* (Vol. 22, pp. 175–210). San Diego: Academic Press.

Newman, G. A., Edwards, J. E., & Raju, N. S. (1989). Organizational development interventions: A meta-analysis of their effects. *Personnel Psychology, 42,* 461–489.

Oakes, P. J. (1987). The salience of social categories. In J. C. Turner, M. A. Hogg, P. J. Oakes, S. D. Reicher, & M. S. Wetherell (Eds.), *Rediscovering the social group: A self-categorization theory* (pp. 117–141). Oxford, England: Basil Blackwell.

O'Brien, G. E., & Owens, A. G. (1969). Effects of organizational structure on correlations between members' abilities and group productivity. *Journal of Applied Psychology, 53,* 525–530.

O'Dell, J. W. (1968). Group size and emotional interaction. *Journal of Personality and Social Psychology, 8,* 75–78.

O'Reilly, C. A., Caldwell, D. F., & Barnett, W. P. (1989). Work group demography, social integration, and turnover. *Administrative Science Quarterly, 34,* 21–37.

Parker, G. M. (1990). *Team players and teamwork: The new competitive business strategy.* San Francisco: Jossey-Bass.

Parker, G. M. (1994). *Cross-functional teams: Working with allies, enemies, and other strangers.* San Francisco: Jossey-Bass.

Patterson, M. L., & Schaeffer, R. E. (1977). Effects of size and sex composition on interaction distance, participation, and satisfaction in small groups. *Small Group Behavior, 8,* 433–442.

Rice, F. (1994). How to make diversity pay. *Fortune, 130,* 78–86.

Ridgeway, C. L. (1988). Gender differences in task groups: A status and legitimacy account. In M. Webster & M. Foschi (Eds.), *Status generalization: New theory and research* (pp. 188–206). Stanford, CA: Stanford University Press.

Rosenberg, S., Erlick, D. E., & Berkowitz, L. (1955). Some effects of varying combinations of group members on group performance measures and leadership behaviors. *Journal of Abnormal and Social Psychology, 51,* 195–203.

Scharf, A. (1989). How to change seven rowdy people. *Industrial Management, 31,* 20–22.

Schein, E. H. (1983). The role of the founder in creating organizational culture. *Organizational Dynamics, 7,* 13–28.

Schneider, B. (1987). The people make the place. *Personnel Psychology, 40,* 437–453.

Schoggen, P. (1989). *Behavior settings: A revision and extension of Roger G. Barker's Ecological Psychology.* Stanford, CA: Stanford University Press.

Schutz, W. C. (1958). *FIRO: A three-dimensional theory of interpersonal behavior.* New York: Rinehart.

Shaw, M. E. (1981). *Group dynamics.* New York: McGraw-Hill.

Shepperd, J. A. (1993). Productivity loss in performance groups: A motivation analysis. *Psychological Bulletin, 113,* 67–81.

Shiflett, S. (1979). Toward a general model of small group productivity. *Psychological Bulletin, 86,* 67–79.

Singh, J. V., & Lumsden, C. J. (1990). Theory and research in organizational ecology. *Annual Review of Sociology, 16,* 161–195.

Slater, P. E. (1958). Contrasting correlates of group size. *Sociometry, 21,* 129–139.

Stasser, G., Kerr, N. L., & Davis, J. H. (1989). Influence processes and consensus models in decision-making groups. In P. Paulus (Ed.), *Psychology of group influence* (pp. 279–326). Hillsdale, NJ: Lawrence Erlbaum Associates.

Stasser, G. M., & Taylor, L. A. (1991). Speaking turns in face-to-face discussions. *Journal of Personality and Social Psychology, 60,* 675–684.

Steiner, I. D. (1966). Models for inferring relationships between group size and potential group productivity. *Behavioral Science, 11,* 273–283.

Steiner, I. D. (1972). *Group process and productivity.* New York: Academic Press.

Swezey, R. W., & Salas, E. (Eds.). (1992). *Teams: Their training and performance.* Norwood, NJ: Ablex.

Terborg, J. R., Castore, C. H., & DeNinno, J. A. (1976). A longitudinal field investigation of the impact of group composition on group performance and cohesion. *Journal of Personality and Social Psychology, 34,* 782–790.

Thomas, E. J., & Fink, C. F. (1963). Effects of group size. *Psychological Bulletin, 60,* 371–384.

Tindale, R. S., & Larson, J. R. (1992a). Assembly bonus effect or typical group performance? A comment on Michaelsen, Watson, and Black. *Journal of Applied Psychology, 77,* 102–105.

Tindale, R. S., & Larson, J. R. (1992b). It's not how you frame the question, it's how you interpret the results. *Journal of Applied Psychology, 77,* 109–110.

Tsui, A. S., Egan, T. D., & O'Reilly, C. A. (1992). Being different: Relational demography and organizational attachment. *Administrative Science Quarterly, 37,* 549–579.

Tziner, A., & Eden, D. (1985). Effects of crew composition on crew performance: Does the whole equal the sum of its parts? *Journal of Applied Psychology, 70,* 85–93.

Vogt, J. F., & Griffith, S. J. (1988). Team development and proactive change: Theory and training implications. *Organization Development Journal, 6,* 81–87.

Watson, W. E., Kumar, K., & Michaelsen, L. K. (1993). Cultural diversity's impact on interaction process and performance: Comparing homogeneous and diverse task groups. *Academy of Management Journal, 36,* 590–602.

Watson, W., Michaelsen, L. K., & Sharp, W. (1991). Member competence, group interaction, and group decision making: A longitudinal study. *Journal of Applied Psychology, 76,* 803–809.

Wegner, D. M. (1987). Transactive memory: A contemporary analysis of the group mind. In B. Mullen & G. R. Goethals (Eds.), *Theories of group behavior* (pp. 185–208). New York: Springer-Verlag.

Weingart, L. R. (1992). Impact of group goals, task component complexity, effort, and planning on group performance. *Journal of Applied Psychology, 77,* 682–693.

Weldon, E., & Weingart, L. R. (1993). Group goals and group performance. *British Journal of Social Psychology, 32,* 307–334.

Wicker, A. W., Kirmeyer, S. L., Hanson, L., & Alexander, D. (1976). Effects of manning levels on subjective experiences, performance, and verbal interaction in groups. *Organizational Behavior and Human Performance, 17,* 251–274.

Wiersema, M. F., & Bantel, K. A. (1992). Top management team demography and corporate strategic change. *Academy of Management Journal, 35,* 91–121.

Williams, K., Harkins, S., & Latané, B. (1981). Identifiability as a deterrent to social loafing: Two cheering experiments. *Journal of Personality and Social Psychology, 40,* 303–311.

Wood, W. (1987). Meta-analytic review of sex differences in group performance. *Psychological Bulletin, 102,* 53–71.

Yamagishi, T. (1992). Group size and the provision of a sanctioning system in a social dilemma. In W. B. Liebrand, D. M. Messick, & H. A. Wilke (Eds.), *Social dilemmas: Theoretical issues and research findings* (pp. 267–288). Oxford, England: Pergamon.

Yetton, P., & Bottger, P. (1983). The relationships among group size, member ability, social decision schemes, and performance. *Organizational Behavior and Human Performance, 32,* 145–159.

Zaccaro, S. J. (1984). Social loafing: The role of task attractiveness. *Personality and Social Psychology Bulletin, 10,* 99–106.

Zaccaro, S. J., Foti, R. J., & Kenny, D. A. (1991). Self-monitoring and trait-based variance in leadership: An investigation of leader flexibility across multiple group situations. *Journal of Applied Psychology, 76,* 308–315.

Zajonc, R. B. (1976). Family configuration and intelligence. *Science, 192,* 227–236.

Ziller, R. C. (1972). Homogeneity and heterogeneity of group membership. In C. McClintock (Ed.), *Experimental social psychology* (pp. 385–411). New York: Holt, Rinehart & Winston.

2

SOCIAL COMPENSATION AND THE KÖHLER EFFECT: TOWARD A THEORETICAL EXPLANATION OF MOTIVATION GAINS IN GROUP PRODUCTIVITY

Wolfgang Stroebe
Utrecht University

Michael Diehl
University of Tübingen

Georgios Abakoumkin
University of Patras

Early research on group productivity was characterized by the conviction that individuals are more productive in groups than when working alone. Thus, Shaw (1932) claimed to have demonstrated that individuals were better able to solve problems in groups than individually. Osborn (1953) developed brainstorming rules that were assumed to help groups produce creative ideas. The search for the magical quality that enabled groups to improve the productivity of their members stimulated research in this area and made it a fascinating enterprise.

The decline in interest in small-group research began during the 1950s and 1960s when Marquart (1955), Lorge and Solomon (1955), and others demonstrated that the alleged superiority of groups over individuals disappeared when proper baselines were used. Thus, Marquart showed that Shaw's (1932) problem-solving groups did no better than "nominal groups." Such nominal groups consisted of the same number of individuals who worked alone and were credited with a solution whenever one of them solved the problem. Even more damaging were the findings of Taylor, Berry, and Block (1958), who found that brainstorming groups produced considerably fewer ideas than the same number of individuals working by themselves. This type of evidence led Steiner (1972) to formulate his well-known "law" that the actual productivity achieved by a group was equal to their potential productivity *minus* losses due to faulty processes.

This statement has often been misinterpreted. Because potential productivity has been erroneously equated with the performance of nominal groups, Steiner's (1972) statement has been taken to imply that people will *never* perform better in groups than they do individually. This seemed to be consistent with research findings that overwhelmingly favored motivation losses (for a review, see Baron, Kerr, & Miller, 1992). The most widely reported motivation loss in group performance was the Ringelmann effect, which originally became known through a review published by Moede in 1927 in the German journal *Industrielle Psychotechnik*. Ironically, in this article, Moede also summarized the findings of a set of studies conducted by Otto Köhler (1926, 1927), which in fact demonstrated *gains* in group productivity. Until recently, these findings have been completely overlooked (Witte, 1989).

Although we also discuss motivation losses, the main emphasis of this chapter is on motivation gains. We begin with a brief review of Steiner's (1972) theory of group productivity. We then analyze the conditions under which motivation losses have been found in groups and contrast these with the conditions under which motivation gains have been observed. Our discussion of motivation gains is based mainly on the work of Köhler (1926). We first describe Köhler's original studies and his interpretation of these findings. We then discuss alternative theoretical interpretations in the light of a series of empirical studies that we have been conducting over the last few years.

STEINER'S THEORY OF GROUP PRODUCTIVITY

According to Steiner (1972) the productivity of a group is determined by three classes of variables: demands (e.g., requirements imposed by the task, or by the rules under which the task must be performed), resources (i.e., all relevant knowledge, skills, or tools possessed by group members), and process (i.e., all intrapersonal or interpersonal actions by which people transform their resources into a group product). The potential productivity of a group reflects the maximum level of productivity that can be achieved if the group makes optimal use of its resources. Potential productivity can be inferred from an analysis of task demands and resources, because it depends only on these two types of variables.

Steiner (1972) developed a classification of tasks that allows for the prediction of potential group productivity for unitary tasks, that is, tasks that cannot be broken down into different subtasks. The actual productivity of groups depends on the way in which individual inputs are related to the group product. For tasks such as generating as many ideas as possible in brainstorming groups, collecting money for charity, rowing a boat, or running a relay, individual inputs are added together (*additive tasks*). Thus, the group product is determined by the individual contributions of *all* group members. There are other tasks, however, where group productivity depends solely on the performance of the *best* or *worst* group member. For example, solving problems, remembering certain facts, or putting the garbage into the garbage can are *disjunctive tasks* where group productivity depends on the best (most intelligent, most retentive, or most accurate) group member. On the other hand, going on a bicycle tour or jointly writing a chapter are *conjunctive tasks* where the worst (usually the slowest) group member determines a group's productivity.

Estimates of the potential group productivity for such unitary tasks have been based on information about individual performance on a given task (e.g., average individual performance or distribution of individual performances). Task-specific models are then used to predict the potential group productivity from knowledge of individual performance. For example, according to the additive tasks model, potential group productivity should equal the average individual performance multiplied by the number of group members. For disjunctive and conjunctive tasks, the probability to solve the task will equal the probability that at least one group member (respectively all the group members) will be able to solve the task. Empirically, motivation gains should therefore occur when individuals exert more effort in groups than they do individually (given that the tasks they work on are of a nature where increases in motivation result in increased performance; i.e., simple or well-learned tasks; Zajonc, 1965).

MOTIVATIONAL LOSSES IN GROUP PERFORMANCE

Empirical Evidence

The study of Ringelmann (1913) was the earliest demonstration of motivation losses in groups (Kravitz & Martin, 1986). Ringelmann had individuals and groups of two, three, or eight men pull on a rope as hard as possible. The average force (in kilograms) was: individuals—63 kg; two-person group—118 kg; three-person group—160 kg; eight-person group—248 kg. Thus, although group productivity increased with increasing group size, the addition of new members to the group brought diminishing returns. For example, instead of 126 kg, as expected from an additive model, the two-person group pulled only 118 kg. The performance of eight-person groups was less than half of the 504 kg one would have predicted on the basis of one's knowledge of individual performance.

At least part of the productivity loss in the Ringelmann (1913) study is due to faulty coordination. Thus, it is unlikely that all group members pulled exactly at the same time and/or in the same direction. However, the importance of motivation losses for this type of task was clearly demonstrated by Ingham, Levinger, Graves, and Peckham (1974), who showed a performance decrease even for subjects who were led to believe that the confederates of the experimenter standing behind them were group members pulling the rope, when in fact their individual performance was being measured. Ingham and colleagues found that the effort exerted by subjects decreased in small groups (i.e., one to three persons) with increasing perceived group size.

Some years later, Latané, Williams, and Harkins (1979) replicated these effects with a different task. Their subjects had to cheer as loudly as possible under conditions where subjects either believed that they cheered alone or as part of groups of different sizes. Consistent with the earlier studies, Latané and his colleagues found that individual motivation decreased with increases in apparent group size. Latané and his colleagues called this motivation loss *social loafing*. Subsequent research has indicated that social loafing effects are not restricted to motor tasks but also occur when groups are performing perceptual or cognitive tasks (e.g., Petty, Harkins, & Williams, 1980; Szymanski & Harkins, 1987).

Free Riding and the Economics of Group Productivity

Stroebe and Frey (1982) proposed an economic theory of group productivity that attributed this type of motivation loss to differences in incentive structure between individual and group performance. For individuals working on their own, there is usually a fairly direct relationship between performance and reward. For example, within the limits of his or her ability, the grade of a student working on a project is determined by the effort he or she puts into the task. The relationship between performance and reward is much less direct for students working on a project in a group. If individual contributions are not identifiable, a student's grade will depend on the efforts of his fellow students as much as on his or her own effort.

Obviously, such differences in the correlation between individual performance and individual reward can be eliminated by choosing a reward structure that assures that individual shares in the group product are proportional to members' contributions. However, a distribution of the group product according to the individual inputs is frequently impracticable, either because individual contributions are not identifiable (e.g., group rope pulling), or because groups feel that scrutinizing individual contributions might create tensions and antagonism and thus disrupt intermember relations. To avoid such tensions, groups often choose the equality principle and agree to give the same share to all members, irrespective of the value of individual contributions.

Once a group has adopted equality as the principle of reward allocation, the group product becomes a "public good" (Buchanan & Tullock, 1962; Samuelson, 1954). The difference between private goods (e.g., a bicycle or a cup of coffee) and public goods (e.g., clean air or a military victory) lies in the ease with which those who have not contributed to the production of the good can be excluded from consumption. This inability to exclude noncontributors from the consumption of public goods creates a temptation to free ride, that is to profit from the

2. SOCIAL COMPENSATION AND THE KÖHLER EFFECT

activities of others without making a fair contribution of one's own. According to Stroebe and Frey (1982), the temptation to free ride increases with increasing group size. This positive relationship is mediated by the size-related variation in two factors that directly influence group members' willingness to contribute to the provision of the public good: perceived identifiability and perceived effectiveness.

Perceived identifiability refers to the question whether individual contributions can be monitored by other group members. If individual contributions are identifiable to other group members, the group member has to consider additional rewards or costs in his decision whether to contribute to the provision of the public good. By noticeably not contributing, the free rider is likely to violate a group norm and to incur negative sanctions. Furthermore, he or she is likely to encourage others to free ride, which may decrease the chance that the public good will be produced.

Perceived effectiveness refers to the individual member's perception of the difference it would make to the group and to him or herself if he or she decided to contribute. According to Stroebe and Frey (1982), perceived effectiveness can be separated into two mechanisms, which are both related to group size: First, if success or failure depends on the group productivity reaching or surpassing a given criterion (e.g., reaching a victory), individual control over the production of the public good decreases with increasing group size. Thus, whereas in small groups individual members can produce the total group product by themselves, if they want to, this is typically not possible for the more sizable products expected from large groups. Second, because in large groups not all individual contributions are typically required for the group product, members may feel that their particular contribution is dispensable. The difference between control and dispensability can be clarified by considering task structure as an additional variable. For disjunctive tasks, where the group is credited with a solution if one member has solved the problem, dispensability of individual contributions increases with increasing group size. At the same time, however, individual control over the production of the group product remains unaffected by changes in group size.

Strategies to Reduce the Free Riding Effect

A classic strategy to reduce the temptation to free ride, which is recommended by political scientists, involves the privatization of the public good (e.g., Orbell & Dawes, 1981). For example, overgrazing of the commons can be prevented by dividing up the commonly owned land and selling the pieces to the owners of the herds. In cases of group products, "privatization" would imply a change in reward structure that assures that the group product is distributed in shares that are proportional to individual inputs. However, this kind of equitable distribution would necessitate scrutinizing individual contributions. As we argued earlier, this is often not desirable or feasible for group members.

Increasing the identifiability of individual contributions is a second strategy that according to the economic model of group productivity should lower the temptation to free ride. Especially with the kind of tasks used in studies of social loafing, for which it is difficult or even impossible for group members to tell how much other members are contributing, increasing perceived identifiability should decrease social loafing or free riding.[1] This hypothesis was supported in a study by Williams, Harkins, and Latané (1981), who varied group size and identifiability independently, using the shouting task. Their findings indicate quite clearly that performance loss varied as a function of identifiability and not group size. The performance loss typically observed with increasing group size disappeared when group members were led to believe that their individual output could be monitored, whereas individual performers who thought that their output could not be monitored showed the kind of performance loss typically observed in three- to four-person groups. Later research has further demonstrated that it is not the identifiability of contributions per se that reduces the temptation to free ride, but rather the possibility of evaluation that identifiability makes possible. If individual contributions are identifiable but for some reason cannot be evaluated (e.g., because comparison with the performance of other group members is not possible), social loafing might still occur (Harkins, 1987; Harkins & Szymanski, 1987).

A third strategy that should reduce the temptation to free ride according to the economic model of Stroebe and Frey (1982), would involve making individual contributions indispensable. The role of dispensability as a mediator of free riding has been demonstrated in a series of experiments conducted by Kerr and Bruun (1983). Dispensability was manipulated by varying task demands and subjects' self-perceived ability. Subjects were led to believe that their ability to perform a group task was either higher or lower than that of the other group members. Task demand was manipulated by telling subjects that a monetary price had been offered for the group that performed best. Depending on the experimental condition, subjects were told that either the score of the highest scoring member (disjunctive task) or that of the lowest scoring member (conjunctive task) would count as the group product. As expected, conjunctive task demands encouraged free riding among high-ability subjects but not among low-ability subjects, who must have perceived their own contributions as indispensable. Low-ability subjects were more likely to free ride with disjunctive tasks. Here high-ability subjects, whose performance was essential for the group effort, showed substantially less performance loss (for a somewhat different manipulation of dispensability, see also Harkins & Petty, 1982, Experiment 3).

---

[1]Our definition of "free riding" differs from that suggested by Kerr (e.g., Kerr & Bruun, 1983). Kerr restricted the term *free riding* to motivation losses caused by perceived dispensability of individual contributions, and used *social loafing* for motivation losses due to low identifiability. In line with most economists, we use free riding as the general term to refer to all motivation losses that result from the inability to exclude noncontributors from the consumption of a public good. According to our definition of the concept, social loafing is one form of free riding.

A fourth strategy suggested by the economic theory of group productivity would involve increasing the value of the public good. This strategy is most likely to be effective under conditions where individual members have control over the production of the public good. If the group members feel that their own efforts will hardly increase the probability that the good will be produced, they are unlikely to exert a great deal of effort, regardless of the value of the good. Whereas perceived control over the production of the public good should decrease with increasing group size for additive tasks, it should be independent of group size for disjunctive tasks.

That the provision of collective incentives for good performance can reduce productivity loss in small groups has been demonstrated in a study by Shepperd and Wright (1989). In this study subjects had to generate uses for an object either individually or as part of an aggregate in which individual contributions would be anonymous. Much less motivation loss occurred when individuals or groups were offered a reward for individually or collectively producing up to a certain standard, than when no such reward was offered.

A final strategy to reduce the temptation to free ride involves the reduction in the costs of the individual contribution to a public good. According to the economic model, the temptation to free ride should be stronger, the greater the individual costs of contributing to the public good. If there are no costs involved for the individual in contributing to the public good, he or she should not be tempted to free ride. In line with this reasoning, Diehl and Stroebe (1987) argued that the failure to find strong evidence for free riding in their brainstorming groups was due to the fact that student subjects who are already committed to participating in an experimental session (i.e., no time costs) enjoy producing ideas rather than perceiving it as costly.

MOTIVATION GAINS IN GROUP PERFORMANCE

Although the conditions under which (laboratory) groups typically work might favor motivation losses, there is no theoretical reason why individuals should not work harder in groups than they do individually. The theoretical and empirical analysis of the factors that are responsible for motivation losses in groups performed previously makes it possible to design group settings in which motivation losses are unlikely to occur. Once one has succeeded in eliminating motivation losses, the addition of incentives to the group setting that were not present in the individual situation should result in motivation *gains* in group productivity.

In the following, we present two research programs that have identified inequality in the distribution of relevant abilities among group members as a factor that can facilitate motivation gains in groups. If groups are formed of members who differ in their ability to perform the required task, and if success in this task is important for the group members, then two types of motivation gains are likely to occur: (a) The stronger members of the group might work harder to compensate for the low performance of the weak member, and (b) the weaker member of the group might work harder under group than individual conditions in order to avoid being responsible for group failure.

Social Compensation in Groups

Social compensation effects were recently studied by Williams and Karau (1991). Expressed in the terminology of the economic model of group productivity, Williams and Karau suggested that a group member will work harder in a group setting than individually if the following conditions are given: (a) The production of the public good is very important, (b) the task is additive, (c) the individual perceives control over the production of the public good, and (d) the other group members are unable or unwilling to contribute to the production of the good.

Williams and Karau (1991) conducted three experiments to test these hypotheses. Subjects in these studies had to brainstorm on uses for an object under conditions where their performance would be assessed individually or as part of a two-person group. When subjects were led to believe that their co-workers were unable or unwilling to contribute to the group product, subjects produced substantially more ideas when working in a group rather than individually. Thus, when subjects knew that they would be evaluated jointly with their partners as part of a group, they exerted more effort than they would have done individually to compensate for their partners' low productivity.

This type of social compensation is only likely to occur under conditions where a capable group member is *able* and *willing* to compensate for the weaker member(s) of the team. In all the experimental settings created by Williams and Karau (1991), the additive task structure and the small group size (i.e., dyads) made it possible for the stronger group member to compensate for the weaker one. If groups had been larger or if the task had been conjunctive, it would have been much more difficult or even impossible for the stronger group members to compensate for the weaker members of their team. If the task had been disjunctive, compensation would not have been necessary. Furthermore, as Williams and Karau (Experiment 3) demonstrated, compensation effects occurred only when subjects considered the task as meaningful.

Beyond Social Compensation: The Köhler Effect

When Williams and Karau (1991) conducted their research, they were unaware of the fact that more than 60 years earlier, Otto Köhler (1926, 1927) had demonstrated with dyads or triads working on a conjunctive task, that group performance depended on the relative individual performance of the group members. Process gains were observed for dyads and triads formed of members who showed moderate discrepancies in ability level. However, these process gains cannot be explained in terms of social compensation, because Köhler used a conjunctive task for which it was difficult or impossible for the stronger member to compensate for the weaker one. The process gains observed in the studies of Köhler must therefore be attributed to increases in the motivation of the weaker member. It appears that the weaker members worked harder in the group than individually, probably to avoid the embarrassment of lowering the group product. Thus, social compensation is only one of the processes contributing to process gains in groups that are characterized by moderate inequality in member abilities. Furthermore, Köhler also demonstrated that there are limits to these effects. Group performance was only higher than the sum of individual performances for groups with moderate discrepancy in ability. If members were very dissimilar or very similar in individual performance, no evidence for process gains was found and the usual group process losses were observed. In the following section we describe these studies and then present our own interpretation of the Köhler effect.

The Köhler Effect: The Original Studies

In a series of articles published in the journal *Industrielle Psychotechnik*, Köhler (1926, 1927) reported the results of four experiments using three different types of physical tasks. We describe these studies in this section.

Experiment I. In his first experiment Köhler (1926) used a weight-lifting task. Subjects in this study were 72 male members of a rowing club who, over a period of several weeks, individually or in dyads repeatedly lifted a weight until they were exhausted. The weight had to be lifted 75 cm and then let down and the performance was tacted by a metronome (2-sec tact). The weight had to be lifted via a pulley (Fig. 2.1). The end of the rope was attached to a crossbar. The crossbar was pulled either by the individual subject or jointly by the dyad. A 41-kg weight was used for individuals and a 82-kg weight for dyads. The distance that the weight was lifted was used as the dependent variable. Because, in the group condition, the weight could only be lifted if both members were able to pull according to the criterion, the task can be considered conjunctive.

Subjects alternatively performed the task individually or as dyads. Figure 2.2 presents the relationship between the individual and group performance averaged over a sizable but unknown number of trials. The y axis reflects the ratio of the group performance to the arithmetic mean of the two individual performances ($\times$ 100). A value of 100 indicates that the dyad performed at the level of their averaged individual performance. Values greater than 100 reflect performance gains of group over individual performance. The x axis depicts the relationship of the individual performances of the two individuals forming the dyad, expressed as the ratio of the performance of the weaker to that of the stronger individual ($\times$ 100). Thus, if both lifted the weight the same distance during individual testing, the ratio would be 100. A ratio of 50 means that during individual performance, the

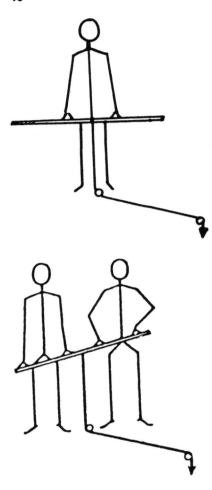

FIG. 2.1. Position of individuals and dyads in the weight-lifting task (Arbeitsgruppenversuch) of Köhler's first experiment. From Köhler (1926).

weaker individual pulled the weight only half the distance lifted by the stronger subject.

Results indicate that, depending on the relative strength of the two individuals forming the dyad, group performance varied between 70% and 135% of the average of the individual performances. When the two group members were either equal or very unequal in strength, there was a process loss. However, when group members were moderately unequal, there was a gain in group over individual performance. With a 25% difference in the weight-lifting ability of the two members of the dyad, the performance gain reaches a maximum of 35%. Thus, the group performance was 35% above the average individual perform-ance. If Köhler (1926) had used the proper baseline for his comparison, that is, the performance of the weaker member rather than the average of the individual inputs of both members, the group gain would have been even more marked.

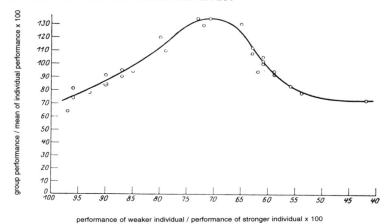

performance of weaker individual / performance of stronger individual x 100

FIG. 2.2. Performance of dyads (group performance divided by the arithmetic mean of the two individual performances) depending on the relative strength of their members (performance of the weaker individual divided by the performance of the stronger individual) in Köhler's first experiment. From Köhler (1926).

Experiment 2. In a second study Köhler (1926) compared the performance of individuals to that of three-person groups. The task was the same as in Experiment 1. The three-person groups had to lift a weight of 123 kg. Two of the members of three-person groups took the lever at each end, with the middle member gripping it in the middle, where it was connected to the rope (Fig. 2.3). Members were arranged in a way that the strongest and weakest members held the outside positions, with the middle member also being of medium strength.

Results for the three-person groups were consistent with the findings for two-person groups (Fig. 2.4). Within the range of 180% to 160% (sum of the individual performance of the two weaker members divided by the best member

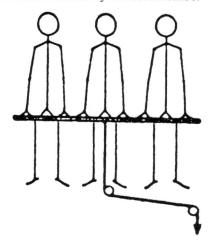

FIG. 2.3. Position of the members of three-person groups in the weight-lifting task (Arbeitsgruppen-versuch) of Köhler's first experiment. From Köhler (1926).

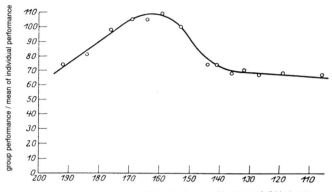

FIG. 2.4. Performance of triads (group performance divided by the arithmetic mean of the three individual performances) depending on the relative strength of their members (individual performance of the two weaker members divided by the individual performance of the best member) in Köhler's second experiment. From Köhler (1926).

× 100), group productivity reached approximately 110% of the individual performances. This performance increase is substantially smaller than that observed for two-person groups, a difference that could be due to an increase in coordination losses as well as a decrease in identifiability in the three-person group.

Experiment 3. In a third study Köhler (1927) used a hand wheel with levers attached at each side. Sixty-five subjects took part in this experiment. They turned the wheel either alone or in two-person groups, with each individual holding one of the levers. Subjects had to turn the wheel tacted in a 2-second tact by a metronome for as long as possible. In turning the wheel they had to overcome the resistance created by a mechanical brake. Despite the difference in task, the results of this study were comparable to those of the first two experiments. Again, groups composed of moderately unequal members performed above their average individual performance, whereas extremely unequal groups and equal groups both showed a performance loss.

Experiment 4. In a fourth study Köhler (1926) used the same subjects who performed in Experiments 1 and 2. They were asked to pull individually, in two-person or in three-person groups against a dynamometer. Subjects had to pull a rope that was connected to the measuring device above the subject via ropes fixed to the floor. Individuals or groups had to pull this lever, which extended only 30 cm above the floor, as hard as they could for exactly 5 seconds. This was repeated twice and results for the three trials were averaged.

Results were analyzed in the same way as for the weight-lifting experiment. However, for this task no variation of the group performance in relation to the ratio of individual performance was observed. Instead, performance losses could

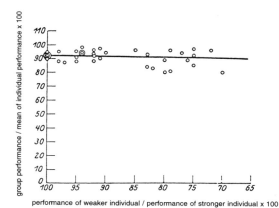

FIG. 2.5. Performance of dyads (group performance divided by the arithmetic mean of the two individual performances) depending on the relative strength of their members (performance of the weaker individual divided by the performance of the stronger individual) in the fourth experiment. From Köhler (1926).

be observed for all groups (Figs. 2.5 and 2.6). The results of two-person groups were at 90% of the mean of their individual performance and those of three-person groups at 80%. This failure of Köhler (1926) to find performance gains in groups for this particular task suggests that conjunctive task structure, high identifiability, and unequal strength are necessary but not sufficient conditions to produce group performance gains. All of these conditions were present in the dynamometer study, and yet, no performance gains occurred.

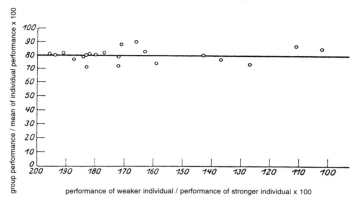

FIG. 2.6. Performance of three-person groups (group performance divided by the arithmetic mean of the two individual performances) depending on the relative strength of their members (performance of the two weaker individuals divided by the performance of the stronger individual) in the fourth experiment. From Köhler (1926).

There are a number of differences between the two tasks that may be responsible for the failure to find a group performance gain. Köhler (1926) reasoned that the time interval of 5 seconds available for the task was too short to allow the development of a leadership structure. Another reason could be that motivation gains are more likely to influence performance for persistence tasks, where subjects have to decide themselves when they are too exhausted to continue, than for a task where only short bursts of energy are required.

Theoretical Interpretations of the Köhler Effect

Competition for Leadership. Köhler (1926, 1927) offered two explanations for his findings. One explanation was in terms of leadership. He suggested that when both members of a dyad are of equal strength, there will be a competition for leadership. An unchallenged leadership can develop only under conditions of unequal strength, where the stronger member assumes the leadership position. Köhler argued that groups need a leader to perform above the individual level because a leader can coordinate individual performance and motivate group members. The problem with this interpretation is that it cannot account for the curvilinear relationship between group performance and relative strength. Because the leader should be the less challenged the greater the difference in the strength of the two members, this assumption would lead one to expect a monotonic rather than a curvilinear relationship between discrepancy in strength and group performance.

Interpersonal Resonance. Köhler's (1926, 1927) second interpretation was in terms of "interpersonal resonance." He suggested that a moderate discrepancy in strength created optimal conditions for "mutual influence and resonance." Under these conditions, the stronger subject somehow motivates the weaker subject to work harder while at the same time increasing his own performance. The problem with this interpretation is that it leaves the nature of the process of interpersonal resonance unspecified. Why would there be a resonance with moderate inequality and not when both members are equal in strength? Furthermore, because the weight-lifting task is a conjunctive task, it seems unlikely that the performance difference was due to an overexertion of both members of the dyad. Although the stronger individual might have been able to compensate somewhat for the weaker member by levering the crossbar, this is a rather awkward way to lift a weight of 82 kg.

Status Incongruency. Witte (1989) attributed the Köhler effect to uncertainty in the relative status of the two collaborators. Witte suggested that in small groups there is typically a clear status hierarchy, depending on the relative performance of group members. He further assumed that with the type of tasks used by Köhler, there is a critical range that would allow a reversal of status and thus induce competition. Outside this range, subjects see no possibility or no need for a reversal of status. Although it seems reasonable that subjects perceive a greater possibility to reverse the status hierarchy at moderate rather than extreme inequality, we would have thought that, according to this hypothesis, competition should be strongest when both are equal in their performance and thus have the same chance of succeeding in their bid for first position.

Goal Comparison. Our own interpretation of the Köhler effect is based on goal-setting and social comparison theories (Stroebe, Diehl, Abakoumkin, & Arnscheid, 1990). We reasoned that individuals who are asked to perform a novel task want to do a "good job," without really knowing what kind of performance is expected. They work hard and over time develop some individual standard for what they consider an adequate performance. If these individuals are then asked to work in a group, they will compare their performance with that of the other group members. When groups are formed of individuals who are equal in their performance, they will feel that their standard is validated by the other group members who perform at the same level. If, on the other hand, groups are formed with members of unequal strength, social comparison processes should induce pressure toward a reduction in the discrepancy in performance standards. Whether the discrepancy will be reduced through a decrease in the performance of the stronger member or in an increase in the performance of the weaker member will depend on the perceived importance of the task. If the task is considered important, the weaker member is likely to feel embarrassed and to try very hard to match the performance level of the stronger member. If, on the other hand, the task is considered unimportant and irrelevant, then the stronger member is likely to reduce his or her performance to the level of the weaker member.

According to Köhler (1926, 1927), the subjects in his study were motivated. Thus, the group performance increase under conditions of moderate inequality of individual performance would have been due to a performance increase of the weaker group member. The performance decrease under conditions of more marked inequality would be due to the fact that the weaker subject is no longer able to compensate for the discrepancy. Because subjects have to perform at the same level due to the conjunctive nature of the task, the stronger subject is forced to lower his or her performance to the level of the weaker subject.

REPLICATING THE KÖHLER EFFECT: THE TÜBINGEN STUDIES

Experiment I

The aim of the first study was merely to see whether we could replicate Köhler's (1926, 1927) findings of process gains in groups in which members were moderately unequal in strength. We therefore built a weight-lifting apparatus that replicated the essential aspects of the Köhler task even though it was constructed along somewhat different lines. A weight of 38 kg was used for individuals and of 76 kg for dyads.

The experiment took place in two sessions. Because the groups were to be formed from members who were either equal in individual performance (1:1) or moderately different (1: .7), we had to run all the individual trials first. Forty-eight male students who were paid for their participation served as subjects, 12 pairs in each condition.

Most of our subjects suffered from intense muscle pain after the first session and were rather unwilling to participate in the second phase of the experiment. Although we had hoped to motivate subjects by merely promising information on the performance of other individuals and groups, we decided to offer a monetary reward ($70) for the three best groups, in order to motivate subjects and assure their further cooperation. Because no monetary rewards had been offered for individual performance, the financial inducement was confounded with the individual versus group manipulation. This did not pose a major problem, however, because we were interested in the compensation effect rather than an individual versus group main effect.

Table 2.1 presents the performance data of individuals and dyads performing the weight-lifting task. The average of the individual performances of the two subjects who later formed the dyad were used as a measure of individual performance. A two-factor (relative strength × group vs. individual performance) analysis of variance (ANOVA) conducted on these performance measures resulted in an interaction that just failed to reach the 5% level of significance ($p < .06$). When the conjunctive instead of the additive model is applied (i.e., when the performance of the less capable member is used as a baseline instead of the average performance of both group members) this interaction effect becomes highly significant. Thus, in line with the findings of Köhler (1926, 1927) groups composed of members who differed moderately in their strength (inferred on the basis of their individual performance) performed significantly better than groups whose members were of equal strength.

A comparison of the group performance with the individual performance of the "weaker" and the "stronger" member of the unequal dyad indicates that the

TABLE 2.1
Means (M) and Standard Deviations (SD) of Individual and Group Performance in the Weight-Lifting Task (Experiment 1)

Relative Strength (Time 1)	Individual Performance (Time 1)	Group Performance (Time 2)
Unequal (1 : .7)	M 45.08	M 52.82
	SD 17.81	SD 22.02
Equal (1 : 1)	M 42.28	M 39.36
	SD 16.84	SD 15.30

group performance is at the level of the "stronger" member (difference .61 m) and far above the performance of the "weaker" member (difference 16.10 m). Thus, the performance increase observed for unequal dyads in the group situation was due to the greater exertion of the "weaker" member of the dyad, who on average lifted the weight 16 m farther or more than 20 times more often (21.5 × .75 m) than he did during individual trials.

The results of our first experiment are in line with an interpretation in terms of goal comparison. In the condition of unequal strength, group performance resembled the individual performance of the stronger member, thus indicating that the weaker member was motivated and able to increase his performance to the level of his partner. Expressed in terms of goal comparison theory, he adopted the performance level of his partner as his own performance goal. In the condition of equal strength neither member of the dyad seemed to be motivated to increase his performance. This indicates that the task did not evoke competition (i.e., a motive to be better than one's partner).

Experiment 2

Because in addition to the health risk, the weight-lifting task did not allow us to measure independently the performance of the individual group members when working under group conditions, we borrowed an idea from Köhler (1927) and used turning a hand wheel as the task for our second experiment. However, unlike in the original experiment where subjects had to turn the wheel in a timed 2-second rhythm, our subjects had to turn the wheel as fast as they could for a period of 10 minutes. This task was quite strenuous because in turning the wheel, subjects had to overcome the strong resistance created by an electromagnetic brake. The number of rotations of the wheel was automatically counted, and this information was relayed to a computer. Because in the individual as well as in the group condition subjects worked in individual rooms on separate wheels, we were able to measure individual performance even under group conditions.

Again, the experiment took place in two sessions, with groups formed after the individual trials from members who were either equal (1:1) in individual performance or moderately different (1:.7). The 36 male students who served as subjects were paid for their participation. The amount of pay was not fixed but depended on their individual performance during individual sessions and on the group performance during group sessions. In order to make the task conjunctive, the members of a dyad were told that they both had to turn their wheels at an approximately equal speed. Continuous feedback was given on the discrepancy in their individual performances via a graphic representation on a monitor. To motivate subjects to adjust their speed to each other, they were told that rewards would be discontinued for periods during which the discrepancy in their performance increased beyond a certain limit marked on the screen.

TABLE 2.2
Means (M) and Standard Deviations (SD) of the Sums of Individual Performances Under Individual
and Group Conditions in the Wheel-Turning Task (Experiment 2)

Relative Strength (Time 1)	Individual Performance (Time 1)	Group Performance (Time 2)
Unequal (1 : .7)	M 2873.00	M 3004.67
	SD 311.92	SD 459.87
Equal (1 : 1)	M 2851.00	M 3071.22
	SD 363.85	SD 318.59

Table 2.2 presents the sum of the individual performances under individual
and group conditions. A two-factor (relative strength × group vs. individual)
ANOVA performed on these data resulted in a significant main effect of the factor
Group Versus Individual. Subjects performed significantly better in groups than
they did in individual sessions. There was no indication of an interaction. Thus,
unlike with the weight-lifting task, dyads of unequal strength did not perform
better than dyads with equal strength, when an additive model was used. However, if we apply the conjunctive model and use the performance of the weaker
member of each dyad as a baseline, instead of the sum of the performances of
both members, we again find a significantly greater performance increase under
conditions of unequal rather than equal strength.

The discrepancy between these findings and those of the weight-lifting experiment becomes quite apparent when we compare the individual performance
of the stronger and the weaker member of each dyad under individual and group
conditions (Table 2.3). Under conditions of equal strength both members of the
groups show a slight performance increase. However, under conditions of unequal strength, there is a much more marked increase in the performance of
the weaker member, which is to some extent compensated for by a performance
decrease of the stronger member. Findings under both conditions are inconsistent with the findings of Experiment 1.

TABLE 2.3
Means (M) and Standard Deviations (SD) of the Differences of the Stronger and Weaker
Group Members Under Individual and Group Conditions in the Wheel-Turning Task
(Experiment 2)

Relative Strength (Time 1)	Stronger Member	Weaker Member
Unequal (1 : .7)	M -152	M +283
	SD 105.02	SD 117.48
Equal (1 : 1)	M +101	M +120
	SD 69.84	SD 69.70

Two factors may have been responsible for our failure to replicate the findings of Experiment 1: First, in contrast to the weight-lifting task, where the performance of dyads did not improve under conditions of equal strength, members of equal-strength dyads in the wheel-turning task seemed to compete with each other. This competition led to an increase in performance comparable to that observed under conditions of unequal strength. Second, whereas with the weight-lifting task the weaker member of dyads of unequal strength increased his performance sufficiently to allow the stronger member to maintain his performance at the level at which he had worked individually, such an increase did not occur with the wheel-turning task.

The failure of the weaker group member to increase his performance to the level of the stronger member under group conditions could have been due to the fact that he already performed near to his maximum during the individual condition. Therefore, he may have been unable to manage the 30% performance increase that would have been necessary to match the performance of the stronger member. This would imply that dyads reached their optimal performance at a lower level of discrepancy with the wheel-turning than the weight-lifting task. For example, if one assumes that an individual's actual performance in the individual condition was about 90% of his potential productivity, allowing for a further increase of only 10%, then the maximum group productivity should have been reached with a performance ratio of 1: .9. Because this maximum is above the ratio of .7 chosen for the unequal dyads in this study, it would have been missed in the present design. To investigate this possibility we conducted a further experiment in which the ratio of performances was manipulated at more than two levels.

Experiment 3

In our third experiment we varied the performance ratios across three levels, namely .6, .8, and 1.0. The task was also performed under additive as well as under conjunctive task conditions. According to the goal comparison model, the curvilinear relationship between group performance and ratio of group members' individual performances should occur only under conjunctive conditions, where the performances of the two members are yoked. Under additive conditions, where members' performance is allowed to vary freely, there should be a monotonically positive relationship between group performance and individual performance ratios.

The experiment was conducted in two sessions. More than 100 high school students aged 15–17 years participated in the first session, in which the individual performance of each subject was assessed. On the basis of their individual performances 96 subjects were combined into 48 dyads reflecting three different ratios of performance (1: .6 vs. 1: .8 vs. 1:1). Forty-seven of these dyads participated in the second session in which they performed under either conjunctive or additive task conditions. The task was the same as in Experiment 2, except that the duration of the performance was extended by 5 minutes. Subjects had to turn a hand wheel as fast as they could for 15 minutes in individual and in group sessions. In the group session the members of the dyad again worked in separate rooms. They were told that their individual performances would be combined into a joint group performance.

As in the previous experiment, subjects received continuous feedback about the discrepancy in their performance through a graphic presentation on a monitor. Under conjunctive task conditions subjects were instructed not to deviate more than 30 revolutions from their partner's performance. A warning signal was given on the screen whenever the discrepancy between partners increased beyond this limit, indicating that payments were discontinued for this period. Under additive task conditions, subjects received the continuous feedback (without the warning signal) and were told that performance discrepancies did not matter. Payment of subjects depended on their individual performance at Session 1 and their group performance at Session 2.

Table 2.4 presents the performance data for individuals and dyads as the sum of the individual performances. A three-factor (relative strength × additive vs. conjunctive task × group vs. individual performance) ANOVA with repeated measures for the last factor revealed only a significant main effect for individual versus group performance. None of the other main effects or interactions reached significance. Hence, as in the previous experiment, there was an improvement in performance from individual to group session and this performance increase was independent of the ratio of members' individual performance or the manipulation of conjunctive versus additive task conditions. These findings do not support our assumption that the failure to find evidence for the Köhler effect with the wheel-turning task was due to the fact that the optimal level of discrepancy for this task was lower than that for the weight-lifting task.

TABLE 2.4
Means (M) and Standard Deviations (SD) of the sums of Individual Performances Under Individual Versus Group and Additive Versus Conjunctive Task Conditions in the Wheel-Turning Task (Experiment 3)

Relative Strength	Individual Performance		Group Performance	
	Additive	Conjunctive	Additive	Conjunctive
1 : .6	M 3566.13	M 3551.25	M 4419.38	M 4195.75
	SD 309.99	SD 383.31	SD 394.31	SD 669.69
1 : .8	M 3767.57	M 3533.13	M 4568.29	M 4193.38
	SD 385.35	SD 588.97	SD 499.64	SD 849.93
1 : 1	M 3355.50	M 3590.63	M 4498.50	M 4375.25
	SD 431.11	SD 705.99	SD 488.59	SD 473.41

What then is the difference that could have been responsible for the difference in findings? We would like to suggest that the failure to find a curvilinear relationship between relative strength of group members and performance is due to the joint effect of two features of the wheel-turning task as used in our experiment: (a) the absence of a tacted rhythm and (b) the presence of continuous information about the discrepancy in individual performance.

In all of the experiments in which the Köhler effect was found, subjects had to perform according to tacted rhythm. Thus, in the weight-lifting experiment, they had to pull weights in a 2-second tact. In Köhler's version of the wheel-turning task, each turn of the wheel also had to follow a timed rhythm. Thus, the original task is for most parts an optimizing task, where subjects have to produce "some specific most preferred outcome" (Steiner, 1972, p. 16), namely to turn the wheel according to the tact. Maximizing only takes place at the end of the period of performance when persistence becomes an issue. In contrast, subjects in our study were instructed to turn the wheel as fast as they could, thus transforming the whole exercise into a maximizing task. This difference, together with the fact that subjects received continuous feedback about their relative performance, induced competition.

Continuous feedback of performance discrepancies in a maximizing task encourages social comparison, as a consequence of the "unidirectional drive upwards" postulated by social comparison theory. The motive to compete should be the stronger the more similar individuals are in their performance levels (Festinger, 1954; Rijsman, 1974). Diehl and Arnscheid (1992) therefore suggested that in the wheel-turning task, *in addition to* the goal comparison motive (i.e., "to be no worse than the other"), the motive to compete with the other was evoked. Whereas the motive "to be no worse than others" is induced in the weaker member by both tasks, the competition motive "to be better than others" is evoked in both members but only for maximizing tasks and when continuous performance feedback is given.

The two motives are differentially related to discrepancy in strength: The motive of the weaker member "to be no worse than others" is positively related to discrepancy.[2] It should increase with increasing discrepancy between the performance of the weaker members and that of their partners. The motive "to be better than others" is negatively related to discrepancy. It should be strongest in dyads of equal strength and should decrease with increasing performance discrepancy for both the weaker and the stronger member. Consistent with these assumptions, the increase in the performance of the stronger member in the group as compared to individual trials of Experiments 2 and 3, was smallest

---

[2]The positive relationship between the motive of the weaker member "to be no worse than others" and the discrepancy between the performance of the weaker and of the stronger member should hold only within the range where the stronger member is still being considered a comparison person. Increases in discrepancy beyond this range are likely to be associated with decreasing motivation.

TABLE 2.5
Percentage of Performance Gains and Losses for the Weaker and Stronger Member of the Dyad
Under Additive Versus Conjunctive Task Conditions in the Wheel-Turning Task (Experiment 3)

Relative Strength	Stronger Member		Weaker Member	
	Additive	Conjunctive	Additive	Conjunctive
1 : .6	+.99	- 3.63	+61.89	+55.67
1 : .8	+13.91	+11.43	+31.54	+35.18
1 : 1	+32.21	+24.71	+37.48	+26.90

under conditions of unequal strength and greatest when strength was equal. In contrast, the performance of the weaker members improved least when partners were equal in strength and most when they were unequal (Tables 2.3 and 2.5).

This interpretation leaves one aspect of our findings unexplained, namely the failure to observe an interaction between task structure and performance ratio in Experiment 3. Whereas a monotonic increase of group performance with increasing discrepancy in individual performance levels was expected for the additive task, we had predicted a curvilinear relationship for the conjunctive task. When the discrepancy becomes too large for the weaker members to match the performance of the stronger members, the stronger members should be forced to lower their performance on a conjunctive task. But even under conditions of high performance discrepancy and conjunctive task, the performance decrement in Experiment 3 was only 3.6%. Hence, the conjunctive task conditions did not force the stronger group member to reduce his performance substantially.

This failure to find the predicted decline in the performance of the stronger member even at high levels of discrepancy might have been due to a relatively low performance level in the individual session, which enabled the weaker members to keep up with their stronger partners, thus enabling the stronger members to maintain their high level of performance. Whereas individual members on average achieved approximately 145 rotations per minute under individual conditions in Experiment 2, they managed only an average of 120 rotations per minute in Experiment 3. The reasons for the relatively low performance during individual sessions in Experiment 3 are somewhat unclear. It seems plausible, however, that subjects paced themselves more in the individual sessions, when they knew that they had to perform for 15 rather than 10 minutes.

Experiment 4

That the wheel-turning task evokes interpersonal competition due to its continuous performance feedback was further corroborated in an additional experiment in which 48 of our subjects of Experiment 3 participated. They were combined into 24 new dyads and assigned to two conditions of differing strengths on the basis of the ratios of their individual performance. All dyads worked under conjunctive task conditions but with two different types of feedback. To check whether continuous feedback stimulated competition, a second feedback condition was induced in which feedback was only given when performance discrepancy came near the prescribed limit. In these cases a "+" or a "−" on the monitor screen indicated whether one had to improve or decrease performance. Although performance improved in all experimental conditions, increments in performance were significantly lower under conditions of reduced feedback than under conditions of continuous feedback.

If we accept the assumption that our failure to replicate the Köhler effect with the wheel-turning task was due to the absence of a time-tacted rhythm and the presence of continuous performance feedback, then the wheel-turning task used here is inappropriate for testing the goal comparison model. Although we could have followed the example of Köhler (1926) and changed the wheel-turning task into a persistence task by prescribing a certain speed of rotation, we decided to develop a new task that, like the weight-lifting task, required persistence, but without endangering the health of our subjects.

Experiment 5

This experiment was conducted by Ruess (1992). Our search for a useful and safe physical persistence exercise yielded the following task. Subjects were instructed to stretch out one of their arms horizontally as long as they could. In order to reduce this performance to a reasonable time period subjects had to wear a band around their wrists that weighed 1 kg. Subjects sat on vertically adjustable chairs so that their shoulder level could be held constant. They had to hold their arms above a string that connected two stands at 1 m above the floor. When subjects lowered their arms, the string was broken and the task finished.

Subjects were male members of sport clubs and high school sport teams who were signed up in 36 dyads. All subjects participated in an individual session and in a group session. The order of individual and group sessions was reversed for half of the subjects. Subjects used both arms alternately. One half started with the dominant and the other half with the nondominant arm, thus counterbalancing use of both arms in individual and group session.

Individual performance was measured as the amount of time each subject was able to hold his arm in the prescribed position. In line with Köhler's (1926, 1927) research, potential group performance was calculated as the average of both group members' individual performance, and actual group performance was assessed as the performance of the weaker member of the dyad, that is to say the performance of that person who dropped his arm first. The relative strength of both members was calculated for each dyad as the ratio of the stronger member's performance (denominator) to the weaker member's per-

TABLE 2.6
Means (M) and Standard Deviations (SD) of Individual and Group Performance in the Arm-
Stretching Task (Experiment 5)

Relative Strength	$\leq .650$	$> .650 - \leq. 840$	$> .840 - \leq. 908$	$> .908 - \leq. 955$	$> .955 - \leq. 967$	$> .967$
Individual Performance	M 230.92 SD 33.36	M 285.00 SD 56.42	M 273.50 SD 100.32	M 270.42 SD 60.71	M 283.42 SD 40.96	M 247.67 SD 37.32
Group Performance	M 205.33 SD 62.50	M 264.67 SD 34.04	M 290.50 SD 82.42	M 239.83 SD 81.52	M 275.67 SD 68.39	M 191.67 SD 73.09

formance (numerator). On the basis of these performance ratios we created six levels of relative strength (<.650 vs. >.650 – <.840 vs. >.840 – <.908 vs. >.908 – <.955 vs. >.955 – <.967 vs. >.967).

Table 2.6 presents the performance data for individual and group sessions for the six performance ratio conditions. A two-factor (relative strength × individual vs. group performance) ANOVA with repeated measures on the last factor yielded a significant main effect for individual versus group performance and a significant interaction. Thus, individual performance was superior to group performance but this difference between individual and group performance depended on the relative strength of group members.

Planned contrasts were conducted, to compare (a) the two conditions of extreme performance ratios (<.650 and >.967) with each other, and (b) both extreme conditions against the four conditions of more moderate performance ratios. These contrasts showed no significant difference between the extreme conditions, but a significant difference between the extreme and the moderate performance ratio conditions. Thus, there is a curvilinear relationship between the differences in individual and group performance and relative strength of the group members. A curve fit leads to the quadratic function ($y = -0.0272x^2 + .1660x + .7522$) depicted in Fig. 2.7.

The results of Experiment 5 replicated Köhler's findings regarding the typical curvilinear relationship between the ratio of group performance to the average of the two individual performances and the relative strength of its members. That our empirical data did not produce as smooth a curve as we are used to from Köhler is probably due to the fact that the performance of our subjects was measured only once under individual and once under group conditions. In contrast, Köhler's subjects performed the task repeatedly over a period of several weeks or even months as part of the winter training of the rowing club.

The maximum ratio of group performance to individual performance was only 1.096 and occurred for dyads with performance ratios between .840 and .908. This performance gain of about 10% is considerably smaller than that found either by Köhler (35%) or by us in our first experiment (17%). The fact that the performance maximum occurred for dyads with only a 10% difference in levels

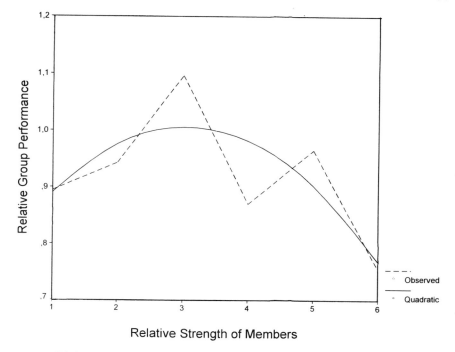

FIG. 2.7. Performance of dyads (group performance divided by the arithmetic mean of the two individual performances) depending on the relative strength of their members (performance of the weaker individual divided by the performance of the stronger individual). Levels 1 to 6 reflect these performance ratios from unequal to equal strength (Experiment 5).

of individual performance suggests a relatively high performance in the individual condition, thus there was only a small discrepancy between actual and potential individual productivity.

DISCUSSION AND CONCLUSION

Our review of research on the relationship of group productivity to individual productivity presented evidence for both motivation losses and motivation gains in group performance. Whereas the conditions under which motivation losses occur are well known, and theoretical explanations of social loafing and free riding are widely accepted, the determinants of motivation gains are less well understood.

All the motivation gains discussed in this chapter are the result of interpersonal comparison processes. Therefore, we restrict our discussion and conclusions to the effects of perceived performance discrepancies on the motivation to contribute to a group product. With regard to performance discrepancies in dyads, two instances are possible: (a) The group members can differ considerably in strength, or (b) they are of equal or nearly equal strength. In the case of differences in strength, one has to distinguish between stronger and weaker members because their situations are quite different. Thus, there are three different positions members of dyads can hold vis-à-vis their partners: They can be better, worse, or equal. Corresponding to these three constellations, three kinds of motivation gains have been observed: (a) social compensation, (b) the Köhler effect, and (c) interpersonal competition.

Social compensation refers to the increased effort of members of very small groups who work on additive tasks and who realize that their partners are not able or motivated to contribute to the group product. Under such circumstances the stronger members perceive their contributions as nearly as indispensable as under conjunctive task conditions. Provided that the group product is important and meaningful to the stronger members, they will compensate for the weaker members' low performance. The theoretical explanations presented by Williams and Karau (1991) refer to the motive to enhance the group's status or the stronger member's status within the group. How social compensation relates to the perceived performance discrepancy between group members and how group performance relates to the sum of individual performances was not investigated by these authors. This was the central research question of the studies on the Köhler effect.

The Köhler effect refers to an increase in group—relative to individual—performance under conditions of moderately unequal strength. This performance increase is due to an increase in the motivation of the weaker member who tries to match the performance of the stronger partner. Because there is a limit to the discrepancy in strength that can be compensated for through increases in motivation, a curvilinear relationship between group performance and relative strength of group members was typically observed with the conjunctive tasks used by Köhler. As our own research indicates, this curvilinear relationship seems to be restricted to physical persistence tasks.

Thus, the conditions under which the Köhler effect could be reproduced appeared at first to be much more restricted than we had expected on the basis of our goal comparison model. On the basis of this theory, we had predicted that the weaker member of a dyad should be motivated to reach the stronger member's performance level not only on persistence tasks but also on other maximizing tasks, provided the task was considered important. Furthermore, in dyads, an improvement in the performance of the weaker individual should also occur for additive tasks where the weaker member should perceive his or her contribution as nearly as indispensable as with conjunctive tasks.

Closer inspection of our data suggested that the Köhler effect in fact occurred under these conditions, but together with, and masked by, the effects of interpersonal competition. Interpersonal competition occurred in our experiments with the wheel-turning task in dyads of equal or nearly equal relative strength under conjunctive as well as additive task conditions. Interpersonal competition is based on the motive to be better than others, and should be evoked in all instances where there is a possibility to reverse an existing rank order (Witte, 1989). The chance to reverse an existing rank order is maximal with partners of equal strength.[3] Quantitative predictions about the strength of the competition motive can be derived from a model of performance comparison processes developed by Rijsman (1974) and based on Festinger's (1954) theory of social comparison.

As Diehl and Arnscheid (1992) pointed out, Rijsman's (1974) performance comparison model can explain interpersonal competition but not the Köhler effect, whereas the goal comparison model can explain the Köhler effect, but not interpersonal competition. However, both models make predictions about the effect of relative strength of two comparison persons on their joint performance. Therefore, in all instances where both effects occur and combine additively (as in the wheel-turning tasks of Experiments 2 and 3) a strong performance gain should be observed that is independent of group members' relative strength.

In cases where social competition is the only motive, performance gains should be maximal when individual performance discrepancies are minimal. In contrast, the motive to be no worse than the partner, which is responsible for the Köhler effect, should result in maximal performance gains when there is a moderate discrepancy in individual performance. Although we are not yet able to predict the level of discrepancy at which the maximum performance increase can be expected, it appears plausible that this ratio depends on the ratio of the actual performance of weaker members under individual conditions to the level of their potential productivity. The ratio should be the smaller, and consequently the Köhler effect the greater, the more the individual performance of the weaker members falls below their level of potential productivity. If their actual productivity under individual conditions is equal to their potential productivity, no performance gains can be expected.

To conclude, like motivation losses, the category of motivation gains subsumes several different processes, driven by a variety of motives that we are only beginning to understand. These motives are induced by the distribution of relative strength within the group and thus add performance incentives that are not present under conditions of individual performance. It should therefore be feasible to extend the economic theory of group productivity into an overall framework that would allow us to account for motivation gains as well as losses.

ACKNOWLEDGMENTS

The research reported in this chapter was supported by a grant from Deutsche Forschungsgemeinschaft to the first and second authors. The authors are grateful to Margaret Stroebe for helpful comments on an earlier version of this chapter.

---

[3]Competition is likely to have been facilitated in our studies by the fact that there was no established rank order between group members with regard to physical performance.

REFERENCES

Baron, R. S., Kerr, N., & Miller, N. (1992). *Group process, group decision, group action.* Buckingham: Open University Press.

Buchanan, J. M., & Tullock, G. (1962). *The calculus of consent.* Ann Arbor: University of Michigan Press.

Diehl, M., & Arnscheid, R. (1992). Die Wirkung der Wahrnehmung und Interpretation von Leistungsunterschieden zwischen Gruppenmitgliedern auf die Gruppenleistung [The effect of the perception and interpretation of performance discrepancies between group members on group performance]. In L. Montada (Ed.), *Bericht über den 38. Kongreß der Deutschen Gesellschaft für Psychologie in Trier* [Report on the 38th Congress of the German Society for Psychology in Trier] (Vol. 2, pp. 157–165). Göttingen: Hogrefe Verlag.

Diehl, M., & Stroebe, W. (1987). Productivity loss in brainstorming groups: Towards the solution of a riddle. *Journal of Personality and Social Psychology, 53,* 497–509.

Festinger, L. (1954). A theory of social comparison processes. *Human Relations, 7,* 117–140.

Harkins, S. (1987). Social loafing and social facilitation. *Journal of Experimental Social Psychology, 23,* 1–18.

Harkins, S., & Petty, R. (1982). Effects of task difficulty and task uniqueness on social loafing. *Journal of Personality and Social Psychology, 43,* 1214–1229.

Harkins, S., & Szymanski, K. (1987). Social loafing and social facilitation: New wine in old bottles. In C. Hendrick (Ed.), *Review of personality and social psychology* (Vol. 9, pp. 167–188). Beverly Hills, CA: Sage.

Ingham, A. G., Levinger, G., Graves, J., & Peckham, V. (1974). The Ringelmann effect: Studies of group size and group performance. *Journal of Experimental Social Psychology, 10,* 371–384.

Kerr, H. L., & Bruun, S. E. (1983). Dispensability of member effort and group motivation losses: Free-rider effects. *Journal of Personality and Social Psychology, 45,* 78–94.

Köhler, O. (1926). Kraftleistungen bei Einzel- und Gruppenarbeit [Physical performance in individual and group situations]. *Industrielle Psychotechnik, 3,* 274–282.

Köhler, O. (1927). Über den Gruppenwirkungsgrad der menschlichen Körperarbeit und die Bedingung optimaler Kollektivkraftreaktion [On group efficiency of physical labor and the conditions of optimal collective performance]. *Industrielle Psychotechnik, 4,* 209–226.

Kravitz, D. A., & Martin, B. (1986). Ringelmann rediscovered: The original article. *Journal of Personality and Social Psychology, 50,* 936–941.

Latané, B., Williams, K., & Harkins, S. (1979). Many hands make light in the work: The causes and consequences of social loafing. *Journal of Personality and Social Psychology, 37,* 822–832.

Lorge, I., & Solomon, H. (1955). Two models of group behavior in the solution of eureka-type problems. *Psychometrika, 20,* 139–148.

Marquart, D. I. (1955). Group problem solving. *Journal of Social Psychology, 41,* 103–113.

Moede, W. (1927). Die Richtlinien der Leistungs-Psychologie [Principles of the psychology of performance]. *Industrielle Psychotechnik, 4,* 193–209.

Orbell, J., & Dawes, R. (1981). Social dilemmas. In G. Stephenson & J. H. Davis (Eds.), *Progress in applied social psychology* (Vol. 1, pp. 37–65). Chichester, England: Wiley.

Osborn, A. F. (1953). *Applied imagination.* New York: Scribner.

Petty, R., Harkins, S., & Williams, K. (1980). The effects of diffusion of cognitive effort on attitudes. An information processing view. *Journal of Personality and Social Psychology, 38,* 81–92.

Rijsman, J. B. (1974). Factors in social comparison of performance influencing actual performance. *European Journal of Social Psychology, 4,* 279–311.

Ringelmann, M. (1913). Recherches sur les moteurs animés: Travail de l'homme [Research on animate sources of power: The work of man]. *Annales de l'Institut National Agronomique, XII,* 1–40.

Ruess, M. (1992). *Ausdauerleistung in Dyaden: Eine Untersuchung zum Köhler-Effekt* [Persistence in dyads. A study of the Köhler-Effect]. Unpublished diploma thesis, University of Tübingen, Tübingen, Germany.

Samuelson, P. A. (1954). The pure theory of public expenditure. *Review of Economics and Statistics, 36*, 387–390.

Shaw, M. (1932). Comparison of individuals and small groups in the rational solution of complex problems. *American Journal of Psychology, 44*, 491–504.

Shepperd, J. A., & Wright, R. A. (1989). Individual contributions to a collective effort: An incentive analysis. *Personality and Social Psychology Bulletin, 15*, 141–149.

Steiner, I. D. (1972). *Group process and productivity.* New York: Academic Press.

Stroebe, W., Diehl, M., Abakoumkin, G., & Arnscheid, R. (1990, October). *The Köhler effect: Motivation gains in group performance.* Paper presented at the annual meeting of the Society of Experimental Social Psychology, Buffalo, NY.

Stroebe, W., & Frey, B. S. (1982). Self-interest and collective action: The economics and psychology of public goods. *British Journal of Social Psychology, 21*, 121–137.

Szymanski, K., & Harkins, S. (1987). Social loafing and self-evaluation with a social standard. *Journal of Personality and Social Psychology, 55*, 891–897.

Taylor, D. W., Berry, P. C., & Block, C. H. (1958). Does group participation when using brainstorming facilitate or inhibit creative thinking? *Administrative Science Quarterly, 3*, 23–47.

Williams, K., Harkins, S., & Latané, B. (1981). Identifiability as a deterrent to social loafing. Two cheering experiments. *Journal of Personality and Social Psychology, 40*, 303–311.

Williams, K. D., & Karau, S. J. (1991). Social loafing and social compensation: The effects of expectations of co-worker performance. *Journal of Personality and Social Psychology, 61*, 570–581.

Witte, E. H. (1989). Köhler rediscovered: The anti-Ringelmann effect. *European Journal of Social Psychology, 19*, 147–154.

Zajonc, R. B. (1965). Social facilitation. *Science, 149*, 269–274.

3

STATUS CONGRUENCE IN SMALL GROUPS

Henk A. M. Wilke
Vakgroep Sociale en Organisatiepsychologie

One of the most conspicuous aspects of groups is that they have structure. This appears from a study of Bales (1950), who observed problem-solving groups having group members who were previously unacquainted with one another. He established that some group members were more active in making problem-solving attempts than others. These group members were also most frequently addressed, and afterward their ascribed leadership was higher than that of group members who were less active (Stein & Heller, 1979).

Group structure may be defined as the relationship among members of the group. The elements are the group members. In groups, several relationships may be distinguished, such as the patterning of communication, attraction, prestige, and competence (see Collins & Raven, 1969, for a discussion of prominent models of group structure). From a cognitive view, Markus and Zajonc (1985) argued that structure, such as group structure, is based on previous experiences. Moreover, structure, being a cognitive representation, does give rise to subsequent inferences. Others (e.g., Moscovici, 1985) maintain that the perception of structure and the subsequent inferences are socially mediated; that is, representations are social in nature in that they allow one to get a grip on reality in a way that communication with others is possible.

As Bales (1950) has demonstrated in problem-solving groups, a task and a social-emotional dimension may be distinguished in the perception of the group members themselves, and in their actual behaviors. On both dimensions group members are ordered by the amount of impact they have on the performance of the group. This ordering implies that on a specific dimension some group members have a higher position or a higher status than other group members. When a group member has a higher or lower position than another one, this group member has status advantage or status disadvantage vis-à-vis the other, respectively.

Status differentials between members of a problem-solving group are part and parcel of the group structure. De Soto (1960) argued that structures are characterized by previously learned formal properties. Concerning the learning of influence relations among group members, it has been shown that when group members have to learn influence relationships within a given group, they learn faster when the presented pair-wise relations are transitive or asymmetric; that is, when they have to learn that A has more influence than B, and that B has more influence than C, subjects infer that A has more influence than C. In accordance with a cognitive view on cognitive representations, he maintained that the task of having to learn a hierarchal pattern of group relationships triggers the expectation of transitive relations. When, subsequently, these relations are presented in a transitive way, they are learned faster than when they are presented in a symmetric or reciprocated way. In the latter case, influence relations have to be learned; but subjects get to know that at one moment of time, A has more influence than B, but at a later moment are informed that B has also more influence than A. Reciprocation (see Markus & Zajonc, 1985) is then involved.

In this chapter we focus on consequences of status differentials in small problem-solving groups. Status differentials refer to structures or cognitive representations implying transitive relations among group members. In small groups, several dimensions of categorization or representation may be involved, each of them referring to possible resources that may be involved, such as the group members' ability to reward or to punish, the respect group members may invoke, the competence and expertness group members may have, and so forth (see, e.g., Fiske & Taylor, 1991; French & Raven, 1959). On each of these dimensions, group members may be ordered, that is, assigned status positions. These status differentials give rise to the group structure on that dimension, which may or may not agree with the group structure on another dimension of categorization, as Bales (1950) indicated while observing that the group members who scored highest on the task dimension were not the highest scorers on the social-emotional dimension in his problem-solving groups.

ELEMENTS OF GROUP STRUCTURE

A group structure may be more or less complex. Complexity refers then to the number of elements, that is, the number of group members, and the relations between elements. In this section, we describe elements and dimensions that are of importance in view of the empirical findings and theoretical ideas pre-

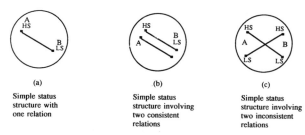

FIG. 3.1. Simple group structure.

sented in the section Status Differentials and Social Influence. The most simple structure is depicted in Fig. 3.1(a).

In Fig. 3.1(a) there are two members (A, B) differing in status (high status vs. low status). Only one status dimension, relation, is involved. As compared with Fig. 3.1(a), Figs. 3.1(b) and (c) are somewhat more complex in that group members do differ on two *dimensions*. To give an example, in Fig. 3.1(b) group member A is superior with regard to ability and prestige as compared with B, whereas in Fig. 3.1(c) A is superior to B as regards ability, but inferior to B as regards prestige.

Status differentials may be constant, but may also vary in time; that is, status differentials may be more or less stable. For example, if in Fig. 3.1(a) A is more able at T1, and also at T2, then the status differentials are more stable in comparison with, when at T1, A is more able, but at T2 it is group member B who appears to be the more able group member. (In)stability then refers to the likelihood that the same status position on dimensions of comparison will be occupied by the same persons over time.

Dimensions of social representations are *evaluative* in nature. For example, having greater competence, more behavioral outcomes, or more influence are evaluated more positively than having less competence, fewer behavioral outcomes, or less influence (for an account, see Fiske & Taylor, 1991). Consequently, group members who score higher on positively evaluated dimensions have greater *status advantage* and their position is evaluated more positively than the position of group members who have status disadvantage.

Status differentials may differ in *size*. For example, if on a competence test A obtains a score of 10 (is maximum), and B a score of 4, the size of the status differentials is more pronounced than when A obtains a score of 10 and B a score of 9.

A specific pattern of interrelationships as depicted in Fig. 3.1 not only serves as a description of an existing pattern of relations within a group, it also has a prospective significance for that group when new dimensions of comparison are introduced. More specifically, it is proposed here that all existing or antecedent patterning of interrelations, such as A has status advantage and B has status disadvantage on the antecedent dimension X (e.g., ability), will be generalized to a subsequent dimension of comparison Y (e.g., A should have more behavioral outcomes than B). Generalization from the antecedent status differentiation on X to a subsequent status differentiation on Y depends on the perceived relevance of dimension X for dimension Y. This tendency to generalize from status differentiation on an existing (antecedent) dimension of comparison to status differentiation on a relevant other dimension is called *status congruence*. When group members perceive that the *relevance* of the antecedent dimension X for dimension Y is less, then status congruence implies that, given a status differentiation on X, status differentiation on the consequent dimension Y is weaker in case of less relevance, or even *absent* if X is considered to be irrelevant concerning dimension Y.

We argue that the status congruence perspective is important to understand, how in groups antecedent status differentiation will affect status differentiation on another status dimension. In the next sections, we show that status congruence can explain emerging influence differentials in small groups, the allocation of subsequent outcomes in task groups, group members' contributions and harvesting behavior in social dilemmas, and coalition formation as well.

Until now, the latter topics have been investigated separately. To integrate their research findings, we propose in the present chapter that they all involve situations in which group members try to achieve a match between status differentiation on an antecedent dimension and a possible status differentiation on another dimension of comparison.

STATUS DIFFERENTIALS AND SOCIAL INFLUENCE

The emergence of influence differentiation in small groups was established by Bales (1950). In an attempt to explain why influence differentiation in small groups does emerge, Berger and his coworkers (Berger et al., 1980) proposed that influence differentials are caused by antecedent status differentiation, such as competence differentials. To investigate this, two-person task groups are formed in which first status differentials are induced on an antecedent dimension. Thereafter, status differentials on another dimension—mostly acceptance of influence—are measured. To be more concrete, two subjects are simultaneously invited to the lab. In the lab they are placed in two separate cubicles. It is explained to them that they are participating in a study on group problem solving and that they can communicate by means of electronic equipment. First, they have to participate in an individual task that involves judging whether there are more black than white squares in a "grid" containing white and black squares. After this task they receive (bogus) feedback about their individual performances; for example, A is more competent than B. Subsequently, the group task is administered. Last, they are requested to give a definite judgment. The dependent variable is the number of times a group member gives up his own judgment in favor of another group member's judgment. This is approximately the experimental situation introduced by Berger and his coworkers (see, e.g., Berger, Rosenholz, & Zelditch, 1980). From their research it appears that high-status (= high-competence) group members accept *less* influence than low-status—that is, low-competence—group members.

Employing another type of setup, Ridgeway, Berger, and Smith (1985) found evidence for their prediction that high-status members exerted *more* influence than low-status members. In this setup, A and B are informed about their competence; that is, status differentials are arranged. Thereafter, A and B are requested to perform a collective task consisting of several trials. On each trial these subjects are instructed to respond as soon as one of them knows the correct answer, and the subject who responds first determines the group response. It appeared that the group member having status advantage responded faster than the group member having status disadvantage, which was assumed to be indicative of the exertion of influence. So it appears that high-status group members accepted less, but exerted more influence in two-person groups in which there was intragroup stability and in which the antecedent dimension of status differentials—that is, contrast sensitivity—was highly relevant for the collective task, because this task also implied contrast sensitivity. Moreover, because this task was rather ambiguous, group members had no reason to doubt the legitimacy of the status assignment made by the experimenter. The question is now how to explain that high-status group members accept less, but exert more influence than low-status group members. In the following we argue that subjects strive for congruence between status differentials on the antecedent contrast sensitivity dimension and status differentiation on a subsequent dimension, that is, influence.

Sampson (1969; see also Homans, 1961) proposed that group members strive for status congruence, because status incongruence is experienced as a displeasing state of affairs (see also Bacharach, Bamberger, & Mundell, 1993; Heider, 1958). Sampson suggested that group members do expect certain rankings—for example, a higher ranking on competence—to go with other rankings—for example, a higher ranking on social influence. Sampson gave the example that people expect power and prestige to be in accordance with wealth. In a similar vein, Homans discussed why more powerful members in groups are expected to contribute more than less powerful members: Group members expect that the ranking on contributing to the group should accord with the ranking on power; in doing so they adhere to the general rule of "noblesse oblige."

Dimensions of comparison are evaluative in nature, and a high position on a positively evaluated dimension will be associated with a high position on another positively evaluated dimension. From empirical literature (e.g., Butler, 1992; see also Festinger, 1954) it appears that having greater competence is preferred over having less competence, suggesting that a high position on competence is evaluated more positively than a low position on competence. Other literature (e.g., Bruins & Wilke, 1993) suggests that people prefer more over less exertion of influence; that is, a high position on exertion of influence is evaluated more positively than a low position. Because status congruence implies that a high position on one positively evaluated dimension, in this case competence, will be associated with a high position on another positively evaluated one—that is, exertion of influence—it seems plausible that group members having greater competence exert more influence than group members having less competence.

In a similar vein, it may be explained why group members having greater competence accept *less* influence than group members having less competence. If we take into account that acceptance of influence or conformity appears to be a negatively evaluated dimension (De Gilder, 1991), or conversely that non-conformity is a positively evaluated dimension, it follows that a high position on competence will be associated with a low position on conformity or acceptance of influence.

Intragroup Stability

In small groups in which group members' status differ on competence, these differences may be stable. What will happen when intragroup status differences are unstable? This question was part of an experimental research program carried out by De Gilder (1991; see also De Gilder & Wilke, 1990, 1994). Half of the subjects had to perform an acceptance of influence task, the other half an exertion of influence task as described previously. In all dyadic task groups, group members were informed about their individual performance on a pretask. Bogus feedback as to high and low status was provided. In half of the group it was pointed out that assigned positions would not change (stable); in the other half it was suggested that it was rather likely that positions might change (unstable). Replicating previous research, it was established that high-status subjects accepted less, but exerted more influence than low-status subjects. Moreover, it was indicated that the influence differences between high- and low-status subjects were greater in the stable conditions, suggesting that instability of status positions—that is, intragroup instability—attenuates the effect of status differentials on social influence measures. Therefore, we may conclude that *status differentiation* on the consequent dimension is weakened when status differentials on the antecedent dimension are suggested to be unstable in comparison to a stable assignment of status differentials on the antecedent dimension of comparison.

Ridgeway (1989) made a distinction between two sources of *legitimation* of an association between competence differentials and behavioral differentiation. Support may come from peers, who may actively support the association or who are expected to support that association. This is called *endorsement*. Support may also be expected from or actually may be provided by a higher authority. In our view these sources of legitimation are related. For example, in the experiment of De Gilder and Wilke (1990), it was the experimenter who expressed that the competence differentials were associated with influence differentials, and it may be assumed that, consequently, endorsement or no endorsement of the association from the other group member was expected. So, it seems plausible to posit that stability of the association between competence differentials and influence differentials is evoked by endorsement and/or by authorization, whereas intra-group instability is elicited by a lack of legitimation either from peers or from a higher level authority, respectively.

Relevance of Status Dimensions and More Antecedent Status Dimensions Involved

In many experiments (see De Gilder & Wilke, 1994) it has been shown that in task groups competence differentials give rise to influence differentials. However, it has also been shown that differentiation on other antecedent dimensions, such as ethnicity and gender (see Broverman, Vogel, Broverman, Clarkson, & Rosenkrantz, 1972), give rise as well to influence differentials. For example, it has been shown that, in task groups in which men and women participated, men accepted less influence than women. Why do status differentials on dimensions, which at first glance are not very relevant for the task at hand lead to differentiation on a subsequent dimension, and why is the influence differentiation in this case weaker than when competence differentials are induced explicitly? These questions were answered by Berger et al. (1980). They made a distinction between specific and diffuse status dimensions. Status differentials on diffuse dimensions, such as gender, ethnicity, and vocal expression, are culturally associated with high or low ability but are not self-evidently related to particular tasks, whereas status differentiation on specific antecedent dimensions, such as competence differentials to solve contrast-sensitivity tasks, are directly associated with the particular task, for example, the collective task to solve contrast-sensitivity tasks. Berger et al. posed that status differentials on an antecedent dimension directly relevant for the task have a more profound effect on influence differentials than status differences on a diffuse (less relevant) dimension. Thus, given status differentials on an antecedent dimension, the greater the *relevance* of that antecedent dimension with regard to the *task* at hand, the stronger the subsequent influence differentiation.

How will status information on more dimensions be processed? Or how will multiple pieces of status information affect influence acceptance or conformity? This question refers to the "balancing-combining" issue. Balancing is the focusing on dimensions on which one ranks higher and the discounting of those on which one ranks lower (see Lemaine, Kasterstein, & Personnaz, 1978), and it is believed to emerge from the motivation to present oneself in a "self-maximizing" way.

Combining (see, e.g., Berger & Fisek, 1970) occurs when one individual uses all of the status information one possesses to infer an aggregated or general status position. The underlying motivation is that individuals want to estimate the relative status positions as correctly as possible and to make use of all available status information.

The evidence appears to favor the combining hypothesis (see De Gilder, 1990). For example, competent women accepted more influence than competent men, but less than incompetent men (Pugh & Wahrman, 1983; Wagner, Ford, & Ford, 1986). Similar results were found when subjects received inconsistent information about race and competence (Cohen & Roper, 1972; Riordan & Ruggiero, 1980; Webster & Driskell, 1978), race and confidence (Sev'er, 1989), and age and competence (Knottnerus & Greenstein, 1981).

In a recent version of the combining hypothesis (Berger, Blackwell, Norman, & Smith, 1992), two subsets of information are taken into account: (a) positive information about an actor—for example, A is more competent than B; A is male, B is female; and (b) negative information about an actor—for example, A has less seniority, and less confidence than B. Furthermore, it is assumed that separate pieces of status information are not added together; rather, according to the principle of diminishing effects, two pieces of status information have less effect (on acceptance of influence) than double the effect of one piece of information. Moreover, the *relevance* of the status differentiation for the task is weighed. For example, if A is more competent on an antecedent dimension that is quite relevant for the task, then the effect is greater than if A has greater seniority than B, a dimension that is of less relevance for the task. Last, a group member's aggregate status is determined by subtracting the weighed subset of negative information. Berger et al. found that the higher a group member's aggregate status, the less likely a group member will conform or accept influence. This means that when more antecedent dimensions of comparison between actors are involved, the status positions on these dimensions are taken into account and weighed for relevance, and that the definite aggregate status differentials form the base for status differentiation on the subsequent dimension.

For the status relations depicted in Fig. 3.1, these insights imply that status congruence is pursued between differentiation on an antecedent status dimension and influence differentials. When only highly task-relevant (or specific) status information is available, the observed influence differentials are more conspicuous in Fig. 3.1(b) than in Fig. 3.1(a), and relatively stronger as compared with when positions on two status dimensions are inconsistent, as is the case in Fig. 3.1(c). When some of the dimensions are low-relevant (or diffuse), the size of the (behavioral) influence differentials also depends on the weighting of these dimensions as for their relevance for the task at hand. The effect of status differentials on influence differentials is discounted by low relevance of the status dimension(s) involved, because aggregate status differentials are weaker. When there are dimensions involved in which group members score equally—for example, A's competence or confidence is equal to B's competence or confidence—these "equating" dimensions do not affect influence differentials (for empirical evidence, see Hembroff, Martin, & Sell, 1981; Martin & Sell, 1980; Webster, 1977).

In the following, we show that the pursuit of status congruence is important for explaining the allocation of behavioral outcomes in other areas, notably in the domain of social dilemmas and in the domain of coalition formation. Before we do so, it is necessary to be somewhat more explicit about the nature of influence differentials. As we argued before, greater acceptance of influence may be considered to be experienced as more negative, whereas greater exertion of influence may be experienced as more positive than a lower rate of exertion of influence. In our view, influence differentials may be considered as the behavioral outcomes in task groups: Acceptance of influence and exertion of influence are the negative and positive behavioral outcomes group members allocate in order to achieve the collective tasks; that is, status congruence then implies that group members having greater (aggregated) status feel entitled to higher behavioral outcomes than group members having a lower (aggregated) status. Therefore, group members having status advantage exert more, but accept less, influence in task groups in which group members have to pursue a cooperative goal, that is, in groups in which status congruence serves the attainment of the group task in an efficient way.

PERFORMING TASKS AND THE ALLOCATION OF BEHAVIORAL OUTCOMES

Quite often in task groups, after completion of their task, group members have the opportunity to divide task outcomes, such as a prize or a budget. In the section after this one, we deal more extensively with coalition formation and social dilemma settings, which are pertinent to the question of how outcomes will be divided among group members. In the present section we argue that behavioral outcomes during the achievement of the group task, such as influence differentials, will be allocated in a status congruent way in view of an efficient production of the task, whereas behavioral outcomes derived from the production of the task are also allocated in a congruent way, but then in view of fairness considerations.

In coalition formation and decision making in social dilemma situations there exists a conflict between individual interests (coalition formation) and a conflict between individuals and collective interests (public choice). In coalition formation there are group members who have to compete for scarce resources (such as cabinet posts), whereas in social dilemma situations individual group members can profit most if they contribute as little as possible, which is detrimental to the group as a whole. Such a conflict of interests makes the allocation of outcomes more salient than in task groups; that is, it is proposed that the division of behavioral outcomes is more salient in groups involved in a conflict of interests than in a group whose primary goal is to achieve a cooperative product. By implication, in task groups the main focus is on how to reach the group goal in an efficient way, whereas in groups that are involved in a conflict of interests the main emphasis is on how to allocate behavioral outcomes in a fair way.

In a similar vein, Sampson (1969) made a distinction between "mastery" and "justice" as two concerns that follow from status structure and that lead to behavioral outcomes. Mastery is involved when group members seek behavioral control over their environment, such as a task. It pertains to coordinating resources to learn about the environment, so that environmental control will be achieved. Simultaneously, mastery over the environment through the control of valuable resources leads to behavioral outcomes, and the allocation of these outcomes evokes the question of fairness. In cooperative task groups as discussed in the previous section, the question of mastery is salient. In groups in which the allocation of the behavioral outcomes themselves is salient, fairness considerations are evoked. The allocation of outcomes may then give rise to a potential conflict, because usually the scarce group outcomes acquired by one member cannot be acquired by another group member.

How do fairness considerations operate? With Homans (1961; see also Sampson, 1969) we maintain that status congruence is also here the basic mechanism. The general idea of distributive justice is that group members with greater perceived investments, such as competence, are entitled to more behavioral outcomes than group members with lower perceived investments (see also Adams, 1965). As we reasoned before, there are many dimensions on which investment differentials or status differentials may be expressed, such as competence, ethnicity, seniority, and need. When the allocation of outcomes is salient, it is also then important to know the perceived relevance of the dimensions on which status differentials do occur in view of the allocation of behavioral outcomes. Moreover, when there are more relevant dimensions on which status differentiation occurs, status information weighed for relevance will be aggregated, and group members having a higher status will be entitled to higher outcomes (for a more systematic statement, see Berger, Fisek, Norman, & Wagner, 1983).

Deutsch (1975) observed that several fairness principles may be distinguished and that these principles are prevalent in specific situations. The equity or distributive justice principle, predicting that behavioral outcomes should be allocated in proportion to the investments of group members, is likely to be applied in the workplace. The need principle, implying that behavioral outcomes should be allocated in proportion to need, is likely to be applied in close relationships, such as those in families. The equality principle, suggesting that behavioral outcomes should be allocated equally, is likely to be applied in political settings (think of one person, one vote). This distinction between principles and the observation that these principles are applied in specific settings is in agreement with a status congruence explanation if the relevance of antecedent status dimensions is taken into account. In the workplace, competence, seniority, and the functional level of workers are considered as highly relevant antecedent dimensions. In families, it is the differentiation on the need dimension that entitles dependent children to higher behavioral outcomes (e.g., pocket money) than the parents. Equality may be pursued in voting, because every citizen is equal on the dimension of citizenship, whereas other dimensions on which citizens may differ are considered to be of less or no relevance. Equality of outcome allocations may also be achieved when there is a relevant dimension on which group members may differentiate, but when in a specific situation group members actually do not differentiate, status differentiation does not occur. For example, in a workplace workers A and B may be equally competent; therefore, their superior is likely to decide to pay them the same salary.

Congruence between differentiation on an antecedent dimension and differentiation on a subsequent dimension, such as the allocation of outcomes, may be considered from two perspectives: the outcome coordination perspective and the consistency perspective. The *outcome coordination perspective* was stressed by Homans (1961), Walster, Berscheid, and Walster (1976), and Leventhal (1976). Homans assumed that an equity or fairness norm is useful for establishing and maintaining long-term relationships. He suggested that if outcomes are scarce, then all will pursue the maximization of their own outcomes, and people may come into conflict. This potential conflict may be solved by introducing a norm to the effect that one takes in proportion to what one gives. The *consistency principle* places more stress on the need to organize cognitions in a consistent way. As an example, the "just world" hypothesis of Lerner, Miller, and Holmes (1976) suggests that people assume that one ultimately gets what one deserves; in other words, the outcomes are consistent with investments. This notion operates in two directions: If a person makes positive investments, it is assessed that he deserves positive outcomes; conversely, if a person recieves positive outcomes, one infers that she has made positive investments. As we have suggested elsewhere (Wilke, 1983), these perspectives are not incompatible if it is assumed that the utility of status congruency to solve or to prevent potential conflict between group members is agreed upon and, thus, learned in specific situations, and that what is learned may become part of an internalized repertory that group members may apply in new settings similar to the situation in which the rules of conduct are learned.

In sum, status congruence is also pursued in settings in which the behavioral outcomes have to be explicitly divided by individual group members. If group members are faced with a potential conflict about scarce resources, they are likely to adhere to fair arrangements to prevent a conflict. Fair arrangements are agreed upon by consensus about the relevance of antecedent dimensions on which differentiation may occur, and by the assignment of the behavioral outcomes involved so that status congruence may be realized. Fair arrangements learned in the past or fairness principles imply also the pursuance of status congruence. Thus, the pursuance of status congruence is not restricted to task situations in which group members seek mastery concerning the collective task, but may also explain group members' allocation of scarce resources. In mastery situations status differentials on relevant dimensions are associated with influence differentials during the task, in order to master the task in an efficient way; in situations characterized by a potential conflict of interests, status positions on relevant dimensions will be associated with outcome differentials, in order to create fair arrangements which, in turn, may prevent the outbreak of an intragroup conflict.

STATUS DIFFERENTIALS IN SOCIAL DILEMMAS

In the following, we deal with social dilemmas, choice situations in which there is a conflict between the group members' own interests and the interests of the group as a whole. We explain what social dilemmas are. We make a distinction between symmetric and asymmetric social dilemmas. By presenting empirical evidence, we show that group members tacitly coordinate their choices in a way that status congruence is realized in accordance with their perception of the achievement of fairness.

A social dilemma (see Dawes, 1980; Hardin, 1968; Messick & Brewer, 1983) occurs when there is a conflict between individual and collective interests. We distinguish between two types of social dilemmas: public good dilemmas (PGD) and resource management dilemmas (RMD). Public good dilemmas are choice situations in which individuals can contribute to a public good, such as joining a union or donating to a charity fund. In such a situation it is most attractive for individuals to free ride on the contributions of others. However, if all individuals concerned act likewise, no public good will be provided and all will be relatively worse off than if they had contributed. In resource management dilemmas, individuals share a common source from which individual group members can harvest. The size of common sources—such as the collective energy reserves or clean air—is limited so that exhaustion due to overconsumption may be the consequence. The dilemmic character of this choice situation is that it is in the collective interest to cut down energy consumption or air pollution, yet in the individual interest to consume excessively.

How do individuals deal with these dilemmas? As for PGDs, Samuelson (1954, 1955) concluded that as a result of free riding, an optimal provision of public goods is almost impossible. In a similar vein, Hardin (1968) accepting the principle of nonsatiety of economic greed, discarded the possibility of cooperative and responsible behavior in RMDs. However, on empirical grounds both assertions appear to be untenable. In daily life, one may observe that unions are established and that measures are taken to conserve collective sources. Moreover, research on decision making in small groups has shown that group members do contribute to the collective interest (Van der Kragt, Dawes, Orbell,

Braver, & Wilson, 1986) and that they are willing to maintain the group resource (Samuelson, Messick, Rutte, & Wilke, 1984), suggesting that they are willing to coordinate their efforts in order to act in the interest of the group as a whole. That fairness considerations are of importance for their decisions appears from the high correlations between own choice, the choices expected from other group members, and the choice one considers fair.

As for group structure, two situations have been investigated. In symmetric games, players occupy identical positions; that is, no status differentiation is introduced. In asymmetric games, players vary in position; that is, status differentiation is involved. In both situations, choice behavior may be explained by status congruence.

In PGDs, *symmetric* situations, group members are usually equal as for their endowments to contribute to the public good. An example is the study by Van der Kragt et al. (1986), who found that group members of equal endowment were either likely to contribute unanimously (although it was not always necessary to provide for the public good) or not to contribute in a unanimous way, in both cases resulting in equal final outcomes. In a symmetric RMD, Allison and Messick (1990) found in a study in which no communication among group members was allowed, that group members who could harvest from a resource anchored their decisions to the rule that all group members should take an equal amount of the shared resource, implying that equal final outcomes were being pursued.

Thus, when in PGD and RMD group members occupy identical positions, or stated differently, when no status differentiation on an antecedent dimension is involved, behavior outcomes are allocated in such a way that equal final outcomes are realized, supporting status congruence.

Can status congruence also explain choice behavior in PGDs and RMDs when *asymmetry* or status differentiation is involved? This is an important question. In real life, situations of asymmetry seem more prevalent than situations of symmetry. In PGDs some members may have more interests in the public good than others and some members may have to spend more endowments than others. Similarly, in RMDs, some members may have more reason to maintain the collective source than others and some may have more access to the collective source than others.

Olson (1965), departing from the rational choice idea that in PGDs one should only contribute to a public good when the interest in the public good exceeds the costs, suggested that in small groups characterized by inequality of interests (or asymmetry) there is a greater likelihood that one member may gain from seeing that the public good is provided for even if he must entail the costs alone. Marwell and Ames (1979) found for four-person groups in which there was one member who could provide the public good all by himself, high-interest group members contributed more than low-interest group members. However, results of other studies (e.g., Wit, Wilke, & Oppewal, 1992) in which for all group members contributing was less attractive than not contributing, indicated that when contributing is not the rational choice, high-interest group members contributed more than low-interest members, suggesting that it is not the weighing of costs of contributing and compensating rewards if the public good is achieved that is responsible for the greater contributions of high-interest group members.

Studies investigating asymmetry in RMDs also indicate that group members having status advantage are more cooperative than group members having status disadvantage (see Van Dijk, 1993). For example, in an asymmetry study of Van Dijk and Wilke (1993b) employing a RMD and a PGD in one design, it appeared that high-status members were more cooperative than low-status members; that is, high-status members took fewer points from a collective source and contributed more to the public good than did group members having status disadvantage. Those results may be explained by the notion of status congruence, if it is assumed (a) that having status advantage (e.g., interest in the public good or in the collective resource from which a greater interest can be harvested) refers to status differentiation on a positively evaluated dimension, (b) that contributing to a public good or leaving resources in a collective resource is also a positively evaluated dimension, and (c) that in order to prevent conflict, differentiation on a positively evaluated dimension should agree with a differentiation on the dimension of cooperation. Together these data are indicative of what Homans (1961) described as the adherence to the norm of fairness, implying noblesse oblige.

So, it appears that group members having status advantage do contribute more to the group than group members having status disadvantage. In addition, the relevance of the dimensions on which status differentiation may be expressed appears to moderate the relation between initial inequalities and final outcomes. In Van Dijk and Wilke (1993b), the four subjects were promised 33%, 33%, 17%, and 17% interests in the public good. Half of the subjects were informed that inequalities of interests were assigned by chance. The other half was informed that they were based on previous task expenditure. It appeared that high-interest group members contributed more than low-interest members. As for the final outcomes group members acquired—that is, the total outcomes consisting of what one kept and what one received from the linear public good—it appeared that in the task expenditure condition the inequalities in final outcomes between high- and low-interest group members were greater than when the inequalities were less relevant, that is, were based on chance.

In Van Dijk and Wilke (1991) inequalities were based on endowments. Group members received 30, 30, 10, and 10 points that they could contribute to the public good. Again, these endowment differentials were based either on chance or on task expenditure (cf. Messé, Vallacher, & Phillips, 1975). Subjects could contribute endowments to a linear public good. The individual contributions were multiplied by two, resulting in a group pay-off that was distributed equally among the four group members. It appeared that high-endowment group members contributed more than low-endowment group members. A high positive correlation was observed between the own contribution and the contribution one considered to be fair. Concerning final outcomes, the inequality between high- and low-interest group members was greater in the more relevant (task expenditure) than in the less relevant (chance) condition.

It may be concluded that status congruence explains the harvesting and contributing behavior in RMDs and PGDs, respectively. In symmetric dilemmas in which no status differentiation is involved, group members strive for equal final outcomes and they also consider this the fair thing to do. As for asymmetric dilemmas, group members having status advantage contribute more to the public good than group members having status disadvantage in PGDs. In a similar vein, group members in RMDs having status advantage are more cooperative. This they expressed by leaving more resources in the collective pool than status disadvantage group members. As for the final outcomes group members achieved, it appears that the difference in final outcomes between high- and low-status members is more conspicuous when the antecedent dimension of differentiation is more relevant—that is, is based on task expenditure—than when the differentiation in status is based on a less relevant antecedent dimension, that is, on chance. Thus, in situations in which there is a conflict between individual and collective interests, group members do coordinate their final outcomes in a way that is congruent with their status positions on the antecedent dimension.

COALITION FORMATION

In RMDs and PGDs, every group member has access to the collective source and may profit from the public good, respectively. That no one can be excluded from the consumption of the collective resource is called *nonexcludability*. Coalition formation is also a choice situation. However, contrary to the choice situation in social dilemmas, the focus is not on the provision or maintenance of the collective good, but on an existing collective resource from which some group members may be *excluded*; that is, excludability is one of the main features of coalition formation.

Coalition formation usually involves explicit *bargaining* over the division of group outcomes, such as bargaining over the division of cabinet posts and the allocation of group outcomes to some members, while other group members are excluded. In social dilemmas no explicit bargaining over the maintenance and the provision of a collective good is usually involved. The results presented in the previous section may be ascribed to "tacit bargaining," that is, accommodating or coordinating one's choice behavior with the behavior of other group members. Both situations are called *mixed-motive situations*. They differ, however, in the type of conflict concerned. Whereas choice behavior in social dilemmas refers to a conflict between individual and collective interests, coalition formation situations refer to a conflict between the interests of individual group members that can usually only be resolved when some group members cooperate in order to acquire all group outcomes, while excluding others who do not become a part of the coalition and who are consequently excluded from the consumption of group outcomes.

A common property of asymmetric social dilemmas and coalition formation is that from the very beginning there exist *status differentials*. This property allows us to continue our argument about status congruence and the moderating effect of the relevance of the dimension on which the status differentials are expressed.

Coalition formation is a broad topic. It may be approached from an ethological (see De Waal, 1985), from a political (see De Swaan, 1985; Mokken & Stokman, 1985), and from a social-psychological (see Komorita, 1984) perspective. The emphasis may be on computational models (see, e.g., Komorita, 1984; Van der Linden & Verbeek, 1985), and be more empirically oriented (see Wilke, 1985b). Multiparty coalitions imply N-person groups or multiparty systems that may vary in size. For the present purpose, we have chosen to deal with coalition formation from a social-psychological point of view. We discuss empirical data, which are collected in studies investigating behavior in three-person groups. Two out of three members may then form a coalition, while excluding the third member; that is, simple-majority situations (see Komorita, 1984) are discussed. In these situations, group members who differ in resources are invited to collect as many coalition outcomes as possible, which two of them may acquire by forming a coalition. This situation implies a mixed-motive situation because group members compete for scarce group outcomes, a conflict of interests that may be resolved by the cooperation of two members and the exclusion of the third member.

In coalition formation, several types of initial status differences may be distinguished. Noteworthy is type V (Caplow, 1956): In a three-person group A has four, B has three, and C has two resources. The rule is that a two-person coalition is formed if coalition members can make an agreement on the division of coalition outcomes. In this type V three possible coalitions can be made: (4, 3), (4, 2), and (3, 2). A conservative coalition involves a coalition between the two strongest coalition members (4, 3). A coalition is called a revolutionary coalition, if the two weakest members (3, 2) make a coalition. What are the circumstances in which these types of coalitions are formed?

In a number of experimental studies (e.g., Caldwell, 1971; Kelley & Arrowood, 1960; Vinacke & Arkoff, 1957; Wilke, Meertens, & Steur, 1973) a pachisi board game is presented in which group members A, B, and C are assigned by chance, on speeds 4, 3, and 2, respectively. The progress of each player is defined by multiplication of the value of a die—to be cast by the experimenter—with the group member's speed. All players move on each throw. The rules of the game are that when no coalition is formed, 4 is the winner and that at any moment a coalition between two group members can be formed; and, in that case, their speeds are added so that they can be confident about receiving a symbolic prize for winning the game. Employing the pachisi board format, a preponderance of revolutionary coalitions is found and the coalition outcomes are divided somewhere between proportionality (60%–40%) and equality (50%–50%), results that are replicated when other setups are employed, such as a poker game (e.g., Chertkoff, 1966), a stockholder's simulation (Chertkoff & Braden, 1974), and a convention game (Gamson, 1961; Wilke, 1968). Thus, in various settings a preference for revolutionary coalitions has been found. It has also been found that coalition outcomes on the average are divided between proportionality and equality. Although these settings vary widely in many aspects, they have one property in common: Weights, speeds, and status differences are assigned by chance. Anderson (1967) observed that in the standard pachisi board setting no attempt has been made to legitimize the distribution of resources.

A preponderance of conservative coalitions has been observed in a number of other studies (e.g., Chertkoff, 1966; Cole, 1969; Cole & Barnett, 1978; Wahba, 1972a, 1972b). In the study of Cole and Barnett, in Game 1 of a ball-throwing experiment, players learn the players' competence. In Game 2, a coalition of two players is allowed to compete against a third player. It appeared that (a) subjects selected a stronger rather than a weaker player, and (b) coalition outcomes were divided in a proportional way. Cole and Barnett concluded from their results that when status differentials are based on achievement, conservative coalitions are likely to be formed more frequently.

In a number of experimental studies (Messé, Vallacher, & Phillips, 1974/1975; Murnighan, 1978; Wilke & Pruyn, 1981) conservative coalitions and revolutionary coalitions have been observed. In the experimental study of Messé, Vallacher, and Phillips (1975), three-person groups played a standard pachisi board game. In the input-relevant condition the group members who received the weights 4, 3, and 2 had worked during 2, 1.5, and 1 hour, respectively. In the no-input condition the weights or speeds were assigned randomly. It appeared that in the input-relevant condition, conservative coalitions were formed more frequently, whereas in the no-input condition revolutionary coalitions were formed, suggesting that conservative coalitions are formed when the initial asymmetry in resources is relevant. Consistent with the status congruence argument are then also the results of the division of coalition outcomes: They are more often allocated in proportion to the initial asymmetry (see Wilke & Pruyn, 1981). Further evidence of the proposition that it is the relevance of the initial status differences that matters to a great extent, is provided by results of a study of Wilke, Van Knippenberg, and Bruins (1986). This study was a scenario study. Subjects had to estimate the probability that a specific coalition would be formed. In each of the scenarios, actors' positions on a dimension were described. For example, it was described that the actors differed on a local contest and that they obtained the grades of 9, 7, and 5 (on a 10-point scale, 10 being the maximum). Other status differences were 8-7-6 and 7-7-7. The other factor was relevance, having three levels: direct, not established, and irrelevant. Relevance was realized by specifying the prestigious regional tournaments to which two of the actors could be sent as delegates. For example, when the status differentials were expressed as grades on a running contest, it was suggested that two delegates could be sent to a running tournament (relevant), to a math contest (irrelevant), or to a tournament the nature of which was not specified (not-established). Subjects were requested to predict which two members would be sent to the regional tournament. It appeared that (a) conservative coalitions were expected to have a higher probability when the differentiation was more relevant, and (b) under the condition of high relevance, the 9-7-5 differentiation led to higher estimated probabilities of conservative coalitions than 8-7-6, which, in turn, led to higher ones than in a 7-7-7 differentiation.

Thus, conservative coalitions are formed when there is differentiation on an antecedent dimension or variable that is of high relevance for the subsequent dimension, in this case, of coalition formation. When this is the case, a strong association between status differentials concerning resources and coalition outcomes may be expected (see Wilke & Pruyn, 1981). In contrast, revolutionary coalitions are formed when resources are assigned randomly in pachisi board, poker, and convention games. For a pachisi board game, Kelley and Arrowood (1960) rendered it likely that 4 overestimates his weight (because 4 can win the prize when no coalition between 3 and 2 is formed) and that consequently 4 is excluded from further coalition formation. This reasoning may apply to coalition formation employing a pachisi board game but cannot explain the formation of coalitions in, for example, convention games, in which this extra advantage of 4 is not available. Moreover, measures taken before playing a pachisi board game reveal that players are well aware that they are equal concerning their chance to become a member of the coalition (see Wilke & Mulder, 1974). Another explanation was also proposed by Kelley and Arrowood, who suggested that subjects have learned in the past that a greater weight and more resources mostly mean more control over coalition outcomes. However, if that were true, then according to the status congruence reasoning presented earlier, conservative coalitions should be formed.

Although not definitive, our preliminary explanation is related to the distinction between a conflict of interests and a cognitive conflict. When group members' resources are relevant in view of coalition outcomes, they have to solve their cognitive conflict in a way that status congruence is served, that is, by forming conservative coalitions. However, when resources are not deemed directly relevant for the division of coalition outcomes, then the coalition situation is more characterized by a conflict of interests, especially in view of explicit bargaining. If players would acknowledge in public that their resources are irrelevant, no coalition is possible (usually three-person coalitions are excluded), and no coalition outcomes can be obtained. Moreover, the bargaining process would take forever. Therefore, we reason that status congruence is applied as a rhetorical tool during the bargaining, to make a distinction among players where no differentiation is perceived. Within the congruence rhetoric as a tool to create cognitive clarity, a conflict of interests is rather severe. During bargaining group members base their claims on proportionality, which means that 4 and 3 should divide the coalition outcomes based on the proportion of 4:3; 4 and 2 in the proportion 4:2, and 3 and 2 in proportion of 3:2. If players are then to pursue maximization of outcomes, which is reasonable given their conflict of interests, the (3, 2) or the cheapest winning coalition (Gamson, 1964; Riker, 1962) is most probable. That players act as if their resources are unequal, but look through it, can be seen also from the allocation of coalition outcomes, which are usually between an equal and a proportional division.

In sum, when resources are relevant for the division of outcomes, conservative coalitions are formed, because one departs from status congruence in order to solve a cognitive conflict. However, when antecedent resources are considered to be irrelevant, revolutionary coalitions are likely to occur. One uses status congruence as a rhetoric in forming (revolutionary) coalitions, because otherwise no coalition outcomes would be forthcoming. However, within the boundaries of status congruence as a rhetorical tool, coalitions are made as to maximize personal outcomes.

DISCUSSION

A group structure may be defined as a *description* of the existing interrelationships between group members. It involves dimensions of comparison and the ordering of group members on these dimensions. The ordering on a specific dimension is called the status differentiation on that dimension. An existing or antecedent status differentiation is not only a description of the present interrelationship within a certain group; it involves also a *prescription* of how group members have to be ordered on emerging dimensions of comparison. Status congruence is the tendency to generalize from status differentiation on antecedent dimensions of comparison to subsequent dimensions of comparison, in which inter alia depends on the perceived relevance of the antecedent dimension of comparison for the subsequent dimension of comparison and the evaluation of the antecedent and subsequent dimensions.

In this chapter, the tendency to generalize from antecedent dimensions of comparison to subsequent dimensions of comparison—status congruence—has been shown to be of importance in several areas of research that until now have not been integrated into one framework. Two kinds of consequent dimensions may be distinguished. In groups, during task performance, group members have to decide how much influence each of the group members will have in view of an *efficient* solving of the task. Having to allocate scarce outcomes, group members have to decide how many outcomes each of the group members is entitled to in view of a *fair distribution of outcomes*. These two kinds of consequent dimensions are of paramount importance, because they refer to the two basic dimensions of task groups. As Katz and Kahn (1966) observed, groups have to accomplish two functions: They have to perform their tasks in an efficient way and they have to maintain their internal coherence by allocating group outcomes in a fair way.

How do groups fulfill these two functions? We have argued that in groups members depart from the existing status structure and that the antecedent status differentiation will be projected on the subsequent dimension of concern in a way that—depending on the relevance of the antecedent dimension for the subsequent dimension and the evaluation of these dimensions of comparison—the subsequent status differentiation is congruent with the status differentiation on the antecedent dimension. We have shown that both functions are served when group members depart from status congruence.

In the section Status Differentials and Social Influence, we have presented experimental results showing that group members having status advantage exert more, but accept less, influence than group members having status disadvantage. This is efficient, because the achievement of the group task is served when members having more resources are allowed to have a greater impact on the group product. Moreover, we have shown that the perceived (in)stability and the availability of multiple pieces of antecedent status information moderates the projection of antecedent status information on subsequent dimensions, such as acceptance and exertion of influence.

In the other sections we have dealt with the allocation of group outcomes that may be considered another dimension of comparison. Following Homans (1961), it has been suggested that outcome differentials will be based on status differentiation on an antecedent dimension of comparison, such as investments and need, depending on the relevance of the antecedent dimension for the subsequent dimension of comparison.

In social dilemmas, which refer to a conflict between individual and collective interests, group members are not led by maximization of their personal gains. Instead, they tacitly coordinate their efforts in a way that fairness will be established. For symmetric social dilemmas in which group members are equal on an antecedent dimension of comparison—for example, endowment, access, and interests—it appears that group members strive for equal outcomes, and they consider this also the fair thing to do. When group members differ on an antecedent dimension—that is, when status differentials are introduced (in asymmetric social dilemmas)—then outcome allocation is made congruent with the antecedent status differentials if these status differentials are made relevant: High-status members are more cooperative than low-status members, and concerning their final outcomes, high-status members obtain higher final outcomes than do low-status members. When the antecedent dimension of comparison is not perceived as relevant in view of the allocation of outcomes, high and low status end up with equal final outcomes, and they consider this as fair.

Behavior of group members in coalition settings in which group members do differentiate on an antecedent dimension of comparison, which is assumed to be of relevance for the subsequent dimension of comparison—that is, outcomes allocated—shows that congruence is pursued: Group members having more resources more often are included in the coalition, and coalition outcomes are divided in agreement with resource differentials. However, when resource differences on the antecedent dimension are deemed to be of no relevance, the status congruence mainly serves as a rhetorical tool, and group members act in a way that maximizes their own behavioral outcomes.

To what extent does status congruence imply the continuation of an existing status structure? From the foregoing it may be decided that in isolated situations in which the environmental challenges and, thus, the nature of the task remains constant, the relevance of antecedent status differentiation for the subsequent status differentiation will be constant or may even be amplified. Amplification of status differentials seems plausible because status differentiation on T1 gives rise to influence and outcomes differentials, which, in turn, may increase the aggregated status differentials at T2, which, in turn, may lead to greater influence and outcome differentials. However, there are many circumstances that render a rigid group structure rather unlikely. First, groups are rarely constant in composition. The joining of new members and the leaving of old members may lead to a revision of the antecedent status differentiation. Second, the group task may change because of environmental demands put on groups, having as a consequence that the status differentiation may be less relevant or irrelevant for the consequent influence and outcome differentiation. Third, groups are usually part of larger structures, such as organizations and societies. These larger structures may also affect the relevance of the antecedent status differentials in view of subsequent dimensions of comparison, which are introduced by these larger structures. Fourth, some group members may leave the group and join other groups, because in other groups greater behavioral outcomes may be acquired (for further discussion, see chapter 4 in this volume).

REFERENCES

Allison, S. T., & Messick, D. M. (1990). Social decision heuristics in the use of shared resources. *Journal of Behavioral Decision Making, 3*, 195–204.

Anderson, R. E. (1967). Status structures in coalition bargaining games. *Sociometry, 30*, 393–403.

Bacherach, S. B., Bamberger, P., & Mundell, B. (1993). Status inconsistency in organizations: From social hierarchy to stress. *Journal of Organizational Behavior, 14*, 21–36.

Bales, R. F. (1950). *Interaction process analysis*. Reading, MA: Addison Wesley.

Berger, J., Blackwell, J. W., Norman, R. Z., & Smith, R. F. (1992). Status inconsistency in task situations: A test of four status processing principles. *American Sociological Review, 57*, 843–855.

Berger, J., & Fisek, M. H. (1970). Consistent and inconsistent status characteristics and the determination of power and prestige orders. *Sociometry, 33*, 287–304.

Berger, J., Fisek, M. H., Norman, R. Z., & Wagner, D. G. (1983). The formation of reward expectations in status situations. In D. M. Messick & K. S. Cook (Eds.), *Equity theory* (pp. 127–168). New York: Praeger.

88   WILKE

Berger, J., Rosenholtz, S. J., & Zelditch, M., Jr. (1980). Status organizing processes. *Annual Review of Sociology, 6*, 479–508.

Broverman, J. K., Vogel, S. R., Broverman, D. M., Clarkson, F. E., & Rosenkrantz, P. S. (1972). Sex role stereotypes: A current appraisal. *Journal of Social Issues, 28*, 59–78.

Bruins, J., & Wilke, H. A. M. (1993). Upward power tendencies in a hierarchy: Power distance theory versus bureaucratic rule. *European Journal of Social Psychology, 23*, 239–254.

Butler, R. (1992). What young people want to know when: Effects of mastery and ability goals on interests in different kinds of social comparisons. *Journal of Personality and Social Psychology, 62*(6), 934–943.

Caldwell, M. (1971). Coalition in the triad introducing the element of chance into the game structure. *Journal of Personality and Social Psychology, 20*, 271–280.

Caplow, T. (1956). A theory of coalitions in the triad. *American Sociological Review, 21*, 489–493.

Chertkoff, J. M. (1966). The effects of probability of success on coalition formation. *Journal of Experimental Social Psychology, 2*, 169–177.

Chertkoff, J. M., & Braden, J. L. (1974). Effects of experience and bargaining restrictions on coalition formation. *Journal of Personality and Social Psychology, 30*(1), 169–177.

Cohen, E. G., & Roper, S. S. (1972). Modification of interracial interaction disability: An application of status characteristic theory. *American Sociological Review, 37*, 643–657.

Cole, S. G. (1969). Examination of the power-inversion effect in three-person mixed-motive games. *Journal of Personality and Social Psychology, 11*(1), 50–58.

Cole, S. G., & Barnett, L. L. (1978). The subjective distribution of achieved power and associated coalition formation behavior. In H. Sauermann (Ed.), *Coalition forming behavior* (pp. 40–54). Tübingen, Germany: J. C. B. Mohr.

Collins, B. E., & Raven, B. H. (1969). Attraction, coalitions, communication and power. In G. Lindzey & E. Aronson (Eds.), *The handbook of social psychology* (Vol. IV, 2nd ed., pp. 102–204). Reading, MA: Addison-Wesley.

Dawes, R. M. (1980). Social dilemmas. *Annual Review of Psychology, 31*, 169–193.

De Gilder, D. (1991). *Expectation states theory.* Unpublished doctoral thesis, Leiden University, Leiden, Netherlands.

De Gilder, D., & Wilke, H. A. M. (1990). Processing sequential status information. *Social Psychology Quarterly, 53*(4), 340–351.

De Gilder, D., & Wilke, H. A. M. (1994). Expectation States Theory and the motivational determinants of social influence. In W. Stroebe & M. Hewstone (Eds.), *European Review of Social Psychology* (Vol. 5, pp. 243–269). London, UK: Wiley.

De Soto, C. B. (1960). Learning in a social structure. *Journal of Abnormal and Social Psychology, 60*, 417–421.

De Swaan, A. (1985). Coalition theory and multi-party systems. In H. Wilke (Ed.), *Coalition formation* (pp. 229–262). Amsterdam: North-Holland.

Deutsch, M. (1975). Equity, equality and need: What determines which value will be used as the basis of distributive justice? *Journal of Social Issues, 31*, 137–149.

De Waal, F. B. M. (1985). Coalitions in monkeys and apes. In H. Wilke (Ed.), *Coalition formation* (pp. 1–28). Amsterdam: North-Holland.

Festinger, L. (1954). A theory of social comparison processes. *Human Relations, 7*, 117–140.

Fiske, S. T., & Taylor, S. E. (1991). *Social cognition.* New York: McGraw-Hill.

French, J. R. P., & Raven, B. (1959). The bases of social power. In D. Cartwright (Ed.), *Studies in social power* (pp. 150–167). Ann Arbor, MI: Institute for Social Research.

Gamson, W. A. (1961). An experimental test of a theory of coalition formation. *American Sociological Review, 26*, 565–573.

Gamson, W. A. (1964). Experimental studies of coalition formation. In L. Berkowitz (Ed.), *Advances in experimental social psychology* (pp. 82–110). New York: Academic Press.

Hardin, G. (1968). The tragedy of the commons. *Science, 162*, 1243–1248.

Heider, F. (1958). *The psychology of interpersonal relations.* New York: Wiley.

Hembroff, L. A., Martin, M. W., & Sell, J. (1981). Total performance inconsistency and status generalization: An expectation states formulation. *The Sociological Quarterly, 22*, 421–430.

Homans, G. C. (1961). *Social behavior: Its elementary forms.* New York: Harcourt Brace.

Katz, D., & Kahn, R. L. (1966). *The social psychology of organizations.* New York: Harcourt Brace.

Kelley, H. H., & Arrowood, A. J. (1960). Coalition in the triad: Critique and experiment. *Sociometry, 23*, 231–244.

Knottnerus, J. D., & Greenstein, T. N. (1981). Status and performance characteristics in social interaction: A theory of status validation. *Social Psychological Quarterly, 44*, 338–349.

Komorita, S. S. (1984). Coalition bargaining. In L. Berkowitz (Ed.), *Advances in experimental social psychology* (Vol. 18, pp. 184–247). New York: Academic Press.

Lemaine, G. (1974). Social differentiation and social originality. *European Journal of Social Psychology, 4*, 17–52.

Lemaine, G., Kasterstein, J., & Personnaz, B. (1978). Social differentiation. In H. Tajfel (Ed.), *Differentiation between social groups: Studies in the social psychology of intergroup relations* (pp. 269–300). London: Academic Press.

Lerner, J., Miller, D. T., & Holmes, J. G. (1976). Deserving and the emergence of forms of justice. In L. Berkowitz & E. Walster (Eds.), *Advances in experimental psychology* (Vol. 9, pp. 134–162). New York: Academic Press.

Leventhal, G. S. (1976). The distribution of rewards and resources in groups and organizations. In L. Berkovitz & E. Walster (Eds.), *Advances in experimental social psychology* (Vol. 9, pp. 92–129). New York: Academic Press.

Markus, H., & Zajonc, R. B. (1985). The cognitive perspective in social psychology. In G. Lindzey & E. Aronson (Eds.), *The handbook of social psychology* (Vol. I, 3rd ed., pp. 137–236). New York: Random House.

Martin, M. W., & Sell, J. (1980). The marginal utility of information: Its effects upon decision-making. *Social Psychology Quarterly, 21*, 233–242.

Marwell, G., & Ames, M. (1979). Experiments on the provision of public goods, I: Resources, interest, group size, and the free-rider problem. *American Journal of Sociology, 84*, 1335–1360.

Messé, L. A., Vallacher, R. R., & Phillips, J. C. (1974/1975). Equity and coalition formation in triads. *Personality and Social Psychology Bulletin, 1*, 249–251.

Messé, L. A., Vallacher, R. R., & Phillips, J. C. (1975). Equity and the formation of revolutionary and conservative coalitions in triads. *Journal of Personality and Social Psychology, 31*, 1141–1146.

Messick, D. M., & Brewer, M. B. (1983). Solving social dilemmas: A review. In L. Wheeler & P. Shaver (Eds.), *Review of personality and social psychology* (Vol. 4, pp. 11–44). Beverly Hills, CA: Sage.

Mokken, R. J., & Stokman, F. N. (1985). Legislative analysis: Methodology for the analysis of groups and coalitions. In H. Wilke (Ed.), *Coalition formation* (pp. 173–228). Amsterdam: North-Holland.

Moscovici, S. (1985). Social influence and conformity. In G. Lindzey & E. Aronson (Eds.), *The handbook of social psychology* (Vol. II, 3rd ed., pp. 347–426). New York: Random House.

Murnigham, J. K. (1978). Strength and weakness in four coalition situations. *Behavioral Science, 23*, 195–209.

Olson, M. (1965). *The logic of collective action.* Cambridge, MA: Harvard University Press.

Pugh, M. D., & Wahrman, R. (1983). Neutralizing sexism in mixed-sex groups: Do women have to be better than men? *American Journal of Sociology, 88*, 746–762.

Ridgeway, C. L. (1989). Understanding legitimation in informal status orders. In J. Berger, M. Zelditch, Jr., & B. Anderson (Eds.), *Sociological theories in progress: New formulations* (pp. 131–159). Newbury Park, CA: Sage.

Ridgeway, C. L., & Berger, J. (1986). Expectations, legitimation, and dominance behavior in task groups. *American Sociological Review, 51*, 603–617.

Ridgeway, C. L., Berger, J., & Smith, L. (1985). Nonverbal cues and status: An expectation states approach. *American Journal of Sociology, 90*, 5, 955–978.

Riker, W. H. (1962). *The theory of political coalitions*. New Haven, CT: Yale University Press.

Riordan, C., & Ruggiero, J. (1980). Producing equal-status interracial interaction: A replication. *Social Psychology Quarterly, 43*, 131–136.

Sampson, E. E. (1969). Studies in status congruence. In L. Berkowitz (Ed.), *Advances in experimental social psychology* (Vol. 4, pp. 225–270). New York: Academic Press.

Samuelson, D., Messick, D. M., Rutte, C. G., & Wilke, H. (1984). Individual and structural solution to resource dilemmas in two cultures. *Journal of Personality and Social Psychology, 47*, 94–104.

Samuelson, P. A. (1954). The pure theory of public expenditure. *Review of Economics and Statistics, 36*, 387–389.

Samuelson, P. A. (1955). Diagrammic exposition of a theory of public expenditure. *Review of Economics and Statistics, 37*, 350–356.

Sev'er, A. (1989). Simultaneous effects of status and task cues: Combining, eliminating or buffering? *Social Psychology Quarterly, 52*, 327–335.

Stein, R. T., & Heller, T. (1979). An empirical analysis of the correlations between leadership status and participation rates reported in the literature. *Journal of Personality and Social Psychology, 37*, 1993–2002.

Van de Kragt, A. J. C., Dawes, R. M., Orbell, J. M., Braver, S. R., & Wilson, L. A. II (1986). Doing well and doing good as ways of resolving social dilemmas. In H. Wilke, D. Messick, & C. Rutte (Eds.), *Experimental social dilemmas* (pp. 177–202). Frankfurt/Main, Germany: Lang GmbH.

Van der Linden, W. J., & Verbeek, A. (1985). Coalition formation: A game theoretic approach. In H. Wilke (Ed.), *Coalition formation* (pp. 29–114). Amsterdam: North-Holland.

Van Dijk, E. (1993). *Coordination in asymmetrical social dilemmas*. Unpublished doctoral thesis, Leiden University, Leiden, Netherlands.

Van Dijk, E., & Wilke, H. (1991). De invloed van de legitimiteit van middelen-asymmetrie op de contributie aan een publiek goed [The influence of the legitimacy of endowments asymmetry on the contribution to a public good]. In J. van der Pligt, W. van der Kloot, A. van Knippenberg, & M. Poppe (Eds.), *Fundamentele sociale psychologie, deel 5* (pp. 222–242). Tilburg, Netherlands: Tilburg University Press.

Van Dijk, E., & Wilke, H. (1993a). Afstemmingsregels in sociale dilemma's: Verschillen tussen geef- en neem-situaties [Decision rules in social dilemmas]. In W. van der Kloot, A. P. Buunk, N. Ellemers, & J. van der Pligt (Eds.), *Fundamentele sociale psychologie, deel 7* (pp. 171–183). Tilburg, Netherlands: Tilburg University Press.

Van Dijk, E., & Wilke, H. (1993b). Differential interests, equity, and public good provision. *Journal of Experimental Social Psychology, 29*, 1–16.

Vinacke, W. E., & Arkoff, A. (1957). An experimental study of coalitions in the triad. *American Sociological Review, 22*(1), 406–414.

Wagner, D. G., Ford, R. S., & Ford, T. W. (1986). Can gender inequalities be reduced? *American Sociological Review, 51*, 47–61.

Wahba, M. A. (1972a). Coalition formation under conditions of uncertainty. *The Journal of Social Psychology, 88*, 43–54.

Wahba, M. A. (1972b). Expectancy model of coalition formation. *Psychological Reports, 30*, 671–677.

Walster, E., Berscheid, E., & Walster, G. W. (1976). New directions in equity research. In L. Berkowitz & E. Walster (Eds.), *Advances in experimental social psychology* (Vol. 9, pp. 1–42). New York: Academic Press.

Webster, M. A., Jr. (1977). Equating characteristics and social interaction: Two experiments. *Sociometry, 40*, 41–50.

Webster, M. A., Jr., & Driskell, J. E., Jr. (1978). Status generalization: A review and some new data. *American Sociological Review, 43*, 220–236.

Wilke, H. A. M. (1968). *Coalitieformatie in triades*. Rotterdam, Netherlands: Bronder.

Wilke, H. A. M. (1983). Equity: Information and effect dependency. In D. M. Messick & K. S. Cook (Eds.), *Equity theory* (pp. 47–60). New York: Praeger.

Wilke, H. A. M. (Ed.). (1985a). *Coalition formation*. Amsterdam, Netherlands: North-Holland.

Wilke, H. A. M. (1985b). Coalition formation from a socio-psychological perspective. In H. Wilke (Ed.), *Coalition formation* (pp. 115–172). Amsterdam, Netherlands: North-Holland.

Wilke, H., Meertens, R., & Steur, Th. (1973). Uncertainty and power inversion in coalition formation: Again strength is weakness. *British Journal for Social and Clinical Psychology, 12*, 38–45.

Wilke, H., & Mulder, M. (1971). Coalition formation on the gameboard. *European Journal of Social Psychology, 1*(3), 339–355.

Wilke, H., & Mulder, A. (1974). A comparison of rotation versus non-rotation in coalition formation experiments. *European Journal of Social Psychology, 4*(1), 99–102.

Wilke, H., & Pruyn, J. (1981). Billijkheidstheorie en coalitieformatie [Fairness theory and coalition formation]. *Gedrag, 9*(3), 159–170.

Wilke, H., Van Knippenberg, A., & Bruins, J. (1986). Conservative coalitions: An expectation states approach. *European Journal of Social Psychology, 16*, 51–64.

Wit, A. P., Wilke, H. A. M., & Oppewal, H. (1992). Fairness in asymmetric social dilemmas. In W. Liebrand, D. Messick, & H. Wilke (Eds.), *Social dilemmas: Theoretical issues and research findings* (pp. 183–197). New York: Pergamon.

CHAPTER

4

LEADERSHIP:
MICRO–MACRO LINKS

Jorge Correia Jesuíno
ISCTE—Lisbon

Leadership is currently defined as a process of influence involving a leader—the agent who exerts influence—and the followers—the agents subjected to that influence. By influence is meant that some change occurs in the target agent (followers) as a consequence of some act performed by the source agent (the leader). Influence, in these broad terms, is an outcome of power. The capability of the leader to influence the followers is another way of saying that the leader has power over the followers.

But it is also current in the literature to distinguish between power and influence or, at least, between different types of power. It is also well known that the similar concept of authority means, according to Weber (1947), legitimate power. Weber also distinguished between three sources of legitimation: the traditional, the legal, and the charismatic. The last one is a personal source of power, whereas the first two are positional sources. Leadership is most often related to the more personalized facet of exerting power and/or influence.

At the core of the distinction is the idea that influence induces change through persuasion rather than through any form of coercion. Barnard (1938), for example, distinguished between authority of position and authority of leadership. For Parsons (1963) the crucial differentiating criteria are the collective bindingness in the case of power and its absence in the case of influence. The use of influence in cases of noncompliance with decisions and recommendations would not result in coercive sanctions.

Influence is thus a medium of persuasion. This implies, still in accordance with Parsons (1963), invoking collectively relevant justifications of the agent of influence, which, in general, invokes consideration of collective interest transcending those of the particular units involved and usually includes the call to what is at some level defined as a matter of moral obligation.

Parsons' (1963) distinction is, thus, more subtle and more demanding. Personalized power and *a fortiori* the charisma are not enough for distinguishing power and influence. Personalized power is still power in the sense that exerting it does not require justifications and in the sense that noncompliance incurs some form of coercive sanction, such as the withdrawal of esteem by the leader.

Parsons (1963) invoked the "common belongingness in a Gemeinschaft type of solidarity as the primary basis of mutual influence, which is for influence systems the equivalent of gold for monetary and force for power systems" (p. 368). Leadership can be exerted either through power or influence media or rather, simultaneously through both.

We can also quote Habermas (1984/1981) who, elaborating on Parsons (1963), distinguished two types of media, or rather communication actions: those aiming at the social integration, requiring illocutionary acts (Austin, 1962) and dependent on the binding effects of using language with an orientation to mutual understanding; and the steering media aiming at the functional integration, such as money and power, that guide interaction through the agent's intervention in the situation of the target, through perlocutionary acts. For Habermas, communicative actions consist of "those linguistically mediated interaction in which all participants pursue illocutionary aims, and *only* illocutionary aims, with their mediating acts of communications" (p. I-295). On the other hand, "strategic action are those interactions in which at least one of the participants wants his speech acts to produce perlocutionary effects on his opposite member" (p. 295). Analogous distinctions can also be found if we turn from sociologists and philosophers to social psychologists who have studied social influence and leadership processes.

Moscovici (1976, 1979), for example, introduced a distinction between two models of influence—the functionalist model and the genetic, the former characterized by asymmetric (power) relations between the source and the target, aiming at producing the social control of the system, whereas in the genetic model the aim is social change and relationships between source and target are symmetric (no power differences). We return to this dichotomy later, which apparently equates leadership with hierarchy (see also Moscovici, 1985) and power, limiting the influence processes to horizontal relationships. But leadership can also take place within a horizontal (influence) system, whenever some asymmetry between a source and a target can be identified. Symmetry of power does not imply symmetry of influence (see also chapter 3 in this volume).

An alternative criterion for distinguishing power from influence was proposed by Turner (1985, 1991) through the self-categorization theory. Briefly stated, the theory relates the distinction between influence and power with the distinction between ingroup and outgroup, between "self" and "others." As summarized by

Turner (1991), "the social categorization of others, implies that one would not expect to be influenced by them, agree with them or feel uncertain when confronted by their different views. Power refers to the process of social control over self exercised by people socially categorised as different from self. Put simply power represents counter-normative and influence pro-normative influence" (p. 172).

More examples could be added showing how the various authors propose subtle nuances of how influence and power relate to each other in the leadership process. The conceptual field in this domain is still and probably will continue to be unstable and fuzzy, crossed by multiple "language games"—that is, by different theoretical approaches—yet close enough to belong to the same "family." Plural discourses in social sciences may be a "way of life" but not necessarily a weakness. On the contrary, they contribute to a greater diversity of perspectives, as a requisite of the diversity and complexity of their object (Ashby, 1968).

In this chapter, an attempt is made not so much to integrate the different models so far proposed but rather to establish bridges between them, showing their continuities and discontinuities, as well as conceptual isomorphisms hidden behind diverse terminologies. In the same vein links are also proposed between different levels of analysis where leadership processes take place, such as small groups, organizations, or even societies, but also between the laboratory and the real world. Rather than proposing another alternative model, preference was given here to a conceptual framework, a sort of map with some more salient itineraries that to a certain extent may help simplify the intricacies of the territory. Such a map can be drawn in successive steps, adding successive layers of complexity.

In the first layer, or the first map, an influence process is simply defined as an action of an agent—the source aimed at producing some change—in the beliefs, attitudes, values, behaviors, of another agent, the target, be it an individual or a group (see Fig. 4.1). By outcomes of the influence action, it is meant here the effects studied by social psychologists in various fields such as social influence, persuasion and attitude change, group decision making, conflict and negotiation, and leadership. It includes among others phenomena like conformity, convergence, innovation, polarization, groupthink, bystander apathy, compliance, obedience, resistance, cooperation and competition, identification and adaptation.

In the leadership literature, the source is the leader and the target is the follower or followers. But what seems to specify leadership among other influence processes is the stable and sustained asymmetry between leader and followers, between the source and the target within the social influence field. It is this asymmetry that probably led to shift the study of leadership processes

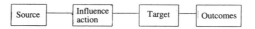

FIG. 4.1. Basic model of influence process.

toward the figure of the leader, and to the paradoxical situation of separate developments within the same area of analysis.

Leadership is defined as an influence process, but researchers of social influence do not seem to be interested in studying how social influence is exerted by leaders and what kind of outcomes they cause on followers. Researchers of leadership also seem to ignore the discoveries achieved by their colleagues on social influence processes. This reciprocal ignorance is not, as evidence shows, an idiosyncrasy of social influence and leadership studies. The same occurs with other paradigms within the same field such as persuasion and attitude change or even, although to a lesser extent, with group processes. In the case of leadership processes, the divorce from the social influence research can also be due to methodological reasons. Social influence has been studied mainly, at the laboratory level, using experimental designs, which necessarily implies a focus on instant processes and on their molecular variants and subtleties. Laboratory studies are most of the time one-shot observations examining static relationships between variables rather than the evolving processes over time, as those taking place through the interactions between group members.

There is, however, an alternative approach in social psychology where this methodological approach has been adopted. Systematic observation of groups in experimental settings was an endeavor undertaken by Robert Bales in the late 1940s. The groups under observation were task groups; that is, they had a specific goal to attain and no appointed leader, and the setting was nonhierarchical.

Among other things, Bales was interested in observing the processes and the interaction pattern leading to the emergence of a leader, that is, of someone recognized by the group members as the most influential one in "locomoting" the group toward its objective. According to the findings of Bales (1950), the emergent leaders display, as a rule, typical behavior such as addressing the group as a whole, receiving information, and giving suggestions.

Bales (1950) also found that emergent task leaders are not necessarily the most popular, in the sense of being liked or preferred as friends. Those findings led to the famous and classic distinction between instrumental and socio-emotional interactions, and the corresponding instrumental leader and socio-emotional leader. These two dimensions are still today, after 50 years of extensive research, the two main dimensions of leadership behavior.

Here we have a situation where no power differences exist, at least at the onset of the group interaction, but where nevertheless a leadership process takes place giving rise to the emergence of a leader. Research on leadership also made attempts to identify the personality traits that might contribute to this emergence of leaders in nonhierarchical groups. Such research has not, however, been very conclusive (Bass, 1981; Stogdill, 1974) and is not pursued here. At any rate, it can be asked what could possibly be the amount of influence exerted by the just-emerged leader on future tasks of the same group. This kind of observation is not common, even within the empirical tradition initiated by Bales (1950).

It is only in very recent times that researchers acknowledged the need to observe groups over time, although under the controlled conditions of the laboratory (Gersick, 1988, 1989; McGrath, 1993). It is not very hazardous to hypothesize that emergent leaders will most likely reinforce their capital of influence, or that members will tend to look to them for advice and direction. In a word, emergent leaders tend to become legitimate leaders, and once the legitimation group is achieved, the influence they subsequently exert over the group is an outcome of legitimate power. The emergence of leaders could thus be interpreted as the emergence of power as an outcome of leadership. The power recognized and conferred to the leader is a personal power; that is, it depends on his or her specific skills as an expert, or at least as the most expert among the group members for the task underway, and also on more effective factors such as emotional appeal (French & Raven, 1959).

We are now at a second level of analysis that could be schematically represented as suggested in Fig. 4.2. What the figure attempts to describe is the process taking place in nonhierarchic task groups where the personal expertise of some member in giving direction to the attainment of goals contributes to his or her emergence as the leader and, once this asymmetry of influence established, it will tend to be maintained in future interactions with the group members. Although this may be the case in most of the situations, it is not excluded that in some cases the group may attain its objectives without any of its members emerging as a leader. In such cases the leadership is distributed by its members, who may or may not be able to coordinate their efforts and skills in order to attain the objectives of the group.

Still in accordance with the earlier findings of Bales (1950), the emergence of a leader is not, as a matter of fact, a necessary condition for the locomotion of the group toward its objectives. The decisive factor is rather the pattern of interactions so that instrumental interactions—exchange of information, opinions, and suggestions—occur at significantly higher rates than the expressive interactions—level of stress and conflict between members. Groups with a high level of conflict may be blocked in their locomotion toward the objectives. Such situations are less likely with the emergence of a leader (see chapter 7 of this volume). The skills of the leader are therefore not only related with the specific task of the group but mostly with his ability to coordinate the interactions in order to reduce the process losses (Hackman, 1987; Steiner, 1972).

This second level of analysis suggests, therefore, that power, under its mild guise of personal skill, may moderate the influence processes occurring in a

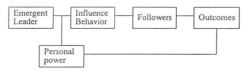

FIG. 4.2. Influence of personal power in the emergence of leader.

task group. Such an effect only becomes salient when the observation is processed on the pattern of interactions taking place along the locomotion of the
group toward its objectives. Those findings are obviously dependent on the
research methodology adopted. Effects taking place over time do not seem to
be easily grasped by experimental designs; they require instead systematic
observational techniques and accurate descriptions.

But the experimental method can also be used for studying leadership processes in groups. The pioneer study conducted by K. Lewin and his associates
R. Lippit and R. K. White (1939) is the first and maybe still the most important
research ever done on leadership using the experimental method. The design
conceived by Lewin in this famous experiment consisted of manipulating the
group climate through the behavior styles of confederates, a role enacted in the
first essays by his research associates themselves. These confederates were
formal leaders, performing the role of monitors of groups of male adolescents,
with specific tasks to perform. Such an experimental setting is a hierarchy with
the implicit assumption about the legitimacy of the power exerted from a formal
position. The experiment of Lewin is also, from that standpoint, a first study on
organizational leadership. We are now at a higher level of analysis where influence processes are moderated by positional rather than personal power and
where followers are designated as subordinates (see Fig. 4.3).

The difference between *position power* and *personal power* is critical for the
leadership process. The influence behavior is now an outcome of power, of
legitimate power, which means that acts of influence (such as the rules adopted
for coordinating the group activities) do not emerge from an outgoing process
that may or may not lead to the emergence of a leader, but are instead imposed
at the outset by the authority of its formal leader. It is this authority that
quasi-automatically assures the acceptance of the influence behavior. Outcomes
may, however, contribute to confirm and force the authority of the formal leader,
but may also undermine his or her legitimacy. In this last case, position power
may become less legitimate and more coercive and expressive. In extreme
situations it may even become "naked power," which may be a symptom of
weakness rather than strength.

In their experiment, Lewin et al. (1939) manipulated three different leadership
behaviors: the autocratic, the democratic, and the laissez-faire. Each one of
those styles corresponds to different levels of legitimacy. In the autocratic
climate it was found that the outcomes in terms of efficiency were not lower
than those observed in the democratic climate. The advantages of democratic

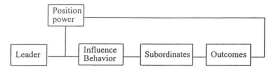

FIG. 4.3. Formal power and leadership process.

leadership were found to be related to innovation and creativity of solutions and also in the lower levels of stress and conflict between group members. In the long run, whereas the autocratic leadership may be undermined by the rising level of conflict and eventually to resistance to complying, the democratic leadership may be reinforced acquiring a higher level of legitimacy. In contrast, in the laissez-faire climate, in which formal leaders apparently abdicate exercising influence, the group tends to disrupt. Laissez-faire is not the same situation as leaderless groups working in a nonhierarchical setting. Of course, informal leaders can also emerge in hierarchical systems, but this is also a symptom of the relative lack of legitimacy of formal leaders.

If the Lewin et al. (1939) research paradigm on leadership shows, on the one hand, that the experimental method may be adequate for studying leadership processes, it also suggests, on the other hand, that the experimental method has severe limitations in the types of variables that can be manipulated. An experimental design is by its own nature a static situation with its pattern of independent and dependent variables linked by linear causal relations. For Graumann (1986), an attentive reader of K. Lewin, those experiments on leadership represent a return to and, to a certain extent, a yielding to the Aristotelian way of thinking.

Instead of the dynamics of a field, instead of the genetic process of an autonomous system that seems to characterize the Lewinian field theory, we have now a rather functional structure of static variables regulated, at best, by a feed system linked to its outcomes. From that standpoint, the Lewinian paradigm on leadership, although decisive for opening the way to the study of organizational leadership, also contributed to its divorce from the ongoing research on social influence processes.

Organizational leadership research has, as a matter of fact, focused on leader behavior relating it directly to the group outcomes, while group processes, although supposed to mediate the influence exerted by the leader, are bypassed and sealed in a sort of a black box. Besides, research on organizational leadership usually does not adopt experimental designs, being mainly conducted in natural settings and oriented to practical concerns of leadership effectiveness through selection and training of leaders. This is another reason for the divorce between leadership research and research conducted by experimental social psychologists on social influence processes.

It is our conviction that this situation could be overcome and links could be established between these separate fields with benefits for both sides. And it is also our conviction that leadership processes, occurring as they do in hierarchical as well as nonhierarchical settings, in articulating influence and power media offer an ideal opportunity for observing to what extent those links could be extended to contiguous but still separate disciplines such as social and organizational behavior.

In Fig. 4.4 a final map is proposed as a simplified attempt for integrating these separate approaches. The map can be read as formed by successive layers or

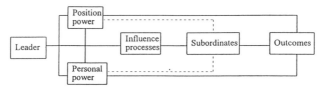

FIG. 4.4. An integrated map of leadership processes.

levels of embeddedness. At the core of the map we have the social influence processes studied in experimental social psychology, such as conformity, normalization, and innovation. The level represented in the lower half is related to emergent leadership in nonhierchical task groups. In those situations, leaders make and simultaneously are made by the groups. From this standpoint they are an outcome of the group interaction, a social construction, to which they critically contribute to give form, in a sort of "bootstrapping" logic creating an asymmetry within a Lewinian group field. Still another level is represented in the upper half of the map related to hierarchy of power positions occupied by appointed formal leaders. At this level of organizational leadership, a great variety of forms of power, either isolated or combined with social influence processes, can be conceived (see chapter 3 of this volume).

For example, power can be directly exerted over the subordinates without any mediating influence process. The autocratic climate studied by Lewin et al. (1939), suppressing the lateral interactions between the group members, gives experimental evidence to this sort of process and expected outcomes. In contrast, in the democratic climate, lateral interactions were encouraged, which might have helped to release social influence processes among group members, thus amplifying the leadership effect.

The model also proposes that position and personal power are linked and can reinforce each other. Legitimate power could be considered as a boundary modality of power, articulating position and personal power. Legitimate power is, in itself, an outcome of a legitimation process, achieved through the acceptance and confirmation of the target subjects. Legitimation is thus contingent on the personal assets of leaders. Personal power can also be reinforced to the extent to which leaders are able to use their positions for mobilizing resources, that is, to exert influence upward (Kanter, 1983; Kotter, 1988; Pelz, 1951).

From this standpoint, appointed leaders, in order to be confirmed by their subordinates, also seem subject to the same bootstrapping logic described for emergent leaders. Of course, and once again, leaders can limit their action to prescribed roles of their position, which amounts to saying that leadership in this case is a function of social control rather than social change. Most situations of organizational leadership combine, quite presumably, both forms and dynamics of power and influence, of social control and social change.

In the next sections, an attempt is made to describe those trade-offs between influence and power and the links that can be established between micro- and macroprocesses.

SOCIAL INFLUENCE AND LATERAL LEADERSHIP

Social influence has been studied through several independent paradigms such as social facilitation, conformity, convergence, attitude change, persuasion, group polarization, and minority influence. Attempts at an integration of the field have been proposed by formal theories such as social impact theory (Latané, 1981; Latané & Wolf, 1981), the extended group situation theory (Witte, 1987, 1990; see also Witte in Vol. 1 of this set), and also by substantive theories such as the theory of conversion behavior (Moscovici, 1976, 1980, 1985), the self-categorization theory (Turner, 1982, 1985, 1991; Turner, Hogg, Oakes, Reicher, & Wetherell, 1987) and, more recently, the conflict elaboration model (Pérez & Mugny, 1993, see also chapter 7 of this volume). Although with partial overlaps, each one of these theories has its own focus and philosophical background, and none of them seems to have succeeded in unifying the various specific findings of social influence research. Somewhat intriguing is the scarcity of accounts of leadership processes that can be observed within the different paradigms studied under the heading of social influence.

Moscovici as well as Turner did not ignore leadership processes, but they both tended to analyze it in very schematic terms, confounding or reducing it to the use of power either formal or informal. As it is claimed here, power is usually necessary for leadership, but we can have power without leadership as we can have leadership without power. What is specific in leadership processes is the mix of power and influence, it is this specificity that justifies its study within the social influence framework.

Social influence theories have been dominated by what Turner (1991) designated as the "dual-process model," that is, the informative–normative distinction introduced by Deutsch and Gerard (1955). As claimed by Turner, the dual-process model has been evoked for exploring processes such as the Asch and Sherif situations, but is also present in the "elaboration likelihood model" of Petty and Cacioppo (1986), in the "persuasive arguments" theory proposed in the polarization literature (Burnstein & Vinokur, 1973, 1975, 1977), and also in the theory of "conversion behavior" (Moscovici, 1980) where the author apparently evolved from his former "genetic theory" (1976).

The dual-process model has its former origin in a seminal text of Festinger published in 1950, where the author proposed an explanation for the "pressures for uniformity" that occur in groups. It is in this article that Festinger introduced the well-known and controversial distinction between "physical reality" and "social reality." Whereas the physical reality can be directly tested and validated by the individual subject, the social reality designates those situations where the judgment of the subject can only be validated by other subjects. A consequence of this notion of social reality is that individuals are more influenced by the majority when the situation is more uncertain or ambiguous, but also they deviate more from a majority already acquired.

But these two situations are not necessarily equivalent. According to Moscovici (1985), for example, uncertainty is not a cause for the differences of individual perceptions, beliefs, or judgments, but rather an effect of those differences. In other words, it is because individuals do not agree with others' perceptions and beliefs that reality becomes uncertain. Social influence is thus a process of reducting as well as creating social conflict rather than a process of reducting some sort of external uncertainty. In his genetic theory, Moscovici (1976) came very close to integrating social influence processes in a theory of leadership when he proposed "behavior styles" as the main source of social influence. In the Asch situation, for example, it is the consistency of the confederates, rather than the simple majority, that exerts pressure on the experimental subject. Whenever a minority disagrees with a majority, a tacit negotiation is likely to be pursued in order to reach some sort of compromise.

Explaining social influence by the behavior style of influence is, to a certain extent, acknowledging the importance of the normative influence, not of the group, but of someone that consistently challenges the group norms and proposes alternatives. Such a figure is obviously a leader. His or her influence derives therefore less from the informational content of his or her judgment than from his ability to mobilize the group members to reexamine their own judgments and norms. The theory of behavior styles is also closely linked to the role of dissent in social change. As argued and empirically evidenced by Moscovici (1976, 1985), innovation is a social influence process triggered by "active minorities," and their success in introducing change is due to the "consistency" of their behaviors.

Promising as it was, the genetic theory did not produce a leadership theory, and instead, it apparently came to be replaced by the dual-process model as expressed in the subsequent distinction between "compliance" and "conversion" as two independent processes of social behavior (Moscovici, 1980). Compliance is now considered an outcome of power, not influence, leading to a "public" change in behavior but not necessarily in attitude, whereas conversion reflects a "private" change, whatever the public behavior.

In other words, the exercise of power aims at social control, at changing the "overt behavior" rather than at a "readiness to act" (Cartwright, 1965), and therefore cannot be considered a modality of social influence. In contrast the conversion process came to be considered by Moscovici (1980) no longer as an outcome of a social conflict negotiation, but as a cognitive individual process of reformulating or revising a judgment as a consequence of being stimulated by a divergent opinion. In other words, it is now the cognitive rather than the social that seems to acquire priority in the process of solving a social-cognitive conflict.

Implicit in this position, as suggested by Turner (1991), is the acceptance not only of the distinction between normative and informative influence, but also and most important, that the latter actually corresponds to social influence. Underlying this conception is the idea, probably somewhat implicit in Festinger

(1950), that the physical reality is the paradigm of science or, better said, of the "Cartesian" scientist able to decipher the "secrets of nature" using his own mind, without any social mediation. This notion of physical reality was criticized by Tajfel (1969), who argued that even physical reality is a product of society. Modern concepts of science seem to greatly depart from this naive Cartesian position. Anyway, the mainstream social psychology with its accent on the lower levels of analysis (Doise, 1982) always comes back to a model that greatly reduces the role of social mediating factors.

To consider the "informative influence" as paradigmatic of social influence processes, and the "normative influence" as only an instance of social control is to accept that a belief or a judgment and, *a fortiori*, a change of a belief or on a judgment, is an exclusively private, individual affair and that social mediation is only instrumental for conveying information. From this standpoint it is difficult to see what could be the difference, in terms of information processing, between the physical and social reality. As rightly argued by Turner (1991), "the trend has been to interpret all validity testing as if it were a kind of physical reality testing—even where the judgments are about issues, attitudes, and beliefs far removed from the simple perceptual or physical tasks that Festinger had in mind . . . Implicitly, a physical reality testing models of informational (subjective) validity has been adopted to the exclusion of social model" (p. 150).

The claim is made here that this trend can also be explained by the paradigms and situations used in studying social influence processes. In his seminal article of 1950, Festinger distinguished two sources of pressure for uniformity: one is the social reality just discussed, and the other is the "group locomotion," a clear Lewinian concept, expressing the idea that pressures may arise because uniformity is perceived as instrumental for group progression toward some goal. This second source, or situation, was not actually developed by either Festinger himself or the social psychologists interested in social influence processes.

Leadership is not, however, only a question of exerting some mix of power and influence, but, perhaps more important, it is giving direction to a group, whether the goals are previously set or (rather) enacted by the group itself.

Locomotion is thus related to a "commitment to action," that is to say to choice (decision). And when we talk of choice it is still important to distinguish between well-defined and ill-defined decision problems (Abelson & Levi, 1985). The key characteristic of ill-defined decision problems is uncertainty, classically defined as the inability to assign specific probabilities to outcomes. This is, however, a sort of "objective" uncertainty, in the sense of being independent of the agreement or disagreement of the group members who have to take some choice about the issue under consideration. The contention of Moscovici (1985) that uncertainy is an effect rather than a cause of social conflict does not seem to take these situations of objective uncertainty into account.

The crucial distinction between judgment and decision is, therefore, in the "commitment to action." Judgment may precede, although not necessarily, the decision. Whatever the case, a judgment is always reversible and revisable, whereas a decision is irreversible. A decision process always involves an element of arbitrariness; "final reasons for a particular decision or a proposed decision can never be given" (Jacques, 1976, p. 301). Group locomotion is a decsion task, involving influence processes that probably cannot be reduced to the dichotomy of informational versus normative influence, derived from the experimental paradigms of normalization, conformity, and innovation. Once again, this dichotomy seems to result from the disjunctive distinction between power and influence, not recognizing that a synthetic mix of both processes is at work in the leadership and decision processes.

Processes are not independent of the context. In the judgmental tasks such as discriminating perceptions of length or color, the informational component can probably acquire more salience, but this does not mean that in more complex tasks, and namely in those where uncertainty can never be completely reduced, the normative component does not have to be combined with the information gathered.

Turner has proposed an alternative that tries to solve the puzzles implied by the dual-process model. In his self-categorization theory (SCT), he advanced the concept of "referent informational influence" (1991) to express "the need of people to reach agreement with others perceived to be interchangeable in respect of relevant attributes (psychological ingroup members in the given situational about the same stimulus situation in order to validate their responses as correct, appropriate, and desirable" (1985, p. 113).

In the referent information influence (RII), both normative and informative influences are united at a higher level of abstraction. The process involves a sort of dialectical circle. The information conveyed is about the group norms to which the subject has chosen to identify himself. The process is thus distinct from bare conformity with group norms: first because social identification is not imposed on the subject, but taken on by his own choice; second, because the criteria attributes are not necessarily deduced from the group category—they can also be induced from one or more individual members (Tajfel, 1959, 1972). This inductive aspect of categorization implies that any member can be perceived as paradigmatic or prototypical, which amounts to saying that group norms are constructed once again through a sort of bootstrapping dynamic.

This process of mutual influence leading to the formation of group norms can be observed in paradigms such as the autokinetic effect or the polarization phenomenon. In both cases the social influence process can be described in terms of negotiation, each member of the group making concessions in order to reach an agreement. But there are important differences between these two situations due to the different tasks assigned to group members. In the polarization paradigm, group members are jointly involved in the pursuit of a goal and are invited to reach a consensus about an issue submitted by the experimenter. This is a situation described by Festinger (1950) as "group locomotion," or in other words, a situation of lateral leadership within a nonhierarchical setting. The amount of group polarization could thus be considered as a measure of the leadership effect.

In strict coherence and in theoretical terms convergence can also be considered as a leadership effect, a sort of "minimal leadership effect," in parallel with the forming of group norms. In convergence we find a leadership process without leader, which could be designated as "distributed leadership." Normalization and group polarization could be compared in terms of negotiation strategies in which normalization corresponds to a distributive negotiation and polarization to an integrative negotiation.

The distinction herein proposed between distributed and lateral leadership tries to follow the same underlying logic. It is not only a question of degree, but also a question of level of analysis. Whereas in the convergence paradigm group norms are formed at the interpersonal level, in the polarization paradigm norms are reconstructed at the group level. It is this transition to the group level through group discussions that triggers the shift to an integrative process of negotiation and to a parallel process of lateral leadership. Emergent leaders, those who defend more extreme positions toward the predominant direction, are also the more instrumental in "locomoting" the group toward its auto-transcendent norm. For Turner and his associates (Turner et al., 1987), the group converges to the more prototypical member—that is, to the member that best represents the future norm of the group—in terms of what they designated as meta-contrast ratio: The more an individual differs from outgroup members and the less from ingroup members, the better he or she represents the ingroup.

Turner (1991) claimed that the advantage of his theory is that it integrates into one unified explanation both polarization and convergence on the mean. However, the theory faces the difficulty of invoking the ingroup–outgroup logic in a situation where the outgroups are "hidden"; that is, "they are implicit in the response scale employed to measure subject attitudes" (p. 168). This "tour de force" is the consequence of a theory grounded on the minimal group paradigm where interactions between group members are not considered for explaining group processes.

A different position is taken by Moscovici (1985; Moscovici & Doise, 1992), who argued that it is precisely the interaction process, the group discussion, that can explain the locomotion of the group toward that more prototypical member. In accordance with this line of thought the convergence and polarization processes do not only differ in degree, as claimed by the "unified" theory of Turner (1991). Groups converge not because their most prototypical member coincides with the mean but because, as widely confirmed by empirical evidence, the group interaction is constrained by some physical or psychological barriers. For example, in a hierarchical context, formal leaders may contravene the spontaneous, informal, emergent lateral leadership process likely to produce a polarization effect. The literature on the polarization phenomenon frequently fails to make this distinction between these two different leadership processes that can be simultaneously enacted in the group. It is, however, through this dual process, combining power and influence, that a link can be established between the microlevel of the group and the macrolevel of the organization.

To conclude, a theory of leadership processes can benefit from the "apports" of research on social influence, namely in its most recent development proposed by Moscovici and Turner. The genetic theory of Moscovici (1976) in displacing the forms of influence for the behavior style is this first step for establishing a link between social influence and leadership. Furthermore, his theory of innovative influence gives another important contribution toward integrating the role of dissent behavior in the leadership processes aimed at changing the direction of the group.

Another important contribution comes from Turner's (1982, 1985, 1991; Turner et al., 1987) self-categorization theory, mainly for the concept of referent informational influence, reconciling at a higher level of analysis the informative and normative components of the influencer's communicative action. On the other hand, the SCT could be helpful in explaining the leader's group centrality in terms of prototypicality.

Leadership processes also show how these two apparently divergent approaches to social influence processes are less antagonistic than complementary when examined in the wider context of group locomotion. In such situations, the influence exerted on group members has to do with decisions about goals involving uncertainties never entirely reduced by information processing. So, and by the same token, a theory of leadership processes also reveals the shortcomings of the theories of social influence in their rather reductionist approach to the role of power either in social control or in social change.

POWER AND VERTICAL LEADERSHIP

It has been argued that leadership involves a mix and a trade-off between influence and power. The phenomenon of polarization could be used to illustrate such a trade-off. An asymmetry of influence leads the group to converge to an extreme and to the emergence of a leader not only in the sense of being the most prototypical member, but also in the sense of being the most competent and convincing in leading the group to acknowledge and accept his or her positions (Kelley & Thibaut, 1969).

One-shot experiments do not allow us to make predictions about the weight of those emergent leaders on future group decisions. But we can speculate based on some empirical evidence (Hollander, 1960) that once confidence is won, for example, after showing competence, emergent leaders would tend to be confirmed and reinforced by group members. According to this view it could be argued that influence is not only an outcome of power but also a way to acquire power. Once in power the leader acts no more as an emergent leader but as a recognized authority. To some extent he has gained power, enabling him to exert a sort of "referent normative influence" over his followers. This is not the case in the discussion of choice dilemmas, because the most extreme group member clashed over the discussion on several items.

The faces of power and the ways to acquire it are certainly various. We are concerned here only with situations involving locomoting groups as those where a process of leadership becomes more salient. We have seen that social influence is closely related to uncertainty, be it a cause or an effect of a sociocognitive conflict. Organizations, as claimed by some specialists (Simon, 1962; Thompson, 1967), can be considered as a strategy for reducing uncertainty, for stabilizing certain segments of the environment. Organizations are not one-shot groups, but natural groups or even "groups of groups," focused on very specific segments of recurrent uncertainty. Uncertainty is due either to complexity or ignorance about cause–effect relationships. It is uncertainty that makes decision making problematic and always involving an element of arbitrariness, where influence and power have the last word. Organizations can also be considered as attempts to minimize this element of arbitrariness in the process of decision making.

This is achieved through the classic processes of differentiation and integration (Lawrence & Lorsch, 1967). Differentiation is the process of structuring the activities by specializing functions, standardizing procedures, and distributing authority along the hierarchy. Integration is the complementary process of coordinating the differentiated activities. Structural differentiation can be conceived as a way of rationalizing the complexity of different functions and activities. Simon (1962) saw the hierarchy as an "architecture of complexity" and illustrated it with the metaphor of the two watchmakers: Hora, the more successful, first makes 10 subassemblies of 100 pieces each, whereas Tempus attempts to use the 1,000 pieces, 1 by 1, until the completion of his work. Hora's advantage is obvious: Every time he is interrupted he only needs to redo 1 of the 10 subassemblies, whereas Tempus has to start it all over from the beginning.

Another well-known metaphor—the black box—can be invoked here. Each subassembly, once finished, is a black box, something that can be sealed, something that can be considered as taken for granted, to which it is neither necessary nor useful to continuously reexamine or validate. A "scientific fact" as provocatively argued by Latour and Woolgar (1979) could also be considered as a black box. As a matter of fact, scientific progress would be impossible if we had to verify everything in every detail.

An organization can thus be conceived of as a system of interacting black boxes, whose combination and control is achieved through a structure of power, where "macro actors are micro actors seated on top of many (leaky) black boxes" (Callon & Latour, 1981, p. 286). Power in organizations, in this sense, is a technique of control and coordination, very close to the relational legal mechanisms of bureaucratic legitimating described by Weber (1947). Power becomes authority. And authoritative leadership is a technical role performed by legitimate leaders (or, better said, managers) enforcing norms—another instance of black boxes—"in-differently" (Barnard, 1938) accepted and complied to by subordinates. The underlying influence mechanisms are here, as a rule, the conformity to a majority (a black box again); but small, incremental innovations may also take place and are functional to the regulation of the system through the mechanisms of idiosyncratic deviations of confirmed competent leaders (Hollander, 1960).

This image of the organization, as a mechanic and rational metaphor (Morgan, 1986) is certainly an "ideal type" and was so conceived by Weber (1947). But even as an ideal type the model does not seem to contemplate the problems of the integration process, considering them as automatically granted by the virtues of rational differentiation. The more sophisticated version proposed by Parsons (1951, 1968, 1969) does not seem to go much further in considering the effectiveness of collective actions as expressed in decision-making ability and the standard of coordination as the acceptance and observance of decisions. But the Parsonian theory is important because of the emphasis given to the capacity of mobilizing resources—capital, labor, and land—for goal attainment, and also in recognizing that coordinating decisions, that is, integration of the system, deal particularly with people who, unlike financial resources, have to be motivated, making the coordination of activities difficult.

As a matter of fact, motivation, expressed as willingness to comply, is linked with the extent to which resources are made available, and it is here that the exercise of power faces its major problems. In the more recent literature, a distinction is sometimes made between management and leadership, where management has to deal with the different actions and functions that contribute to give direction to total social systems, and leadership is apparently more related with a person and her ability to influence other people to comply "over and above the routine directives of the organization" (Katz & Kahn, 1978; Mintzberg, 1973). Whatever the designation, either as manager or as leader, the ability to mobilize and allocate resources is a critical concern for the coordination of the system, and determinant for the distribution of power along the hierarchic chain.

As persuasively argued by Callon and Latour (1981), social scientists are oblivious to the material alliances that macroactors make in order to be seated at the top of a chain of black boxes. Interactions within the organizational framework are mediated not only by individuals and groups but also by material resources as well as socio-technical systems. Technical expertise and the subsequent ability of controlling "zones of uncertainty" (Crozier, 1963; Pfeffer, 1986) is a critical source of "lateral power" as well as "vertical power" in organizations.

As already stated, organizations attempt to reduce uncertainty by structuring functions and distributing authority along the hierarchy. In accordance with the studies at Aston (Pugh, 1976), these two factors can be combined yielding four different organizational formats (see Fig. 4.5). Compared with the well-known classification proposed by Mintzberg (1979), it could be said that "technostructures" are the configurations where both structuring and centralization are high,

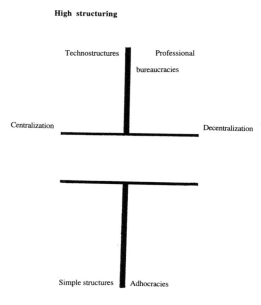

FIG. 4.5. A typology of organizational formats.

"professional bureaucracies" are where structuring is combined with decentralization, "simple structures" are where centralization is high and structuring is low, and "adhocracies" are where both structuring and centralization are low. Each one of these configurations is characterized by specific coordination mechanisms that can be interpreted in leadership terms reflecting, at the macrolevel, the mix of power and influence already found at the microlevel.

In the technostructure, or "full-bureaucracy" in the Aston terminology, the coordination is achieved through the use of rules and procedures enforced by a "chain of command" operated by authoritative "legitimate" leaders. The power basis is the "position," and influence is implicit in the legitimating process underpinning the structure. In the "professional" or "work-flow" bureaucracies, the coordination is achieved by "standardized skills," which correspond, in terms of power bases, to the "expert power," which also implies that influence processes are at work in creating and confirming the expertise of leaders. "Simple structures" or "personnel bureaucracies" rely on more discretionary uses of power, either coercive or referent, and a minimal use of influence. Finally in "adhocracies" or "implicitly structured organizations" such as networks, the coordination is by "mutual adjustment," using a more personal power basis and influence.

Trade-offs and continuities can also be discerned between these focus configurations. Simple structures can evolve or change along the vertical or horizontal axis of power, toward either bureaucratic formats or network formats. But the reverse trend can also be observed. Much less likely are the transitions along the diagonals toward opposite formats—between network and full bureaucracies or between simple structures and professional bureaucracies. Lateral power—that is, power not associated with formal positions and most prominent in "professional bureaucracies" and "networks"—is, nevertheless, a form of power that combines with influence but cannot be reduced to it. Influence is a way of acquiring power in the sense of one seeing one's own expertise acknowledged, which can be reflected in the weight that actors have in the process of decision making. In organizational formats that rely on uncertainty reduction by structuring activities, expert power is focused on the strengthening and technical improvement of norms in order to contribute to the efficient regulation of the systems.

Political games (Crozier, 1963) and intergroup behavior (Tajfel, 1978, 1982) are also likely to pervade in such configurations where the logic of lateral power very often prevails over the logic of vertical power. In contrast, in systems governed by vertical power, such as full-bureaucracies, the standardized norms are not sufficiently legitimated for dispensing a more explicit use of coercion in order to assure the compliance of its members.

In simple structures, power is also concentrated at the top but not mediated by structuring or standardization of activities. The legitimating sources are here, to recall Weber (1947), tradition and charisma. Tradition as a source of legitimate power can be observed in the "families," a metaphor often used to designate the simple formats headed by a "father." Most entrepreneurial activity starts in this way.

Charisma is a more enigmatic process, ignored by the literature on leadership for decades but experiencing today an enormous upsurge in attention, not only in the pop literature of business, but also as a central topic in leadership research. Charisma is a typical modality of personal power. In terms of the French and Raven (1959) classification, it is an extreme form of reference power. In a full bureaucracy the power is shared between the experts and the managers. Considering the process of organizational decision making as a continuum starting with the "identification" of the problems, "design" of alternatives, and "choice" (Simon, 1965), it can be argued that experts exert power and influence at least at the upstream stages of this process by elaborating and screening the alternatives submitted for choice (Mintzberg et al., 1976). The elimination of this source of power and influence amounts to concentrating the power exclusively at the top, and this can be achieved either through naked power (force) or through charisma.

The distance between one and the other is short, however. A subtle distinction sometimes proposed between "good" and "bad" charisma, as, for example, between "mosaic" and "totemic" leaders (Moscovici, 1981), is not so much a distinction in processes as in their embeddedness in the context where they take place. Appeals to charismatic leadership as a way of overcoming the "frozen" bureaucracy and energizing the system have the implicit aim of changing the organizations from a group of groups into one sole family, clan, community, or culture.

In terms of Turner's (1982, 1985, 1987; Turner et al., 1987) SCT, this corresponds to the fusion of different groups in only one ingroup. The intergroup theory as originally developed by Tajfel (1978, 1982) conceived of groups as separate and discontinuous entities, a model that can be considered adequate, at best, for describing the processes of the relatively "free-floating" groups that form the social fabric of society.

But an organization as a group of groups is more and less than a society; more because it is more integrated and less because it is more restrictive of alternative options for self-categorization. Within organizations, boundaries between groups tend to be fuzzy. To some extent this is a condition for integration. The logic of bureaucracy aims at avoiding such fuzziness as a source of continuous ambiguity, and this is achieved through differentiation. But differentiation alone is not enough.

It could, however, be asked whether such a fusion with its corresponding suppression of lateral leadership effects would not be detrimental to change processes and a way of generating more top-down conformity or even groupthink than bottom-up innovation. Besides, the dichotomy between ingroups and outgroups, at the organizational level of analysis, is perhaps too simplistic and requires some qualifications. Organizational behavior has here a chance to complement and widen the findings of experimental social psychology.

A social system is not a mechanical system. It always requires some "interpolation of structures" (Katz & Kahn, 1978) in order to assure the continuity of differentiated but interdependent functions. Integration is then a leadership process and organizational leaders are located in vertical and horizontal interfaces that give continuity and coherence to the system. Leaders are "linking-pins" (Likert, 1961), "spanning-boundary" roles (Thompson, 1967) whatever the level at which they operate, be it at the top, the middle, or the bottom of the hierarchy, and at each level along both the vertical and horizontal axis of power and structuring.

The situation looks, therefore, more complex than the dichotomous distinction between ingroup emergent leaders, as their most influential members, and outgroup formal leaders exerting a counternormative power (Turner, 1991). Formal leaders within organizations do not have an easy task when it comes to self-categorizing themselves in terms of social identity. Nor is it easier for group members to categorize their formal leaders using criteria such as the metacontrast ratio. A common strategy for leaders in dealing with these ambiguous and mixed-motive situations is to use the logic of integrative negotiation, appealing to the superordinate objectives that can unify the divergent groups.

An earlier contribution along these lines was offered by the famous experiments conducted by Sherif with groups of adolescents—the Robbers Cave paradigm (Sherif, 1966). The ingenious critical incidents "created by Sherif that transformed prior competition into cooperation could be reinterpreted as a sort of 'ecological influence' " (Cartwright, 1965, p. 19), motivating members to change their categorization frameworks and thus enabling the group to locomote toward its own objectives.

I am not trying to dispute the relative merits of the theory of interdependence versus the theory of social identity (see chapters 9 and 10 of this volume). Most likely they are both valid and reconcilable at the higher level of organizational processes. Social categorization can be considered either as a cause or as an effect of interdependent group behavior, the relations between both processes being probably more circular than linear. In any case, and this is the conclusion emerging so far from the various approaches examined, leadership in organizations has as its primal function the aligning of the various organizational segments toward a common direction and achieves this purpose through a mix of power and influence, in variable proportions, contingent on the various organizational configurations and processes.

A promising approach seeking to integrate the socio-psychology of group process within organizational settings was proposed by Bales, Cohen, and Williamson (1979) with their SYMLOG theory. It may be recalled that it was Bales (1950) who first carried out systematic observations of the group interaction processes and who first identified the two main dimensions of leadership behavior—the instrumental and the social-emotional (expressive). The SYMLOG theory is a rather complex extension and elaboration of those first observations. In its present form groups are conceived as "interactive gestalts," that can be systematically "observed" through the images/perceptions that members form of each other. Those images can be represented in a sort of Lewinian field with three orthogonal dimensions: dominance/submission (UD), friendly versus unfriendly (PN) and task oriented versus social-emotional (FB). An important feature of the theory is that group members may perceive themselves as more or less unified with or polarized from one another. Leadership is then defined as the "ability to unify a diverse group of people to work effectively as a team toward a common purpose under varied and often difficult conditions, through the elimination of scapegoating, the maximization of mediation, and the judicious use of power" (Bales & Koenigs, 1992, p. 2).

Polarization in this context means that group members may not agree with each other or share the same values, which may give rise to some conflict of variable intensity. Such a conflict is not, however, considered undesirable; on the contrary it can be a source of creativity and social change, a view also strongly advocated by Moscovici. When the task of leaders is defined in terms of "group unification" it must therefore be understood that such unification is not to be carried out through "pressures to uniformity," but rather by an "integrative negotiation" aimed at "resolving conflict and preserving productive levels of tension" (see chapter 7 of this volume). Leaders are defined as "mediators" making a "judicious" use of power. The dynamics of leadership processes can be better understood through the graphic representation of the SYMLOG space (Fig. 4.6).

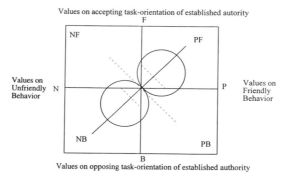

FIG. 4.6. The SYMLOG space–field diagram.

The field diagram has only two dimensions, FB and PN, which roughly correspond to the two dimensions of instrumental and social-emotional, group interactions and group leadership. The new SYMLOG theory introduces a third dimension—dominance versus submission (UD)—which is represented in the field diagram by circles whose diameter is proportional to the amount of this dimension for each image. A moderate amount of dominance is a necessary but not a sufficient condition for leadership. It only reflects the minimum willingness for exerting an active role on the group. But more important than the amount of dominance is the relative "position" of the leader as perceived by the other group members.

The four quadrants of the SYMLOG space are related with the four main styles of leadership processes. Two of them, the autocratic process (NF) and the democratic process (PF), are already familiar. Formal leaders in hierarchic settings are usually perceived as located in those quadrants, and ideal images mostly in the PF quadrant. In contrast NB and PB images are less often associated to leaders. B is the pole of "opposite values," that is, the pole of "dissidents."

Congruent with the theory of innovation proposed by Moscovici, it could be said that the NB quadrant corresponds to the image of "rigidity" whereas the PB quadrant corresponds to the image of "flexibility" (Moscovici, 1976; Mugny, 1982). Innovation can be initiated by minority members opposing the established authority, provided that they are consistent enough in sustaining their positions. The SYMLOG theory, however, goes a step further in suggesting that this process of social change implies a restructuring of the entire gestalt, through alliances and coalitions—the progressive persuasion of proximal members—and also through the action of mediating leaders (PB) seeking the commitment of both sides.

The theory of unification-polarization also displays some points in common with Turner's self-categorization theory. A unified group corresponds to the notion of ingroup and a polarized group is one split in two groups that perceive each other as outgroups. The categorization is, however, a very flexible and variable process, contingent on the specific context (task) in which it takes place.

Dissidents unable to introduce change in the group may thus experience authority as power exerted from an outgroup, whereas members of the ingroup may experience the "same" authority as legitimate process of influence to which they willingly adhere. But, more important, it can now be seen that intermediate positions between ingroups and outgroups may be related with leadership, assuring the mediation and transition to more stabilized and effective interactive gestalts.

The unification-polarization theory, although not very popular within the mainstream social and organizational psychology, offers a very comprehensive framework for describing and explaining group leadership processes occurring within and between multiple levels of human interaction, such as individuals, groups, organizations, or even societies.

To summarize and conclude, power and leadership are closely related, mostly in organizational contexts where hierarchy is, as a rule, one of its main features. Leadership is not, however, reducible to power. Only in rather extreme circumstances is group locomotion carried out through naked power. More currently, organizational leadership is exerted through a combination of power and influence processes. Social influences contribute to the achievement of personal power, in terms either of expertise or personal appeal, or both, and personal power contributes by its turn to legitimate positional power. The exercising of organizational leadership can thus be considered as a continuous two-way process, bottom-up from influence to power and top-down from power to influence. The more they reinforce each other, the more legitimate the leadership exerted, and the more effective their outcomes in terms of motivation of organization members will be.

MOTIVATION AND LEADERSHIP

Motivation is another construct closely related to leadership as well as to power and influence. To lead is to motivate, that is, "directing" and "energizing" (Cranach, 1986; see also chapter 6 of this volume). The explanation that Moscovici and Doise (1992) proposed for the polarization phenomenon, in terms of group commitment, could also be interpreted in terms of motivation. The more motivated the group members, the more they will polarize. To use the concept of motivation is to introduce another language game. But there are continuities and overlaps across different games, at least if they are close enough. To approach leadership from a motivational perspective is also a way of establishing continuities between the microlevel of groups and the macrolevel of groups of groups.

Regarding the polarization and accepting the causal effect of commitment, it could be asked what mechanisms and processes contribute to "energetize" the group. There are various factors that may contribute and one of them is probably the "leadership effect." How can a leader "energetize" a group? A plausible answer is, once again, suggested by Cranach (1986): "[T]he group's specific pattern of leadership forms a part of the group identity. As a result, the leader becomes a target of projection and is put into the constant focus of attention. These are the reasons why the leader exerts such an impact on the group processes of motivation and regulation: The leader serves as a standard (Sollwert) in the cybernetic system" (p. 131). This quote reminds us once again of Turner's self-categorization theory—another language game. The leader is prototypical, the most central figure in the group, a reference, the norm. His or her ability to transmit energy to the group depends on his or her ability or willingness to be committed to the action. The leader is an emotional amplifier of the group whose appeals and example are critical for mobilizing the group.

To a certain extent this is also the normative influence at work but now concentrated and symbolized in the figure of the leader. But the leader's functions are not limited to endowing the group with energy. The leader also is supposed to give direction, to steer the group toward its objectives. From this standpoint, to lead is to motivate or rather, to persuade people to accept both the goals and the ways to achieve them. This mix of emotional and cognitive components in the leadership functions—resembling the dual-process model of social influence research, and also the Bales distinction between instrumental and socioemotional interactions, and maintained under several guises and designations in the subsequent literature—probably corresponds to the deep-seated dichotomy in behavior between cognition and affect.

One of the most comprehensive models of leadership linking macro- and micro- organizational levels was proposed by Katz and Kahn (1978). They distinguished three basic types of leadership processes occurring at the corresponding levels of organizational hierarchies. They are, from top down: (a) originating of structure—introduction of structural change or policy formulation, (b) interpolation of structure—supplementing and piecing out of structure, and (c) applying existing structure—routine application of prescribed remedies for predicted problems. The model also posits that each process at different hierarchical levels is coupled with specific cognitive and emotional abilities and skills. For top echelons the required skills are systems perspective and charisma; for intermediate levels they are subsystem perspective and human relations skills; and finally for lower levels they are technical knowledge and understanding of system of rules and equity in use of rewards and sanctions. The model amplifies and differentiates stages in a process of decision making also observable in small groups as goal choices, political choices, and execution, related either with task-group locomotion or with group maintenance.

Skills required are also specified in accordance with hierarchical level, but an isomorphy can also be established with power and influence processes at the small-group level. In their normative model Katz and Kahn (1978) proposed a sort of distribution of power and influence so that at the bottom what prevails is conformity and compliance through the use of power, at the middle of the hierarchy lateral influence leads to convergence and integration, whereas at the top the focus is on differentiation, either internal or external to the system, through innovative processes.

This distribution of roles is certainly very schematic. The mix of influence processes varies with the specific type of configuration. In simple structures, a situation close to small-group configurations, the different leadership roles are, as a rule, centralized in the figure at the top, although leadership processes might differ along the Lewinian axis anchored by autocratic and democratic climates. In professional bureaucracies, usually decentralized, lateral power and influence are most likely the prevailing processes within the organization. Integrative negotiations may, however, produce synergy through the polarization group processes. These same dynamics can be found in complex formats such as adhocracies, where mutual adjustment is the prevailing coordination mechanism. In adhocracies, also designated as "innovative organizations," the innovation becomes particularly relevant, requiring a special sensitivity to innovative processes such as openness to dissent (Moscovici & Doise, 1992; Nemeth & Staw, 1989). Different configurations and corresponding distribution of power and influence processes also contribute to give differential weight to the role of the overall organizational leadership. Where lateral processes prevail, leadership also tends to be dispersed or rotate among interacting actors. Weick (1979), possibly having in mind the "loosely coupled" configurations typical of universitarian organizations, used the metaphor of the orchestra conductor to suggest that "while he may presume that he (the conductor) and the baton produced an ordered performance, in actuality they probably are minor contributors to the outcome. Of more importance are the bonds and mutually supportive relationships that have been built up among small subsets of the musicians" (p. 8).

In the same vein, Cohen and March (1974) persuasively argued how the exercise of leadership is ambiguous in "organized anarchies," the expression here used to describe typical processes such as "garbage can" decisions that pervade in organizations such as universities. In contrast, vertical leadership is enhanced in simple structures as well as in the bureaucratic formats that seem to inspire the Katz and Kahn (1978) model. It is, however, within this framework that, implicitly or explicitly, more theories of organizational leadership have been developed. Those theories usually have as a framework the lower levels of hierarchy and aim at identifying in detail the right mix of power and influence to get compliance and, at best, commitment from their subordinates.

Influence tactics are trade-offs of power and influence, or rather of positional and personal power. Yukl (1989) proposed a very comprehensive list of those influence tactics, such as: legitimating tactic, rational persuasion, exchange tactic, personal appeals and ingratiation tactic, inspirational appeals, consultation, pressure tactic, and coalition tactic. These tactics can be used in isolation or combination, some of them working better than the others. The so-called art of leadership has much to do with the skill of the leaders in combining those various forms of influence tactics.

Other authors (e.g., Bell, 1975) suggest that the syntactical structure of communication changes from power to influence statements. Power wielders use modes involving either threats or promises (if you do X, I will do Y, where X and Y may be either positive or negative). In contrast, the syntactical structure of a sanction-free influence statement involves a change from the first-person contingent statement into a second-person construction (if you do X, you will do, feel, experience . . . Y). The forms of manipulation move now to the perception by followers about contingencies of their own choices.

It is this focus on the way followers process the information supplied by leaders that best characterizes the shift from naked power, legitimate power, or even wilder forms of influence. Theories of leadership are increasingly aware of the need to integrate those mediating variables. An earlier example can be found in the path-goal theory of leadership proposed by House (1971), which is both a motivational and a cognitive approach to the leadership processes. According to House, "the motivational function of the leader consists of increasing personal pay-offs to subordinates for work-goal attainment, and making the path to these pay-offs easier to travel by clarifying it, reducing roadblocks and pitfalls and increasing the opportunities for personal satisfaction en route" (p. 324).

This sort of second-person communication approach for motivating subordinates can be interpreted as an influence tactic combining cognitive ingredients of relevant information so that the recipients may make their own decisions of how to apply their skills and effort (Porter & Lawler, 1968; Vroom, 1964). Although motivation is an intrapsychic construct, leaders can be instrumental in clarifying the paths of subordinates for their own goals. More recently, Lord and Maher (1991) developed new approaches to leadership based on the information-processing model of cognitive psychology. It was time to recognize that a better understanding of leadership processes cannot bypass the perceptions of both leaders and their followers.

These new trends in leadership research are also likely to be due to a concomitant shift of focus from lower to higher levels of the organizational hierarchy. As a matter of fact if, in archaeological terms, most theories of organizational leadership deal with lower level transactions involving supervisors and subordinates within a bureaucratic framework, in more recent developments the focus has been moving for higher levels of management and governance and also for alternative forms for structuring activities and roles.

The model of Katz and Kahn (1978) mentions change as a major goal of top echelons of the hierarchy. Nowadays, the topic of change has become a major concern and also a sort of miraculous panacea for solving the problems of organizations. Innovation and creativity are, as a consequence, a priority in the agenda of organizational behavior research. The contribution given by Moscovici and associates with their paradigm of innovative influence are obviously greatly relevant in this context (Nemeth & Staw, 1989). Change in the Katz and Kahn model is what top managers are expected to accomplish for their organizations. This requires, at the cognitive level, "intersystemic" skills or "vision," if we prefer more current concepts (Bennis & Nanus, 1986; Kotter, 1988), and at the affective level, the controversial feature of charisma. The two classic dimensions of leader behavior—the instrumental and the social-emotional—are once again invoked, although under a different guise or, if preferred, recur in a different language game.

Whether top managers are actually decisive in introducing change in organizations is another issue to divide the analysts. For some of them leadership is ambiguous, a "protagonist illusion" (Pfeffer, 1977) or a "romanticized vision" (Meindl, Ehrlich, & Dukerich, 1985). Leaders have at best only a symbolic role in organizations whose changes are, to a far greater extent, dependent on these contingencies of the environment (Lieberson & O'Connor, 1972; Pfeffer, 1978). More recent researchers gathered, however, substantial evidence in favor of the critical importance of leaders for organizational effectiveness (Lord & Maher, 1990, 1991).

The text of Katz and Kahn (1978), published in its first edition in 1966, was really a forerunner. The great triad of the "new leadership," to use an expression proposed recently by Bryman (1992), is formed as a matter of fact by change, vision, and charisma. Links and continuities between micro and macro levels of analysis are possible if we once again accept the metaphor of the black boxes according to which macroactors are no more complex than microactors.

The accent now put on change and innovation could also explain the relevance given to a new dichotomy introduced by Burns (1978), the one opposing transactional to transforming leadership and then widely adopted by authors in organizational behavior (Bass, 1985; Bennis & Nanus, 1986; Peters & Waterman, 1982; Tichy & Devanna, 1986).

For Burns (1978), leadership is also closely related with motivation. Burns is a political scientist, and it is within the framework of political science that his theory was elaborated. But the underlying processes he described also apply to the organizational context. Burns started by distinguishing leadership from power. In exerting power the motives of power recipients are not a first concern. They may or may not be met. What is decisive for the power wielder is the satisfaction of his or her own needs. The situation is different in leadership, in that motives of followers become a matter of concern and a priority. The motives of leaders and followers may or may not converge. When there is no necessary convergence, leadership becomes a sort of bargain "to aid the individual interests of person or groups going their separate way" (p. 425). In contrast, transforming leadership occurs when "whatever the separate interests persons might hold, they are presently or potentially united in the pursuit of higher goals, the realization of which is tested by the achievement of significant change that represents the collection or pooled interests of leaders and followers" (p. 425).

Another difference between power and leadership has to do, according to Burns (1978), with the role of conflict and competition: "Leadership is examined in a condition of conflict and competition" where as "naked power admits of no competition or conflict, there is no engagement" (p. 18). As it may be recalled, conflict is a major issue in the processes of social influence studied at the group and intrapsychic levels (see chapter 7 of this volume). The analysis of two modalities of leadership are carefully examined and documented by Burns in his seminal book, which has enjoyed an enormous success. The next step was due to Bass (1985), who operationalized the concepts and introduced a scale for measuring leadership characteristics. The scale rapidly acquired an enormous popularity, "the kind of prominence that the Ohio State LBDQ enjoyed in the 1950s and 1960s" (Bryman, 1992, p. 121). Bass identified three factors for transformational leadership: (a) charisma, (b) individualized consideration, and (c) intellectual stimulation; and two factors for transactional leadership: (d) contingent reward and (e) management-by-exception.

Following the study of Bass (1985), other authors have developed similar models and instruments focusing mainly on the dimension of charisma found to account for a greater percentage of total variance (Conger, 1989; Conger & Kanungo, 1987; Nadler & Tushamn, 1990). The contrast between transactional and transforming leadership can be and has been variously interpreted. They complement each other and correspond, in the model of Katz and Kahn (1966), to middle and higher hierarchical level, respectively. Through "transactions," basic "contracts" are established between management and employees, and this may be sufficient under conditions of environmental stability. When the situation requires change, transforming leadership becomes prominent. Leaders are then expected to give direction through their intersystemic skills and to energetize through their charismatic traits.

For Burns (1978), charisma does not have the centrality that it came to acquire in the "new leadership" literature. Burns seemed to prefer the labels of *heroes* and *ideologues*, a *distinguo* resembling the one proposed by Moscovici between "mosaic" and "totemic" leaders. "Heroic leadership is not simply a quality or entity possessed by someone; it is a type of relationship between leader and led. A crucial aspect of this relationship is the absence of conflict. . . . Heroic leadership provides the symbolic solution of internal and external conflict" (Burns, 1978, p. 244). This remark by Burns is important and alerts us to the proximity of charisma and naked power. Charisma is a subtle way of suppressing conflict, and this can open the way to conformity and groupthink (Janis, 1972). In contrast "the key elements of ideology are cognition, conflict, consciousness, value and purpose" (Burns, 1978, p. 250). Ideological leaders, like the mosaic leaders described by Moscovici, appeal to reasons and values rather than images. And, most important, they do not suppress conflict, they rise and face it. A tension could then be at work between dimensions like charisma and intellectual stimulation, which is not at all evident in the literature on the new leadership.

It is also worth mentioning that transforming leadership, as conceived by Burns (1978), is a sophisticated construct related to "terminal values" (Rokeach, 1973) and moral development (Kohlberg, 1963; Piaget, 1932). It is through transforming leadership that individuals move from lower to higher stages of ethical behavior. In transforming leadership, the motives of both leaders and followers are no longer separate. They coincide in those higher stages of moral development. But transforming leadership is also very comprehensive and "*common*, because acts of leadership occur not only in the presidential mansion and the parliamentary assemblies, but far more widely and powerfully in the day-to-day pursuit of collective goals through the mutual tapping of leaders' and followers' motive bases and in the achievement of intended change. It is an affair of parents, teachers and peers as well as of preachers and politicians" (Burns, 1978, p. 426). The ethical concern of Burns, this "elevating" people to higher values and motives, was rapidly translated in the new leadership literature in elevating people to the higher goals of the organization.

In this light it is at least arguable that transforming leadership may have the same meaning and implications for Burns as for his immediate followers. Transforming leadership, to be faithful to the original concept, requires a tranformation starting by the leaders themselves, in that they ought to be concerned with the ethical consequences of their decisions. It is probably no accident that ethics and moral leadership are becoming topics of increasing concern in the management and organizational behavior literature. In terms of hierarchical as well as nonhierarchical groups, those higher values could, therefore, be understood in terms of time span (Jacques, 1976), as locomotion of the group to more distant goals into the future. The further the goal distance, the higher the level of abstraction required, and also the higher the level of cognitive and moral development achieved. Long-term goals require decentration, the ability of embedding the self or the group within a broader context, eventually from the point of view of God or the ideal society.

In accordance with these new theories, transforming leadership could be intrepreted as a synthesis of democratic and lateral leadership and transactional leadership as a synthesis of autocratic and distributed leadership. By democratic leadership it is meant here the climate of wide participation of members in group decision, and by lateral leadership the free interplay of social influence processes that facilitate innovation and self-transcendence of groups. This is based on the understanding that the direction of change is not arguable. Allocating harms, such as cutting salaries, restructuring and downsizing, or eliminating benefits, is not easy to carry out, even less so with the "participation" of their victims (Albert, 1992).

Once again and to conclude we see the dialectics of power and influence at work. In Habermasian terms, it also could be said that transactional leadership is empirically motivating people, reinforcing ties through inducement and deterrence, whereas transforming leadership is rationally motivating people, reinforcing trust through knowledge and responsibility.

In natural systems the two leadership macro processes can both be found in a variety of combinations. Although obeying different logics, one pushing to social control and the other pulling to social change, in the best of possible worlds, they can complement each other.

FINAL REMARKS

Leadership was here defined as a motivational function providing direction and energy to the group. Leadership is exercised through power and influence aimed at the locomotion of groups and organizations toward the achievement of their own objectives and goals.

Two different theoretical approaches can be used to derive models for describing and explaining leadership processes: the functionalistic and the genetic. Within the functionalism framework, goals are previously defined, and it is toward their accomplishment that leadership provides direction and energy. Leadership becomes a social control process with a clear-cut role distinction between leader and followers. In contrast, in the genetic perspective, goals do not preexist the group action. They are the outcome of a social construction, which by the same token also contributes to the emergence of leaders as an experience of asymmetries of influence. In the functionalistic or social control approach, influence can be seen as an outcome of power, whereas in the genetic approach the trade-off is reversed, and influence can be seen as way of acquiring power.

Influence modalities also differ in their prevalence within each framework. Conformity prevails in social control, whereas in social construction it is innovation that comes to the foreground. Convergence is common to both, although probably involving different motivational dynamics. Under social control, convergence may result from a distributive agreement splitting the differences; whereas under social innovation, convergence corresponds to an integrative consensus achieved by the group.

The group polarization phenomenon is another paradigmatic situation where both theoretical approaches can be involved. The heuristic importance of this phenomenon resides in the fact that group polarization can result either from groupthink or from group innovation, depending on the "history" leadership processes exerted either from power to influence, or from influence to power.

Catastrophe theory could be invoked here (Stewart & Peregoy, 1983) to illustrate how the same outcome can involve completely different and even opposite processes and aims, which is a strong argument against analyzing isolated processes out of their context (see also chapter 5 of this volume). Functionalistic and genetic approaches may also be considered less as disjunctive alternatives, and more as alternating phases of the same process with trade-offs between the micro innovative processes triggered by minorities and the macro stabilizing processes controlled by majorities.

REFERENCES

Abelson, R. P., & Levi, A. (1985). Decision making and decision theory. In G. Lindzey & E. Aronson (Eds.), *Handbook of social psychology* (3rd ed., pp. 231–309). New York: Random House.

Albert, S. (1992). The algebra of change. In B. M. Staw & L. L. Cummings (Eds.), *Research in organizational behavior* (Vol. 14, pp. 179–229). Greenwich, CT: JAI.

Ashby, W. R. (1968). Variety, constraint and the law of requisite variety. In W. Buckley (Ed.), *Modern systems research for the behavior scientist* (pp. 129–136). Chicago: Aldine.

Austin, J. L. (1962). *How to do things with words.* New York: Oxford University Press.

Bales, R. F. (1950). *Interaction process analysis.* Chicago: University of Chicago Press.

Bales, R. F., Cohen, S. P., & Williamson, S. A. (1979). *SYMLOG—A system for the multiple level observation of groups.* New York: The Free Press.

Bales, R. F., & Koenigs, R. J. (1992). *Images that guide leadership.* San Diego: SYMLOG Consulting Group.

Barnard, C. (1938). *The functions of the executive.* Cambridge, MA: Harvard University Press.

Bass, B. M. (Ed.). (1981). *Stogdill's Handbook of Leadership—A survey of theory and research.* New York: The Free Press.

Bass, B. (1985). *Leadership and performance beyond expectations.* New York: The Free Press.

Bell, D. V. J. (1975). *Power, influence and authority: An essay in political linguistics.* New York: Oxford University Press.

Bennis, W. G., & Nanus, B. (1986). *Leaders: The strategies for taking charge.* New York: Harper Collins.

Bryman, A. (1992). *Charisma and leadership in organisations.* London: Sage.

Burns, J. M. (1978). *Leadership.* New York: Harper & Row.

Burnstein, E., & Vinokur, A. (1973). What a person thinks upon learning he has chosen differently from others: Nice evidence for the persuasive-arguments explanation of choice shifts. *Journal of Experimental Social Psychology, 11,* 412–426.

Burnstein, E., & Vinokur, A. (1975). Testing two classes of theories about group induced shifts in individual choice. *Journal of Personality and Social Psychology, 9,* 123–127.

Burnstein, E., & Vinokur, A. (1977). Persuasive argumentation and social comparison as determinants of attitude polarisation. *Journal of Experimental Social Psychology, 13,* 315–332.

Callon, M., & Latour, B. (1981). Unscrewing the big leviathan: How actors macro-structure reality and how sociologists help them to do so. In K. Knorr-Cetina & A. V. Cicourel (Eds.), *Advances in social theory and methodology toward an integration of micro and macro sociology* (pp. 227–303). Boston: Routledge & Kegan Paul.

Cartwright, D. (1965). Influence, leadership, control. In J. G. March (Ed.), *Handbook of organizations* (pp. 1–47). Chicago: Rand McNally.

Cohen, M. D., & March, J. G. (1974). *Leadership and ambiguity* (2nd ed.). Boston: Harvard Business School Press.

Conger, J. A. (1989). *The charismatic leader: Behind the mystique of exceptional leadership.* San Francisco: Jossey-Bass.

Conger, J. A., & Kanungo, R. N. (1987). Towards a behavioural theory of charismatic leadership in organisational settings. *Academy of Management Review, 12,* 637–647.

Cranach, M. von (1986). Leadership as a function of group action. In C. F. Graumann & S. Moscovici (Eds.), *Changing conceptions of leadership* (pp. 115–134). New York: Springer Verlag.

Crozier, M. (1963). *Le phénomène bureaucratique*. Paris: Seuil.

Deutsch, M., & Gerard, H. B. (1955). A study of normative and informational social influences upon individual judgment. *Journal of Abnormal and Social Psychology, 51,* 629–636.

Doise, W. (1982). *L'explication en psychologie sociale*. Paris: PUF.

Festinger, L. (1950). Informal social communication. *Psychological Review, 57,* 271–282.

French, J. R. P., & Raven, B. (1959). The bases of social power. In D. Cartwright (Ed.), *Studies in social power* (pp. 150–167). Ann Arbor, MI: University of Michigan, Institute for Social Research.

Gersick, C. J. G. (1988). Time and transition in work teams: Toward a new model of group development. *Academy of Management Journal, 31,* 9–41.

Gersick, C. J. G. (1989). Makingtime: Predictable transitions in task groups. *Academy of Management Journal, 32*(2), 274–309.

Graumann, C. F. (1986). Power and leadership in Lewinian field theory: Recalling an interrupted task. In C. F. Graumann & S. Moscovici (Eds.), *Changing conceptions of leadership* (pp. 83–89). New York: Springer Verlag.

Habermas, J. (1984). *The theory of communicative action: Vol. I. Reason and the rationalization of society* (T. McCarthy, Trans.). London: Heinemann Educational Books. (German ed. 1981)

Habermas, J. (1987). *The theory of communicative action: Vol. II. The critique of functionalist reason* (T. McCarthy, Trans.). Cambridge: Dolity Press. (German ed. 1981)

Hackman, J. R. (1987). The design of work teams. In J. W. Lorsch (Ed.), *Handbook of organizational behavior* (pp. 315–342). Englewood Cliffs, NJ: Prentice-Hall.

Hollander, E. P. (1960). Competence and conformity in the acceptance of influence. *Journal of Abnormal Social Psychology, 61,* 361–365.

House, R. J. (1971). A path-goal theory of leader effectiveness. *Administrative Science Quarterly, 16,* 321–339.

Jacques, E. (1976). *A general theory of bureaucracy*. Portsmouth, NH: Heinemann, Gower.

Janis, I. (1972). *Victims of group think: A psychology study of foreign policy decisions and fiascoes*. Boston: Houghton Mifflin.

Kanter, R. M. (1983). *The Changemasters: Innovation for production in American corporations*. New York: Simon & Schuster.

Katz, D., & Kahn, R. L. (1978). *The social psychology of organizations*. New York: Wiley. (1st ed. 1966)

Kelley, H. H., & Thibant, J. W. (1969). Group problem solving. In G. Lindzey & E. Aronson (Eds.), *The handbook of social psychology* (Vol. 4, pp. 1–101). Reading, MA: Addison-Wesley.

Kohlberg, L. (1963). Moral development and identification. In H. W. Stevenson (Ed.), *Child psychology* (pp. 217–232). Chicago: University of Chicago Press.

Kotter, J. P. (1988). *The leadership factor*. New York: The Free Press.

Latané, B. (1981). The psychology of social impact. *American Psychologist, 36,* 343–356.

Latané, B., & Wolf, S. (1981). The social impact of majorities and minorities. *Psychological Review, 88,* 438–453.

Latour, B., & Woolgar, S. (1979). *Laboratory life: The construction of scientific facts*. Princeton, NJ: Princeton University Press.

Lawrence, P. R., & Lorsch, J. W. (1967). *Organization and environment*. Cambridge, MA: Harvard Graduate School of Business Administration.

Lewin, K., Lippit, R., & White, R. K. (1939). Patterns of aggressive behaviour in experimentally created social climates. *Journal of Social Psychology, 10,* 271–299.

Lieberson, S., & O'Connor, J. F. (1972). Leadership and organizational performance: A study of large corporations. *American Sociological Review, 37,* 117–130.

Likert, R. (1961). *New patterns of management*. New York: McGraw-Hill.

Lord, R. G., & Maher, K. J. (1990). Alternative information processing models and their implications for theory, research and practice. *Academy of Management Review, 15,* 9–28.

Lord, R. G., & Maher, K. J. (1991). *Leadership and information processing—Linking perceptions and performance*. Boston: Unwin Hyman.

McGrath, J. (1993). Introduction—The SEMCO workshop—Description of longitudinal study. *Small Group Research, 24*(403), 285–306.

Meindl, J. R., Ehrlich, S. B., & Dukerich, J. M. (1985). The romance of leadership. *Administrative Science Quarterly, 30*(1), 78–102.

Mintzberg, H. (1973). *The nature of managerial work*. New York: Harper & Row.

Mintzberg, H. (1979). *The structuring of organizations*. Englewood Cliffs, NJ: Prentice-Hall.

Mintzberg, H., Raisinghani, D., & Théorêt, A. (1976). The structure of "unstructured" decision processes. *Administrative Science Quarterly, 21*, 246–275.

Morgan, G. (1986). *Images of organization*. Beverly Hills, CA: Sage.

Moscovici, S. (1976). *Social influence and social change*. London: Academic Press.

Moscovici, S. (1979). *Psychologie des minorités actives*. Paris: P.U.F.

Moscovici, S. (1980). Toward a theory of conversion behavior. In L. Berkowitz (Ed.), *Advances in experimental social psychology* (Vol. 13, pp. 209–239). New York: Academic Press.

Moscovici, S. (1981). *L'âge des foules*. Paris: Fayard.

Moscovici, S. (1985). Social influence and conformity. In G. Lindzey & E. Aronson (Eds.), *The handbook of social psychology* (Vol. 2, 3rd ed., pp. 347–412). New York: Random House.

Moscovici, S., & Doise, W. (1992). *Dissension et consensus. Une théorie générale des décisions colectives*. Paris: P.U.F.

Mugny, G. (1982). *The power of minorities*. London: Academic Press.

Nadler, D. A., & Tushman, M. L. (1990). Beyond the charismatic leader: Leadership and organizational change. *California Management Review, 32*, 77–97.

Nemeth, C. J., & Staw, B. M. (1989). The tradeoffs of social control and innovation in groups and organizations. In J. Berkowitz (Ed.), *Advances in experimental social psychology* (Vol. 22, pp. 175–210). New York: Academic Press.

Parsons, T. (1951). *The social system*. Glencoe, IL: The Free Press.

Parsons, T. (1963). On the concept of political power. *Proceedings of the American Philosophical Society, 107*, No. 3, June. Reprinted in Parsons (1969, pp. 352–404).

Parsons, T. (1968). *The structure of social action*. New York: The Free Press.

Parsons, T. (1969). *Politics and social structure*. New York: The Free Press.

Pelz, D. C. (1951). Leadership within a hierarchical organization. *Journal of Social Issues, 7*, 49–55.

Pérez, J. A., & Mugny, G. (1993). *Influences sociales—La théorie de l'élaboration du conflit*. Neuchâtel, Switzerland: Delachaux et Niestlé.

Peters, J., & Waterman, R. H. (1982). *In search of excellence*. New York: Random House.

Petty, R. E., & Cacioppo, J. J. (1986). The elaboration likelihood model in persuasion. In L. Berkowitz (Ed.), *Advances in experimental social psychology* (Vol. 19, pp. 123–205). New York: Academic Press.

Pfeffer, J. (1977). The ambiguity of leadership. *Academy of Management Review, 2*, 104–112.

Pfeffer, J. (1986). *Power in organizations*. Marshfield, MA: Pittman.

Piaget, J. (1932). *Le jugement moral chez l'enfant*. Paris: P.U.F.

Porter, L. W., & Lawler, E. E. (1968). *Managerial attitudes and performance*. Homewood, IL: Irwin-Dorsey.

Pugh, D. (1976). The "Aston" approach to the study of organizations. In G. Hofstede & M. Sami Kassen (Eds.), *European contributions to organization theory* (pp. 62–78). Assen/Amsterdam: Van Gorcum.

Pugh, D., Hickson, D. J., Hinings, C. R., & Turner, L. (1968). Dimensions of organization structure. *Administrative Science Quarterly, 13*, 65–105.

Rokeach, M. (1973). *The nature of human values*. New York: The Free Press.

Sherif, M. (1966). *Group conflict and cooperation*. London: Routledge & Kegan Paul.

Simon, H. A. (1962). The architecture of complexity. *Proceedings of the American Philosophical Society, 106*, 467–482.

Simon, H. A. (1965). *The shape of automation*. New York: Harper & Row.
Simon, H. A. (1974). *Administrative behavior*. New York: Macmillan.
Steiner, I. D. (1972). *Group processes and productivity*. New York: Academic Press.
Stewart, I. N., & Peregoy, P. L. (1983). Catastrophe theory modeling in psychology. *Psychological Bulletin, 94*(2), 336–362.
Stogdill, R. (1974). *The handbook of leadership*. New York: The Free Press.
Tajfel, H. (1959). Quantitative judgements in social perception. *British Journal of Psychology, 50*, 16–29.
Tajfel, H. (1969). Cognitive aspects of prejudice. *Journal of Social Issues, 25*, 79–97.
Tajfel, H. (1972). La catégorisation sociale. In S. Moscovici (Ed.), *Introduction à la psychologie sociale* (Vol. 1). Paris: Larousse.
Tajfel, H. (1978). Intergroup behaviour. In H. Tajfel & L. Frazer (Eds.), *Introducing social psychology* (pp. 401–446). Cambridge, England: Cambridge University Press.
Tajfel, H. (1982). Social psychology of intergroup relations. *Annual Review of Psychology, 33*, 1–30.
Thompson, J. D. (1967). *Organizations in action*. New York: McGraw-Hill.
Tichy, N. M., & Devanna, M. A. (1986). *The transformational leader*. New York: Wiley.
Turner, J. C. (1982). Towards a cognitive redefinition of the social group. In H. Tajfel (Ed.), *Social identity and intergroup relations* (pp. 15–40). Cambridge, England: Cambridge University Press.
Turner, J. C. (1985). Social categorisation and the self-concept: A social cognitive theory of group behaviour. In E. J. Lawler (Ed.), *Advances in group processes* (Vol. 2, pp. 77–122). Greenwich, CT: JAI.
Turner, J. C. (1991). *Social influence*. London: Open University Press.
Turner, J. C., Hogg, M. A., Oakes, P. J., Reicher, S. D., & Wetherell, M. S. (1987). *Rediscovering the social group: A self-categorisation theory*. Oxford, England: Basil Blackwell.
Vroom, V. H. (1964). *Work and motivating*. New York: Wiley.
Weber, M. (1947). *The theory of social and economic organization* (A. M. Stenderson & T. Parsons, Trans.). Edited with an Introduction by Talcott Parsons. New York: The Free Press.
Weick, K. E. (1979). *The social psychology of organizing*. Reading, MA: Addison-Wesley.
Witte, E. H. (1987). Behaviour in group situations: An integrative model. *European Journal of Social Psychology, 17*, 403–429.
Witte, E. H. (1990). Social influence: A discussion and integration of recent models into a general group situation theory. *European Journal of Social Psychology, 20*, 3–27.
Yukl, G. A. (1989). *Leadership in organizations* (2nd ed.). Englewood Cliffs, NJ: Prentice-Hall.

5

EFFECTIVE TEAMWORK— A THEORETICAL MODEL AND A TEST IN THE FIELD

Wolfgang Scholl
Humboldt University, Berlin

The following theoretical model for analyzing the effectiveness of teams working on complex problems is based on a more general theoretical frame of reference for an interdisciplinary analysis of social interaction (Scholl, 1991). It is intended to encompass social systems of any size, from two-person interaction to small groups to organizations and even societies. This may sound overly ambitious but there are some striking parallels at the different system levels that are worthwhile to systematize theoretically and—maybe—to refute them empirically. Figure 5.1 gives an overview of the basic features of this model. For example, the most important variable for the application of the model to reality is the size and differentiation of the social system (in the lower right corner of Fig. 5.1). By following the arrows it can be seen that an increasing size of the system should lessen the congruence between its members, which has a lot of consequences in other variables. It is not necessary to further explicate these consequences of the size effect, because the model is applied here only to group behavior and teamwork. Moreover, in this chapter only the theoretical kernel of the model (including congruence, power exertion, action capability, growth of knowledge and effectiveness; see the shaded area in Fig. 5.1) is explained and tested with empirical data from a field study on innovations. The logic of presentation follows the guideline giving theoretical development the primary weight.

BASIC ASSUMPTIONS

Psychological social psychology today consists of a few middle-range theories (e.g., interdependence theory, lay epistemics; see also Vol. 1) and a lot of minitheories (e.g. self-perception, reactance, dissonance), and much more re-

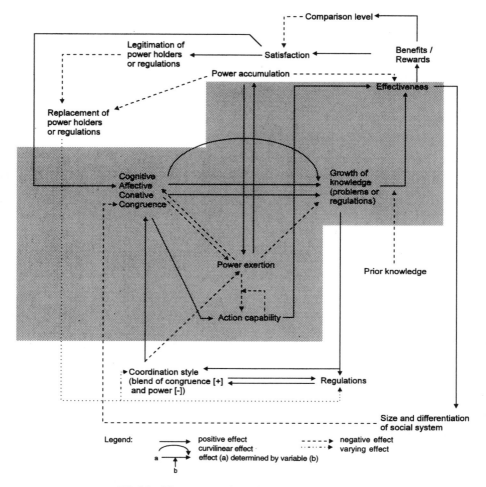

FIG. 5.1. Effectiveness of social systems: basic model.

search is devoted to the latter. Moreover, the bulk of social-psychological research and theory focuses on the individual under social stimulation, whereas the social dynamics between at least two persons get much less attention. Of course, social interaction and social systems like groups are much more complex phenomena than, for example, social cognition, social motivation, or nonverbal cues. Therefore, it is quite understandable that progress in group research is slower (Steiner, 1986) than in less complex areas and that theoretical integration is here far more difficult. On the other hand, because of its practical relevance, group research is carried out not only in social psychology but also in many other (sub)disciplines—for example, organizational psychology, psychiatry, microsociology, communication, education (Fisch, Daniel & Beck, 1991)—which, regrettably, do not take much notice of each other's methods and results. So, group research is scattered, and partial analyses are dominating the field, which are likely to miss again the basic complexity of the phenomenon. Apparently, the diverse partial lines of progress, as useful as they are in themselves, do not preserve or establish theoretical compatibility between themselves; this lowers the chances of theoretical integration and of developing theories appropriate for the systemic and complex properties of groups. Therefore, it seems to be fruitful to supplement this scattered and, if done at all, bottom-up approach with a genuine top-down approach trying to start with a few general and more encompassing theoretical concepts and postulates. That is the approach that I have taken and am presenting here for discussion.

For such a top-down approach it is necessary to use relatively encompassing, molar variables instead of molecular ones; they allow the building of more general hypotheses that may be less prone to circumstantial variations. Inter-dependence theory—with the general variables of benefits, costs, comparison level, alternatives, and matrix transformation—is a case in point. In my search for suitable interaction variables, I had four criteria in mind, presented here in a rank order of descending significance:

- *Universality*, that is, the concepts are relevant for every type and form of interaction and they are based on culturally invariant, eventually biologically predetermined qualities of human beings.
- *Interdisciplinary relevance* and linkability toward biology on the one side and economics and the social sciences on the other.
- *Applicability to all system levels*, that is, for dyads, groups, organizations, and states. This is an unusual but worthwhile goal because many everyday interactions do not take place between individuals, but across different system levels (see also chapter 6 of this volume).
- *Practical relevance*, that is, the usefulness of these concepts in reconstructing approved practical instructions (e.g., the Harvard negotiation concept, Fisher & Ury, 1984; or the discussion guidelines of Hall, 1971) on a general theoretical level.

The basic concepts fulfilling these criteria are presented in the following section.

CHOICE OF CENTRAL THEORETICAL TERMS

Congruence, power, and knowledge seem to me to be the most important interaction variables; the reasons can only briefly be listed, following the aforementioned criteria (cf. Scholl, 1991, for more details).

I. Universality

Numerous studies and reviews (starting with Foa, 1961) have found that the perception of interpersonal behavior can be reduced to two basic dimensions: The first is often termed "love-hostility," "affiliation," "solidarity," or—in my terminology—*congruence*; the second is "dominance-submission," "prominence," or—in my terminology—*power* (for definitions, see the next section). These dimensions are culturally invariant (Lonner, 1980). It is also very interesting that related dimensions have been found—interculturally invariant—in the functional meaning of nonverbal communication, termed "affiliation" and "control" (Argyle, 1975) as well as in the semantic space of verbal communication, termed "evaluation" and "potency" (Osgood, May, & Miron, 1975). These astonishing similarities are apparently rooted in the underlying emotional dimensions[1] of pleasantness (joy/acceptance-sadness/disgust) and dominance (anger/anticipation-fear/surprise) (Traxel & Heide, 1961; cf. already Burt, 1915). These basic emotions are genetically determined and physiologically anchored (Birbaumer, 1983) and they have presumably developed together with social bonding in mammals in a process of coevolution. Hence, it seems worthwhile to rely on these two general dimensions of congruence and power in constructing interaction theories.

Besides congruence and power, a third universal feature of humans is their ability to produce, transmit, and apply *knowledge* for better coping with environmental conditions. Brain volume and intelligence have been successively developed in our phylogenetical line; that is, the heightened potential for knowledge acquisition must have been an evolutionary advantage. Especially important are the social or interactional aspects of knowledge:

- The evolution of intelligence has been primarily stimulated by the complexities of social life, because nonhuman primates plan and carry out complex social-political actions, whereas they normally do not use self-made tools, though their intelligence is sufficient to do that (Cheney & Seyfarth, 1990).

- Through their language capacity, humans can accumulate knowledge and thereby profit from the evolution of social knowledge, which occurs much faster than biological evolution. Through the invention of symbolization and storage and transmission devices (e.g., script, books, telecommunication), the societal production, transmission, and application of knowledge have been enormously broadened and accelerated. So, any individual knowledge is in fact to a very large part transmitted social knowledge.

- Though new and better knowledge can be produced individually to some extent, it must be corroborated and approved socially (cf. Festinger's social comparison theory, 1954); knowledge in that sense is always socially constructed

---

[1]Some researchers prefer to speak of separate basic emotions instead of dimensions of emotions, but the fact remains that the emotional qualities can be ordered on a two-dimensional surface (e.g., Plutchik, 1980).

(see also Berger & Luckmann, 1966) and is distributed in the form of social representations (Farr & Moscovici, 1984).

Because the biological and cultural evolution of knowledge has furthered the survival rate of humans extraordinarily, knowledge should be a central variable determining the effectiveness of coping with any problem.

2. Interdisciplinary Relevance

The links to biology have become apparent in the preceding discussion. The links to the social sciences can best be seen in Etzioni's (1968) book *The Active Society. A Theory of Societal and Political Processes*, in which he gave a synthesis between basic assumptions of political science and sociology. The main variables of his theoretical frame are almost the same as in my work, which owes several ideas to "the active society": knowledge, power, and consensus (a part of congruence). The links to economics are less apparent because mainstream neoclassical theory is too individualistic and rationalistic; yet, evolving new economic approaches usually include the idea of bounded rationality (Simon, 1957), which creates the central problem of the amount and validity of knowledge inherent in human actions; the economics of information are a rapidly expanding subfield. Power is usually an important but not well elaborated variable: The trichotomy of atomistic markets, oligopoly, and monopoly has dominated the discussions, but differentiating advances are made in the new institutional economics. And the amount of congruence or incongruence is not used as a term but lies at the heart of economic game theory with its distinction of zero- and non-zero-sum games and with the problem of cooperation propensity (another part of congruence, see later) in bilateral and social dilemma situations.

3. Applicability to All System Levels

The applicability of these variables to all system levels can be demonstrated very easily: Etzioni's (1968) book shows it for states and societies, Kirsch (1976) and Scholl, Hoffmann, and Gierschner (1993) for organizations, and the following discussion shows it for groups and dyads.

4. Practical Relevance

The relevance of these variables for reconstructing approved practical instructions, needing more than a few sentences, cannot be demonstrated here; but it was analyzed in Scholl (1991) for group moderation techniques, for participation in organizational decision making, for concepts of conflict resolution and negotiation, for communication and many forms of leadership training, and for organizational forms of group work like semiautonomous groups, quality circles, and lean production.

DEFINITION OF THE THEORETICAL TERMS

It can be summarized from the earlier discussion that congruence, power, and knowledge are universal and very central aspects of human interaction, which are highly useful for interdisciplinary discussion and practical application; so, it should be fruitful to use them in theorizing. Yet, this evidence of their general importance does not give a perfect demarcation of these concepts. Therefore, definitions must be guided by additional arguments, which are given briefly in the following paragraphs (see also chapters 3 and 4 of this volume).

Pleasantness is one fundamental emotional dimension; applied to other persons it gives love-hostility, affiliation, solidarity, sympathy, or—in my terms—emotional congruence. This emotional or affective quality between interaction partners is of decisive importance for the interaction process, but it is also strongly connected to cognitive and conative aspects. There are several theories that deal with these connections: for example, balance theory (Heider, 1958), with the cognitive-affective link in subsuming unit and sentiment relations; the theory of reasoned action (Fishbein & Ajzen, 1975), with cognitive- (beliefs) affective- (attitudes) conative (intentions) links; and dissonance theory (Festinger, 1957), with the cognitive-conative link where intentions bias cognitive activity (cf. especially Beckmann & Irle, 1985). So, we have to assume relatively strong consistency effects among cognitive, affective, and conative dispositions toward any object or person (cf. also Insko & Schopler, 1967); therefore, congruence is not only relevant for emotions but also for cognitions and intentions. On the other hand, each of these cognitive, affective, and conative components can be separately altered by other variables such that people who do not like each other may nevertheless have similar beliefs, or such that friends may have incompatible intentions. Therefore, it is useful to maintain this cognitive-affective-conative distinction and to take the empirical connectedness between these distinctive disposition tendencies into account through the differentiation of three types of congruence:

1. *Cognitive congruence* (consensus-dissensus) is defined as the similarity of the relevant cognitions of interaction partners.
2. *Affective congruence* (sympathy-antipathy) is defined as the degree of positivity of the emotions of interaction partners toward each other.
3. *Conative congruence* (cooperation-competition propensity) is defined as the compatibility of the intentions of interaction partners.

By taking consistency effects seriously we have gained three types of congruence that "grow out" of the emotional dimension of pleasantness and are to a certain degree reflected in emotional, nonverbal, and/or semantic signals in interaction. These three forms of dispositional congruence facilitate cooperation, which can be termed *behavioral congruence*. Feelings of love, sympathy, or congruence toward each other can differ within a relationship, but there is always a tendency toward reciprocation as has been shown in attraction research. The same holds for cognitive and conative congruence. So, congruence can be an individual attribute related to another person. More important, though, it can be a relationship or system's property designating the state of affairs between two or more partners, which can be measured, for instance, by averaging the mutual individual congruence.

Anger and fear, as well as anticipation and surprise, mark the second fundamental emotional dimension of dominance, which reflects the interaction quality of "power," "influence," "social impact," or "control." In psychology and the social sciences, power and influence are often almost synonyms in that they both encompass any impact on other people, with the only distinction being that power is an influence potential and influence is actualized power (Argyle, 1992; Cartwright, 1959). The usage of power and influence in this sense is too broad for the formulation of hypotheses, because it entails quite diverging consequences and would encompass almost all social-psychological phenomena. Especially, the conceptual differentiation between power and congruence would almost lose its sense, because consensus building and cooperation—that is, cognitive and behavioral congruence processes—would always be instances of the actualization of power (see also chapter 4 of this volume). In accordance with Partridge (1963), a political scientist, and Etzioni (1968), a sociologist, the definitions of power and influence are differentiated sharply, whereby *power* means a social impact *against* the basic preferences or interests of the interaction partner and *influence* a social impact *in favor of* or at least without hurting those interests (the important distinction between a potential and its exertion is drawn with just these supplementary qualifications). It is true that power and influence are similarly felt as strong and mighty in everyday language, reflected in generic terms like social impact or control. Yet, the proposed differentiation is also reflected in the attributed consequences of influence and power: Influence is seen as responsive, appreciative, and tolerant, whereas power evokes opposite associations (Pelz & Scholl, 1990). It can be shown that power and influence in this sense have several opposite consequences such that this distinction seems to be necessary or is at least more fruitful than the common undifferentiated usage (Buschmeier, 1995; Scholl, 1991; Scholl et al., 1993).

The definition of the third central concept, *knowledge*, seems to be more simple, whereas its measurement may be more difficult. Knowledge is defined as the (relevant) set of representations of the world. They are assumedly built from schemata and their connections. An important distinction is that between "knowing how" or "experience," that is, implicit knowledge contained in learned successful responses, and "knowing that" or "insight," which is explicit knowledge contained in symbolic constructs. Experience and insight often stem from different learning conditions and may be present in differing parts and combinations. Sometimes they cover the same realities and, therefore, may be partly contradictory. For example, a person may be convinced of the intrinsic worth of human equality but may nevertheless try to dominate others and may then deny or excuse this apparent inconsistency. Degrees of relevant knowledge should be differentiated regarding its amount, its consistency, and its validity, but the measurement of these aspects of knowledge can be very difficult, especially if experience is to be included. Of course, difficulties in measurement should be taken as less problematic than excluding highly relevant parts of reality from the theoretical agenda. Learning by trial and error and by the observation of others does often happen without semantic coding and reflection and is often extremely important for effective action.

Two additional variables, which are used in the empirical investigation of the core model, are also briefly introduced (cf. Scholl, 1991). *Effectiveness* includes the appropriateness of goal formation (goals related to needs or interests), the extent of goal achievement (outcomes related to goals), and the efficiency with which the outcomes are realized (benefits minus direct costs or opportunity costs). For empirical comparisons it is usually sufficient to use only suitable parts of this encompassing definition. Very often in the theoretical and empirical literature, effectiveness and knowledge (or the growth of knowledge) are used interchangeably as dependent variables. Yet, they are quite different and should be handled differently, because (a) erroneous assumptions may often point to the same (good or bad) alternatives as correct assumptions, (b) for complex tasks there is often no single right answer and the available knowledge is insufficient to determine it, and (c) the best knowledge does not guarantee that action is taken adequately or, even worse, there is the danger of "paralysis through analysis." This last argument leads to the inclusion of another important variable for effective action: *Action capability* means the ability to perform complete cycles of decision making and implementation. Its first main aspect is the *decision capability*, which includes the abilities to initiate the tackling of a problem, to advance the problem-solving process, and to make a clear-cut decision. The second main aspect is the *implementation capability*, which includes the abilities to guarantee a proper realization and to secure the acceptance of the measures taken.

THEORETICAL POSTULATES AND DERIVATIONS

What are the main determinants of the effectiveness of groups working on complex tasks? No clear answer to this question has been developed in the group literature as far as I know. Research in the tradition of Steiner's (1972) typology of tasks is—in my opinion—not applicable to *complex tasks* like the development of a new product, the introduction of a computerized logistics system, or the preparation of a new traffic plan; these are most probably discretionary tasks for which no clear predictions are made. Social decision schemes in the tradition of Davis (1973; see also Vol. I) do not provide a sufficient answer because they refer only to one of at least four necessary—and in practice intermixed—stages in teamwork, that is, orientation and preliminary problem definition, information processing, decision making, and implementation. The Hackman and Morris model (1975; see also Hackman, 1987) gives basically a framework that shows some similarities with the model proposed here but it contains no specified theory. Finally, there exist several more or less approved hypotheses about antecedents of effective teamwork but they usually are singular input–output contentions and neither specify the mechanisms via which they affect the output, nor are they integrated or at least harmonized with other relevant hypotheses. This holds, for instance, for the advantages of cooperative versus competitive conditions (D. W. Johnson, Maruyama, R. T. Johnson, Nelson, & Skon, 1981) or of controverse instead of concurrent information processing (Hall, 1971; Janis, 1972), hypotheses that have never been taken up jointly (but see later and chapter 7 of this volume). The development of the effectiveness model from Fig. 5.1 meant to find a new way for theory building in interaction and group psychology, which owes a lot to mathematical sociology (especially to Blalock, 1969, 1971). Its theoretical kernel is briefly explicated.

The main direct determinants of group effectiveness in the proposed model are (a) the growth of knowledge during the group process, and (b) the capability for coordinate action. It seems to be evident that a *growth of knowledge* is beneficial for a better solution of the task problem at hand. At least, this is the implicit assumption behind most group problem-solving studies, but the growth of knowledge has seldom been conceptualized and measured as a variable in relation to others. In the model, the impact of the growth of knowledge on effectiveness is moderated by the amount of previous knowledge (cf. Fig. 5.1). For the solution of relatively simple tasks (like those in most group experiments) the growth of knowledge should be less important than for those complex tasks that are the primary domain of teamwork in practice; for routine tasks no more knowledge is necessary at all. It is also proposed that the importance of a growth of knowledge for effectiveness is not as high as often assumed (see the arguments a–c in the earlier effectiveness paragraph), and that additional determinants other than pure chance must be taken into account. The *capability* for coordinate *action* is another, often neglected independent source of effectiveness because member efforts must be coordinated in every phase of the group process. Sometimes, people just think too much; that is, they invest excessively in the growth of their knowledge but do not come to grips with practical demands (see earlier argument c). The importance of a sufficient action capability is usually overlooked in group research presumably because (a) experimental tasks are often very simple, (b) the decision capability is largely manufactured by the experimenter and his instructions, and (c) most experiments have no implementation stage. In contrast, for complex tasks in practice the problems of knowledge acquisition are always coexistent with the problems of securing the decision and implementation capability.

If we look on the *determinants of action capability*, which encompass mainly the problems of coordination, there seem to be two principal possibilities: Coordination can be brought about by *conative congruence* (i.e., the mutual readiness to cooperate) or by *power*. It is relatively easy to take collective action if people are unanimous or are willing to cooperate, but, if not, power can be used to bring "deviators," "procrastinators," or "egocentrics" into line. (Power exertion in that sense is closely related to group pressure, conformity pressure, or normative influence.) Yet, our empirical results (see later) and a closer look on the consequences of power exertion lead to a further theoretical differentiation: If the action capability is already relatively high, power exertion will be seen as unnecessary and illegitimate and will produce reactance, which in turn will lower the action capability. But if the action capability is relatively low, power exertion will cause less resistance or will even be accepted and can successfully bring order into chaos and thereby raise the action capability to a medium level. It follows that conative congruence (cooperativeness) and power can substitute each other to a certain degree to secure action, but a high action capability cannot be reached without substantial congruence.[2] It follows, too, that power exertion will always tend to move the action capability to a medium level regardless of its prior level.

The most important postulates of the model concern the *determinants of the growth of knowledge*. How is new knowledge produced through interaction? According to Steiner (1972), the number of the team members has a curvilinear impact on the growth of knowledge because the knowledge potential is too low from very few members, and the process losses become too high with too many members. This idea is transferred to cognitive congruence (consensus-dissensus). If team members have basically the same opinions and the same experiences—that is, if they have almost the same knowledge—they cannot learn very much from each other and are not stimulated to produce new ideas or to elaborate diverse opinions.[3] The same consequence will hold if members *practice* cognitive congruence; that is, instead of a fruitful controverse discussion, concurrent thinking prevails (see Janis, 1972, on groupthink and the related literature; see also Vol. I). On the other hand, if team members are too different in their concepts and implicit assumptions, the exchange of ideas and opinions would be very laborious, irritating, and time consuming; in the words of Piaget

---

[2]Etzioni (1968) advanced a similar but seemingly different hypothesis: Power and consensus (= cognitive congruence) can substitute each other to a certain degree in order to secure the steering capacity (action capability) of a society *but some power exertion is always necessary.* Yet, this difference in hypotheses dissolves if one takes the size of the considered social system into account, see Fig. 5.1: The greater the size of the social system the less congruence will prevail in it such that also according to our hypothesis congruence alone cannot secure a sufficient action capability.

[3]The literature on group heterogeneity is based on a similar but broader and more diffuse idea.

(1976), too many accommodations instead of the easier assimilations would be necessary such that it becomes too difficult to learn from each other. Festinger's (1954) social comparison theory yields the appropriate conclusion that people will compare their opinions primarily with those persons to whom similar opinions are attributed. My hypothesis, then, is that not only the number of participants but also their cognitive congruence have a curvilinear impact on the growth of knowledge (see Fig. 5.2). Indirect empirical support for the latter hypothesis comes from Driver and Streufert (1969).

The model also assumes a direct *linear* impact of the other two components of congruence on the growth of knowledge. Affective congruence (mutual sympathy or a good group atmosphere) and conative congruence (cooperativeness) are both expected to further a deep, open, and unbiased exchange of ideas and opinions and thereby to support the growth of knowledge (cf. Fig. 5.1 for the three causal paths from congruence to the growth of knowledge). That cooperation furthers group effectiveness is well documented in the literature (e.g., D. W. Johnson et al., 1981). But that this happens partly via a larger growth of knowledge and partly via an improved action capability, as the effectiveness model here assumes, has not been previously shown. As argued earlier, the three components of congruence are supposed to have high interdependencies between each other. From these hypotheses concerning *the interdependent congruence components and their relation to the growth of knowledge* an important problem for teamwork can be derived: The optimal values in the three components of congruence for the growth of knowledge are difficult to achieve because they lead to inconsistencies that are likely to be solved through suboptimal value combinations: High affective congruence and high conative congruence are likely to lead—via consistency effects—to the display of high cognitive congruence, eventually through a suppression of diverging opinions, the well-known

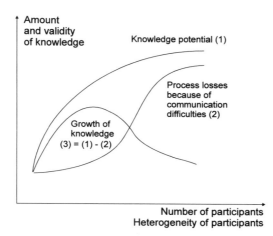

FIG. 5.2. Learning through communication.

groupthink effect (Janis, 1972; Smith, Petersen, D. W. Johnson, & R. T. Johnson, 1986). Or, strongly diverging opinions are maintained and exchanged but cannot be assimilated in due time; as a result of consistency effects, sympathy and cooperativeness are shrinking and harmful competition (see D. W. Johnson et al., 1981, for a meta-analytic review) comes into play. That controversial discussions from *medium cognitive incongruence*, which take place in a climate of *high affective and conative congruence*, are needed for the optimal growth of knowledge poses severe practical problems that are presumed to be one main reason for bad discussions and ineffective teamwork.

Another important determinant of the growth of knowledge and effectiveness is *power exertion* (in the defined narrow sense: a social impact on another person against his or her interests); it is assumed in the model that *power exertion hampers the growth of knowledge*, whereas influence (a social impact on another person in line with his or her interests) furthers it. The reasoning for this postulate is the following (Scholl, 1992): People exerting power often stop discussions if they see their interests endangered; others with deviant opinions come under conformity pressure or are driven out; information is held back or manipulated in favor of a preferred course of action; the less powerful are often reluctant to express their opinions freely. In all these cases the free exchange of information and opinions, which is necessary for an optimal growth of knowledge, is impeded or terminated. The relation of power to knowledge has—as far as I know—never been explicitly specified in social psychology, presumably because it makes sense only with the narrow definition of power given earlier. Of course, the empirical literature gives some hints in this direction: A negative effect of power on knowledge production has been found, for instance, by Torrance (1955), Maier (1967), and Fodor and Smith (1982). Much indirect evidence has been assembled in participation research (Kiessler & Scholl, 1976; Miller & Monge, 1986): Participation and power neutralization lead to more relevant knowledge and higher productivity. The poverty and invalidity of knowledge production through power exertion tends to grow *over time*: (a) Power exertion is often accompanied by a devaluation of the victims (Kipnis, 1976) so that their future ideas and remarks are devalued too; (b) if the likelihood of false decisions is raised by power exertion, a subsequent correction is even less likely because of a self-esteem saving escalation tendency (Brockner et al., 1986) of the power wielder, which can hardly be corrected by the less powerful actors; and (c) the use of expert power in manipulating the perception of others leads after a while to the same distorting effect in the power wielder because he begins to believe in his own propaganda (Higgins, 1981). These tendencies (a–c) are already contained in the model in that they increase the strength of the negative effect of power exertion on the growth of knowledge. They have been neither modeled nor investigated separately. The following side effects of power exertion on the growth of knowledge are explicitly stated in the effectiveness model: (d) Power exertion is often used for augmenting one's power potential, which raises the likelihood of further power exertion (Kipnis, 1976) with its detrimental effects on knowledge[4]; (e) the exertion of power often leads to reactance (Brehm, 1966) and thereby to a decline of sympathy and cooperativeness (affective and conative congruence) with negative effects on information exchange and knowledge production; and (f) antipathy and competitiveness (affective and conative incongruence) in turn raise the likelihood of power exertion and thus reinforce the negative effect on the growth of knowledge.[5] All arguments taken together, the total effect of power exertion on the growth of knowledge should be relatively strong. This hypothesis is perhaps the most important in the effectiveness model because of its clear-cut and severe consequences for any social system. Economic and political theory assume a comparable detrimental effect of centralized planned economies or centralized dictatorial systems—that is, of power—on system effectiveness, but precise hypotheses and investigations are rare in these areas, too. We look for the empirical results of our investigation in the next paragraph.

A FIELD STUDY ON INNOVATIONS

A first test of the expounded central aspects of this model was undertaken as part of a larger study on innovation and information (Scholl et al., 1993). In 16 firms 21 successful and 21 unsuccessful innovation cases were intensively studied; in each firm we chose, together with executives, one or two successful as well as one or two unsuccessful completed product and process innovations, such that the difference in success cannot be attributed to general organization or industry characteristics, but rather has to be sought in the innovation process itself. After the 3 to 10 most important members of each innovation project were interviewed, a questionnaire was given to them measuring the variables of the model. The rate of return was quite good with 79%. A preliminary version of the questionnaire was applied in the first cases and then completely revised such that 142 responses from 36 innovations are the basis for the following test of the effectiveness model. Because the primary focus of this article is on theoretical perspectives, no details of the measurement are given here (see Scholl et al., 1993). All variables of the core model have been measured with several questions yielding acceptable to very good reliabilities (Cronbach's alpha = .60–.96). The face and construct validities also seem to be satisfactory with one exception. Because the (very reliable) measure for the growth of knowledge

---

[4]These effects have not been investigated empirically but they are included in the model; see Fig. 5.1.

[5]These hypotheses (e) and (f) are included separately in the model as a causal feedback loop to antipathy and competitiveness and back to power exertion; its summary effect has been empirically investigated, see later.

showed some very unlikely correlations with other variables, the presumption originated that our subjects eventually did not, and maybe could not, report appropriately gains in knowledge but perhaps primarily gains in certainty.[6] Because also the correlation between growth of knowledge and effectiveness was not significant, whereas the case stories showed vividly the importance of a proper growth of knowledge, a proxy variable was sought. One main part of our innovation study dealt with information pathologies in innovation processes (encompassing all things that can go wrong with the production, transmission, and application of information: Scholl, 1990; Wilensky, 1967). So, from the rich material on information pathologies a summary index was built and used as a proxy for the growth of knowledge; it is assumed that information pathologies impede a proper growth of knowledge such that there should be a high inverse association between them. All empirical results concerning the growth of knowledge are thus based on the proxy variable measurement of information pathologies. They should be a very good indicator of process losses (in the sense of Steiner, 1972) during the production of knowledge but not of the knowledge potential; therefore, no curvilinear relationship (which is derived from the difference between potential production and process losses; see Fig. 5.2) can be expected with cognitive congruence; and, not surprisingly, no curvilinear relationship was empirically obtained with this proxy. So, one of the most critical parts of the model could not be properly tested; this shall be done next with a suitable experiment. The assumed causal relations of the effectiveness model are tested with simple Spearman rank-correlations, which should have the predicted sign and should be significant. Statistically more precise would have been a nonrecursive path analysis, but the quality of measurement was not unequivocally high for all variables so that the less sophisticated, but more robust, correlational test was preferred.

TEST OF THE EFFECTIVENESS MODEL: EMPIRICAL RESULTS

The results of this correlational study mainly support the model. The obtained correlations at the individual level are shown in Fig. 5.3, those at the group level—where individual values were averaged per innovation team—in Fig. 5.4.[7] They are altogether relatively similar; therefore I concentrate my report on the individual level (Fig. 5.3), but some comments about differences on the group

---

[6]Moreover, these growth of knowledge items were the only self-report items. Though gains in knowledge seem to be most visible to the concerned people themselves, the likelihood of biased perception is especially high in self-perception.

[7]For convenience and readability the following signs are used to report the obtained significance level of the correlations: *** = $p < .001$; ** = $p < .01$; * = $p < .05$. At the case or group level with the much lower n of 35–36, the additional significance level of $^{+} = p < .10$ is used. The abbreviation n.s. means nonsignificant.

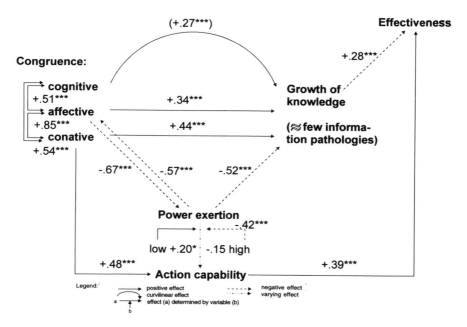

FIG. 5.3. Core model of teamwork, individual level, $n = 130–134$ (*** indicates $p < .001$, * indicates $p < .05$).

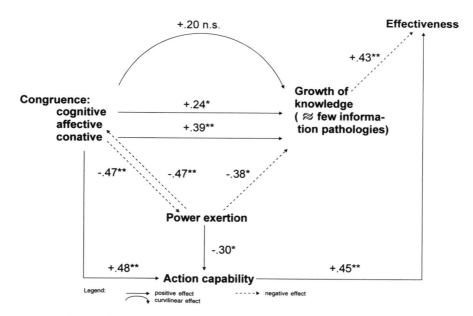

FIG. 5.4. Core model of teamwork, group level, $n = 35–36$ (** indicates $p < .01$, * indicates $p < .05$, n.s. = not significant).

level (Fig. 5.4) seem to be noteworthy. As predicted, the success of the innovation (as subjectively estimated on several dimensions by the main participants)—that is, the effectiveness of teamwork—is positively but not highly (+.28***) correlated with the growth of knowledge (inversely measured by few infomation pathologies) and with the action capability (+.39***). The first correlation is even lower than expected, but this may result from the indirect measurement used. Though a more encompassing and, therefore, better measure of the growth of knowledge may yield a somewhat higher correlation with effectiveness, both correlations underline the previously stated inadequacy to equate the growth of knowledge with effectiveness: The first correlation is (and will be even with improved measurement) not high enough to carry the whole weight, the second is too substantial to be ignored. On the group level both correlations are a bit stronger (+.43***, +.45***; see Fig. 5.4). Because effectiveness is a genuine group-level variable, the higher group-level correlations may simply reflect that the most appropriate system level for the hypothesized effects is not the individual in interaction but the group itself. This may hold with regard to the cumulative effects of information pathologies and the joint problems of coordination for the action capability. Because a more objective measure of innovation success[8] was used on the group level, the higher correlations may also—at least partly—stem from more valid measurement.

The correlation between cognitive congruence and few information pathologies as a proxy for the growth of knowledge is linear and low (+.27***) in the individual model and even insignificant (+.20 n.s.) in the group model, a result that has been already attributed in the last section to the lack of the knowledge potential component; that is, the test of this hypothesis is inconclusive. The results with the other two components of congruence confirm the theoretical expectations: The growth of knowledge is positively correlated with affective congruence or sympathy (+.34***) and even stronger with conative congruence or cooperativeness (+.44***). On the group level the values are a bit lower (+.29* and +.39**). It may be speculated that groups are not as vulnerable to incongruence and the resulting information pathologies, because it is unlikely that all dyadic relationships are incongruent (statistically the averaging procedure reduces the respective variances). The assumed consistency effects between the three components of congruence should produce high correlations between them, which is, in fact, the case, as can be seen from the left side of Fig. 5.3. Because affective and conative congruence were measured in the same way with polar terms in the semantic differential format, their intercorrelation (+.85***) may be a bit overestimated. The measurement of cognitive congruence used a

---

[8]Here a dichotomous classification is used differentiating between successful and unsuccessful innovations as the measure of effectiveness. It is not only based on the averaged subjective estimates of the main participants but also on statistical business reports for the product innovations, on the case reports about the functioning of the process innovations, and for both on the final management judgment.

quite different format and was somewhat indirect in asking for similarities in education and opinions; therefore, its correlations with affective (+.51***) and conative (+.54***) congruence may be a bit underestimated. (Because consistency effects are strictly individual events, it is meaningless to look at the same correlations on the group level.)

The assumed strong negative effect of power exertion on the growth of knowledge, measured by a low rate of information pathologies, is mirrored in a high empirical correlation (−.52***), which is a clear-cut corroboration of the most important assumption of the model. On the group level, the related correlation is somewhat lower (−.38*), nevertheless supporting the hypothesis. Again, the negative effect in some dyadic relations may be ameliorated in groups by some other dyadic relationships with less power exertion. Conative incongruence (uncooperativeness) is assumed to be an important cause of power exertion; affective incongruence (antipathy) is seen as an important consequence of power exertion. Via consistency effects between affective and conative congruence, cause and consequence should reinforce each other: The obtained high correlations between power exertion and conative congruence (−.67***) as well as affective congruence (−.57***) are in accordance with these causal assumptions. They further elucidate the key role of power exertion in the deterioration of interpersonal relations *and* its direct and indirect negative effects on the growth of knowledge. Even on the group level the respective correlations (−.47**; −.47**) are relatively high, as can be seen from comparison with the other correlations in Fig. 5.4.

The last, but not least important, results to report are the determinants of the action capability: Coordination is easy if conative congruence is high, which is corroborated by the remarkable correlation of +.48*** (the same correlation was obtained for the group level). Though power exertion seemed to be an appropriate alternative to secure the action capability, the correlation is negative (−.42***). Because conative congruence with its negative correlation with power exertion and its positive correlation with action capability may have overlaid the direct causal effect from power exertion onto the action capability, a partial correlation was computed holding conative congruence constant. The partial correlation was substantially lower and not significant (−.15, n.s.) but tended, nevertheless, to the negative side; that means that power exertion is generally not a good means to raise the action capability, even if folks and, especially, some managers think so. A further analysis showed that the overall negative association could be separated into a positive correlation (+.20*) for low to median values of the action capability and a slight negative correlation (−.15, n.s.) for high values.[9] This result led to a theoretical correction of the model, which is already included in Fig. 5.1 and has been described in the section Theoretical Postulates and Derivations: Power

---

[9]If the frequently chosen median value would have been included into the higher part of the action capability, the negative correlation would have been higher than the original whole-range correlation.

exertion can only raise the action capability from very low to medium values, thus it may have an emergency function to secure some minimum action capability needed for coordinate collective action.

CONCLUDING REMARKS

The empirical results in the field of innovation teams in organizations are encouraging in that they mainly support the theoretical model. It seems to be very promising not only for group research but also as an integrative model for some core aspects of social interaction at different system levels. Of course, much more research is needed in order to test and refine the presented theory of effective social interaction, specifically as follows:

• Especially needed are experimental tests of the consistency dynamics among cognitive, affective, and conative congruence and their effects on the growth of knowledge; most important for that test is the independent manipulation of at least three levels of cognitive congruence crossed with at least two levels of conative congruence. This shall be done in the next project.

• Further tests in the field are also necessary with improved measurement quality and more exogenous prediction variables in order to be able to compute and test an overidentified nonrecursive path model.

• Very valuable refinements are possible with detailed interaction process studies though they are extremely expensive.

• Additional tests and theoretical refinements are worthwhile for most of the single hypotheses of the model. The causes and consequences of power exertion (in the here more narrowly defined sense) especially could be fruitfully further explored as our results show (Buschmeier, 1995; Scholl & Willinghöfer, 1993).

REFERENCES

Argyle, M. (1975). *Bodily communication*. London: Methuen.
Argyle, M. (1992). Soziale Beziehungen. In W. Stroebe, M. Hewstone, J.-P. Codol, & G. M. Stephenson (Eds.), *Sozialpsychologie—Eine Einführung* (pp. 232–257). Berlin: Springer.
Beckmann, J., & Irle, M. (1985). Dissonance and action control. In J. Kuhl & J. Beckmann (Eds.), *Action control: From cognition to behavior* (pp. 129–150). Berlin, Heidelberg, New York: Springer.
Berger, P. L., & Luckmann, T. (1966). *The social construction of reality*. Garden City, NY: Doubleday.
Birbaumer, N. (1983). Emotionstheorien—Psychophysiologische Ansätze. In H. A. Euler & H. Mandl (Eds.), *Emotionspsychologie. Ein Handbuch in Schlüsselbegriffen* (pp. 45–52). München, Germany: Urban & Schwarzenberg.
Blalock, H. M. (1969). *Theory construction. From verbal to mathematical formulations*. Englewood Cliffs, NJ: Prentice-Hall.
Blalock, H. M. (Ed.). (1971). *Causal models in the social sciences*. Chicago: Aldine-Atherton.
Brehm, J. W. (1966). *A theory of psychological reactance*. New York: Academic Press.

Brockner, J., Houser, R., Birnbach, G., Lloyd, K., Deitcher, J., Nathanson, S., & Rubin, J. Z. (1986). Escalation of commitment to an ineffective course of action: The effect of feedback having negative implications for self-identity. *Administrative Science Quarterly, 31,* 109–126.

Burt, C. (1915). *General and specific factors underlying the primary emotions* (Report No. 85). Presented at the meeting of the British Association for the Advancement of Science, Manchester, England.

Buschmeier, U. (1995). *Macht und Einfluß in Organisationen.* Göttingen, Germany: Cuvillier.

Cartwright, D. (1959). A field theoretical conception of power. In D. Cartwright (Ed.), *Studies in social power* (pp. 1–47). Ann Arbor: University of Michigan Press.

Cheney, D. L., & Seyfarth, R. M. (1990). *How monkeys see the world.* Chicago: University of Chicago Press.

Davis, J. H. (1973). Group decision and social interaction: A theory of social decision schemes. *Psychological Review, 80,* 97–125.

Driver, M. J., & Streufert, S. (1969). Integrative complexity: An approach to individuals and groups as information-processing systems. *Administrative Science Quarterly, 14,* 272–285.

Etzioni, A. (1968). *The active society. A theory of societal and political processes.* New York: The Free Press.

Farr, R. M., & Moscovici, S. (Eds.). (1984). *Social representations.* Cambridge, England: Cambridge University Press.

Festinger, L. (1954). A theory of social comparison processes. *Human Relations, 7,* 117–140.

Festinger, L. (1957). *A theory of cognitive dissonance.* Stanford, CA: Stanford University Press.

Fisch, R., Daniel, H. D., & Beck, D. (1991). Kleingruppenforschung—Forschungsschwerpunkte und Forschungstrends. *Gruppendynamik, 21,* 237–261.

Fishbein, M., & Ajzen, I. (1975). *Belief, attitude, intention and behavior.* Reading, MA: Addison-Wesley.

Fisher, R., & Ury, W. (1984). *Das Harvard-Konzept. Sachgerecht verhandeln—erfolgreich verhandeln.* Frankfurt: Campus. (Original title: Getting to yes)

Foa, U. G. (1961). Convergences in the analysis of the structure of interpersonal behavior. *Psychological Review, 68,* 341–353.

Fodor, E. M., & Smith, T. (1982). The power motive as an influence on group decision making. *Journal of Personality and Social Psychology, 42,* 178–185.

Hackman, J. R. (1987). The design of work teams. In J. W. Lorsch (Ed.), *Handbook of organizational behavior* (pp. 315–342). Englewood Cliffs, NJ: Prentice-Hall.

Hackman, J. R., & Morris, C. G. (1975). Group tasks, group interaction process, and group performance effectiveness: A review and a proposed integration. In L. Berkowitz (Ed.), *Advances in experimental social psychology* (Vol. 8, pp. 45–99). New York: Academic Press.

Hall, J. (1971, May, June). Decisions, decisions, decisions. *Psychology Today,* pp. 51–54 resp. pp. 86–88.

Heider, F. (1958). *The psychology of interpersonal relations.* New York: Wiley.

Higgins, E. T. (1981). The "communication game": Implications for social cognition and persuasion. In E. T. Higgins, C. Herman, & M. Zanna (Eds.), *Social cognition: The Ontario Symposium* (Vol. I, pp. 343–392). Hillsdale, NJ: Lawrence Erlbaum Associates.

Insko, C. A., & Schopler, J. (1967). Triadic consistency: A statement of affective-cognitive-conative consistency. *Psychological Review, 74,* 361–376.

Janis, I. L. (1972). *Victims of groupthink: A psychological study of foreign policy decisions and fiascoes.* Boston: Houghton Mifflin.

Johnson, D. W., Maruyama, G., Johnson, R. T., Nelson, D., & Skon, S. (1981). Effects of cooperative, competitive, and individualistic goal structures on achievement: A meta-analysis. *Psychological Bulletin, 89,* 47–62.

Kiessler, K., & Scholl, W. (1976). *Partizipation und Macht in aufgabenorientierten Gruppen—Ein Feldexperiment zur Therie der organisatorischen Bedingtheit von Gruppenprozessen.* Frankfurt, Germany: Haag & Herchen.

Kipnis, D. (1976). *The powerholders.* Chicago: University of Chicago Press.

Kirsch, W. (1976). *Organisationale Führungssysteme.* München, Germany: Planungs- und Organisationswissenschaftliche Schriften.

Lonner, W. J. (1980). The search for psychological universals. In H. C. Triandis & W. W. Lambert (Eds.), *Handbook of cross-cultural psychology* (Vol. 1, pp. 143–204). Boston: Allyn & Bacon.

Maier, N. R. F. (1967). Assets and liabilities in group problem solving. *Psychological Review, 74,* 239–249.

Miller, K. I., & Monge, P. R. (1986). Participation, satisfaction, and productivity: A meta-analytic review. *Academy of Management Journal, 29,* 727–753.

Osgood, C. E., May, W. H., & Miron, M. S. (1975). *Cross-cultural universals of affective meaning.* Urbana: University of Illinois Press.

Partridge, P. (1963). Some notes on the concept of power. *Political Studies, 11,* 107–125.

Pelz, J., & Scholl, W. (1990). *Entwicklung eines Verfahrens zur Messung von Sympathie, Einwirkung, Macht-Einfluss-Differenzierung und Interesse. SEMI.* Universität Göttingen: IWSP-Bericht 17.

Piaget, J. (1976). Piaget's theory. In B. Inhelder & H. H. Chipman (Eds.), *Piaget and his school* (pp. 11–23). New York: Springer.

Plutchik, R. (1980). *Emotion: A psycho-evolutionary synthesis.* New York: Harper & Row.

Scholl, W. (1990). Die Produktion von Wissen zur Bewältigung komplexer organisatorischer Situationen. In R. Fisch & M. Boos (Eds.), *Vom Umgang mit Komplexität in Organisationen* (pp. 107–128). Konstanz, Germany: Universitätsverlag.

Scholl, W. (1991). *Soziale Interaktion: Ein interdisziplinärer Bezugsrahmen* (2., verb. Aufl.). Universität Göttingen: IWSP-Bericht 20.

Scholl, W. (1992). The social production of knowledge. In M. von Cranach, W. Doise, & G. Mugny (Eds.), *Social representations and the social bases of knowledge* (pp. 37–42). Bern, Switzerland: Huber.

Scholl, W., Hoffmann, L., & Gierschner, H. C. (1993). *Innovation und Information. Wie in Unternehmen neues Wissen produziert wird.* DFG-Abschlußbericht (Mimeo). Berlin: Humboldt Universität.

Scholl, W., & Willinghöfer, U. (1993). *Macht und Einfluß als Formen sozialer Einwirkung: Eine theoretische und empirische Analyse.* Unpublished manuscript, Humboldt Universität, Berlin, Germany.

Simon, H. A. (1957). *Models of man.* New York: Wiley.

Smith, K. A., Petersen, R. P., Johnson, D. W., & Johnson, R. T. (1986). The effects of controversy and concurrence seeking on effective decision making. *The Journal of Social Psychology, 126,* 237–248.

Steiner, I. D. (1972). *Group process and productivity.* New York, London: Academic Press.

Steiner, I. D. (1986). Paradigms and groups. In L. Berkowitz (Ed.), *Advances in experimental social psychology* (Vol. 19, pp. 251–289). New York: Academic Press.

Torrance, E. P. (1955). Some consequences of power differences on decision making in permanent and temporary 3-man groups. In A. P. Hare, E. F. Borgatta, & R. F. Bales (Eds.), *Small groups, studies in social interaction* (pp. 482–491). New York: Knopf.

Traxel, W., & Heide, H. (1961). Dimensionen der Gefühle. Das Problem der Klassifikationen der Gefühle und die Möglichkeit seiner empirischen Lösung. *Psychologische Forschung, 26,* 179–204.

Wilensky, H. L. (1967). *Organizational intelligence.* New York: Basic Books.

6

TOWARD A THEORY OF
THE ACTING GROUP

Mario von Cranach
University of Berne

Human institutions exist primarily for the purpose of executing plans that their members, as individuals, would be unable or unwilling to execute. When the plans that form their raison d'être *are taken away—finished, frustrated, outlawed, outgrown, completed, whatever—the group may disband.*

(G. A. Miller, Galanter, & Pribram, 1960)

ABOUT THIS CHAPTER

Many different viewpoints must be brought together to build a comprehensive and realistic—or realistic because comprehensive—group theory. On the other hand, some options may be incompatible so that we have to make a choice between them. Both of these aims—integration and selection—call for a statement of the underlying *Weltbild*. As far as groups are concerned, my own theory is based on these preassumptions: that human groups are highly developed living systems, that they exist in the context of other social systems and of environments, that they exist largely through their own activity, and that they are involved in constant development, so that their present state must be explained from their history. Thus the basis of our theorizing are systems theory, action theory, and the spare beginnings of what might be a theory of social coevolution. In order to bring these preassumptions to a point, I have formulated three principles, both as theoretical baselines and as heuristic signposts for empirical research. The *principle of multilevel organization* states that human affairs tend to be simultaneously organized on many levels, the individual level and several social levels. The *principle of self-activity* says that human individuals and social systems act on their own, on the basis of internal energy and internally stored information, although of course in interaction with their environment. The *principle of historicity* states that important human affairs, including individual and social structures, processes, and future development, can only be understood in the context of their historical embeddedness; the present and the future are understood from the past. The meaning of these statements becomes more clear in the course of my presentation.

My statements are material for what we call a "frame theory": a rather wide frame for a variety of more specific theories that would otherwise lack connection. (A frame theory should show how different theories, concepts, and findings fit together, what is their meaning in a larger context, and what is still missing.) In preparing this chapter, I have restricted my discussion to theoretical viewpoints.

My chapter consists of four main parts. The first part is directed at the question: What is a group? Here I propose somewhat of a definition and describe the properties of groups that are most important for this theory. In the second part, I concentrate on the core of my theory, the organization of group action. Here I need to take a look at ongoing developments of the theory of individual action, which are essential for our enterprise. In the third part, I outline some of the relationships between group action, group structure, and group process. In the fourth part, I illustrate the usefulness of my theory as a frame for other research and theories.

The more central notions I formulate as theses. Some of these may sound trivial, but I have experienced that they have very nontrivial consequences if taken seriously. Let me point out my indebtedness to a large literature in various disciplines, which I cannot mention specifically. None of my ideas is really new. All of them have been stated in one or many places, although there may be some novelty in their combination and application. I also owe much to my students and coworkers, above all to Guy Ochsenbein and Franziska Tschan Semmer.

WHAT IS A GROUP?

Let me begin with a statement.

I. Definition of Groups

The term *group* refers to a particular class of small social systems with specific properties.

This (rather parsimonious) definition has a number of implications. As a social *system*, the group shares a number of properties with other living systems: structure, process, function, matter, energy, information, boundary, instability,

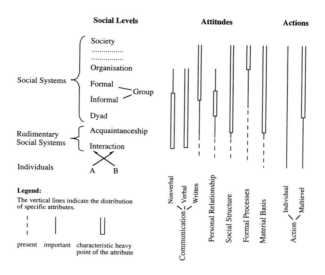

FIG. 6.1. Human self-active systems: A classification of levels (vertical lines indicate qualitative characteristics).

self-activity, self-reference, and development, to name just a few (e.g., Jantsch, 1979; J. G. Miller, 1978). For a *social* system, synergy and interaction must be added. All of this is discussed in a large literature, and the theory of systems is still developing rapidly. It is also implied that there are other classes of social systems, of which groups are one, and that these classes have their own specific properties. Therefore, a group is seen as different from a dyad or an organization, and so on (see Fig. 6.1). If this is accepted, we can no longer lend the name of group to all kinds of human aggregations as is often done in the social sciences.

Furthermore, the definition contains the assumption of super- and subsystems' relationships, which is elaborated in Thesis 3.

Finally, the term *small* in the definition is important; it is related to number, but not in an unequivocal way. A constituent characteristic of groups is personal relationship (Fig. 6.1), which delimits the size but is not restricted to "face-to-face" contact.

Within the broad class of groups, there are, however, many different types.

2. Group Types

Group types differ in their characteristics and external relationships.

Of course, there are many group typologies in the literature (e.g., McGrath, 1984). Which one we prefer depends on our research goals. But it is essential that relevant differences not be neglected in theory and research practice. (Thus, the findings from an experimental ad hoc group cannot be applied to the family without thorough justifications.) Argyle's (1969) observation—"Recent books have overlooked the obvious but extremely important differences between these different kinds of groups" (p. 240)—is to an extent still true.

3. The Importance of Supersystems and Subsystems

Groups are normally embedded into larger social systems, and they consist of smaller units and individuals. These super- and subsystems can have very different characteristics, and the groups' relationships with them can be very different. These particular circumstances codetermine to a large extent the group processes and structures.

Let us begin with an example. A military platoon has a rather strict hierarchy, not because its members have so decided; it is enforced on this group by its supersystem. The platoon is embedded into a tight-knit multilevel order of supersystems—company, battalion, regiment, division, brigade or army, and so on, and the hierarchical principle acts down from the highest superunit to the individual actions, thoughts, and feelings. When we read in the footnote of a scientific article: "The subjects were marines. They had been convinced by their sergeant to volunteer for this experiment," then we know what "voluntary" means in this context. Or, to use another example, groups in organizations tend to be *formal* groups, because formalization is a characteristic of organizations. But in the business organization, the impact of the supersystem on the groups will be less pervasive than in the military, and voluntary associations (as, e.g., the Swiss Alpine Club) will still have more difficulty exercising strict control over their member groups. It is the total pattern of the supersystem–subsystem relationship that matters. On the other hand, the processes of groups tend to be much influenced by the personality characteristics of their members. That is the major reason why life can be like hell in one platoon and tolerable in another. We come back to this problem when we discuss group development.

Now, we come to a very important point:

4. Groups Are Acting Units

Groups are acting units, they act as a whole. They exist to act, and they cease to exist if they cease to act.

This is my version of G. A. Miller et al.'s (1960) notion, cited in the beginning. There are many references to group action in the social sciences, but often not as explicit as I would like for them to be. I want to emphasize three ideas: that groups act as a whole, which is more than just the action of the group members, which is why we need a "theory of the acting group." This implies the distinction of a group level from an individual level and the idea of a multilevel organization. Furthermore, the statement declares action as the reason for the groups' existence. Let me also hint to the fact that similar statements can be formulated for other kinds of social systems, for example, for the organization (v. Cranach & Tschan, 1990).

5. Levels of Group Processes

Group processes occur simultaneously on the group level and on the individual level. In many cases, processes of the social supersystem and of the group's social subsystems are also involved.

In this statement I say more about the problem of levels. The principle of multilevel organization applies to all kinds of processes, not only to actions; I illustrate this assumption with the example of knowledge or "social representations." And what I say here about groups is also true for other social systems: Individual processes are always involved; processes of other levels are important according to the given structural conditions. Thus, in the case of groups it depends on the way in which the group is embedded into a social supersystem: Is it part of an organization? And it is important how the group is structured into subunits: Does it contain dyads or coalitions? (Compare also Thesis 3.)

6. Group History

The multilevel history of groups is essential for the understanding of their functions, structures, and processes.

What is history? In our context it can be defined as the temporal aspect of the information elaboration that underlies human self-construction. This sounds as complicated as it is, and it would take another article for a more comprehensive explanation. In short, of course there are real events, which have their place and order on the arrow of physical time. On each level "history" transforms notions of these events into beliefs about the past that explain the present and form the basis of aspirations for the future, of which goals form an essential part. That is, in short, why historicity must be an important principle in an action approach.

The first idea that this statement conveys is that history is also a multilevel process. It proceeds, often with different intensity and speed, on all of the social levels that I have distinguished. Thus, a group has its own history (consider the Kennedy family), but this is also created by the history of its supersystems (the United States and its upper class) and the biographies of its individual members.

The statement further expresses the conviction that, without reference to the specific group history, its present and future cannot be completely understood—a request that is more easily formulated than translated into empirical research, as I regretfully admit.

7. Group Development

Groups develop in a process of multilevel coevolution.

Development is partly ongoing history. Therefore, this statement is a useful illustration of Thesis 6. The word *coevolution*, which I borrowed from biology, hints to the coordination of the multilevel process. Basically, it results from mutual influence, for example, through the transfer of information from one level to the next.

How can we imagine such processes? Figures 6.2a and 6.2b illustrate the case. On each level, we concentrate on two parts of the developing system, action and knowledge. Then, we can observe a kind of dialectical interplay between the two, which can be described in the sentence: Action changes knowledge, and knowledge influences action. (If this reminds you of Piaget, you are not quite wrong.) The result is developmental change. By mutual linkages between the levels, their development is coordinated into the coevolutionary process.

Theories of individual learning and development, of socialization, of social change (e.g., by minority influence), and others can be introduced into this schema, an illustration of what we mean by the term *frame theory*.

GROUP ACTION

General Characteristics and Types

I have stated that action is essential for a group's existence (Thesis 4). Let me now describe these functions in more detail.

8. Functions of Group Action

The actions of groups serve the following functions: (a) to achieve effects in the groups' environment and on its supersystems (outwardly directed function), (b) to create, maintain, and adapt its own structure and processes (inwardly directed function), (c) to fulfill the needs of their supersystems (supersystem-directed function), and (d) to fulfill the needs of its own super- and subsystems and of its individual members (subsystem-directed function).

Similar functions were noted by McGrath (1990).

This classification is rough, but useful. Outwardly—and inwardly—directed functions characterize individual action and the action of systems in general (e.g., Parsons & Shils, 1951). The importance of the outwardly directed function is obvious. It is also well known that, as an aspect of their development, groups have to work more or less constantly on their internal problems. In fact, any change in the relationship with the outer world requires an inner adaptation, and vice versa. We might go further and say that a social system that does not

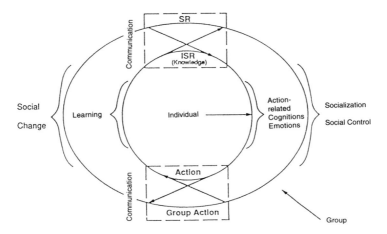

FIG. 6.2a. Nested circular processes in multilevel social coevolution. SR = social representations, ISR = individual social representations.

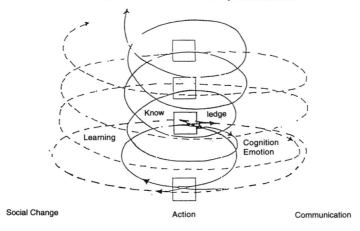

FIG. 6.2b. Coevolution of individual and group. □ = link between levels; — individual processes; --- group processes.

develop will sooner or later cease to exist. The member-directed function can also be regarded as a subfunction of the inwardly directed one, but because it is perhaps the most often cited, it merits its own name. It is sometimes over-looked that it also refers to social subsystems. The four mentioned functions are not necessarily compatible, but may contradict each other and give rise to conflicts. These can be compared to "inherent paradoxes" (Murnigham & Cou-lon, 1991; Smith & Berg, 1987) and are a source of group development.

We are approaching now the central part of this chapter: the detailed analysis of group action. Before I begin to consider this matter, let me briefly discuss a methodological question. How can we profit from similarities between actions on various levels, and where are the limits for comparison? This merits a thesis:

9. Similarities and Differences Between Actions on Different Levels

As a heuristic device it is assumed that, as far as there exist homologies and analogies, actions on different levels tend to be similar. They tend to be different insofar as their underlying structures are different.

Here we treat an example of what is called "self-similarity" in systems theory. Homology (the presence of the same underlying information) and (functional) analogy (the compared structures or processes serve the same functions) are the two conditions that produce similarity between systems (for a more profound discussion, see v. Cranach, 1976). As a heuristic for the derivation of hypotheses, we can change the direction of reasoning: Wherever we can assume homology or analogy, we can search for similarity on another level. Thus findings on the individual level can be used as a basis for hypotheses on the social one and vice versa. Similar procedures can be used in the comparison of different social levels (e.g., groups and dyads). On the other hand, groups and dyads are not the same. Where we find established differences between the structure of systems on different levels, we can expect to find other related differences in structures and processes.

Let me illustrate this heuristic by an example. Individual cognition and group communication are both means of action-related information elaboration. They are to an extent homologous (communication is based on individual cognition and vice versa) and analogous (they serve similar functions). Therefore I expect them to be similar in those areas where homology and analogy can be inferred, for example, the similarity of sequential processes in action. (Compare Thesis 17.) However, performing many actions at the same time is difficult for the individual and easy for the group: I expect differences in the frequency and organization of multiple action. More examples for this heuristic are presented later.

What is group action? Like in the case of individual action, most of us are used to thinking of a behavior that is directed toward an end goal. Goal-directed action is what I myself have been studying for some time (v. Cranach, Kalbermatten, Indermühle, & Gugler, 1982). This topic has, in fact, dominated for decades the study of individual action as well as motivation and volition. Today I should like to argue, like some critical voices have before, that this view is by far too narrow. On the group as well as on the individual level, there is a variety of long-term and short-term activities with very different characteristics. The ratiomorph goal-directed action is only one of these types, although a prominent one in our civilization.

In the following paragraphs, I propose the outline of a classification of group actions. It is based on criteria that I have taken partly from the field of individual action. However, I cannot go very much into the detail, not only for reasons of time and space but also because this is an unfinished task that I would prefer to discuss in a small circle, rather than presenting it to a distinguished readership.

First of all, there are activities in which groups can be involved over a long time span:

10. Long-Term Activities[1]

We distinguish two kinds of long-term activities of groups: (a) *Recurrent themes* refer to topics that appear again and again in the group's everyday life, and (b) *long-term projects* are directed at unitary purposes that occupy the group over extended periods. Both of these contain and organize group actions of various types.

The importance of recurrent themes, like family meals, harvesting on the farm, or high school examinations, is obvious. They serve outwardly and inwardly directed functions, which are essential for the maintenance of the group. First, they are normally the solution of a constant problem and are, therefore, of a high practical value. Furthermore, and due to their recurrent nature, they not only give structure to the flow of time, but also symbolize the stable existence of the group (the common meal expresses the cohesion of the family). Therefore, they form points of attachment for the development of rituals.

Long-term projects are equally important. Their function is—beyond the achievement of long-term practical purposes—more in progress, change, and development than in maintenance. Building a house, traveling through a foreign continent, joining a transocean race, performing an ambitious research project are outstanding events in the life of the family, the crew, or the research team, even if other voyages, regattas, or projects have been done before. The meaning of the event is in its uniqueness, and often rituals are attached to the beginning or end. (The laying of the foundation stone.)

Recurrent themes and long-term projects are, however, not totally unrelated: A theme can become a project when its routine character is disturbed, for example, by unexpected difficulties; a series of projects may become themes as the novelty wears off.

Themes as well as projects comprise and are constructed of group actions of various types. Whether they differ in this composition (e.g., more routine actions in themes, more goal-directed actions in projects) is a question for empirical research.

Let us now proceed to group actions.

---

[1]I have borrowed the term *theme* from Pulver (1991) and the term *project* from Little (1983).

11. Group Actions and Acts

Group actions are short- (and middle-) term group activities that have an identifiable object. Group actions that are socially well defined as to situation, acting group, organization, and purpose are called group acts.

Group action is considered to be a short-term activity; but there is no objective way to distinguish short and long term. The decision depends on how the group itself defines the action, and that again may depend on many factors of its life circumstances. (The experienced time span of small children or of day laborers is restricted.) Something like the "unity of time, location, and action," old criteria from the theory of drama (Lessing's famous "Hamburger Dramaturgie") may play a role. The assumption of an object (a kind of a reference point) as a defining characteristic of actions is a general point in action theories. The term *group act* has been introduced for the sake of completeness, but I cannot deal with the act-action problem (Harré & Secord, 1972) in the present chapter. Let me only mention that the definition of a specific act may be different within different systems and at different levels.

Now we are ready to turn to the problem of action types:

12. Group Action Types

According to differences in important characteristics, I make a distinction among the following types of group action: (a) primary goal directed, (b) routine goal directed, (c) trial-and-error goal directed, (d) meaning oriented, (e) process oriented, and (f) agitated group action.

This typology is not based on theory. It is more an abstraction from group actions that can be more or less often observed in daily life. Most probably there are more types. There is some analogy to the typology of individual actions about which we know a little bit more (v. Cranach, 1994a; v. Cranach, Blatter, & Gerber, 1993).

What are the characteristics of these types? Up to now I have identified the following: (a) the kind of object (concrete or abstract), (b) the purpose (achievement of results, organization of the process of action itself, or creation of social meaning), (c) the function (outwardly, inwardly, or member directed), (d) the characteristics of steering, and (e) the characteristics of energizing. There is not enough space to go into the details of these types or to describe the characteristics and their various dimensions. Let us instead consider as an example the Christmas evening of a young Swiss family: father, mother, and two small children.

The organization of the Christmas evening is a recurrent event; still as long as the children are small and the problems are new and changing, it might be considered as a *project* for the family. Most of the preparing acts that go on during the weeks, days, and hours before will be of the *goal-directed* type, either *primary* (buying presents, decorating the tree) or *routine* (cooking the meal, setting the table). We deal with the organization of goal-directed action in a later paragraph. Let us now look at the other types. The ritual of singing Christmas songs or reading from the Bible in front of the candle-lit tree are cases of *meaning-oriented actions*: Their purpose is the creation of religious meaning (though the children are glancing sidewards to the table with the presents); the object is *concrete* (performing manifest behavior) and *abstract* (producing religious ideas and feelings); the function is the reinforcement of the family bonds in the Christian community and the religious enlightenment of the members, so it is as well *outwardly as inwardly as member directed*. The steering of the action will be *role related* (family roles, but also influenced by family habits, traditions, and social representations—social control); and its energizing is based on the *supersystems actions* (Christmas time in Switzerland), but also on the emotional involvement of the family members (*relationship*). In case these people like to sing and sing well (which is rare), the singing may have a *process-oriented* component: The steering and energizing processes melt into a unitary recurrent pattern, making the action self-rewarding and self-maintaining as far as the text of the songs allows.

Let us now perform a dramaturgical intervention: The Christmas tree starts burning (we are still using candles in Switzerland). This event will cause a fast change in the action type into a *goal-directed action* (if the father is a professional fire fighter) or more probably into *agitated action*. The latter will be *result oriented* (to put out the fire), *outwardly* and *inwardly* directed (put out the fire and save the children), *steered* more or less *according to a plan* by *leadership* (somebody takes the initiative), or *self-organization*, whatever that means in this case. The *energizing* occurs by strong affect resulting in *impulsive motivation*.

Goal-Directed Action of Groups

We have published a number of articles on this topic (v. Cranach, 1990, 1992; v. Cranach, Ochsenbein, & Tschan, 1987, 1989; v. Cranach, Ochsenbein, Tschan, & Kohler, 1987; v. Cranach, Ochsenbein, & Valach, 1986; v. Cranach & Tschan, 1990; Tschan & v. Cranach, 1990) and others are in preparation. Similar ideas were proposed by Wekselberg (1992) and Larson and Christensen (1993). The following statements, which contain the essence of the theory, are based on the theses from the section Group Action, especially Theses 3, 4, and 5. Here we must also introduce the concept of the *task* as a *demand that requires an act from an agent*. Tasks are more or less *structured*: They contain information about goals, plans, and other features of the act. Depending on the extent of the specification, they also tend to be *sequentially* and *hierarchically* structured. Now I am in the position to state:

13. Group Tasks

Goal-directed action is based on tasks that the group receives from its super- or subsystems or that it poses for itself.

No further explanation seems necessary. I should, however, remind you of the group task classifications by Steiner (1972) and McGrath (1984).

The information that is normally contained in the task refers to two basic types of functions, which have to be realized in the action and its parts.

14. Steering and Energizing

Steering functions give an action its direction. Energizing functions provide the action with energy.

This distinction concerns the functions that given action-related information elaboration processes may subserve. Steering processes say where it shall go, energizing processes influence the energy that makes the system move. (Energy, as far as action is concerned, is a physiological concept on the individual level; energizing processes are individual information elaboration—e.g., a "resolve"— or group communication—e.g., a "command.") Both are relevant for all systems levels—in our context, both the individual and the group level.

In the psychological treatment of individual motivation and volition, both of these functions tend to be treated together without much distinction (e.g., Heckhausen, 1989). In fact, they are often simultaneously realized in the same process: for example, the idea "now it's time to get out of bed" on the individual level, or the demand "please help me to put the table over there" on the group level. But there are also cases where both functions are served separately by different action parts. Thus individuals can form goals and plans in their leisure time, almost on stock, which they execute later at the proper opportunity ("next time I go to Zürich, I shall phone Mary and arrange to have lunch with her"). On the group level there are many examples in which a "precommand" contains the steering, and an "execution command" the energizing information (the commands "ready about" and "lee-o!" in our sailing example given later). Therefore, and for the sake of conceptual clarity, let us keep the two functions apart.

Let us now turn to the structural and processual components of group action.

15. Group Action Structure

Group action is (like all goal-directed actions) sequentially and hierarchically organized. Its particular group character results from the projection of the task structure on the group structure.

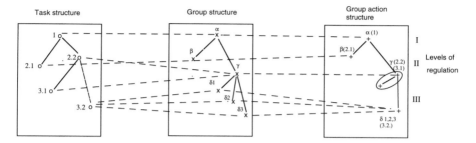

FIG. 6.3. The (logical) group action structure as a combination of task structure and group structure. Arabic numbers refer to the logical task structure. Greek letters refer to the hierarchically organized role structure of the group. Both are combined in the "group action structure" with its "levels of regulation" (Roman numbers). (Note that γ performs task from two levels.)

This statement deals with the logical structure of group action, something like a blueprint of the act. (See Fig. 6.3.) First, I say that the sequential-hierarchical structure of individual goal-directed action is also characteristic for group action: It reflects the basic properties of a control structure.[2] But the structure of group action is more: The division of subtasks (task 1 with the subtasks 2.1 and 2.2, the latter consisting of 3.1 and 3.2) is now transformed into a social division of work (α has to do 1, β has to do 2.1, γ has to do 2.2 and also 3.1, etc.). To give an example from sailing: The skipper of the yacht (α) is responsible for the general decisions about the ship's course and maneuvers (1); he uses information about the ship's position and the direction of the harbor (2.1) from the navigator (β), a "staff" position. If he decides to turn (1), he may leave the execution of the maneuver (2.2) to the helmsman (γ) who coordinates the operations of the rudder (3.1), which he does himself, and of the sails (3.2) by crew members (δ 1–3).

But who does the "projection"; who assigns tasks to positions? In case the group is already structured, the assignment will follow the existing role prescriptions and hierarchies. In case of uncertainty, task assignment is an important function of leadership. If no structure should exist (which is only probable in new groups), the group structure is created in view of the task structure. Finally, if the task structure does not fit the existing group structure and the task cannot be rejected and is important, a new or second group structure is likely to be created. Or, in case of emergency, the group structure may be simplified in order to allow fast and efficient action. These considerations are, of course, points of departure for the formation of hypotheses.

---

[2]The model of sequential-hierarchical organization goes back to systems logic (e.g., G. A. Miller et al., 1960) and has been explicitly used in most treatments of action problems (e.g., Carver & Scheier, 1981; Gallistel, 1980; Powers, 1973). In the psychology of work it has become a leading principle (Hacker, 1978, 1986; Volpert, 1982). For reasons of space, we cannot represent this well-known model in detail.

These assumptions have important consequences. For example, because groups have different structures, their group action structures will also be different. Consider the case of group goals: Many textbooks repeat that a group goal is a goal shared by its members. From our viewpoint, that statement is misleading: Instead, a group goal has to be represented in the position that is appropriate according to the group structure. (In case of an excursion of a friendship group or voluntary organization, everybody will know where it goes, and also everybody wants it. But in the military unit, only the officer may know where they march, and often even he doesn't know why.)

16. Two-Level Processes of Group Action

The processes of group action, information-elaboration and execution, are based on the group action structure. Both run off at least at two levels. The levels of information elaboration are individual cognition and emotion, and intragroup communication. The processes of execution are individual actions, and their coordination in cooperation.

This thesis is, first, a consequence of the general action principle: Action-related information-elaboration processes steer and energize action. Second, it is an application of the idea of multilevel organization to the problem of group action. The individual components, cognition and individual action, are only meaningful in the context of the group processes. The simple example of the turn of the sailing yacht illustrates these processes (Fig. 6.4). The navigator calculates the ship's

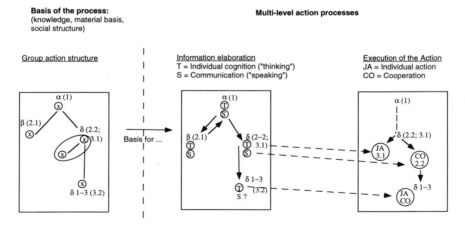

FIG. 6.4.   The multi(two)level group action process. On the basis of the group action structure (see Fig. 6.3) group action proceeds through multi- or two level information elaboration, which steers multi(two)level execution of the act. Note that in our example α (1) is not involved in the execution.

position and the new course and announces it to the skipper. The skipper considers the situation, before he orders the new course to the helmsman. The helmsman considers the speed of the yacht and other factors and gives the appropriate commands to the crew members; he operates the rudder appropriately and in coordination with the shift of the sails, and so forth. (More elaborate examples can be found in v. Cranach et al., 1986; Hacker, 1986; Tschan, in preparation.)

17. Sequential Order of Action-Steering Information

As a heuristic it is assumed that the components of group action—steering on the various levels—serve different steering subfunctions. These are situational orientation, goal determination, choice of plans, starting the execution, control of execution, stopping the action, end evaluation, and consumption of the results. In extended actions they tend to run off in recurrent loops. Their detailed organization depends on the task and group structure, the situation, and other factors.

This is a heuristic proposition and only in the second line a statement of facts. But the phenomenon has been described in political science (Snyder, Ruck, & Sapin, 1962), regarding individual action (Thommen, Ammann, & v. Cranach, 1988; Tomaszewski, 1978) and problem solving (Dörner, 1989). It has been empirically investigated (Tschan, 1995) and it also seems to correspond to a social representation in our culture (ongoing research). I propose that it applies to all levels of group action. The special circumstances of regularity are, however, hardly known, and the empirical investigation is difficult because of unclear units and functions, superimpositions, double-functions, omissions, and so on.

Another important feature of group information processes is their openness.

18. Degree of Openness of Group Communication

Group communication can be more open or covered. Its *degree of openness* is related to the perceived difficulty of the task or its execution, to the necessity of transfer of action-related information between group members, and to conflicting individual action-related cognitions and emotions.

First, I propose that communication varies along a dimension of openness. In earlier articles we have distinguished between four classes that are similar (see Thesis 9) to a division of individual action-related cognitions (Table 6.1) that we have theoretically and empirically investigated (v. Cranach, 1983; v. Cranach & Ochsenbein, 1985; Ochsenbein, 1989; Ochsenbein, v. Cranach, & Tschan, in preparation). Furthermore, the thesis maintains that the degree of openness is of functional importance. Primary goal-directed action demands full communication, whereas in the routine case information will be merely indicated or even not communicated. Empirical hypotheses derived from this assumption have been tested. Of course, openness is also related to structural circumstances (e.g., the group's relationship structure).

TABLE 6.1
Degrees of Conscious Representation and of Communication in Analogy

The Individual: Degrees of Conscious Representation (v. Cranach, 1983)	*The Group: Degrees of Communicability of Individual Cognitions and Emotions*
1. Fully conscious: The individual is aware and can report about. Problems are accessible to rational and voluntary control and meta-cognitive elaboration.	1. Fully communicated: Open to group discussion and problem solving, distribution of action-related cognitions, flexibility, creative solution of internal problems.
2. Subconscious cognitions at the fringe of consciousness, which can easily become fully conscious. Useful in the context of routine	2. Hardly mentioned cognitions which are only indicated, which seem unproblematic: Can be fully discussed, if the need arises. Mostly routine problems.
3. Non-conscious cognitive and emotional processes, which are not represented, but can become so under specific conditions. Higher order planning and meta-cognitions impossible. Fast and efficient lower level acting.	3. Not communicated: Cognitive and emotional processes which are not communicated, but processed by individuals according to group structure. Fast and efficient outward directed adaptation, little inward directed adaptation, little flexibility, if higher levels of information-processing are required.
4. Unconscious cognitions and emotions which are repressed according to psychoanalytic defense processes and hardly accessible. Under no cognitive and voluntary control, fractionated, no meta-cognitions, lead to neurotic behavior.	4. Uncommunicable (unspeakable): Problems under taboo; which sometimes bother all or many group members, are eventually secretly discussed in subgroups. Leading to neurotic group structure and in the end unefficient group action.

The case of the taboo is special and merits its own thesis.

19. Communication Taboo[3]

The group communication of information that seems to endanger the group, its structure, or features that are important to it, can be explicitly or implicitly forbidden. The elaboration of this information on other levels remains possible. Under short-term perspectives, a taboo protects the group. In the long run, it inhibits the improvement of deficient aspects and, thus, the group's development. Taboos tend to spread to other topics.

Let me illustrate this thesis by a commonplace example. Father drinks too much and misbehaves when this is mentioned. Therefore, there is silent agreement not to touch the topic in his presence (when the whole family is gathering). That does not hinder the other family members from thinking about it or even from referring to the matter in dyadic encounters. Thus, father's authority is publicly maintained, although silently doubted, and scenes that are frightening to all are

---

[3]This thesis is based on the research of Guy Ochsenbein (Ochsenbein & Schaerer, 1994).

prevented. On the other hand, father cannot receive support in his fights against the drug. If, in consequence of his drinking, his professional situation is also deteriorating, this will be another forbidden topic. The situation becomes worse, family members think about leaving, and the family may sooner or later dissolve. Note that communication taboos tend to be restricted to one or certain levels, and that they do not prevent information processing, action, and development on other levels (in view of his father's weakness, the oldest son develops a strong sense of responsibility); that everybody may be interested in maintaining the taboo; and that it can be protective in the short term and only harmful in the long term. The situation becomes really dangerous when the group adopts the general rule and strategy to regulate its problems by taboos.

These are some of the problems of action steering. Let us now turn to energizing.

20. Group Action Energizing

The group elicits, maintains, or inhibits individual energizing processes through the exertion of social influence or power. Direct energizing social influence is exerted through action-related verbal or nonverbal communication. Mutual direct influence between group members can result in positive or negative feedback processes. Indirect energizing social influence results from the group's relationship structure. Direct energizing power is exercised through commands and directives. Indirect energizing power is exercised through group norms; this can also occur in coordination with the group's environment.

As already stated in Thesis 14, I consider energizing as a primarily individual affair. The group codetermines the process in various ways. I have distinguished between influence and power. Influence is conceived as a persuasive communication that considers the interests or values of the target person and does not contain coercion; in contrast, power is based on the threat of sanctions, and the required action can be against the interest of the actor (see chapter 5 of this volume).

Furthermore, I have distinguished between direct and indirect forms. Direct influence consists of admonition, demands, and encouragement; indirect influence of the effect of examples and in processes that have been studied under the title of social facilitation, inhibition, loafing, and so forth. The relationship structure of the group and the so-called group atmosphere seem to have a considerable energizing effect. An example of negative feedback in direct influence is the control of individual effort in groups of industrial workers.

The effects of direct power are obvious. Indirect power through norm systems is often combined with constraints from the group structure (sometimes referred to as "structural violence") and with enforcement from the socially constructed features of the material environment (e.g., the combination of direct power, structural power, and environmental forces that seems to reign on board navy ships).

Let us finish this with the consideration of knowledge.

21. Group Action-Related Knowledge
and Group Memory

Knowledge is processed (stored, encoded, elaborated, decoded) on the group and on the individual level (social and individual social representations). Its primary function (besides others) is the organization of action. A multilevel knowledge presupposes a multilevel memory.

This statement is based on the general relationship between knowledge and action: Action is steered through knowledge, and knowledge is changed through action (Thesis 7). This is the point where the theories of group action and of social representations come together (v. Cranach, 1992, 1994b; Thommen, v. Cranach, & Ammann, 1992). Socially shared knowledge concerns as well specific actions—for example, goals—as also general principles of functioning of a given group. Social representations (Farr & Moscovici, 1984) are knowledge on a social level; if transferred to the individual level ("individual social representations"; Thommen et al., 1988), they are part of the individual knowledge. The notion of group knowledge presupposes a group memory. Here Wegner's (1986) theory of "trans-active memory" can serve as a point of departure. An important hypothesis in this context concerns the fact that the information–elaboration characteristics of a system influence its knowledge processes and hence contents. Knowledge plays an important role in group action (e.g., shared goal representations) and in development (Thesis 7). Self-referent knowledge ("group beliefs"; Bar-Tal, 1990) is of particular importance and constitutes an analogue to the individual self-concept.

GROUP ACTION: ITS RELATION TO GROUP
STRUCTURE AND PROCESSES

I consider group action a key to the understanding of group phenomena in general. Thus, it is also one of the important determinants of group structure. Let us first draw a more complete picture.

22. Determinants of Group Structure

Group structure results from the interaction of the structure of the task, the impact of the supersystem, the characteristics of members, the existing "traditions," the history of the group, and the constraints of the environment.

This is only an enumeration of factors; their relative importance is different in different cases. They interact in a complex way. These processes are partly of a circular nature, as in our model of development (Figs. 6.2a and 6.2b). Let me take an example from my teaching to illustrate their interaction. Many of my students will become psychology teachers in professional institutions. In a course on "teaching psychology to nonpsychologists," I aimed to give them more insight into the problems of construction and improvement of curricula. As is normal in our department, this was done in form of a seminar; I gave the students the task "to construct a psychology curriculum" (*impact of the supersystem*). The whole course had to fit into the spatial and temporal reality of our department. Some students choose the "nursing school" as an example. Very soon they found out that a curriculum is based on educational goals and choice of content, which must depend, in the given case, on the professional requirements of nursing. Furthermore, the instruction in psychology must fit into the nursing school curriculum in general. Thus, the *structure of the task* slowly emerged. The students then formed subgroups to study these various aspects; the results were coordinated in plenary sessions (*group structure*). It turned out that several of the students had a background as teachers or students of educational science (*member characteristics*). As experts, they tended to grow into an informal *leadership role* (*group structure*). From general cultural *traditions* and experience (*group history*) they soon tended to introduce the (changing) roles of chairperson, minutes secretary (formal group structure), and so on. It should be mentioned that all this was not developed fast or smoothly, but in processes of trial, error, and conflict; but finally it was worked out.

Let me end this section with a few more abstract considerations. Supersystem and member characteristics are aspects of the multilevel organization of group events. (To the importance of member characteristics see chapter 1 of this volume.) Traditions can be considered as a specific kind of knowledge ("social representations" or "group beliefs"; see Thesis 21). And in the case of an already existing group, what matters will be the "group action structure" rather than the task structure.

After having placed group action into the context of factors that determine group structure, I am now looking at the various structural aspects that have been distinguished in the social sciences: role, hierarchy, status, leadership, power, norm, and communication. They are all somehow related to group action, and in these dynamic relationships I distinguish between the effects of structure on action and the reverse, of action on structure.

Let me begin with the concept of role. In social psychology, role has been defined as the behavior of a tenant of a position that is based on the expectations of the group (Shaw & Costanzo, 1970); similar also Jaspars and Lamb (1986). In the context of my theory, behavior is action and position is a place in the group action structure. So I arrive at the following thesis:

23. Roles

Roles depend on the task structure and are part of the group action structure. They form the basis of work division in group action.

Of course, role theory is a very broad set of concepts. Some of them can be reformulated as important parts of my theory, others are less relevant. The concept of role expectation, for example, describes an important part of the group action guiding cognitions and communications. Role conflict refers to the intraindividual conflict in regard to incompatible group actions, but this conflict tends to have its basis in the group structure or its relation to super- or subsystems. (In German factories, the "Industrie-Meister"—something like a foreman—is simultaneously a worker and part of the management; this double reference is likely to create role conflict.) These are examples of the effect of role upon action. The reverse may be seen in the increasing specialization (role development) that can be observed in groups when a new action is performed.

Let me finally hint to the fact that the group as a whole is likely to have a role in its social supersystem (e.g., Katz & Kahn, 1978).

Within group action, hierarchies are closely connected to roles, a consequence of the sequential-hierarchical structure of group action. Different roles refer to superordinate and subordinate partial tasks that differ in their relative influence on other partial tasks, in their range of discretion, in their degrees of freedom, and so on; all of these are related to hierarchical differences. Hierarchies, however, are normally not restricted to the execution of single tasks. They tend to be connected with task sets and to freeze into the enduring structures of social systems. Social hierarchies, if not strictly controlled, tend to be replicated in new actions. On the other hand, hierarchical aspects of tasks that are vital for the group tend to radiate to other tasks and to the group structure.

As a general rule, higher hierarchical positions with more access to more highly valued activities are less likely to be involved in less prestigious work and more likely to get a greater share of the group product; in short, they have a higher status (see chapters 3 and 4 of this volume). (The captain is responsible for the ship's fate in general, but usually he will not wash the dishes. And, of course, he earns more money than the cook's aid.) Thus, group action is closely related to the status order of the group, which, once established, provides stability. Summing up, we arrive at the thesis:

24. Hierarchy and Status

Hierarchy and status are derived from the whole set of long-term group activities, and related to particularly important aspects of group action. In primary group action, they influence the distribution of roles.

In another article, I discussed the relationship between group action and leadership (v. Cranach, 1986). The reader is referred to that article, but we can summarize here: Leadership, a specific role, is an indispensable function of group action, the fulfilling of specific higher order subtasks of steering (as goal determination, elaboration of plans, decision making, etc.) and of energizing (ordering, encouraging, resolving conflicts, etc.). The exercise of power (although undesirable in our culture) is sometimes necessary to grant these functions. All this does not prevent democratic forms of leadership and the social control of power. All in all:

25. Leadership and Power

Leadership is a function of group action, and power is an indispensable attribute of leadership.

Let me, however, add a few remarks about power. First, I find it remarkable that the discussion of power in social psychology refers mostly to individual power. It is not much debated that power is often located in the group as a whole (as, e.g., when "majority influence" forces an individual to act against his own interest). Second, much of the power that acts upon the group and its members comes from the social supersystem and its representatives. Thus much of the power that determines my own professional life comes from a nested set of social systems. There exists a whole cascade of power in which I have the position of a lower ranking part: The minister cuts the university budget; the loss is distributed by the faculty (of which I am a member); then by the institute's directory (of which I am a member); until I finally know how much money my chair has lost. Finally, I have to tell a coworker that he has to cut his position by about 20% in the coming year. Third, once we have understood that power is not just an individual attribute but a systemic property, many assumptions of the theories of power must be adapted to these conditions. To mention an example, the assumptions about the sources of power (e.g., French & Raven, 1959) can be adapted to the group and other social systems as well.

26. Personal Relationships

Personal relationships and group action structure and results are mutually influencing each other. Personal relationships are an object of inwardly directed group action.

This is a very important issue although it is often neglected in research on group action; it plays, however, a big role in consulting. The concept of personal relationship refers to the emotional relations between group members, the amount of their mutual liking and disliking, and how they handle their interpersonal problems. This pattern is often assessed by sociometric methods (Moreno, 1934, and the work that has been done in this context; see also Nehnevajsa, 1973). It is influenced by and should fit to the group action structure (who has to cooperate with whom). Because it codetermines communication, it can have an impact on group action steering. Observations of real working groups suggest that it may be one of the important determinants of motivation in group action (see also chapters 3 and 4 of this volume).

Because it is so important and interesting for group members, personal relationships are a target of many acts that the group directs toward its own functioning and structure (inward-directed group action).

Let us now turn to characteristics of group structures that are based on specific patterns of knowledge.

27. Conventions, Rules, and Norms

The prescriptive knowledge systems of the groups and their social supersystems— their conventions, rules, and norms—influence and control the actions of groups and their members. They can be changed by group action.

Here we are dealing with a special class of knowledge that is more or less explicitly prescriptive.

I emphasize that many (if not most) of these prescriptions are not derived by the group itself but from the group's supersystems and, finally, the society as a whole. To increase their analytic power, I propose to distinguish between three classes of concepts: The prescriptive character of *conventions* is based on common agreement. *Rules* are conventions that are value related and therefore have a morally binding character. *Norms* are rules that are explicitly reinforced by sanctions (Fig. 6.5). An example of conventions are the specific requirements of politeness in a group; of rules, the expectations of how a conflict should be resolved; of norms, the reinforced expectations of a member's contribution. Conventions are less binding than rules but may become a value in themselves by sheer habit. Rules are less binding than norms. By changes in their prescriptive character, they can be transformed: A rule that loses its value basis becomes a convention; a norm without value, an unjustified coercion. Conventions, rules, and norms are often parts of more comprehensive social representations.

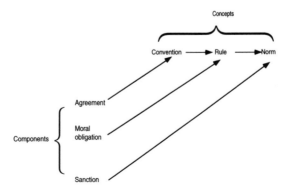

FIG. 6.5. The concepts of convention, rule, and norm and their components.

These prescriptions influence group action in several ways. They delimit the range of possible actions, they refer to possible or aspired actions, and they regulate how actions can be steered, energized, and executed. On the other hand, a spectacular action or an enduring practice may change their character and content.

These considerations should be sufficient to sustain my claim of a strong relation between group action and group structure. I refrain from the treatment of two other structural features, intragroup relationship and group cohesion, which appear to be more difficult and demand more space.

As for communication, I have already discussed it repeatedly in this chapter. Let me, therefore restrict myself to a definition:

28. Communication

Communication is information elaboration at the group level.

Clearly we cannot conceive of any important process at the group level that does not contain communication. From my definition it also follows that communication at the group level must contain communicative individual action at the individual level. Communication is the group action itself if the end goal is problem solving, for example, in some cases of decision making. Here, the act itself consists of the elaboration of information. In actions that are directed toward a concrete goal, communication serves the steering and energizing functions on the group level as I have already described it. Communication networks, as they were studied some years ago (Bavelas, 1950; Shaw, 1964) refer to an abstracted property of the group's role/hierarchy structure.

GROUP ACTION THEORY—AN INTEGRATIVE APPROACH

In a field of thousands of empirical studies based on a great number of small- and middle-range theories, integration becomes urgent. Furthermore, there is a need for a more realistic group psychology—realistic in the sense that it should refer to the real groups "out there," as it is sometimes formulated in scientific discussions. This is how I see the situation. My theory should integrate different approaches and findings by giving them a common frame, and it should help to bridge the gap between science and reality. To demonstrate that it can serve these purposes, let me apply it to important research in the field. For reasons of space, I restrict myself to selected examples, which to an extent also seem to represent different cultural tastes, but certainly different scientific aims: the study of "collective induction," which aims at a formalized small-range theory based on experimental research; the "theory of self-categorization," a middle-range theory about individuals in social systems; and the theory of minority influence, which at least in Moscovici's version generalizes from his own experimental data and a large literature and tends toward a grand societal theory.

Collective Induction in Group Decision Making

In a series of well-designed experimental studies, Laughlin and his coworkers have studied social induction in group decision making (see also Vol. I). The following discussion is based on an article by Laughlin, Vanderstoep, and Hollingshead (1991).

Let us get an overview first. Laughlin and his colleagues (1991) were interested in the problem of why groups perform better than individuals in problem solving and decision making. In addition to two more traditional explanations—namely, that groups perform better than the average individual because they recognize and adopt correct answers if proposed by at least one group member, and that they recognize and reject errors—they assumed that "groups combine member knowledge, skills, and other resources," that they "recognize patterns and relationships collectively that none of their members recognize individually," and that "they may propose correct emergent group responses that no member had previously proposed" (p. 50). In their study, Laughlin et al. compared the achievement of four-person groups in a rule induction task with the best, second-best, and so on, of four independent individuals. In 10 subsequent trials, subjects had to produce a hypothesis about the rules for a sequence of playing cards, before they had to formulate a final hypothesis. In the group situation, each individual had to propose his individual hypothesis before the group as a whole formulated a single group hypothesis. Laughlin et al. distinguished between correct, plausible, and nonplausible hypotheses. In variations of the experiment two, three, or four hypotheses could be formulated in each trial, but only one final hypothesis in the end. Laughlin et al. formulated what they called "social combination models . . . formalizations of the processes by which groups resolve disagreement among their members in proposing a collective response" (p. 52). They are based on the four basic processes of voting, turn taking, demonstration, and generation of a new emergent group response. To give an example: Model 1 combines majority, plurality, and proportionality. Several postulates predict under what conditions the groups should follow what model. Laughlin et al. were, however, "prescinding from structural differences in formal power and individual differences in ability, motivation, persuasiveness, and persuasability" (p. 52). Subjects were 768 college students in introductory psychology courses. They were randomly assigned to the various experimental conditions.

The results show that the groups perform better than the average individual, but that they need more time to fully develop their advantages. Besides recognizing truth and rejecting error, the groups seem to process, in fact, more information than the individuals, and when they have the chance to do so (developing more than one hypothesis on each trial), they perform on the level of the best individual. Furthermore, under conditions of increased disagreement (more different hypotheses proposed) the groups increased their turn taking and their production of emergent group hypotheses—most of which, however, were not correct. "Groups recognized and adopted correct hypotheses if proposed by their members, but they did not form correct emergent hypotheses that no member had previously proposed" (Laughlin et al., 1991, p. 62, which is in disagreement with the previous hypotheses).

At the end of their article, Laughlin et al. (1991) hinted at the examples of scientific research teams; of committees of connoisseurs in the estimation of authenticity of art objects; of staff groups of medical specialists in the evaluation of X rays, CAT scans, and angiographs; and of satellite recognition teams ("their collective inductions may result in war or peace," p. 62) in order to illustrate the importance of their approach.

How does this research fit into my theory of the acting group? I try to answer this question by a step-by-step comparison with our 28 theses, asking each time: How does Laughlin et al.'s (1991) study relate to this particular statement?

First, we find that Laughlin et al. (1991) in fact studied groups in the sense of Thesis 1, "informal groups" in particular (Thesis 2, see Fig. 6.1), the structures and processes of which are not regulated by formal rules. But some of the particular characteristics of this kind of social system are missing or not mentioned. (These shortcomings are a nearly unavoidable consequence of laboratory studies for which Laughlin et al. cannot be blamed.) Personal relationships in particular, which tend to form the glue that keeps informal groups together, seem to be missing. Instead, the groups' coherence is provided by their embeddedness (Thesis 3) into the organization "Department of Psychology of the University of Illinois" and the activity of one of its subsystems, namely the research unit "Laughlin et al."; and this must have consequences for the groups and their members, although nothing in particular is known. What makes these groups particularly interesting cases for us is that they are explicitly designed for the purpose of group action (Thesis 4), namely to acts of the type of problem solving (Thesis 12), and Laughlin et al. considered them explicitly to be acting units and distinguish, as the previous quotations make clear, between the individual and the group level (our "principle of multilevel organization" and Thesis 5; welcome to the club of group action theorists, dear Pat!). The groups have no real history (Theses 6 and 7) of their own, although there must be some development during the course of the experiments; but their multilevel history encompasses the biographies of their members, whose experiences as subjects or members of problem-solving groups remains unknown. Clearly the history of their supersystem "Laughlin et al." as research unit of the psychology department is a very important feature (our discussion of Thesis 13).

How are these groups' activities, namely decision making, related to group action, our next topic? Let us consider the practical examples that Laughlin et al. (1991) provided. The research teams and also the larger scientific community develop and test hypotheses in order to *integrate them in models and theories.* The committees of connoisseurs elaborate their expertises in order to *mandate withdrawal of any questionable objects.* The auditing teams lead to explanations that *enable* the *concerned authorities to meet appropriate steps.* The medical staff groups evaluate their material in order to establish a *diagnosis that guides the further treatment.* Satellite reconnaissance teams provide the material *for decisions about political actions* to be taken by cabinets and security councils. To generalize from these examples, **decisions are parts of actions, they have action consequences,** and this in two ways: A decision can stand on the beginning of action (which act to choose or whether to act at all), or they can occur during an already ongoing act (at a *node*) in order to determine the further *course of action.* Therefore, the agent does not only look backward, at the material at hand, but also forward, namely to the goal, and this goal orientation has a considerable impact upon the ongoing steering and energizing processes. This is a truism in action theory, but often ignored in decision theory because it complicates the matter. In Laughlin et al.'s experiment, there is no action context that gives the decisions their meaning, contrary to the examples used.

Second, we notice that these groups act in the context of a supersystem-directed function (Thesis 8), which is certainly not unimportant for the questions of motivation, which are discussed later. Interesting questions open up in consideration of Thesis 9. The heuristic assumption of an analogy between group communication and individual thinking might lead to the formulation of additional hypotheses about the development of social combination models. Just to give an example (the implications and feasibility of which should be more carefully reflected), let us transfer *dissonance theory* to the group level (see chapter 8 of this volume). We would expect that dissonant communications should lead to a state of tension the amount of which should increase with the importance of the subject of discussion, the number and balance of dissonant opinions, and the feeling that the group had freely chosen the problem (the impact of relative status of group members is discussed later). We do not know what importance the subjects attribute to the experiment, nor how free they feel, but we do know the balance of opinions from the distributions of votes. Because dissonance from balance in a four-member group would be maximal in a two against two situation, pressure for a solution should then be great, and because majority-plurality rules would be useless, emergent group solutions should become more probable—and even more so, if the arguments on both sides were plausible. So we could add a third one to Laughlin et al.'s (1991) two postulates: "The more balanced the opinions and the more plausible the arguments on both sides, the more likely an emergent group solution becomes." Analogous postulates could be added if the factors "importance of the task" and "experienced freedom of choice" should be varied. Of course, we are just playing with ideas now, but this little play has demonstrated the integrating possibilities that are contained in Thesis 9.

What is the meaning of Thesis 10 in relation to Laughlin et al.'s (1991) experiment? For the student subjects, participation is a part of their studies, which are a long-term project. For the researchers, the study is part of another long-term project, their research program on group decision making. On the group level, the act is not related to any superordinated activity for the students, but to a very well defined one for the group of researchers. Thus, although we do not know the subjects' viewpoints, we consider it highly probable that the study's meaning is very different for both parties, and so also their motivation, a matter of course that we should not forget.

There is not much to say in respect to Thesis 11 except that the experiment is obviously a group act for the students. What can we say about its particular type (Thesis 12)? In our typology of individual acts, we have defined the type of the *mental act* that occurs only in the mind; *problem solving* but also the *determined nonaction* are among its subtypes. Mental acts have much in common with goal-directed acts, for example, goals, plans, decisions, process and outcome control, and so forth. On the social level there is of course no mental activity, but communication instead, so that we could define the groups' activity as a *communicative act*, namely *problem solving*, to which we can apply our considerations of goal-directed group actions.

I have already stated that the groups have received their task (Thesis 13) from one of their supersystems in the form of experimental instruction. Of course, there must be steering and energizing (Thesis 14) as the constituting parts of action. How these functions are realized on the group level is elaborated in the following theses. The basis of steering is contained in the group action structure, which relates the hierarchical-sequential structure of the action to the properties of the group. Unfortunately, in the given case the groups have no structures, or else we do not know about it, so that we have to rely only on the task structure, which we do not know either. We could derive it from a task analysis (Hacker & Matern, 1980; Ulich, 1992) if we had more information. But we do not; therefore the analysis of group action as described in Theses 16 and 17, if we had the data and were willing to do it, would remain purely descriptive. Without insertion of the decision into a wider action context its structure will lack important features, as we have already pointed out. Openness of group communication (Thesis 18) is more or less provided by the experimental instruction, and the hypotheses that concern its functions cannot be applied here. It is, however, not unlikely that some of the group members feel under a communication taboo (Thesis 19) as far as the experimental situation, the task, and the person of the experimenter are concerned. In view of the short life of the groups in this experiment, this should not create dramatic consequences, but an influence on the group's action cannot be excluded.

But what are, in the given case, the group analogues to energetization (Thesis 20)? As we have discussed, energetization from a superordinate goal is excluded in this case. There are several other possibilities. First, the group is energized by the experimenter's instruction, his "legitimate" power resulting from the group's embeddedness into the university. Second, the group may develop structural features, for example, personal relationships that bind the loyalty of its members and thus influence their motivation; likewise, negative relations might decrease the individual involvement. Third, a developing leadership structure might contribute to the energizing processes by commands and demands. All of these possibilities can in principle be investigated if the corresponding data are available.

Knowledge (Thesis 21) plays a big role in our case. First, the experimenters, the subjects, and the experimental groups relate to the experiment on the basis of their knowledge about psychology departments and their requirements. Second, the results of the experiments, namely the decision strategies of the experimental groups, are most probably determined by the subjects' social representations of techniques of collective decisions. Majority and plurality are culture-bound decision criteria of Western democracies; in other cultures other criteria—for example, "seniority"—may play a comparable role. It is a very common fallacy of contemporary psychology to present their results *only* as manifestations of human nature even if they are in fact *also* products of social rules; at least, this possibility must be considered. That is why we have formulated Thesis 27.

Our statements, Theses 23–26 refer to structural features of the group, which Laughlin et al. (1991), however, explicitly excluded from this study ("*prescinding from structural differences . . .*"). That is alright in an experimental study; however, we have to expect that these are exactly the properties that are important if not decisive in real cases. Research teams, medical staff groups, and satellite reconnaissance teams are social systems with explicit role distributions and leadership, hierarchies, status and power differences, and personal relationships; and, as any of their members knows, these properties are essential for their functioning. (A collection of empirical studies is provided, e.g., by Moscovici, 1985, pp. 367–373.) To prescind from these features means to decrease the "ecological validity" of a study.

Communication (Thesis 28) finally is the detailed *process* by which the decisions are reached. The social combination models of this study "are essentially formalizations of the processes by which groups resolve disagreement" (p. 52). They "formalize the four theoretical processes of voting, turn-taking, demonstration of the correct response and generation of an emergent group response" (p. 62), as Laughlin et al. (1991) formulated it. In other words, Laughlin et al. studied communication at an already more abstract level, and with considerable success. If particular research interests should demand it, we could return to the more basic level of verbal and nonverbal communication in detail.

Asking ourselves at the end of our exercise what it has shown us, we come to the following results. Putting Laughlin et al.'s (1991) study into the context of our theory makes its character as a study of group action more explicit and opens possibilities to relate it to other theories. It shows how the experiment is embedded into a social environment,[4] and it throws some light on the consequences of neglecting both the social knowledge that forms the basis of the subjects' and groups' actions, and also essential structural features. The results of the study fit, of course, into the frame of the theory.

Self-Categorization

As a second example I now discuss the "self-categorization theory." This is a very well known theory presented by Turner (1985), Turner and Oakes (1986), and Turner, Hogg, Oakes, Reicher, and Wetherell (1987). It is based on Tajfel's "social identity" or "social categorization theory" (Tajfel, 1965, 1982) and sustained by a considerable number of empirical studies (see chapters 9 and 10 of this volume). My present discussion is based on Turner et al. (1987), especially the theoretical chapter 3, and on the article by Turner and Oakes.

Let me begin by elaborating some of the theory's general features, as a basis for the comparison with our own theory.

We consider our theory a frame theory—so did Turner et al. (1987):

> The self-categorization theory takes the form of a series of assumptions leading to hypotheses as to the basic process underlying the psychological group and elaborative hypotheses as to the antecedents and consequences of that process. The general theory of the group process forms a basis for the derivation of "intermediate" sub-theories of the main group phenomena such as attraction, co-operation and influence. . . . These sub-theories are the more detailed analyses of the particular consequences of group formation. (p. 43)

We consider our theory an overcoming of individualism—so did Turner et al.:

> It is shown that the social identity theory (theories) of group behaviour, social influence and group polarization explicitly assumes a functional interaction between psychological and social processes, in contrast to individualism. . . . It is concluded that the social identity concept represents a mechanism of social-psychological interaction and as such demonstrates that social psychology need not be an individualistic science. . . . This paper has several aims: to argue against an "individualistic" and for an interactionist metatheory of social psychology. (Turner & Oakes, 1986, p. 237)

Turner et al. also realized that social systems are phenomenal entities:

> If one thinks of some instance of real-life collective action, an army in battle, a rioting crowd, . . . the participants will often seem to act and feel in spontaneous unitary fashion. . . . They may behave with "one mind," as if in fact they were not a collection of separate individual beings but one supra-organism. . . . Furthermore,

---

[4]It is misleading to assume that experiments are artificial because they are unembedded into the social world: They are always embedded into the specific academic world and culture, but the researchers often do not see the consequences of these connections.

the fact of apparent higher order unity is not something we have to think about, but something we "see" directly.... In the real sense, we see the group as one unity. (Turner et al., 1987, p. 3)

Moreover, Turner et al. (1987) accepted that this unity is not only apparent but real: "Human social behavior ... exists *sui generis,* at its own level of reality, with its own distinctive, emergent forms ..." (p. 4). In a presentation of our theory, we used very similar examples and concluded: "... this is not only an economic way to describe the coordinated acts of individuals. On the contrary, in our mental operations, our perception, thought and memory, we use such social units" (v. Cranach, Ochsenbein, & Tschan, 1987, p. 121). And our whole approach takes it for granted that social systems exist.

So there is a certain similarity of attitude that should facilitate an integration of the two approaches. Where are the differences? First, Turner et al. (1987) seemed to hold different preassumptions of how social psychology can proceed; from these, they arrived at different goals and concepts.

The preassumption from which Turner et al. (1987) seemed to depart in their theorizing is the apparent incompatibility of the undoubted fact that "psychological processes only reside in the individual ... there is no such thing as a 'group mind' " and the reality of groups and their structures and processes. "We are caught, it seems, in a limbo between a psychology which can only be individualistic and a sociology which for precisely that reason can never be psychological, and all the time knowing or 'seeing' that in some sense the group is as psychological as the individual. The issue is how scientifically to retain the psychological reality of the group whilst rejecting both the fallacy of the group mind and the rejection of group life" (pp. 4–5). This is what they called "the master problem of social psychology," the solution of which is "the *raison d'être* of social psychology," and to which they devoted a whole historical chapter. Turner et al.'s solution is self-categorization theory, which explains the existence of the "psychological group." Here lies the basic difference between Turner et al.'s and our approach. We have tried to resolve the same problem by another means, a multilevel approach based on systems theory. (Systems theory, it seems, did not come to Turner et al.'s mind.) I try to show that this approach has some advantages: Among others, it should allow us to integrate self-categorization theory with only a few changes while retaining all of its virtues.

But let us first deal with some of the other preliminaries. What is the aim of self-categorization theory? Turner et al. (1987) took care to distinguish it from its predecessor, social identity theory, and stated: "The current theory ... is focused on the explanation not of a specific kind of group behaviour but of how individuals are able to act as a group at all" (p. 43). And Turner and Oakes (1986) explained: "The self-categorization theory explains group phenomena in terms of the structure and functioning of the social self-concept (the system of cognitive representations of self based upon comparison with other people and relevant to social interaction)" (p. 241). This explanation is preceded by an explanation of the authors' "interactionist" meta-theory (p. 239). It is important to note that the theory is restricted to the object they called "the psychological group." It

> is defined as one that is psychologically significant for the members, to which they relate themselves subjectively for social comparison and the acquisition of norms and values (i.e. with which they compare to evaluate themselves, their abilities, performances, opinions, etc., and from which they take their rules, standards and beliefs about appropriate conduct and attitudes), that they privately accept membership in, and which influences their attitudes and behaviour. In the usual terminology, it is a (positive) *reference* group and not merely a *membership* group as defined by outsiders, i.e., it is not simply a group which one is objectively *in*, but one which is subjectively important in determining one's actions. (Turner et al., 1987, pp. 1-2)

Turner and Oakes (1986) gave a useful summary of their theory, the citation of which finishes this survey:

> Cognitive representations of the self take the form (*inter alia*) of "self-categorizations": a self-categorization is a cognitive grouping of the self as identical (similar, equivalent, interchangeable) to some class of stimuli in contrast to some other class of stimuli. . . . In the social self-concept there are three important levels of abstraction: self-categorization as a human being (the superordinate category) based on differentiations between species, in-group-out-group categorizations (the self as a social category) based on differentiations between groups of people (class, race, nationality, occupation, etc.) and personal self-categorizations (the subordinate level) based on differentiations between oneself as a unique individual and other (relevant) in-group members. There is a functional antagonism between the different levels of self-categorization in terms of their "salience" (the degree to which they are functionally pre-potent in determining self-perception) in any given situation. Self-categories form on the basis of appropriately perceived intra-category similarities and inter-category differences, and also accentuate such similarities and differences as they become salient (Tajfel, 1969). The effect of the salience of one level of self-categorization, therefore, is to minimize the intergroup similarities and intragroup differences which provide the perceptual basis of more superordinate and subordinate levels respectively. . . . It is hypothesized from the above ideas (ignoring for simplicity the human level of self-categorization) that there tends to be an inverse relationship between the salience of in-group-out-group and personal self-categorizations such that self-perception varies along a continuum depicted at one pole by the perception of oneself as a unique person (different from in-group members) and at the other pole by perception of the self as the in-group (identical to other in-group members and maximally different from out-group members). It can be assumed that most of the time people perceive themselves as moderately similar to in-group members perceived as moderately different from out-group members, i.e. that both the in-group-out-group and the personal level of self-categorization are salient to some (inverse) degree. Factors which increase the salience of in-group-out-group categorizations enhance the perceived identity (similarity, equivalence, interchangeability, etc.) between self and in-group members on the stereotypical dimensions which define in-group membership. They

lead to the *depersonalization of individual self-perception* (the stereotypical perception of self as an example of some defining social category). It is hypothesized that
depersonalization is the basic process underlying group phenomena such as social
stereotyping, in-group cohesiveness and ethnocentrism, intragroup cooperation
and altruism, emotional empathy and contagion, social influence processes and
the emergence of social norms. (p. 241)

What are the relationships between self-categorization theory and our theory? Again I have to restrict myself to a few topics, and I may overlook consequences. I also admit that an integration does not make empirical research
easier.

My first argument, of course, as in the other cases discussed, concerns the
undifferentiated use of the term *group*; I feel rather sure that self-categorization
processes will be different on the various levels of our classification and will
lead to different consequences. Being a partner in an interaction or acquaint-
anceship will not produce many results in the normal case, although a person
with many acquaintances will feel more like an insider in his environment and
therefore identify more easily with his quarter, town, and so forth. But to have
known an important person even only casually may already make a difference
("Once I talked to Lenin" may be part of the personal myth of old comrades).
Being a member of a dyad or small group may deeply imprint the personality
of an individual, because personal relationships are so loaded with emotion,
which in turn may influence identification. A purely "cognitive" theory of self-
categorization may miss some points on these levels, but be valid on the level
of the organization as long as it is not of existential importance for the individual.
Furthermore, in most cases dyads are parts of groups that are part of organizations that in turn are parts of even greater units, and so on. The idea of a
hierarchical order of three levels of abstraction (Turner et al., 1987, p. 45, A.6)
can be extended to the stratification of a person's real social world.

A further point is the theory's scope. Turner et al. (1987) were interested in
the "psychological group"; our theory aims at social systems in general. As
Turner et al. seemed to admit (p. 2), not all social systems are positive reference
groups. But that does not mean that membership has no impact on identification.
Consider the anorexic girl who does not want to be a female (because she does
not want to be like her mother?), the youngster who is ashamed of his family,
or the young man who reluctantly and against his intentions serves in the army.
They are all examples of a counteridentification that certainly is related to
self-categorization and has considerable impact on action and group processes,
because these people cannot but act against their intention as unwilling members of the category. For the individual, another type of "depersonalization" (to
be *only opposition*) may result. And this has considerable impact on the social
systems processes, as the plagued family or the troubled military superiors in
our examples will testify. There are the less dramatic cases of indifferent neu-
trality against the membership system that produces less dramatic, but still
long-lasting consequences (the child who is just not very interested in school).

This means that self-categorization theory should be enlarged to embrace, beyond positive reference, membership in general.

Let us next look at the "antecedent conditions of depersonalization" (Turner et al., 1987, p. 51). What I am missing here is the consideration of the consequences of multilevel action. Here we must consider at least two facts: the impact of the activity itself and that of the group action structure. Daily experience encourages us to hypothesize that the more intensively a person is embedded into multilevel action the stronger the depersonalization may be. On the other hand, the lack of the multilevel action for which a system exists may weaken self-categorization and open the gate to alternative categorizations (many historians attribute the mutiny of the German battle fleet in 1918 to its ordered long-term inactivity). Another set of possible hypotheses may be derived from the relationship of multilevel action to the systems action structure (our Thesis 15). In fact, a *focus of self-categorization* might be the *individual's role within the system,* rather than the system itself.

Let me conclude with the extension of self-categorization theory to the social levels. Is there a social analogue to the individual self-concept, and if so, how do these self-referent information-elaboration processes on the various levels interact? (Recall Thesis 9: Communication can be considered a social level analogue to individual cognition.) In Thesis 21, we have referred to Bar-Tal's (1990) "group beliefs," which "are defined as convictions that group members (a) are aware that they share and (b) consider as defining their 'groupness' " (p. 36). In a systematic sense, group beliefs are a particular kind of *social representation* (v. Cranach, 1994), and, as such, they may be encoded in the individual memories of the members and in the transactive or the material memory of the social system. What is important in our present discussion—their content, knowledge about the group, its history, actions, values, and so on—forms the material for the individual self-categorization process. Thus, a concept of a *social-level self-concept* may use group beliefs and individual self-categorization as points of departure.

On the other hand, an integration of the basic ideas of self-categorization theory will force us to enlarge and change our own theory. As it seems at a short glance, this might have an impact on our conceptions of action and roles, knowledge and memory, group cohesion (a concept that is as yet totally missing), group development, and categorization on the group level (something we did not consider before). However, these ideas are not mature, and this chapter must come to an end.

Minority Influence and Group Development

Since the early article by Moscovici, Lage, and Naffrechoux in 1969, numerous studies have been performed in Europe and the United States. Moscovici (1976) presented a comprehensive theoretical framework, the basic propositions of which are still valid. Today, minority influence is seen as an essential part of the broad topic of social influence, conformity, and social change, which is still one of the main problem areas of social psychology; and it represents a well-established field, although of course some research questions have remained open and new questions tend to emerge. I cannot treat such a field in the same detailed manner as in our first example; what I can try to do is to relate some of its main presumptions, concepts, propositions, and procedures to my frame theory. The following discussion is based mainly on two review articles that are not quite new but still representative, the detailed and also critical article by Maass and Clark (1984), and the comprehensive and inspired handbook chapter by Moscovici (1985).

To gain an overview of the field, let me begin with the context of the theory. At the basis of Western conceptualizations of the social is the idea of the autonomous, rational, and self-directed individual. Consequently the question arises how such persons can join in groups and societies. The answer is that social influence makes individualities compatible. There are three different aspects of social influence, wrote Moscovici (1985), which have been studied in different paradigms, although they must be seen in their coherence: normalization, conformity, and innovation. Normalization refers to the gradual mutual adaptation of individuals to establish a common behavioral and intellectual norm. Conformity is the change of feelings, opinions, and behavior on one person's part to adapt to the group. Innovation is the introduction of new ideas about a problem, of new values and behaviors that were not considered by the group before. Innovation is produced by minority influence. Maass and Clark (1984, p. 433) summarized "the central propositions of the theory of minority influence that have been generally supported by research: Minorities will exert influence on the majority when showing a consistent behavioral style that allows the majority to infer certainty and confidence. At the same time, a number of qualifying conditions have been identified under which minority influence is likely to fail. These include (a) a rigid style of negotiation in situations in which the minority's behavior can easily be ascribed to its idiosyncratic psychological characteristics, (b) discordance of the minority's position, (c) a Zeitgeist that is unfavorable to the minority's point of view, and (d) double-minority status." And in their critical evaluation, they drew up the following list: (a) exclusive use of one-shot experiments, omission of field studies, (b) confusion of the definition of key concepts like consistency, rigidity, and so on, (c) negligence of intra- and interpersonal processes combined with, (d) lack of interest in their statistical treatment, and (e) too little theoretical controversy in the theoretical interpretation of the findings. My discussion touches instances of some of these problematic points (see also Witte, chapter 11, Vol. 1).

How does this field relate to my frame theory? Actually, I see many reference points. Let us discuss the two most important ones. First, the superordinated topic of the theory, *social influence, is action.* Social influence processes consist of the exchange of *communicative acts* the goal of which is to convince the recipient to change his knowledge, values, attitudes, opinions, and, finally, actions. These communications can be acts of individuals or social systems, for example, majorities and minorities. The statements of our theory can be applied to them in many of their details. Thus they can be multilevel activities (Thesis 9), embedded into long-term activities (Thesis 10), based on steering and energizing processes (Thesis 14), sequentially and hierarchically organized, and, in the case of an acting group, based on a specific group action structure (Thesis 15), and so forth. Any detailed analysis of influence processes will profit from these viewpoints.

Second, normalization, conformity, and innovation are of course action-related processes. Let me illustrate this with the example of innovation, the most interesting case. Innovation, exactly as Moscovici (1985) described it, is an important part of the development of social systems and of group development (Theses 6 and 7) in particular. Here I feel in close agreement with the aims of the theory of minority influence. It describes in detail one of the processes of multilevel coevolution, namely the transition of knowledge from a lower to a higher systemic level.

Let us now look at this theory's scope. The sources cited did not explicitly state what they consider its range of validity. Both of these articles speak of "groups" in a very indiscriminate way. Moscovici's (1985) discussions indicate that he wanted to apply the theory to all kinds of social systems, from small groups to societies and historical social movements like the student movement of 1968, the Reformation in the 15th century, or socialist parties in capitalist countries. The empirical data, of course, are more or less exclusively derived from the study of small laboratory groups (and most of what we have remarked about the embeddedness of such groups in our first example could be repeated here). And because different kinds of social systems have different structures, functions, and processes (Fig. 6.1), we believe it extremely unlikely that the same principles can be indiscriminately applied to the whole range of them. We believe in the *heuristic value* of *analogies* (Thesis 9), but *under consideration of given differences*.

Similar questions arise when we ask ourselves: What is a minority? The certainly not unmodest hope to find this question answered in the two articles is unfortunately disappointed. The spirit of the theory would make us expect that minorities should be socially defined (in terms of social structure, namely hierarchy, power, prestige and status, resources, etc.), but the studies on minority influence use to our knowledge exclusively numerical definitions. There is the additional difficulty that a minority could be an individual as well as a social system. Moscovici (e.g., 1976, p. 168) seemed to take both possibilities into account, whereas Maass and Clark (1984) seemed to think of individuals—for example, in their definition of individual and double minorities (p. 432). In the context of our multilevel theory a *minority* can be defined as a *subsystem* (be it an individual or a social system, dyad, group, organization, or whatever else) *that has less power in relation to the given question* (which will be action related as we have pointed out, "in relation to the given question" meaning that the subsystem can have minority status in one and majority status in another case). Such a minority can but need not be smaller in number. Sometimes the minority role is played by the numerical majority of subordinates against their small but powerful leadership team. In other cases, the minority role is played by the legitimate but powerless leader who has to convince his reluctant followers. In such a case, the findings about a consistent behavior style, rigidity, the zeitgeist, and so on, can probably be applied in analogy. Thus, our definition of minority enlarges the scope of the theory.

What about "real" minorities? Maass and Clark (1984) seemed to identify them with "double" in contrast to "single" minorities, which they defined as follows: "Single minorities can be defined as individuals who deviate from the majority only in term of their beliefs, such as the antiwar students of the mid-1960ties. Double minorities, in contrast, differ from the majority not only in terms of their beliefs, but also in term of their ascribed category membership ... or social categorization" (p. 432). This is important, but only part of the story. We believe that *the essence of real minorities is that they tend to be structured and acting social systems,* as our theory describes them. This is what Moscovici (1985) considered the reason for the scientific interest in minorities in the 1960s: "From all corners of society movements appeared that wanted to change society and its values. Young people and students, women and ecologists, ethnic and religious minorities, homosexuals and prisoners—*all consolidated into groups,* exerting pressure on the majority. ... All those, in a word who used to be considered deviants now *took a stand as active minorities* ..." (p. 351; emphasis added).

Let us finally discuss another important phenomenon, the definition and explanation of which are not satisfying: the *zeitgeist.* Moscovici (1985) failed to express in his few remarks how much he appreciated the concept. Maass and Clark (1984) defined it as "the direction in which the norm trend evolves" (p. 431). But whose norm trend? The majority's, the minority's? And what is a norm trend, and how do we (and our subjects!) know about it? Paicheler (1976, 1977), who detected the phenomenon, spoke of "the trend of the norms at the global level of society." So this is a multilevel affair: The norm trend on a higher (Thesis 21), the societal level influences the events of the groups under study. But is it necessarily the society at large that must be involved? We expect that trends within other kinds of supersystems might have the same effect. To spell out these assumptions in the terms of our theory: We consider a norm as a specific kind of knowledge (Thesis 27) that is stored on a specific level in a specific memory (Thesis 21). The zeitgeist can be seen as *knowledge about a developmental or action-related tendency on the level of a supersystem of the involved parties.* Thus it constitutes a variable in the multilevel social order, and can only be assessed if we know its carrier system. To give examples, when a reluctant conservative faculty is convinced by some of their younger members that they should elect more women, the zeitgeist can be found at the level of the faculty, of the whole academic system, or of the society at large. Or, perhaps it is unlikely that I can convince my colleagues to consider this theory seriously, because the zeitgeist of the discipline seems to be against it. Of course, these normative trends on higher levels cannot just be postulated, but must be empirically studied and proved.

Let me summarize: Integrating the theory of minority influence into our frame theory might help to clarify some of its concepts and enlarge its scope as far as it concerns the social systems that are our subject. As far as it refers to society at large, it is beyond the focus of this chapter. And two comments on this whole chapter: The discussion of the self-categorization and minority influence theories is perhaps more productive than that of collective induction, probably because our theory, as a frame theory, is meant to be applied to theories rather than to empirical studies; and it is difficult to be impartial against other people's research, but even more so against one's own.

EPILOGUE

I have presented the outlines of a frame theory. I have demonstrated with three examples that it has a certain integrative power and makes missing points visible. Other instances have been mentioned in the text (e.g., social representations and group beliefs—Thesis 21) and dissonance theory. Extending this demonstration to other examples does not seem to be difficult in principle, but rather just a matter of work and printing space. Just to mention a few: The concept of personal relationships is unclear because it sometimes seems to refer to a property, sometimes to a specific class of social systems. In our theory it becomes a structural feature of social systems. Some years ago I outlined the application of group action theory to the topic of leadership (v. Cranach, 1986). Theories and models that concern partial action processes (as, e.g., perception in its function of situational orientation—Thesis 17) might also receive their coordinated place in the multilevel order of group action. And my discussion of self-categorization indicates that intergroup relations are a topic for a multilevel approach. Some proponents of these approaches see an advantage in the restriction to the individual level, but I cannot follow them. Although it is interesting and necessary to study these phenomena as individual processes, this reveals only part of the story. Nobody can be against the study of trees, but that should not mean to negate the wood. Our theory is integrative in two more respects: It demands the incorporation of group types into our field that are presently excluded (e.g., the family), and as a multilevel theory, it puts the group into the frame of other social systems (like, e.g., the organization) that can be treated in an analogous way.

So much about integration. As a further advantage, I consider our theory realistic, in the sense that it aims at the study of real groups. That does not exclude the study of groups in the laboratory; but we should not forget that it is the real groups that are found "in the world out there," and that they tend to possess all of the features that I have treated in this chapter, if not more. To the extent to which certain features are excluded, we can consider a study as unrealistic. It is not my aim to construct the most elegant models, but to describe and explain reality in its complexity.

ACKNOWLEDGMENTS

I am grateful to Peter Beck, Guy Ochsenbein, Adrian Bangerter, Erich Witte, and an unknown "native speaker" for their comments on earlier versions of this chapter.

REFERENCES

Argyle, M. (1969). *Social interaction*. London: Methuen.

Bar-Tal, D. (1990). *Group beliefs: A conception for analyzing group structure, processes and behavior*. New York: Springer.

Bavelas, A. (1950). Communication patterns in task oriented groups. *Journal of the Acoustical Society of America, 22*, 725–730.

Carver, C., & Scheier, M. (1981). *Attention and self-regulation. A control-theory approach to human behavior*. New York: Springer.

Cranach, M. von (Ed.). (1976). *Methods of inference from animal to human behaviour*. Den Haag: Mouton. Chicago: Aldine.

Cranach, M. von (1983). Ueber die bewusste Repräsentation handlungsbezogener Kognitionen. In L. Montada, K. Reusser, & G. Steiner (Eds.), *Kognition und Handeln* (pp. 64–76). Stuttgart, Germany: Klett-Cotta.

Cranach, M. von (1986). Leadership as a function of group action. In C. F. Graumann & S. Moscovici (Eds.), *Changing conceptions of leadership* (pp. 115–134). New York: Springer-Verlag.

Cranach, M. von (1990). Eigenaktivität, Geschichtlichkeit und Mehrstufigkeit. Eigenschaften sozialer Systeme als Ergebnis der Evolution der Welt. In E. Witte (Ed.), *Sozialpsychologie und Systemtheorie* (Vol. 26, pp. 13–49). Braunschweiger Studien zur Erziehungs—und Sozialwissenschaft, Braunschweig, Germany.

Cranach, M. von (1994a). Die Unterscheidung von Handlungstypen—Ein Vorschlag zur Weiterentwicklung der Handlungspsychologie. In B. Bergmann & R. Richter (Eds.), *Von der Praxis einer Theorie—Ziele, Tätigkeit und Persönlichkeit* (pp. 69–88). Göttingen, Germany: Hogrefe.

Cranach, M. von (1994b). Ueber das Wissen sozialer Systeme. In U. Flick (Ed.), *Psychologie des Sozialen. Sprache und soziales Wissen in der Sozialpsychologie* (pp. 22–53). Hamburg, Germany: Rowohlt.

Cranach, M. von, Blatter, Th., & Gerber, P. (1993, September). *Social representations of action types*. Paper presented at the Xth meeting of the EAESP, Lisbon, Portugal.

Cranach, M. von, Kalbermatten, U., Indermühle, K., & Gugler, B. (1982). *Goal-directed action*. London: Academic Press.

Cranach, M. von, & Ochsenbein, G. (1985). "Selbstüberwachungssysteme" und ihre Funktion in der menschlichen Informationsverarbeitung. *Schweiz. Zeitschrift für Psychologie, 44*(4), 221–235.

Cranach, M. von, Ochsenbein, G., & Tschan, F. (1987). Actions of social systems: Theoretical and empirical investigations. In G. R. Semin & B. Krahé (Eds.), *Issues in contemporary German social psychology—History, theories and applications* (pp. 119–155). London: Sage.

Cranach, M. von, Ochsenbein, G., & Tschan, F. (1989). Arbeitsgruppen. In S. Greif, H. Holling, & N. Nicholson (Eds.), *Arbeits- und Organisationspsychologie. Internationales Handbuch in Schlüsselbegriffen* (pp. 109–112). München, Germany: Psychologie Verlags-Union.

Cranach, M. von, Ochsenbein, G., Tschan, F., & Kohler, H. (1987). Untersuchungen zum Handeln sozialer Systeme. *Schweizerische Zeitschrift für Psychologie, 46*, 213–226.

Cranach, M. von, Ochsenbein, G., & Valach, L. (1986). The group as a self-active system (outline of a theory of group action). *European Journal of Social Psychology, 16*, 193–229.

Cranach, M. von, & Tschan, F. (1990). Mehrstufigkeit im zielgerichteten Verhalten von Organisationen. In F. Frei & I. Udris (Eds.), *Das Bild der Arbeit* (pp. 208–226). Bern, Switzerland: Huber.

Dörner, D. (1989). *Die Logik des Misslingens: Strategisches Denken in komplexen Situationen.* Reinbeck, Germany: Rowohlt.

Farr, R. M., & Moscovici, S. (Eds.). (1984). *Social representations.* Cambridge, England: Cambridge University Press. Paris: Editions de le Maison des Sciences de l'Homme.

French, J. R. P., & Raven, B. H. (1959). The bases of social power. In D. Cartwright (Ed.), *Studies in social power* (pp. 607–623). Ann Arbor: University of Michigan Press.

Gallistel, C. R. (1980). *The organization of action: A new synthesis.* Hillsdale, NJ: Lawrence Erlbaum Associates.

Hacker, W. (1978). *Allgemeine Arbeits—und Ingenieurpsychologie. Psychische Struktur und Regulation von Arbeitstätigkeiten* (2. überarb. Auflage). Berlin: Deutscher Verlag der Wissenschaften. Bern: Hans Huber Verlag.

Hacker, W. (1986). *Arbeitspsychologie.* Bern, Switzerland: Huber.

Hacker, W., & Matern, B. (1980). Methoden zum Ermitteln tätigkeitsregulierender kognitiver Prozesse und Repräsentationen bei industriellen Arbeitstätigkeiten. In E. Ulich (Ed.), *Schriften zur Arbeitspsychologie* (Vol. 20, pp. 607–623). Bern, Switzerland: Huber.

Harré, R., & Secord, P. F. (1972). *The explanation of social behaviour.* Oxford, England: Basil Blackwell.

Heckhausen, H. (1989). *Motivation und Handeln.* Berlin: Springer.

Jantsch, E. (1979). *Die Selbstorganisation des Universums.* München, Germany: Carl Hanser Verlag.

Jaspars, J. M. F., & Lamb, R. (1986). Roles: Social psychology. In R. Harré & R. Lamb (Eds.), *Dictionary of personality and social psychology* (pp. 293–294). Oxford, England: Blackwell.

Katz, D., & Kahn, R. L. (1978). *The social psychology of organizations.* New York: Wiley.

Larson, J. R., & Christensen, C. (1993). Groups as problem-solving units: Toward a new meaning of social cognition. *British Journal of Social Psychology, 32*, 5–30.

Laughlin, P. R., Vanderstoep, S. W., & Hollingshead, A. B. (1991). Collective versus individual induction: Recognition of truth, rejection of error and collective information processing. *Journal of Personal and Social Psychology, 61*, 50–67.

Little, B. R. (1983). Personal projects: A rationale and method for investigation. *Environment and Behavior, 15*, 273–309.

Maass, A., & Clark, R. D. (1984). Hidden impact of minorities: Fifteen years of minority influence research. *Psychological Bulletin, 95*, 428–450.

McGrath, J. E. (1984). *Groups: Interaction and performance.* Englewood Cliffs, NJ: Prentice-Hall.

McGrath, J. E. (1990). Time matters in groups. In J. Galegher, E. R. Kraut, & C. Egido (Eds.), *Intellectual teamwork. Social and technological foundations of cooperative work* (pp. 23–62). Hillsdale, NJ: Lawrence Erlbaum Associates.

Miller, G. A., Galanter, E., & Pribram, K. H. (1960). *Plans and the structure of behavior.* New York: Holt.

Miller, J. G. (1978). *Living systems.* New York: McGraw-Hill.

Moreno, J. L. (1934). *Who shall survive? A new approach to the problem of human interrelations.* Washington, DC: Beacon House.

Moscovici, S. (1976). *Social influence and social change.* London: Academic Press.

Moscovici, S. (1985). Social influence and conformity. In G. Lindzey & E. Aronson (Eds.), *Handbook of social psychology* (Vol. II, pp. 347–412). New York: Random House.

Moscovici, S., Lage, E., & Naffrechoux, M. (1969). Influence of a consistent minority on the responses of a majority in a color perception task. *Sociometry, 32*, 365–379.

Murnigham, J. K., & Coulon, D. A. (1991). The dynamics of intensive work groups: A study of British string quartets. *Administrative Science Quarterly, 36*, 165–186.

Nehnevajsa, J. (1973). Soziometrie. In R. König (Ed.), *Handbuch der empirischen Sozialforschung,* 3. Aufl., Bd. 2. Stuttgart, Germany: Enke.

Ochsenbein, G. (1989). Analoge Funktionen offener Informationsverarbeitung in menschlichen selbstaktiven Systemen. *Zeitschrift für Sozialpsychologie, 20*, 27–37.

Ochsenbein, G., Cranach, M. von, & Tschan, F. (in preparation). *Attention and communication in small group action.*

Ochsenbein, G., & Schaerer, M. (1994). *Die Funktion von Tabus in sozialen Systemen. Forschungsberichte aus dem Psychologischen Institut der Universität Bern.* Bern, Switzerland: Eigenverlag.

Paicheler, G. (1976). Norms and attitude change: I. Polarization and styles of behaviour. *European Journal of Social Psychology, 6*, 405–428.

Paicheler, G. (1977). Norms and attitude change: II. The phenomenon of bipolarization. *European Journal of Social Psychology, 7*, 5–14.

Parsons, T., & Shils, E. A. (Eds.). (1951). *Toward a general theory of action.* Cambridge, MA: Harvard University Press.

Powers, W. (1973). *Behavior: The control of perception.* New York: Aldine.

Pulver, U. (1991). *Die Bausteine des Alltags. Zur Psychologie des menschlichen Arbeitens und Handelns.* Heidelberg, Germany: Asanger.

Shaw, M. E. (1964). Communication networks. *Advances in Experimental Social Psychology, 1*, 111–149.

Shaw, M. E., & Costanzo, Ph. R. (1970). *Theories of social psychology.* New York: McGraw-Hill.

Smith, K., & Berg, D. (1987). *Paradoxes of group life.* San Francisco: Jossey Bass.

Snyder, R. C., Ruck, H. W., & Sapin, B. (1962). *Foreign policy decision making. An approach to study international politics.* New York: The Free Press of Glencoe.

Steiner, I. D. (1972). *Group processes and productivity.* New York: Academic Press.

Tajfel, H. (1969). Cognitive aspects of prejudice. *Journal of Social Issues, 25*, 79–97.

Tajfel, H. (Ed.). (1982). *Social identity and intergroup relations.* Cambridge, England: Cambridge University Press.

Thommen, B., Ammann, R., & Cranach, M. von (1988). *Handlungsorganisation durch soziale Repräsentationen: Welchen Einfluss haben therapeutische Schulen auf ihre Mitglieder?* Bern, Switzerland: Hans Huber Verlag.

Thommen, B., Cranach, M. von, & Ammann, R. (1992). The organization of individual action through social representations: A comparative study of two therapeutic schools. In M. von Cranach, W. Doise, & G. Mugny (Eds.), *Social representations and the social bases of knowledge* (Swiss Monographs in Psychology, Vol. 1, pp. 194–201). Bern, Switzerland: Hans Huber.

Tomaszewski, T. (1978). *Tätigkeit und Bewusstsein.* Beiträge zur Einführung in die polnische Tätigkeitspsychologie. Weinheim/Basel, Switzerland: Beltz.

Tschan, F. (1995). Communication enhances small group performance if it conforms to task requirements: The concept of ideal communication cycles. *Basic & Applied Social Psychology, 17*(3), 371–393.

Tschan, F., & Cranach, M. von (1990). Zielgerichtetes Verhalten sozialer Systeme als mehrstufiger Prozess. In R. Fisch & M. Boos (Eds.), *Vom Umgang mit Komplexität in Organisationen. Kon-*

zepte-Fallbeispiele-Strategien. Konstanzer Beiträge zur sozialwissenschaftlichen Forschung. (Bd. 5, pp. 12–41). Konstanz, Germany: Universitätsverlag.

Turner, J. C. (1985). Social categorization and the self-concept: A social cognitive theory of group behavior. In E. J. Lawler (Ed.), *Advances in group processes* (Vol. 2, pp. 77–121). Greenwich, CT: JAI.

Turner, J. C., Hogg, M. A., Oakes, P. J., Reicher, St. D., & Wetherell, M. S. (1987). *Rediscovering the social group. A self-categorization theory.* Oxford, England: Basil Blackwell.

Turner, J. C., & Oakes, P. J. (1986). The significance of the social identity concept for social psychology with reference to individualism, interactionism and social influence. *British Journal of Social Psychology, 25,* 237–252.

Ulich, E. (1992). *Arbeitspsychologie.* 2. Auflage. Zürich: Verlag der Fachverbände. Stuttgart, Germany: Poeschel.

Volpert, W. (1982). The model of hierarchical-sequential organization of action (Paper presented at the XXII International Psychological Congress, Leipzig). In W. Hacker, W. Volpert, & M. von Cranach (Eds.), *Cognitive and motivational aspects of action* (pp. 35–52). Amsterdam: North Holland.

Wegner, D. M. (1986). Transactive memory: A contemporary analysis of the group mind. In B. Mullen & G. R. Goethals (Eds.), *Theories of group behavior* (pp. 185–208). New York: Springer-Verlag.

Wekselberg, V. (1992). *A blueprint of the cooperative theory of groups.* Unpublished manuscript.

INTERPERSONAL INFLUENCE, CONFLICT, AND RESOLUTION

THE CONFLICT ELABORATION THEORY OF SOCIAL INFLUENCE

Juan Antonio Pérez
University of Valencia

Gabriel Mugny
University of Geneva

THE ISSUES IN THE DEBATE

For several decades, social influence phenomena have provided the basis for a great variety of theoretical, experimental, and applied studies (cf. Allen, 1975; Cialdini, 1985; Levine & Russo, 1987; Moscovici, 1985; Mugny, 1982; Paicheler, 1988; Turner, 1991; Zanna, Olson, & Herman, 1987). This diversification has given rise to a debate about explanations (cf. Doms, 1983; Eagly & Chaiken, 1993; Latané & Wolf, 1981; Moscovici, 1976; Tanford & Penrod, 1984; Wolf, 1987).

From this debate it has emerged that the dominant explanations—models or theories—are subject to three kinds of complementary "biases" relating to the expected effects of sources and their levels of influence (cf. Mugny, Butera, Sanchez-Mazas, & Pérez, 1994). Whereas some theories focus on the conformity to majority, expert, or ingroup sources, others put back into the melting pot the studies demonstrating the latent influence of minority, discredited, and outgroup sources. This distinction between manifest and latent influence (Moscovici, 1980) has played a crucial role in more recent research (Wood, Lundgren, Ouellette, Busceme, & Blackstone, 1994), but has also largely complicated the problem of theorizing the multiple social influence processes (Chaiken & Stangor, 1987).

Furthermore, a great variety of tasks has been used, without enough care having been given to the specific consequences of using one task or another (Maass, West, & Cialdini, 1987).

The cumulative and sometimes contradicting experimental evidence (cf. Kruglanski & Mackie, 1990; Maass & Clark, 1984) is such that it has now become imperative to develop a psychosocial model that can account for these various strands within a more encompassing framework. Conflict elaboration theory (CET; Pérez & Mugny, 1993) is an attempt to integrate research on social influence phenomena in order to lead to new insights about the various processes confounded under the generic notion of "social influence."

THE CONFLICT ELABORATION THEORY

This theory initiated from the idea that, in spite of the multiple types of tasks, sources, levels of influence, and processes in which influence operates, all these factors could be understood from a common basic explicative notion: *conflict elaboration.*

Social influence is understood as the modification of what the person or the group would have done in a different way if they had not been exposed to this influence. A fundamental postulate is that influence will be a consequence of any divergence with any other. The notion of conflict elaboration refers to the way people think about this divergence and give it a meaning. The specific elaboration of the conflict is hypothesized depending on the type of task, as well as on the type of source introducing the divergence. The following are three general hypotheses of the CET:

1. Given the same amount of judgment divergence supported *by two different sources,* conflict will be elaborated in two different ways.
2. Given a similar degree of divergence in judgment maintained by the same source *in two different tasks,* conflict will be elaborated in two different ways.
3. Different ways of conflict elaboration will correspond to *different patterns of manifest and/or latent influence.*

Let us first consider how conflict elaboration is elicited in different ways depending (a) on the nature of the task and (b) on the nature of the source. We then see how one specific conflict resolution process in each case leads to a particular pattern of influences resulting from each conflict elaboration. In effect, CET is aimed at predicting the most probable pattern of manifest and latent influences (resolution process), taking into consideration that different types of sources should activate different socio-cognitive dynamics in different types of tasks (conflict elicitation).

Relevant Dimensions of the Tasks

CET postulates the functioning in the "lay epistemology" (Kruglanski, 1989) of specific preconceptions that are ordinarily applied in order to determine the validity of the judgments in a given task. So CET does not describe the task's properties in themselves, but the task dimensions psychologically relevant for subjects faced with a divergence in the social influence encounter (Maggi & Mugny, 1995). Two preconceptions are of particular importance in the study of social influence:

1. One is concerned with whether subjects believe that the task allows for a demonstrably (see Laughlin, 1980) right answer, all others being wrong, or whether they consider it a task in which one cannot determine objectively what is right and what is wrong. On this dimension CET differentiates tasks where relevance of error is high versus low for targets.

2. A second preconception is whether the task is considered by targets as one in which the responses are socially qualifying the targets, that is, define their membership to a given social category rather than to another, or assign them a particular (low versus high) rank position within a category, or whether the task lacks such social implications. On this dimension CET distinguishes socially anchoring tasks from non socially anchoring tasks.

Crossing these two socio-epistemic dimensions we obtain four types of task representations that should account for most, if not all, possible paradigms for the study of social influence: (a) Task: Objective, Nonambiguous (TONA), (b) Task: APtitudes (TAP), (c) Task: OPinion (TOP), and (d) TAsk: Nonimplicating (TANI). Let us consider now how the divergence introduced by a source will be elaborated as one type of conflict or another depending on the specific socio-epistemic preconceptions corresponding to each task (see Fig. 7.1).

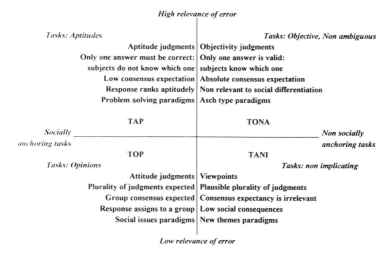

FIG. 7.1. Task dimensions in the conflict elaboration in function of relevance of error and social anchoring.

Task: Objective, Nonambiguous (TONA). TONA are nonanchoring tasks where relevance of error is high. The prototypical study on social influence using this type of task is the well-known conformity paradigm used by Asch (1956).

In TONA objectivity judgments are at stake. Subjects have the certainty that only one answer is valid, that it can be demonstrated which one it is, and that they know it exactly. They therefore expect to find a total consensus, that is, unanimity.

These tasks are not usually relevant to differentiate people socially: Judgments are facts, and different judgments are not conceived as depending on social divisions. In this way, they are non socially anchoring tasks.

Task: APtitudes (TAP). TAP are anchoring tasks where relevance of error is high. The problem-solving paradigms used in several studies of influence (Legrenzi, Butera, Mugny, & Pérez, 1991; Nemeth, 1986) have all the peculiarities of this type of aptitude task.

TAP put at stake aptitude judgments. In these tasks subjects start with the certainty that one answer must be correct or more valid than others; they know that mistakes can be determined objectively, although they do not know exactly which answer is correct and which is not. Subjects can feel the necessity of reaching a consensus, but the absence of agreement among different people does not break any previous expectancy of consensus: Divergence is the most plausible, socially and cognitively, logic. Subjects know that there is a right answer (or at least one better than others) and the first concern would be how to discover it.

In this type of task, social influence is also studied in situations representing an aptitude test (Festinger, 1954), an evaluation of their own abilities. In this manner these are tasks normally used to rank people in terms of their differential aptitudes and are, therefore, socially anchoring tasks.

Task: OPinions (TOP). TOP are anchoring tasks where relevance of error is low. Experiments using social issues (attitudes, values, etc.) are typical of TOP.

They are tasks in which there is no objective way to determine what is right or wrong. The preconception does not imply that there is one right answer. On the contrary, a plurality of differentiated positions is expected and even considered as necessary.

In this type of task a direct correspondence is expected between different opinions and relevant social differentiations (Doise, 1978; Rokeach, Smith, & Evans, 1966). To each group or social category would correspond specific opinions, and vice versa, a specific opinion assigns people to a determined group or social category. In TOP opinions are, therefore, socially anchoring.

TAsk: Nonimplicating (TANI). TANI are nonanchoring tasks where relevance of error is low. They refer to viewpoints and share the same characteristics as the TOP, with an important exception: They refer to tasks where opinions are not indicators of specific social positions. In this way, whereas in the TOP a given opinion reveals a social orientation, in the TANI it only expresses a personal point of view among the plurality of viewpoints, and it generally refers to questions nearly new for the targets, and/or that are of very low social relevance for them. People may feel compelled to be asked for their personal views or preferences, without any social consequence for the self. These judgments have no social anchoring, and error is not relevant. Anyone can express a priori whichever opinion or preference he or she wishes, independent from particular social memberships and correctness. In the TANI, people would have no special expectation to reach or not reach a consensus. The difference in answers from other people is not conflictual in itself. In this way they are socially nonimplicating tasks.

For each task we can summarize the main factors that will shape the conflict elaboration elicited by a divergence of responses in the social influence encounter:

1. In TONA, conflict elaboration will be oriented by the challenging of two preconceptions: Why unanimity is not achieved, and why the source is wrong.
2. In TAP, conflict elaboration will be shaped by people concerned with trying to increase the correctness of their judgments and/or to give the best self-image of their abilities.
3. In TOP, conflict elaboration is shaped by how to the maintain categorical differentiation logic, that is, ingroup agreement and outgroup disagreement, and/or avoidance of negative attributes to the self in the case of a threatening identification.
4. In TANI, because they are not socially implicating tasks, there is no previous fixed norm to give a meaning to divergence.

Type of Sources and Relevant Dimensions

Studies of social influence and persuasion (for a review, see Allen, 1975; Moscovici, 1985; Petty & Cacioppo, 1986) have repeatedly shown that a source can obtain an influence not only by what it says but primarily by what it represents socially, that is, who it is and what its characteristics are. However, few social influence theories have developed a systematic conceptualization of the characteristics of the source, except social impact theory/model (cf. Latané & Wolf, 1981, see also Vol. I; Tanford & Penrod, 1984). In this respect CET considers that source characteristics (mainly number, social identity, and competence) are to be understood in terms of their relevance to the specific socio-epistemic preconceptions of a given type of task. Thus, depending on the type of task, one characteristic or another will be relevant for conflict elaboration:

1. We have seen that in TONA what matters is principally the existence or absence of unanimity. Due to this absolute unanimity expectancy, anyone who

breaks it will always produce a conflict. The most important characteristic of the source is not here whether it is or is not an expert who breaks it, nor whether it is someone who belongs to an ingroup or an outgroup. The important point is whether there is someone (1, 2, 3, or more subjects) breaking unanimity. In this type of task the main key is, then, *the number* of people who compose the source.

2. In TAP the source's *competence* would be of the most importance. Subject would above all try to formulate the most suitable judgments. In consequence, they can try to rely on the indications the source offers due to the credibility of its message (Hass, 1981).

3. With TOP the most relevant characteristic of the source will refer to its *social identity,* its numerical character and even its credibility being of secondary importance. The most important thing is if the source belongs to or does not belong to the same group or social category as the subjects. The point of reference of opinions is located in the entanglement of the membership and reference groups.

4. Finally, in TANI the source characteristics may orient the processing of the message (cf. Eagly & Chaiken, 1993; Petty & Cacioppo, 1986) depending on whether or not they are socially shared credibility heuristics.

Of course, taking into consideration one source dimension more than another for a given type of task does not mean that other dimensions are not of some relevance for other cases. An important postulate of CET is, however, that for specific tasks certain source's attributes are more relevant than others. The point here is that other dimensions can also be important, but in the way they incide on these attributes, in particular through the inferences they can induce in respect to the most relevant dimension.

Conflict Elaboration

In order for the influence produced by a given source to be studied, targets are usually confronted with a divergent response. The amplitude and direction of this divergence help define the amount of the potential influence. Let us consider now the meanings of a divergence (recognized as such by the target) as a function of the type of task and the type of source.

In the case of TONA the *basic conflict* is of a *socio-epistemic* kind: The source's answers do not coincide with what subjects see or know, or expect to see or know. But the conflict will be elaborated also at the level of the social relation with the source. However, it will take a different meaning depending on the majority or the minority status of the source.

A majority source would activate the fear of ridicule, deviation, disapproval, or rejection (Levine, 1989). This can be defined by the notion of *relational conflict.* In fact, besides its basic epistemic nature (the priority remains to be correct), the conflict takes on a complementary relational character. Subjects have to avoid keeping a deviate judgment and may give importance to the restoration of the manifest consensus (Moscovici & Personnaz, 1980).

On the other hand, a minority source will not induce such a relational conflict. First, subjects will not experience a relational pressure as intense as that from the majority, and this pressure is not strong enough to produce a manifest compliance. The target would be especially interpellated because of the lack of total uniformity that questions the basic ground of their preconception, for in TONA unanimity is constitutive of the object. The conflict would not be relational but *epistemic* in nature.

The conflict experienced in TAP is of a competence nature. The divergent point of view defended by a given source may duplicate the *uncertainty* that subjects already feel themselves in approaching the task in isolation.

Confronting highly competent sources, there would be a tendency for subjects to converge. They would hardly question the content of the answer given by the source because their social characteristics suffice as criteria of validity. Conflict is nearly nonexistent, because the source answer is supposed to be a useful contribution for the subjects, like a prosthesis with which they can cope with the task and solve their inaptitude.

When opposed to a source with less competence, targets feel a double fear of invalidity (Kruglanski, 1989): They might make the mistake of adopting an answer with few social assurances, or of setting aside an answer without previously invalidating it, that is, without having been fully convinced socio-cognitively of its inadequacy, in case it might prove to be more correct than their own answer. We can say that it is a *conflict between incompetences*: Those of the source and those of the target.

In TOP also, the conflicts created by a source supporting a divergent judgment take on different meanings, depending now on its ingroup or outgroup category membership. These conflicts of an identity nature can take different forms:

1. When subjects are expecting an agreement, established in an ingroup, and that agreement is not reached, we can talk about a *normative conflict*.

2. When identification with extreme members or deviants from the ingroup imply negative connotations, all proximity with them means the self-attribution of characteristics that threaten the positive self-image (Mugny, Kaiser, & Papastamou, 1983). In this case we can talk of *an identification conflict*. The elements of this identification conflict are, on one hand, the search for a positive social image, and on the other hand, the pressure to maintain the cohesion (Hogg, 1992; see also chapter 9 of this volume) or even the existence of the ingroup.

If the source endorses a divergent point of view and has an outgroup identity, the conflict becomes an *intergroup conflict*. Because the source is an outgroup, subjects could reject it, as a mere effect of categorization. We still have to see what kind of structuring socio-cognitive activities should be developed with this type of conflict for the outgroup to obtain some influence, in spite of this first resistance against it.

Notice already the possible existence of another particular conflict whose importance is dealt with later: In some circumstances, overt discrimination of outgroup and minority sources qualified as "double minorities" (Maass & Clark, 1984) can lead to a *cognitive-cultural conflict,* as long as it is an outgroup minority "protected" by a Zeitgeist that hints negatively its discrimination. It is a cognitive conflict because the mere socio-cognitive functioning of categorization would lead subjects to differentiate themselves from the outgroup; it is a cultural conflict because a set of values of justice and social equality accepted in most societies recriminates the open explicitation of such minority discrimination.

It must be noted that the absence of judgment divergence can also be conflictual, concretely when targets are expecting a difference that does not appear, as in the case of an intergroup setting when a source categorized as outgroup defends, in spite of this, the same point of view as the target. In such a case, the *identity conflict* stems from a contradiction between a similarity of answers and a relevant social differentiation (Lemaine, Lasch, & Ricateau, 1971–1972), and leads to dissimilation (cf. Lemaine, 1975).

In terms of CET we think that the TANI are marked by *avoidance of conflict* (cf. Mugny et al., 1991): One viewpoint or another is a priori without social significance.

Conflict Resolution: Manifest and Latent Influences

Numerous studies on social influence have demonstrated that conflict resolution is to be examined at two levels: The manifest level and the latent level (cf. Moscovici, 1980; Moscovici, Mucchi-Faina, & Maass, 1994; Moscovici & Mugny, 1987; Moscovici, Mugny, & Van Avermaet, 1985; Moscovici & Personnaz, 1980; Mugny & Pérez, 1991; Nemeth, 1986). The main reason for doing this is that, according to the nature of conflict, the manifest answer does not necessarily end up with the conflict created by a given source. In some cases the manifest answer can even induce a new conflict.

A main principle of CET is that virtually any cognitive conflict is also primarily a social conflict. This social conflict is resolved at the level of the (even if only symbolic) social relationship with the source, whereas the cognitive conflict is resolved in the processing of the source's answer and in object examination. Another basic principle of CET is that when the social conflict is intense, no specific consequence of the cognitive conflict will appear before the social conflict is resolved in one way or another.

But these are only general tendencies, and we see now their fluctuations according to the type of task and the type of source. Let us consider, then, the conflict resolution at the manifest level (public, immediate, and direct influence) and at the latent level (private, delayed, or indirect influence; Mugny & Pérez, 1991) that would most probably happen in each task with each source.

Conflict Resolution in TONA

The Majority. In TONA (see Table 7.1), numerical majority sources produce in subjects a perplexity and a relational conflict that absorbs all of their attention. This conflict is usually resolved by partially showing compliance (Kelman, 1958), that is, only manifest consensus restoration. The main socio-cognitive activity is looking for a straight conflict reduction.

Compliance may have a positive connotation if subjects interpret it as a successful ingratiation tactic (Jones & Jones, 1964). In this case no latent change should occur, and the most probable result is that the latent (e.g., private) judgments will be the same as those given before the influence situation. Personnaz (1975–1976, 1979) used the notion of clandestinity to explain this way of keeping at a "secondary" level the personal judgments during the period of influence itself in order to make the resolution of the social conflict possible.

Now, compliance would have negative connotations when subjects understand it as a submission to a social pressure of the majority. Because manifest reactance behaviors (Brehm, 1966) are difficult or psychologically costly (Heilman, 1976), subjects could experience here a double threat for their personal integrity: that of yielding to the other and that of yielding in the face of the perceptive evidence. It can be said that in this case subjects will try to recover their autonomy and enhance their self-image, even if this is possible only at a latent level free from majority pressures.

TABLE 7.1
Conflict Elaboration and Social Influences in Objective Nonambiguous Tasks (TONA)

	Majority	*Minority*
Conflict:	Relational Conflict	Epistemic Conflict
Manifest Elaboration:	Consensus Restoration	Independence
Latent Elaboration:	Threat of Integrity	Object Unicity
Manifest Influence:	Compliance	Self-Conformity
Latent Influence:	Autonomy Recovering	Uniformization
Main Socio-Cognitive Activity:	Straight Conflict Resolution	Objectivation
Other Factors Effect:	Any factor that increases the relational pressure:	
	Increases Compliance	Decreases Uniformization

Specific hypotheses about latent majority influence deriving from CET have been tested using situations close to the Asch (1956) paradigm, where the response is as evident as the fact that the source is wrong. Despite the objective character of the answer, the extent of the influence observed in this type of paradigm is well known. What is the reason? Classically, the effect has been interpreted in terms of informational and normative dependence (Deutsch & Gerard, 1955). The hypothesis of CET is that the socio-epistemic nature of the conflict is responsible for this. It has then been demonstrated that dynamics of influence appear because targets expect unanimity and disappear when this expectation is challenged (Butera, Huguet, Mugny, & Pérez, 1994).

Now, how do we explain why one observes a compliance effect so frequently? CET predicts that it is essentially due to the fact that this basic conflict is deviated from its origins and takes, when confronted with a majority source, a salient relational significance masking the epistemic conflict. It follows that if an ad hoc manipulation succeeds in suppressing the relational or informational pressure (i.e., in eliminating dependence), then latent effects should be observed, because unanimity expectations are not met (Butera et al., 1994; Mugny, 1984). This constitutes a core demonstration in the Brandstätter et al. (1991) experiment. The corollary has also been illustrated: Once some relational dependence is reintroduced, latent effects disappear and manifest influence is the only remainder (Pérez, Mugny, Butera, Kaiser, & Roux, 1991).

The Minority.   In TONA an effect of self-conformity usually appears in confrontation with a minority. With the manifest maintenance of independence, the social conflict is resolved in a comfortable way for the personal identity of the subjects. However, the problem of uniformity of the judgments remains unsolved, because object unicity requires these to be totally consensual (i.e., unanimous) in order to be fully objective. Subjects find themselves in a double impossibility. They are not able to change the source, and they cannot change themselves by adopting the judgment from the source at a manifest level because the source is a minority. Given the epistemic conflict that any (even numerically weak) divergence creates in a TONA, subjects would be led to undertake an objectivation activity; that is, reconstructing in some way the properties of the object, in order to maintain its uniformity, now anchored in the point of view of the minority source. This can explain why when faced with TONA a minority, despite the lack of manifest influence, can modify the latent responses of the targets (Brandstätter et al., 1991; Moscovici & Personnaz, 1980, 1986, 1991; Personnaz, 1981). The change rests here on a representational dynamic that comes from the epistemo-ideologic (Mugny & Doise, 1979) necessity of the unicity of the object.

In TONA the effect of the other dimensions that can differentiate the sources is easy to predict: All factors that increase the relational pressure or facilitate identification with the minority will shift the conflict resolution to a more manifest level and inhibit latent change (Mugny, Butera, Pérez, & Huguet, 1993).

Conflict Resolution in TAP

In TAP (see Table 7.2) a *high-competence source* would generally yield an extensive manifest influence. Based on the uncertainty and inability of the targets, the conflict with competent or expert sources would be resolved by way of informational dependence (Deutsch & Gerard, 1955; Festinger, 1950). Subjects would take for granted that the opposed point of view has more validity than their own and would adopt or imitate it directly, thus resolving both the uncertainty and the social conflict (Butera, Mugny, Legrenzi, & Pérez, 1996). Subjects can eventually look for further confirmation on the latent level. Whether or not it is generalized to related tasks will depend on the intensity of convergent thinking (Nemeth, 1986).

Let us now look at the case of *low-competence sources* in TAP. The conflict they introduce leads to the most various constructivist resolutions. In the first place, given their incompetence, they are not expected to obtain a notable manifest influence, avoidance or distantiation instead. However, subjects remain uncertain—they still do not know the right answer—and are therefore in a conflict between incompetences—the source's, and their own. Due to the fear of invalidity (Kruglanski, 1989), and according to a series of socio-cognitive activities implicated in the process of validation, this conflict between incompetences can induce an important indirect influence on task solving.

First, we must make a distinction between the validity of a response and the validation process. The validity of a response here refers to the social prestige associated with a response due to the prestige of the source itself. The validation

TABLE 7.2
Conflict Elaboration and Social Influences in Aptitude Tasks (TAP)

	High Competence	Low Competence
Conflict:	Nearly Nonexistent	Conflict Between Incompetences
Manifest Elaboration:	Informational Dependence	Social Invalidation
Latent Elaboration:	Confirmation	Fear of Invalidity
Manifest Influence:	Imitation	Distantiation
Latent Influence:	Generalization	Task Solving
Main Socio-Cognitive Activity:	Convergent Thinking	Validation, Divergent Thinking, Decentration
Other Factors Effect:	Majority or Ingroup Accentuate Convergent Thinking	Source Independence Activates Validation Process

process, as Moscovici and Personnaz (1980) understood it, refers to the socio-cognitive operations that subjects undertake to examine the adequacy of what the source says concerning the object properties. Taking into consideration this difference, it can be hypothesized that the expert sources would obtain their influence because their expertise confers validity to their answer. On the contrary, a source without greater expertise than the targets themselves would obtain influence through the validation process.

Three complementary socio-cognitive activities would intervene in this validation process that makes the indirect influence of the low-credibility sources possible:

1. First is the still intriguing observation by Moscovici and Personnaz (1980). They supported that "as a result of trying to see or understand what the minority saw or understood, the majority begins to see and understand as the minority would" (p. 272).

2. The second type of activity is divergent thinking. It is characterized (Nemeth, 1986) by the fact that subjects do more than just convince themselves of the correctness of the minority point of views: "Those exposed to minority views are stimulated to attend to more aspects of the situation, they think in more divergent ways, and they are more likely to detect novel solutions or come to new decisions. . . . There are creative contributions made by dissenting minority, even when it is wrong. Its value lies not so much in the correctness of its position but rather in the attention and thought process it induces" (p. 3). In respect to a minority subjects can concentrate on the task and activate a whole set of abilities, without being "paralyzed" by the dominant solution, as usually occurs when the source is seen as highly competent or when it is seen as a majority.

3. Decentration is another possible socio-cognitive activity that intervenes in the validation process (Huguet, Mugny, & Pérez, 1991–1992). It is related to the ambiguous property of the task and to the source's independence. It lies in the idea that subjects understand that from another perspective different characteristics of the objects might be perceived that also have some probability of being right (Huguet et al., 1991–1992).

From all this, two predictions can be concluded. First, when TAP refer to tasks implicating abilities in creativity, originality, or personal autonomy, the full adoption of the source's response challenges original and autonomous characteristics of the self. High-power, -status, or -number-size sources will probably lose their manifest influence, and certainly their latent influence. In such a case, a less compelling source (i.e., of low expertise, number, or power) will obtain more influence (Crano, 1992). Second, any variable that emphasizes the independent behavior of the source (e.g., belonging to another group) adds properties likely to activate the validation process.

A critical test of these various processes has been the demonstration that in an aptitude task a low-competent source (i.e., a minority) induces a constructivistic activity (Butera & Mugny, 1992; Legrenzi et al., 1991) when targets have a task representation allowing for multiple solutions, whereas imitation of a more credible source (i.e., a majority) model appears when subjects expect that a single correct answer is allowed (Butera, Legrenzi, & Mugny, 1993; Butera et al., 1996). Furthermore, it has been demonstrated that this constructivistic activity is effectively due to simultaneous doubt concerning self-validity and source's validity, that is, to a conflict between incompetences (Butera & Mugny, 1995).

Conflict Resolution in TOP

Let us look at the variety of activities induced by the categorization of the source in the TOP, where the influence implications are of an identity nature (see Table 7.3).

When the source is an ingroup, in terms of CET three types of possible activities can be seen: the self-categorization process, the dynamic of identification, and the indissociation process.

First, an ingroup source can give rise to an intensification of the self-categorization process described by Turner, Hogg, Oakes, Reicher, and Wetherell (1987). The consequence will be an intensification of conformity to the position of the ingroup source and the self-attribution of the response considered as definitional

TABLE 7.3
Conflict Elaboration and Social Influences in Opinion Tasks (TOP)

	Ingroup	*Outgroup*
Conflict:	Normative Conflict Identification Conflict	Intergroup Conflict Cognitive-Cultural Conflict
Manifest Elaboration: Latent Elaboration:	Normative Dependence Ingroup Homogeneity	Social Differentiation Shame of Discrimination
Manifest Influence: Latent Influence:	Conformity Dissimilation No Change Interiorization	Discrimination Conversion
Main Socio-Cognitive Activity:	Self-Categorization Identification Indissociation Paralysis	Categorization Dissociation
Other Factors Effect:	Majority or Competence Accentuate These Dynamics	Minority or Denial Accentuate Dissociation

of the ingroup identity (Abrams & Hogg, 1990; Maass, Clark, & Haberkorn, 1982; Martin, 1988; Mugny & Papastamou, 1982; Volpato, Maass, & Mucchi-Faina, 1990). A process of this type implies normative dependence on the source. Furthermore, when the indirect dimension constitutes a relevant dimension and makes salient the identification with its own category, the manifest influence will be interiorized (cf. Mackie, 1987; Mackie, Worth, & Asuncion, 1990; Turner, 1991; Wilder, 1990). In fact the influence of ingroup source will be greater when that source polarizes the ingroup position (cf. Turner et al., 1987). In this case, influence would be the way to maintain the ingroup homogenization (Turner, 1991).

Now, it is not excluded that an ingroup source produces what can be considered a socio-cognitive paralysis (Sanchez-Mazas, Pérez, Navarro, Mugny, & Jovanovic, 1993). This refers to the resolution of the cognitive conflict by giving the response expected to be given by the ingroup. In this way subjects would not feel the need to elaborate it more at a personalized level, because ingroup homogeneity is reestablished through manifest conformity. This process results in a manifest compliance with the prototypical norm of the ingroup but without any more elaborated nor deeper changes (Pérez, Mugny, & Navarro, 1991).

In fact, it is when the targets are "obliged" to go against their group norm that they can engage in a deeper change, precisely because they do not overtly conform to it. Contrary to self-categorization ideas, deeper changes are here not the result of mere self-categorization, but the consequence of the elaboration of the conflict in an ingroup context, as has been shown in studies bearing on attitudes concerning foreigners (Sanchez-Mazas et al., 1993).

However it is not evident that any divergence felt within the ingroup will be perceived as more prototypical, orienting in its direction the self-categorization process and social influence. In many cases the positions at the margins of the ingroup can be seen as intradeviates and would induce an identification conflict.

So when subjects' activity is essentially focused on the creation of divisions (or subtyping) within their own membership category (Pérez & Mugny, 1985), dissimilation (Lemaine, 1975) can absorb their whole socio-cognitive activity and prevent indirect as well as direct influence. This is a typical case of indissociation (cf. Mugny, Ibáñez, Elejabarrieta, Iñiguez, & Pérez, 1986; Papastamou, Mugny, & Pérez, 1991–1992; Pérez & Mugny, 1987).

The ingroup can obtain more latent than manifest influence when both an intense process of self-categorization and an identification conflict are present. In this case, the target is confronted with the fact that, on one hand, the source's extreme position may be more prototypical of its own category (Mugny & Pérez, 1985), and on the other hand, these extreme positions have negative connotations that the target is not inclined to endorse overtly. This latent influence depends here on the conflict due to the loss of ingroup homogeneity and cohesion.

What happens in TOP when the source is categorized as an outgroup? Two types of activities can produce an open discrimination together with a latent change (i.e., the so-called conversion effect).

With regard to the outgroup, at the manifest level subjects simply could resolve the conflict by maintaining or accentuating social differentiation between groups (cf. Tajfel, 1978). That is, by adopting a divergent point of view they can even increase the discrimination of the outgroup source beyond the discrimination it would receive by the mere fact of being categorized as an outgroup. This outgroup discrimination can, however, bear one or several paradoxical effects.

First, there could exist a shame of discrimination. It is observed nowadays that in many issues discrimination (at least manifest discrimination) is a socially censured behavior. There is a predominant Zeitgeist that connotes negatively any social discrimination, when this is not sufficiently "justified" (Dovidio & Gaertner, 1981). Hence, the resolution on the public level of the conflict created by an outgroup can lead to another cognitive-cultural conflict that can only be resolved at the most latent level.

In several studies, a distinction has been made between manifest racism (subject to current cultural censorship) and latent racism, that is the pernicious form it can take when prevented from overt expression. Several studies address the discrimination of an outgroup minority, in particular anti-Gypsy racism (cf. Pérez, Falomir, Bagueña, & Mugny, 1993). The underlying logic, as in the case of normative conflicts, is that latent racism can only be eradicated by leading individuals to express—even against their own will—a manifest attitude at least tendentially racist. Latent changes can be found as a consequence of the cognitive and cultural conflict—shame of discrimination—elicited by the manifest expression of a culturally prohibited attitude. Specific to this cultural conflict are the normative constrains concerning minority outgroups protected by the cultural censorship. Evidence for this fact is the experimental demonstration that as soon as a minority is given a position of superiority (through appropriate inductions, e.g., high social status), the cultural conflict is deactivated and therefore the latent changes (Pérez, Mugny, Llavata, & Fierres, 1993).

The second socio-cognitive activity whereby an outgroup—and above all an outgroup minority—could produce a conversion effect is the process of dissociation (Pérez & Mugny, 1990). Dissociation refers to the fact that subjects process "in two times" the social and cognitive conflict created by the source. Before they can elaborate the cognitive conflict induced by the positions of the outgroup, they must have resolved the intergroup conflict, in general, at the expense of the outgroup. Only then can subjects focus their attention on the contents of the minority positions, in particular on its organizing principle (Pérez & Mugny, 1986, 1990). It is predicted that the best conditions for the emergence of conversion are when the cognitive conflict is experienced after being dissociated from the social conflict. The paradoxical prediction here is that in case of dissociation, the more intense the conflict (e.g., because of denial; see Moscovici, Mugny, & Pérez, 1984–1985; Mugny & Pérez, 1991; Pérez, Moscovici, & Mugny, 1991; Pérez, Mugny, & Moscovici, 1986; see also Pérez, Falomir, & Mugny, 1995), the more the latent change.

Conclusion

In spite of the considerable extension and variety of research on social influence
and of the number of "local" theories, it appears possible to have a global
overview that integrates the multiple processes at stake under a common dynamic notion, that is, conflict elaboration. Such a conceptualization offers the
opportunity not to deny the validity of relevant theories and paradigms, and to
try to take them all into account. In effect, it suggests refining the particular
conditions (tasks and sources) under which the specific dynamics discovered
by the various scholars in the field of social influence do intervene, without
opposing them in vain controversies.

ACKNOWLEDGMENTS

The theory and research have been carried out with the support from the Swiss
Fonds National de la Recherche Scientifique, from the Spanish Direccion General
de la Investigacion Cientifica y Tecnica, and from the French Centre National de
la Recherche Scientifique.

REFERENCES

Abrams, D., & Hogg, M. A. (1990). Social identification, self-categorization and social influence. *European Review of Social Psychology, 1,* 195–228.
Allen, V. L. (1975). Social support for nonconformity. In L. Berkowitz (Ed.), *Advances in experimental social psychology* (Vol. 8, pp. 1–43). New York: Academic Press.
Asch, S. E. (1956). Studies on independence and conformity: A minority of one against an unanimous majority. *Psychological Monographs, 70*(No. 416).
Brandstätter, V., Ellemers, N., Gaviria, E., Giosue, F., Huguet, P., Kroon, M., Morchain, P., Pujol, M., Rubini, M., Mugny, G., & Pérez, J. A. (1991). Indirect majority and minority influence: an exploratory study. *European Journal of Social Psychology, 21,* 199–211.
Brehm, J. W. (1966). *A theory of psychological reactance.* New York: Academic Press.
Butera, F., Huguet, P., Mugny, G., & Pérez, J. A. (1994). Socio-epistemic conflict and constructivism. *Swiss Journal of Psychology, 53,* 229–239.
Butera, F., Legrenzi, P., & Mugny, G. (1993). De l'imitation à la validation: Études sur le raisonnement. In J. A. Pérez & G. Mugny (Eds.), *Influences sociales: La théorie de l'élaboration du conflit* (pp. 99–120). Neuchâtel, Switzerland: Delachaux et Niestlé.
Butera, F., & Mugny, G. (1992). Influence minoritaire et falsification. A propos de "quelques réflexions psycho-sociologiques sur une controverse scientifique" de B. Matalon. *Revue Internationale de Psychologie Sociale, 5,* 115–132.
Butera, F., & Mugny, G. (1995). Conflict between incompetencies and influence of a low-expertise source in hypothesis testing. *European Journal of Social Psychology, 25,* 457–462.
Butera, F., Mugny, G., Legrenzi, P., & Pérez, J. A. (1996). Majority and minority influence, task representation, and inductive reasoning. *British Journal of Social Psychology, 35.*
Cialdini, R. B. (1985). *Influence: Science and practice.* Glenview, IL: Scott, Foresman.
Chaiken, S., & Stangor, C. (1987). Attitudes and attitude change. *Annual Review of Psychology, 38,* 575–630.

Crano, W. (1992, July). *Context/categorization model of social influence: Minority and majority influence in the formation of a novel response norm.* Poster presented at E.A.E.S.P. & S.E.S.P. Joint Meeting, Leuven/Louvain-la-Neuve, Belgium.

Deutsch, M., & Gerard, H. B. (1955). A study of normative and informational social influence upon individual judgment. *Journal of Abnormal and Social Psychology, 51,* 629–636.

Doise, W. (1978). *Groups and individuals.* Cambridge, England: Cambridge University Press.

Doms, M. (1983). The minority influence effect: An alternative approach. In W. Doise & S. Moscovici (Eds.), *Current issues in European social psychology* (Vol. 1, pp. 1–32). Cambridge, England: Cambridge University Press.

Dovidio, J. F., & Gaertner, S. L. (1981). The effects of race, status, and ability on helping behavior. *Social Psychology Quarterly, 44*(3), 192–203.

Eagly, A. H., & Chaiken, S. (1993). *The psychology of attitudes.* Orlando, FL: Harcourt Brace.

Festinger, L. (1950). Informal social communication. *Psychological Review, 57,* 271–282.

Festinger, L. (1954). A theory of social comparison processes. *Human Relations, 7,* 117–140.

Heilman, M. E. (1976). Oppositional behavior as a function of influence attempt intensity and retaliation threat. *Journal of Personality and Social Psychology, 33,* 574–578.

Hogg, M. A. (1992). *The social psychology of group cohesiveness: From attraction to social identity.* London: Harvester Wheatsheaf; New York: New York University Press.

Huguet, P., Mugny, G., & Pérez, J. A. (1991–1992). Influence sociale et processus de décentration. *Bulletin de Psychologie, 45,* 155–163.

Jones, E. E., & Jones, R. G. (1964). Optimum conformity as an ingratiation tactic. *Journal of Personality, 32,* 436–458.

Kelman, H. C. (1958). Compliance, identification and internalisation: Three processes of opinion change. *Journal of Conflict Resolution, 2,* 51–60.

Kruglanski, A. W. (1989). *Lay epistemics and human knowledge.* New York: Plenum.

Kruglanski, A. W., & Mackie, D. M. (1990). Majority and minority influence: A judgmental process analysis. *European Review of Social Psychology, 1,* 229–261.

Latané, B., & Wolf, S. (1981). The social impact of majorities and minorities. *Psychological Review, 88,* 438–453.

Laughlin, P. R. (1980). Social combination processes of cooperative problem-solving groups on verbal intellective tasks. In M. Fishbein (Ed.), *Progress in social psychology* (Vol. 1, pp. 127–155). Hillsdale, NJ: Lawrence Erlbaum Associates.

Legrenzi, P., Butera, F., Mugny, G., & Pérez, J. A. (1991). Majority and minority influence in inductive reasoning: A preliminary study. *European Journal of Social Psychology, 21,* 359–363.

Lemaine, G. (1975). Dissimilation and differential assimilation in social influence (situations of "normalization"). *European Journal of Social Psychology, 5,* 93–120.

Lemaine, G., Lasch, E., & Ricateau, P. (1971–1972). L'influence sociale et les systèmes d'action: Les effets d'attraction et de répulsion dans une expérience de normalisation avec l'"allo-cinétique". *Bulletin de Psychologie, 25,* 482–493.

Levine, J. M. (1989). Reaction to opinion deviance in small groups. In P. Paulus (Ed.), *Psychology of group influence* (pp. 187–231). Hillsdale, NJ: Lawrence Erlbaum Associates.

Levine, J. M., & Russo, E. M. (1987). Majority and minority influence. In C. Hendrick (Ed.), *Group processes* (pp. 13–54). Newbury Park, CA: Sage.

Maass, A., & Clark, R. D., III (1984). The hidden impact of minorities: Fourteen years of minority influence research. *Psychological Bulletin, 95,* 428–450.

Maass, A., Clark, R. D., III, & Haberkorn, G. (1982). The effects of differential ascribed category membership and norms on minority influence. *European Journal of Social Psychology, 12,* 89–104.

Maass, A., West, S. G., & Cialdini, R. B. (1987). Minority influence and conversion. In C. Hendrick (Ed.), *Group processes* (pp. 55–79). Newbury Park, CA: Sage.

Mackie, D. M. (1987). Systematic and nonsystematic processing of majority and minority persuasive communications. *Journal of Personality and Social Psychology, 53,* 41–52.

Mackie, D. M., Worth, L. T., & Asuncion, A. G. (1990). Processing of persuasive in-group messages. *Journal of Personality and Social Psychology, 58*, 812–822.

Maggi, J., & Mugny, G. (1995). Les préconstruits des tâches d'influence. In G. Mugny, D. Oberlé, & J. L. Beauvois (Eds.), *La psychologie sociale* (Vol. 1, pp. 228–232). Grenoble: Presses Universitaires de Grenoble.

Martin, R. (1988). Ingroup and outgroup minorities: Differential impact upon public and private responses. *European Journal of Social Psychology, 18*, 39–52.

Moscovici, S. (1976). *Social influence and social change.* London: Academic Press.

Moscovici, S. (1980). Toward a theory of conversion behavior. In L. Berkowitz (Ed.), *Advances in experimental social psychology* (Vol. 13, pp. 209–239). New York: Academic Press.

Moscovici, S. (1985). Social influence and conformity. In G. Lindzey & E. Aronson (Eds.), *The handbook of social psychology* (Vol. 2, pp. 347–412). New York: Random House.

Moscovici, S., Mucchi-Faina, A., & Maass, A. (Eds.). (1994). *Minority influence.* Chicago: Nelson Hall.

Moscovici, S., & Mugny, G. (Eds.). (1987). *Psychologie de la conversion.* Cousset, Switzerland: Delval.

Moscovici, S., Mugny, G., & Pérez, J. A. (1984–1985). Les effets pervers du déni (par la majorité) des opinions d'une minorité. *Bulletin de Psychologie, 38*, 365–380.

Moscovici, S., Mugny, G., & Van Avermaet, E. (Eds.). (1985). *Perspectives on minority influence.* Cambridge, England; Paris: Cambridge University Press, Editions de la Maison des Sciences de l'Homme.

Moscovici, S., & Personnaz, B. (1980). Studies in social influence: 5. Minority influence and conversion behavior in a perceptual task. *Journal of Experimental Social Psychology, 16*, 270–282.

Moscovici, S., & Personnaz, B. (1986). Studies on latent influence using spectrometer method: 1. Psychologization effect upon conversion by a minority and a majority. *European Journal of Social Psychology, 16*, 345–360.

Moscovici, S., & Personnaz, B. (1991). Studies in social influence: 6. Is Lenin orange or red? Imagery and social influence. *European Journal of Social Psychology, 21*, 101–118.

Mugny, G. (1982). *The power of minorities.* London: Academic Press.

Mugny, G. (1984). Compliance, conversion and the Asch paradigm. *European Journal of Social Psychology, 14*, 353–368.

Mugny, G., Butera, F., Pérez, J. A., & Huguet, P. (1993). Les routes de la conversion: Influences minoritaires et majoritaires. In J. L. Beauvois, R. V. Joule, & J. M. Monteil (Eds.), *Perspectives cognitives et conduites sociales* (Vol. 4, pp. 195–218). Neuchâtel, Switzerland: Delachaux et Niestlé.

Mugny, G., Butera, F., Sanchez-Mazas, M., & Pérez, J. A. (1994). Jugdments in conflict: The conflict elaboration theory of social influence. In B. Boothe, R. Hirsig, A. Helminger, B. Meier, & R. Volkart (Eds.), *Perception, evaluation, interpretation* (Swiss Monographs in Psychology, Vol. 3, pp. 160–168). Bern, Switzerland: Huber.

Mugny, G., & Doise, W. (1979). Niveaux d'analyse dans l'étude expérimentale des processus d'influence sociale. *Social Science Information, 18*, 819–876.

Mugny, G., Ibáñez, T., Elejabarrieta, F., Iñiguez, L., & Pérez, J. A. (1986). Conflicto, identificación y poder en la influencia minoritaria. *Revista de Psicología Social, 1*, 39–56.

Mugny, G., Kaiser, C., & Papastamou, S. (1983). Influence minoritaire, identification et relations entre groupes: Etude expérimentale autour d'une votation. *Cahiers de Psychologie Sociale, 19*, 1–30.

Mugny, G., Maggi, J., Leoni, C., Gianinazzi, M., Butera, F., & Pérez, J. A. (1991). Consensus et stratégies d'influence. *Revue Internationale de Psychologie Sociale, 4*, 403–420.

Mugny, G., & Papastamou, S. (1982). Minority influence and psycho-social identity. *European Journal of Social Psychology, 12*, 379–394.

Mugny, G., & Pérez, J. A. (1985). Influence sociale, conflit et identification: Étude Expérimentale autour d'une persuasion "manquée" lors d'une votation. *Cahiers de Psychologie Sociale, 6,* 1–13.

Mugny, G., & Pérez, J. A. (1991). *Social psychology of minority influence.* Oxford, England: Cambridge University Press.

Nemeth, C. (1986). Differential contributions of majority and minority influence. *Psychological Review, 93,* 23–32.

Paicheler, G. (1988). *The psychology of social influence.* Cambridge, England: Cambridge University Press.

Papastamou, S., Mugny, G., & Pérez, J. A. (1991–1992). La valeur stratégique de la psychologisation dans l'influence sociale. *Bulletin de Psychologie, 45,* 164–172.

Pérez, J. A., Falomir, J. M., Bagueña, M. J., & Mugny, G. (1993). El racismo: Actitudes manifiestas y latentes. *Revista del Colegio Oficial de Psicologos, 56,* 45–50.

Pérez, J. A., Falomir, J. M., & Mugny, G. (1995). Internalization of conflict and attitude change. *European Journal of Social Psychology, 25,* 117–124.

Pérez, J. A., Moscovici, S., & Mugny, G. (1991). Effets de résistance à une source experte ou minoritaire, et changement d'attitude. *Revue Suisse de Psychologie, 50*(4), 26–267.

Pérez, J. A., & Mugny, G. (1985). Influencia minoritaria sobre las opiniones frente al aborto y los anticonceptivos. *Estudios de Psicologia, 23/24,* 29–54.

Pérez, J. A., & Mugny, G. (1986). Induction expérimentale d'une influence minoritaire indirecte. *Cahiers de Psychologie Sociale, 32,* 15–24.

Pérez, J. A., & Mugny, G. (1987). Paradoxical effects of categorization in minority influence: When being an out-group is an advantage. *European Journal of Social Psychology, 17,* 157–169.

Pérez, J. A., & Mugny, G. (1990). Minority influence, manifest discrimination and latent influence. In D. Abrams & M. A. Hogg (Eds.), *Social identity theory. Constructive and critical advances* (pp. 152–168). London: Harvester Wheatsheaf.

Pérez, J. A., & Mugny, G. (1993). *Influences sociales. La théorie de l'élaboration du conflit.* Neuchâtel, Switzerland: Delachaux et Niestlé.

Pérez, J. A., Mugny, G., Butera, F., Kaiser, C., & Roux, P. (1991). Integrazione tra influenza maggioritaria e minoritaria: Conversione, consenso e uniformita. *Ricerche di Psicologia, 4,* 75–102.

Pérez, J. A., Mugny, G., Llavata, E., & Fierres, R. (1993). Paradoxe de la discrimination et conflit culturel: Études sur le racisme. In J. A. Pérez, G. Mugny et al. (Eds.), *Influences sociales: La théorie de l'élaboration du conflit* (pp. 145–168). Neuchâtel, Switzerland: Delachaux et Niestlé.

Pérez, J. A., Mugny, G., & Moscovici, S. (1986). Les effets paradoxaux du déni dans l'influence sociale. *Cahiers de Psychologie Sociale, 32,* 1–14.

Pérez, J. A., Mugny, G., & Navarro, E. (1991). El efecto de la "parálisis intragrupal": Niveles de categorización del yo y niveles de influencia social. *Anthropos (Suplementos), 27,* 121–132.

Personnaz, B. (1975–1976). Conformité, consensus et référents clandestins: La dépendance en tant que processus annulateur de l'influence. *Bulletin de Psychologie, 29,* 230–242.

Personnaz, B. (1979). Niveau de résistance à l'influence de réponses nomiques et anomiques, étude des phénomènes de référents clandestins et de conversion. *Recherches de Psychologie Sociale, 1,* 5–27.

Personnaz, B. (1981). Studies in social influence using the spectrometer method: Dynamics of the phenomena of conversion and covertness in perceptual responses. *European Journal of Social Psychology, 11,* 431–438.

Petty, R. E., & Cacioppo, J. T. (1986). *Communication and persuasion.* New York: Springer-Verlag.

Rokeach, M., Smith, P. W., & Evans, R. I. (1966). Race and shared belief as factors in social choice. *Science, 151,* 167–172.

Sanchez-Mazas, M., Pérez, J. A., Navarro, E., Mugny, G., & Jovanovic, J. (1993). De la paralysie intragroupe au conflit normatif: Études sur l'avortement, la contraception et la xénophobie. In J. A. Pérez & G. Mugny (Eds.), *Influences sociales: La théorie de l'elaboration du conflit* (pp. 121–143). Neuchâtel, Switzerland; Paris: Delachaux & Niestlé.

Tajfel, H. (1978). Social categorization, social identity and social norms. In H. Tajfel (Ed.), *Differentiation between social groups: Studies on the social psychology of intergroup relations* (pp. 27–60). London: Academic Press.

Tanford, S., & Penrod, S. (1984). Social influence model: A formal integration of research on majority and minority influence processes. *Psychological Bulletin, 2,* 189–225.

Turner, J. C. (1991). *Social influence.* Buckingham: Open University Press.

Turner, J. C., Hogg, M., Oakes, P. J., Reicher, S. D., & Wetherell, M. S. (1987). *Rediscovering the social group. A self-categorization theory.* Oxford, England: Basil Blackwell.

Volpato, C., Maass, A., & Mucchi-Faina, A. (1990). Minority influence and social categorization. *European Journal of Social Psychology, 20,* 119–132.

Wilder, D. (1990). Some determinants of the persuasive power of in-groups on out-groups: Organizations of information and attribution of independence. *Journal of Personality and Social Psychology, 59,* 1202–1213.

Wolf, S. (1987). Majority and minority influence: A social impact analysis. In M. P. Zanna, J. M. Olson, & C. P. Herman (Eds.), *Social influence: The Ontario Symposium* (Vol. 5, pp. 207–235). Hillsdale, NJ: Lawrence Erlbaum Associates.

Wood, W., Lundgren, S., Ouellette, J. A., Busceme, M. S., & Blackstone, T. (1994). Minority influence: A meta-analitical review of social influence processes. *Psychological Bulletin, 115,* 323–345.

Zanna, M. P., Olson, J. M., & Herman, C. P. (Eds.). (1987). *Social influence: The Ontario Symposium* (Vol. 5). Hillsdale, NJ: Lawrence Erlbaum Associates.

8

INFORMATION SEEKING AMONG INDIVIDUALS AND GROUPS AND POSSIBLE CONSEQUENCES FOR DECISION MAKING IN BUSINESS AND POLITICS

Dieter Frey
University of Munich

Stefan Schulz-Hardt
University of Kiel

Dagmar Stahlberg
University of Mannheim

The goal-oriented activities and decisions made by groups in business and politics very frequently involve the search for and evaluation of information. Such search and evaluation processes are not complete once provisional or even final decisions have been reached, but should instead be regarded as ongoing activities. Of considerable interest is the question of whether the search for and evaluation of decision-relevant information are carried out in an unbiased way or whether they are more likely to be "distorted." The model of the "Homo Oeconomicus" suggests, for example, that persons involved in this process very carefully search for and evaluate all information relevant to the problem before reaching a provisional or final decision. However, because persons and groups active in politics and business are subject to the same laws of human information processing as other people, the opposite may indeed be the case: Empirical research on the phenomenon of "groupthink" (Janis, 1972, 1982) and one of the most important theories of social psychology—the theory of cognitive dissonance (Festinger, 1957, 1964)—lead to the conclusion that people involved in a decision-making process prefer and even selectively search for specific information that will support a decision that has already been made or that the actor intends to make.

COGNITIVE DISSONANCE AS A DETERMINANT
OF INFORMATION SEEKING

According to the theory of cognitive dissonance (Festinger, 1957, 1964), once people have reached a preliminary or final decision they are aware that, on the one hand, the selected or preferred option may also be tied to negative aspects and that, on the other, the rejected or nonpreferred alternative may also have positive aspects. Such a cognitive configuration produces an unpleasant state of tension known as cognitive dissonance. According to dissonance theory, individuals strive to reduce this state of tension. One possibility to reduce this cognitive dissonance is an intensified search for information that will make the preferred or chosen alternative appear in a better light, while information conflicting with this alternative is avoided (confirmation bias; cf. Frey, 1986; Frey & Wicklund, 1978).

The present authors have carried out a number of investigations to see whether these theoretical predictions are correct. In a number of diverse experiments subjects were presented with several alternative decisions concerning purchasing, career, and business problems. In one experiment by Frey, Schulz-Hardt, Lüthgens, and Moscovici (1995), for example, subjects had to decide whether or not to invest in a developing country given an equal number of supporting and opposing arguments. The subjects' task in this and other experiments always was to decide in favor of one of the alternatives offered. Following these (usually provisional) decisions, subjects were given the opportunity to select further information relating to their choice from a list of 10 items of information, 5 of which contradicted the subjects' decision and 5 of which supported it. These items of information were declared to be expert opinions. (The subjects were given the opportunity to select as many items as they wished in order to read them at full length, and this enabled us to determine whether they preferred supporting or contradicting information.) The core statement that can be derived from these findings is that the confirmation bias predicted by the theory of cognitive dissonance does indeed occur, as long as the decision to be made involves a high degree of commitment, choice, and importance (cf. Frey, 1981b, 1986, 1991). Under these circumstances, subjects primarily sought for information that supported their preferred or selected alternative. The confirmation bias was amplified (a) among anxious individuals (Frey, Stahlberg, & Fries, 1986), (b) when subjects were placed under time pressure while choosing information (Frey, Bresnitz, & Moscovici, 1993), (c) when the amount of information was increased to the extent that it caused an information overload (Frey, Schulz-Hardt, & Martens, 1993), (d) when the information was provided by experts rather than laypersons (Frey, 1981c), (e) when the decision was irreversible (Frey, 1981d; Frey & Rosch, 1984), and (f) when the search for information was linked to financial costs (Frey, 1981d). Conflicting information was only chosen when it was considered to be either easily refutable or useful for decisions arising at a later stage (cf. Frey, 1982, 1986).

To summarize, the factors enhancing confirmation bias, apart from the already existing cognitive dissonance, burden or overload the cognititve capacities of the decision maker. Thus, the conclusion is warranted that especially under suboptimal conditions a stronger confirmation bias appears in decision making. This selective information seeking, that is, ignoring negative information, can be dangerous in real life. Both in private and public life the avoidance of negative or contradicting information can often have catastrophic consequences, because only a confrontation with and an elaboration of dissonant information enable possible dangers and risks of a decision to be detected. When considering the conditions surrounding decision making in business and politics, the significance of these findings becomes apparent: Nearly all decisions are made under time pressure, involve a confrontation with a high density of complex information, and are tied to further costs when information is acquired from expert opinions or market research. So instead of being immunized against self-serving information seeking, decision makers whose decisions have important consequences for themselves and other people often tend to inform themselves in a distorted manner.

SELECTIVE INFORMATION SEEKING IN GROUPS

Should One Expect Groups to Avoid a Confirmation Bias When Seeking Information?

All of the previously mentioned findings add to our knowledge of the search for decision-relevant information among individuals. However, the question of whether these findings can also be generalized to groups is of great practical as well as theoretical relevance: Most of the decisions made in politics, business, and law are made not by individuals, but by groups of individuals in an institutional context. This is theoretically interesting due to the question of whether processes of cognitive dissonance also affect group decision making, and thus whether the postulates of dissonance theory can also be applied to groups with the same validity. Therefore, it seemed to be of great practical and theoretical significance to investigate if the strength of the confirmation bias depends on whether a decision is made by a whole group rather than by an individual.

As the quality of group decision making is regarded as superior to that of individuals (cf. Hill, 1982), one could assume that the information-seeking processes of groups are carried out in a more objective, well-balanced manner than those of individual decision makers. In contrast, we know from research by Janis (1972, 1982) concerning the phenomenon of "groupthink" that under certain conditions (high cohesion, structural faults, and a provocative situational context) groups exhibit dysfunctional symptoms, such as overestimation of the group, closed-mindedness, and pressure on dissenters. One consequence for the decision-making process is a biased search for and evaluation of information. Empirical investigations concerning groupthink have shown that especially the aforementioned structural faults, including "insulation," "directive leadership," "lack of decision procedures," and "group homogeneity," have proven to be good predictors of groupthink (cf. McCauley, 1989; Park, 1990; Schulz-Hardt, Frey, & Lüthgens, 1995; Tetlock, Peterson, McGuire, Chang, & Feld, 1992). So one should expect that, at least under these conditions, groups underlie a strong confirmation bias while searching for information.

Therefore, in a series of studies we transferred the experimental designs employed in the studies of selective information seeking among individuals to group settings. The groups' task again was to decide between two given alternatives. In contrast to the experiments with individuals, the groups were requested to discuss the problem before deciding which alternative to choose using the majority vote system. It was explicitly emphasized in the experimental instructions that the result of the majority vote would be reversible and that the final decision would be made later on. Following this provisional decision, the groups were invited to determine, once again by using the majority vote system, what kind and how much information they wanted to select from a given amount of information (usually 10 items, of which 5 supported and 5 opposed the decision).

Confirmation Bias in Group Experiments

We conducted our first experiments (see Frey et al., 1995) with New York high school students who had to decide, in groups of three, whether or not to invest in a developing country. Apart from having to reach a preliminary decision, the students were asked to give an indication of their confidence in the correctness of their decision before being given the opportunity to obtain further information according to the procedure outlined previously. Single individuals who had to both reach a decision on the same problem and select information individually served as controls.

The evidence indicates that groups show a stronger confirmation bias than individuals: Groups were both more confident about the correctness of their decision as well as more selective when seeking information. They were more interested in information that supported their group's decision.

These findings clearly prove that cognitive dissonance results in selective information seeking not only among individuals but also, and to a greater extent, among groups. One open question is, therefore, why confirmation bias is more strongly pronounced in group decision making. Possible answers to this question can be derived from the outcomes of the classic experiments on "conformity pressure" within groups: In addition to the already existing motivation to reduce cognitive dissonance, the informal pressure to adjust to the group opinion comes into play that promotes selective information seeking. However, in earlier research conformity pressure in groups in particular has been shown to depend on different additional group characteristics such as homogeneity, group size, and group structure, so that the strength of the confirmation bias can be expected to depend on these factors, too.

Accordingly, our more recent research has paid special attention to those variables that have proven to be relevant to traditional group research. The results are summarized in the subsections that follow.

Homogeneous Versus Heterogeneous Groups. Homogeneous groups (i.e., groups consisting of individuals with the same initial opinions) are consistently not only more confident about their decisions but also show a stronger confirmation bias when selecting decision-relevant information than heterogeneous groups (consisting of individuals with varying initial opinions). At the same time, homogeneous groups underestimate the risk of their decision compared to heterogeneous groups. When group members are tested individually following the group experiment, both majorities and minorities are more selective than the previously measured heterogeneous groups.

The experimental finding of a greater selectivity in homogeneous compared to heterogeneous groups is not trivial. One could expect homogeneous groups to be more willing to look for dissenting information because their confidence in their point of view makes dissenting information appear less threatening and more amenable to counterargumentation. However, the opposite is the case: The more certain they are, and the more they deem themselves to be unanimous or homogeneous in terms of a decision, the more they look for consistent information. In the heterogeneous groups, the minority members probably confront the group with conflicting information and make them more cautious so that they are less confident and less selective.

Relevance of Group Size. In our experiments we varied the size of the groups from two to seven members. For homogeneous groups, it was found that the larger the group was, the greater their perceived confidence in their decision was, while an increase in the confirmation bias could also be observed. Extreme confidence was voiced particularly by the groups with seven members. At least for homogeneous groups it is thus true that the distortion in the selection of information increases rather than decreases with increasing group size. Again, the homogeneous groups behave relatively arrogantly in that they are nearly 100% confident and avoid any confrontation with dissonant information, although they "only" have to make a provisional decision and despite the fact that the ignored dissonant information might be of great importance for their final decision.

Size of the Minority in Heterogeneous Groups. The influence of a minority opinion on information seeking in groups depends on its size. It was consistently shown in all our experiments that by increasing the relative size of the minority within a group, the selectivity of information seeking decreased. If, for example, the minority in a group of five subjects consisted of one person, then the confirmation bias produced by the whole group was greater than when the minority consisted of two people. Nevertheless, it still holds that even in groups with a relatively large number of minority members a confirmation bias bolstering the group decision can be discovered.

Confidence of the Minority in Their Decision.   In heterogeneous groups the confidence of minority members in their opinion also proved to be relevant for the selectiveness of information seeking: Groups with uncertain minority members showed a similarly high confidence in the majority decision and a comparably strong confirmation bias to homogeneous groups. Confident minority members, in contrast, ensured a less selective information-seeking behavior in their group.

Representatives.   In one of our studies, each of the groups was asked to elect a representative who was to make the decision concerning information seeking in place of the whole group. Among these elected representatives the confirmation bias was shown to be more pronounced than among nonrepresentatives, although the results of the nonrepresentatives also indicated a selective-exposure effect for this group. It may be the case that the representatives regard themselves as infallible as a direct consequence of having been elected and thus they want to secure their decision cognitively.

Perceived Competence.   In many of our experiments we also asked the groups about the degree of competence they ascribed to themselves when solving the problems at hand. Using a median split of these self-attributions, we then differentiated between high- and low-competence groups. These analyses revealed that groups who ascribed a high degree of competence to themselves were prone to a higher selectivity than less competent groups. It is possible that the self-attribution of competence merely increased the subjective certainty and, as a result, the selectivity. Thus, regarding oneself as an expert by no means safeguards against perceiving information in a distorted manner—this fact is strengthened by another experimental finding: The subjects participating in our studies consisted not only of students and pupils but also of German managers aged between 30 and 50 years and working in different areas: banks, insurances, industry, mechanical engineering, the car industry, and so on. It was demonstrated that the results for these adult managers do not differ from those of students as far as a higher objectivity among experts is concerned—on the contrary, the selectivity effects among managers are even partially more blatant (cf. Frey et al. 1995).

The Role of Leadership.   In two recently performed experiments we randomly designated one person within groups of three as the leader of the group. This leader was put in charge of coordinating the contributions made to the discussion and was made responsible for directing the selection of information. In this condition a stronger confirmation-bias could be established than with groups of three persons without a leader.

The Influence of Justification Pressure on Selective Exposure. Does the pressure to justify a decision have an effect on information seeking and on the confidence in the decision made? In an experiment by Schulz-Hardt, Castagne, and Frey (1995) groups of three people were asked to justify their decision (by writing an essay concerning the reasons for their decision) or not to do so (controls). In the "justification" condition the participants were also told that their decisions as well as their essays on these decisions would be presented to everybody in an exhibition at the end of the study. It was found that groups under justification pressure were not only more certain about the correctness of the decision but were also more selective (the information seeking took place *after* the essay had been written). Justification probably increases dissonance as well as the feeling of infallibility and therefore confidence and selectivity also increase in order to counteract dissonance.

Other Important Dependent Variables: Evaluation of Decision Alternatives and Evaluation of Information

In nearly all of our experiments we asked subjects to evaluate each piece of information according to its usefulness for decision making. It was generally found that consonant information is evaluated as being more useful than dissonant information, and that furthermore it is perceived as being more credible and more difficult to discredit. Additionally, we asked for an evaluation of both the selected and rejected decision alternative. In general, the chosen alternative was regarded as being less risky than the rejected alternative. Besides the results relating to information seeking, we found a large "spreading-apart" effect in nearly all of our experiments: The chosen alternative increased in attractiveness within groups as opposed to individual testing sessions, whereas the attractiveness of rejected alternatives decreased. These spreading-apart effects as well as the distorted evaluation of information are substantially correlated to the degree of selectivity within the search for information—so the former effects are also heightened by the aforementioned factors: homogeneity, competence, leadership, and so forth.

THEORETICAL MECHANISMS UNDERLYING SELECTIVE INFORMATION SEEKING IN GROUPS

In sum, it is possible to say that confirmation effects tend to appear more frequently in groups than in individual decision makers. The effects of selective exposure to information were shown to be particularly prominent in homogeneous groups and in groups that had a formal leader. These results are in line with current research on groupthink (cf. Tetlock et al., 1992). Other results go beyond our current knowledge of distortive group processes, such as group-think: Confirmation effects and feelings of high competence (indicating an "illusion of invulnerability") are more pronounced in groups that are under pressure to justify their decisions, and in subjects who act as representatives. On the other hand, the confirmation bias in groups is moderated by strong and confident minorities who plead for the alternative decision. Additionally, homogeneous groups are consistently more self-confident and more ignorant with regard to risky aspects of their decisions than heterogeneous groups. Our research shows that the confirmation bias arises not only when information is sought, but also when it is evaluated. How can these findings be explained?

Conformity Pressure in Groups

Taken as a whole, these findings are in agreement with the classic investigations into both conformity pressure in groups and the influence of minorities in groups (cf., e.g., Asch, 1951; Moscovici, 1985; Sherif, 1935). In line with this research, our studies (e.g., Frey et al., 1995) revealed that in heterogeneous groups with a strong or confident minority, the pressure to adjust ones own opinion to that of the group was far less than in homogeneous groups. This indicates that, in addition to the motivation provided by the reduction of dissonance on the individual level, once the homogeneous group has reached a consensus on the "truth," it will exert pressure on its members to conform to this truth. Raising doubts, stating disagreement, or actively promoting dissonant information would endanger the consensually validated truth and is therefore avoided. Thus the homogeneous group is more confident and selective than the heterogeneous group.

A very similar mechanism involved in the extremification of group opinions found in homogeneous groups is that of "shared arguments," which are exchanged among members of a group. Together with group pressure, the need to find a consensus regarding these shared arguments also contributes toward the observed extremification. Shared arguments are less likely to be found in heterogeneous groups, so there is no common view that has to be defended by conformity within the group (see also chapters 5, 10, and 11 in Vol. 1).

Once the pressure to conform abates, as in groups with a confident minority, the confirmation bias observed approaches that of a single person. In the heterogeneous group the minority member forces the group to consider his or her opinion, thus making the group less confident and less selective. At first glance, it may appear inconsistent with dissonance theory that confident subjects and groups are more selective, that is, try to bolster their confidence by selective information seeking. However, Irle's modified version of dissonance theory (cf. Irle, 1975) argues that when subjects strongly believe in the correctness of their decision they display higher dissonance than when they do not have such firm convictions. In order to reduce this dissonance they try to fortify their belief by selective information seeking.

Striving for Harmony

The group discusses a complex problem, then it makes a tentative decision supported by all or a majority of its members. Subsequently, information outlining the strengths and weaknesses of the decision has to be selected. A search for possible weaknesses would endanger the harmony attained after the decision-making process and the controversy would start anew. In order to preserve the state of harmony and to bolster the final decision (cf. Janis & Mann, 1977; Montgomery, 1989; Svenson, 1992) those group members who prefer dissonant information are explicitly or implicitly branded as "disturbers of the peace"—even if only provisional decisions are being considered. The maintenance of harmony offers a high social and emotional feeling to group members: They feel accepted, and the group can develop a highly positive distinctiveness because it can take recourse to an assumed confidence based on the decision-making process and the information seeking.

Social Comparison Processes

If individual group members discover that all the other group members subscribe to the same opinion as themselves, this could be interpreted as a validation of their own judgment in terms of the theory of social comparison processes (Festinger, 1954). The social comparison shows the individual that his or her evaluation seems to be correct, which is why contradicting information may be regarded as unnecessary and/or incredible—the group relies on a simple "consensus implies correctness" heuristic (Maheswaran & Chaiken, 1991). The selective-exposure effect is not necessarily only a motivational, but also a cognitive effect; that is, consonant information appears to be more credible and valid. If all the members of a group subscribe to the same opinion, then the credibility and validity of decision-consonant information increase, and this consonant information is consequently preferred to other alternatives. If, in contrast, minorities in heterogeneous groups point out that another truth may exist, then the credibility of the decision-dissonant information increases.

Diffusion of Responsibility

Every individual relies on the judgment of other individuals while trying to find a decision, which leads to a reduced appreciation of the responsibility held by an individual. Independent critical thinking is relegated to second place, which can result in a higher selectivity. The search for dissonant information is a necessary though aversive duty. In the homogeneous group, each member relies on the others to undertake this duty, and thus the diffusion of responsibility does indeed lead to greater selectivity. In the same way greater confidence arises, because every group member believes that another member could come up with a counterargument—but in actual fact nobody does, thus leading to an increase in overall confidence.

All of these factors lead to a stronger distortion in terms of the confirmation bias in homogeneous groups in particular, whereas in heterogeneous groups with strong minorities a confrontation with contradictory information is unavoidable.

THE RELEVANCE OF THESE FINDINGS FOR BUSINESS AND POLITICS

Groups of experts in business and politics reach decisions that have far-reaching consequences for other people on a daily basis. The research results seem to suggest that these teams and bodies selectively search for information during the decision-making process that proves that they are in possession of the truth. Especially groups that have to justify their decisions to the outside world, which are internally very homogeneous, and that ascribe a high competence to themselves will show such distortions to the highest degree. If one keeps in mind that particularly political parties and groups in the highest ranks of business are expected, even by outsiders, to represent their interests in a consistent way and with a high degree of confidence, it has to be concluded from the current research findings that these groups in particular are vulnerable to selective distortions and the symptoms of groupthink. This applies all the more when one considers that in many cases the decisions have to be made under suboptimal conditions, that is, under time pressure and with a massive information overload. These factors along with the acquisition of information from expert opinions or market research normally involve costs and have been proven to intensify distortions.

Additionally, such groups also appear to be extremely susceptible to another symptom of groupthink: The search for unanimity replaces critical thinking, and evokes the illusion of invulnerability and a pronounced optimism. It induces people to take extreme risks and ignore warning signs. The analysis of historical and political-economic decisions shows the catastrophic consequences of such group processes, for example, Pearl Harbor, the Korean War, the invasion of the Bay of Pigs by Kennedy in 1962, the escalation of the Vietnam War (cf. Janis, 1972, 1982), the Iran-Contra affair (cf. Hart, 1990), the Space Shuttle disaster (cf. Esser & Lindoerfer, 1989; Moorhead, Ference, & Neck, 1991), and so on. The Metallgesellschaft fiasco and the German section of CARE's disastrously planned mission to Goma are two recent German examples of such consequences.

Unfortunately, according to research findings it has to be assumed that especially expert commissions, for example, quality controllers in companies, are not free from such group processes. These groups frequently become euphoric about their problem-solving competencies so that they overlook certain danger signals. While reaching a decision, they are convinced of the correctness and truthfulness of their point of view. Information is then merely processed through a filter, which can, among other things, consist of "mindguards" whose function (and aim) it is to protect the group from contradictory or confusing information.

However, the fact that individuals and groups are prone to such processes should not be viewed exclusively in negative terms. These processes can be of decisive importance both for the ability to act (cf. Beckmann & Irle, 1985) and for providing the energy with which a goal is pursued, and can thus occasionally ensure the organism's ability to survive. It should be mentioned that the observed selectivity may be a rational principle: Selectivity is significant, especially in those areas where it is difficult to objectively find correct decision alternatives. Selectivity in this case could be described as a meaningful judgment heuristic, which may lead to mistaken judgments under certain conditions. Many successful innovations would probably never have been undertaken if all the opposing information had been taken into account (cf. Frey, 1991; Wicklund & Frey, 1981). The danger of the possible far-reaching negative consequences of wrong decisions made on the highest level, however, suggests being cautious and vigilant when warning signals occur that should be taken into account. Particularly the research findings relating to the influence of minorities in decision making show the familiar call for a strong and loud opposition in pluralistic and democratic systems in a new light. Thus, coalitions of different, but internally homogeneous groups seem, in contrast to the frequently taken view that too many cooks spoil the broth, to be desirable in terms of good decision making.

HOW CAN SELECTIVE INFORMATION SEEKING AND ITS NEGATIVE CONSEQUENCES BE PREVENTED?

Psychological knowledge can contribute toward the avoidance of selective information seeking and distortive group processes, such as groupthink, by conveying the insights it has derived (based mainly on research conducted by Janis) and by providing appropriate training: Supplying knowledge about the laws of human information processing and dynamic group processes promotes the transparency necessary for providing individuals and groups with the opportunity to reflect upon their own actions. Furthermore, on the basis of theories and research findings, strategies can be developed and scientifically evaluated that are well suited to effectively counteracting the negative consequences of these processes. From these strategies, in turn, institutional structures can be derived that may assist in applying the acquired knowledge:

1. The formal or informal leader should be impartial; that is, he or she should not prematurely favor any particular solution.

2. The formal or informal leader of a group should encourage all members to be critical and to come up with counterproposals by searching for alternatives; he or she should also be in the position to handle criticism concerning his or her own standpoint constructively. A climate of "nobody is perfect" entailing the rejection of a notion of absolute truth should be promoted. The result is a greater receptivity toward new ideas and a reduced danger of relying on particular experts. In addition, it communicates the philosophy that striving for harmony is inappropriate because it can be a source of mistakes. Existing harmony should be regarded as suspect in decision making.

3. Ideally, groups should be heterogeneous; minorities should be equipped with the highest professional and social competence.

4. The diffusion of responsibility within the group should be preempted by making all group members responsible for the consequences, but especially for the *process* of the group decision—thus averting the danger of entrapment (a dysfunctional decision-making process characterized by the inability to stop a losing course of action; cf. Brockner, 1992).

5. Ideally, several groups should try to find solutions to the problem under consideration in order to investigate whether different decisions are made. Deviations should then be analyzed critically and worked through together. In this way, one can avoid that single individuals dominate the entire group opinion. The groupthink phenomenon can thus still occur within these small subgroups, but when the teams try to reach an agreement, a discussion of the entire spectrum of arguments and alternatives will automatically follow because each small group must present its opinions to the others.

6. Within the group, one or more persons could play the devil's advocate (Herbert & Estes, 1977). The task of the devil's advocate is to exercise constructive criticism and thereby create an atmosphere in which others are invited to follow suit. An examination of disadvantages of the preferred alternative allows for an adequate consideration of the problem and should provide the best solution. It is important that the role of the devil's advocate is rotated so that it is not associated with one particular person. Another, more extensive formal decision technique is that of "dialectical inquiry" (Mason, 1969; Mitroff & Emshoff, 1979). Both techniques lead to a superior decision quality (cf. Schwenk, 1990).

7. Different experts who are not involved in making the decision can be invited to every meeting and then be requested to criticize the group members' opinions. Being external onlookers, they would assume the function of the devil's advocate, and due to their external standing, they are not subject to the peril of conformity and cohesion. A constant accompaniment of the group by an external commentator would also be useful.

8. As our results show, confirmation bias is often accompanied by a neglect or underestimation of possible risks. Techniques of psychological risk modeling

can be used for transforming abstract risks into concrete ones that should be better considered during the decision-making process.

9. The mesh of relationships and the dynamics within the group should not be underestimated. Prestige, fear of losing face, internal formation of coalitions, personal likes and dislikes, the repression of weaker members, although irrational, frequently determine decision making, can lead to the avoidance of specific information, and should accordingly be made transparent and counteracted.

10. Constructive competition and controversy while using adequate decision procedures (see earlier this section) should be promoted, as well as critical-rational discussions for finding the best solution. There should be a struggle for ideas to create new solutions instead of a power struggle, which would create new problems. The quality of the solution should be the focus of concern instead of a quick solution that underestimates possible pitfalls—silence can be dangerous.

11. Neither the justification of investments already made nor the fear of negative sanctions should prevent the revision of opinions and decisions. Even if the best strategy seems to have been found, every member should express any remaining doubts as clearly as possible and the question should be reconsidered once more before the final decision is reached. This should prevent making hasty decisions. In the general euphoria of having found a good solution, the disadvantages related to the chosen alternative or the hasty decision are easily overlooked. Thus, an adequate amount of time should be invested in making a decision; this time can be made up later when the decision is put into practice.

12. Every group member should regularly discuss the problem with other individuals within and/or outside the institution and should relate their reaction to the problem to the group. This is another way of receiving new inputs from the outside and of preventing a conspiracy.

13. "Strategic planning of decision making": All possible action scenarios, especially with regard to a broader time perspective, should be elaborated and played through and possible interventions considered (e.g., "what if . . ."). This includes generating and evaluating worst-case scenarios.

14. "Working under a norm of flexibility and a culture of critical rationalism": Instead of praising consistency as the mean characteristic of successful decision makers and relying on the stereotype of good decision makers being infallible, it should be clear that nobody is perfect, mistakes are normal, and nothing is so clear that it cannot be criticized. Recognizing and correcting mistakes is a central feature of success, as well as learning from them. It is of great importance that all the group members are aware that the presence of unanimity may heighten spirits and contribute to more self-confidence and satisfaction, but that it provides absolutely no guarantee of "truth" or "correctness." Groups are by no way immune to thinking errors resulting from a distorted search for and evaluation of information.

REFERENCES

Asch, S. E. (1951). Effects of group pressure on the modification and distortion of judgments. In H. Guetzkow (Ed.), *Groups, leadership, and men* (pp. 177–190). Pittsburgh: Carnegie.

Beckmann, J., & Irle, M. (1985). Dissonance and action control. In J. Kuhl & J. Beckmann (Eds.), *Action control: From cognition to behavior* (pp. 129–150). Berlin, Heidelberg, New York, Tokyo: Springer.

Brockner, J. (1992). The escalation of commitment to a losing course of action: Toward theoretical progress. *Academy of Management Review, 17*, 39–61.

Esser, J. K., & Lindoerfer, J. S. (1989). Groupthink and the Space Shuttle Challenger accident: Toward a quantitative case analysis. *Journal of Behavioral Decision Making, 2*, 167–177.

Festinger, L. (1954). A theory of social comparison processes. *Human Relations, 7*, 114–140.

Festinger, L. (1957). *A theory of cognitive dissonance*. Stanford, CA: Stanford University Press.

Festinger, L. (1964). *Conflict, decision, and dissonance*. Stanford, CA: Stanford University Press.

Frey, D. (1981a). The effect of negative feedback about oneself and cost of information on preferences for information about the source of this feedback. *Journal of Experimental Social Psychology, 17*, 42–50.

Frey, D. (1981b). *Informationssuche und Informationsbewertung bei Entscheidungen*. Bern, Switzerland: Huber.

Frey, D. (1981c). Postdecisional preference for decision-relevant information as a function of the competence of its source and the degree of familiarity with this information. *Journal of Experimental Social Psychology, 17*, 51–67.

Frey, D. (1981d). Reversible and irreversible decisions: Preference for consonant information as a function of attractiveness of decision alternatives. *Personality and Social Psychology Bulletin, 7*, 621–626.

Frey, D. (1982). Different levels of cognitive dissonance, information seeking, and information avoidance. *Journal of Personality and Social Psychology, 43*, 1175–1183.

Frey, D. (1986). Recent research on selective exposure to information. In L. Berkowitz (Ed.), *Advances in experimental social psychology* (Vol. 19, pp. 41–80). New York: Academic Press.

Frey, D. (1991). Informationssuche und Informationsbewertung bei Einzelund Gruppenentscheidungen und mögliche Auswirkungen auf Politik und Wirtschaft. In D. Frey (Ed.), *Bericht über den 27. Kongreß der Deutschen Gesellschaft für Psychologie in Kiel 1990, Kongreßband II* (pp. 45–56). Göttingen, Germany: Hogrefe.

Frey, D., Bresnitz, H., & Moscovici, S. (1993). *Time pressure in decision making and information seeking*. Unpublished manuscript.

Frey, D., & Rosch, M. (1984). Information seeking after decisions: The roles of novelty of information and decision reversibility. *Personality and Social Psychology Bulletin, 10*, 91–98.

Frey, D., Schulz-Hardt, S., Lüthgens, C., & Moscovici, S. (1995). *Group homogeneity and groupthink: The influence of preliminary preferences on distorted group decision-making processes*. Manuscript submitted for publication.

Frey, D., Schulz-Hardt, S., & Martens, T. (1993). *Amount of available information and information seeking after tentative decisions*. Unpublished manuscript.

Frey, D., Stahlberg, D., & Fries, A. (1986). Reactions of high and low anxiety subjects to positive and negative self-relevant feedback. *Journal of Personality, 54*, 694–703.

Frey, D., & Wicklund, R. (1978). A clarification of selective exposure: The impact of choice. *Journal of Experimental Social Psychology, 17*, 621–626.

Hart, P. 't. (1990). *Groupthink in government: A study of small groups and policy failure*. Amsterdam: Swets & Zeitlinger.

Herbert, T. T., & Estes R. W. (1977). Improving executive decisions by formalizing dissent: The corporate devil's advocate. *Academy of Management Review, 2*, 662–667.

Hill, G. W. (1982). Group versus individual performance: Are N+1 heads better than one? *Psychological Bulletin, 91*, 517–539.

Irle, M. (1975). *Lehrbuch der Sozialpsychologie.* Göttingen, Germany; Toronto; Zürich: Hogrefe.

Janis, I. L. (1972). *Victims of groupthink.* Boston: Houghton Mifflin.

Janis, I. L. (1982). *Groupthink* (rev. 2nd ed.). Boston: Houghton Mifflin.

Janis, I. L., & Mann, L. (1977). *Decision making—A psychological analysis of conflict, choice, and commitment.* New York: The Free Press.

Maheswaran, D., & Chaiken, D. (1991). Promoting systematic processing in low-motivation settings: Effect of incongruent information on processing and judgment. *Journal of Personality and Social Psychology, 61*, 13–25.

Mason, R. O. (1969). A dialectical approach to strategic planning. *Management Science, 15*, 403–414.

McCauley, C. (1989). The nature of social influence in groupthink: Compliance and internalization. *Jounal of Personality and Social Psychology, 57*, 250–260.

Mitroff, I. I., & Emshoff, J. R. (1979). On strategic assumption-making: A dialectical approach to policy and planning. *Academy of Management Review, 2*, 662–667.

Montgomery, H. (1989). From cognition to action: The search for dominance in decision making. In H. Montgomery & O. Svenson (Eds.), *Process and structure in human decision making* (pp. 23–49). Chichester, England: Wiley.

Moorhead, G., Ference, R., & Neck, C. P. (1991). Group decision fiascoes continue: Space Shuttle Challenger and a revised groupthink framework. *Human Relations, 44*, 539–550.

Moscovici, S. (1985). Innovation and minority influence. In S. Moscovici, G. Mugny, & E. van Avermaet (Eds.), *Perspectives on minority influence* (pp. 9–51). Cambridge, England: Cambridge University Press.

Park, W.-W. (1990). A review of research on groupthink. *Journal of Behavioral Decision Making, 3*, 229–245.

Schulz-Hardt, S., Castagne, T., & Frey, D. (1995). *How to present a consistent world: Autistic decision making under self-justification.* Unpublished manuscript.

Schulz-Hardt, S., Frey, D., & Lüthgens, C. (1995). Wege ins Desaster: Groupthink, Entrapment und ein dissonanztheoretisches Modell des Entscheidungsautismus. In K. Pawlik (Ed.), *Bericht über den 39. Kongreß der Deutschen Gesellschaft für Psychologie in Hamburg 1994* (pp. 409–414). Göttingen, Germany: Hogrefe.

Schwenk, C. R. (1990). Effects of devil's advocacy and dialectical inquiry on decision making: A meta-analysis. *Organizational Behavior and Human Decision Processes, 47*, 161–176.

Sherif, M. (1935). *The psychology of social norms.* New York: Harper & Row.

Svenson, O. (1992). Differentiation and consolidation theory of human decision making: A frame of reference for the study of pre- and post-decision processes. *Acta Psychologica, 80*, 143–168.

Tetlock, P. E., Peterson, R. S., McGuire, C., Chang, S., & Feld, P. (1992). Assessing political group dynamics: A test of the groupthink model. *Journal of Personality and Social Psychology, 63*, 403–425.

Wicklund, R. A., & Frey, D. (1981). Cognitive consistency: Motivational vs. non-motivational perspectives. In J. Forgas (Ed.), *Social cognition: Perspectives on everyday understanding* (pp. 141–163). New York: Academic Press.

9

SOCIAL IDENTITY, SELF-CATEGORIZATION, AND THE SMALL GROUP

Michael A. Hogg
University of Queensland

Social identity theory is often viewed primarily as a theory of large-scale inter-category behavior that has only passing relevance for intragroup phenomena, particularly processes that occur in small interactive groups. My aim in this chapter is to try to dispel this view. I want to show how social identity theory, particularly its recent extension and development as self-categorization theory, potentially has a great deal to say regarding the small group. But I also want to highlight the way in which characteristics of small groups may pose challenges for these theories.

The first two sections are overviews of social identity theory and self-categorization theory. The next two sections describe the potential relevance of these theories, and the more general intergroup perspective that they represent, to explanations of small-group phenomena. The face-to-face characteristics of small groups may raise new issues for these theories. The following seven sections deal with specific phenomena and processes that occur in small groups and describe how social identity and self-categorization theory can approach their explication: conformity and group polarization, group cohesiveness, group-think, social loafing, intragroup differentiation, roles and group socialization, and leadership. A slightly more detailed treatment, illustrated by description of recent studies, is given of group cohesiveness. The chapter concludes with a summary of some potential issues and directions posed by small groups for social identity theory.

SOCIAL IDENTITY THEORY

Origins

Social identity theory has its origins in early work in Britain by Henri Tajfel on social factors in perception (e.g., Tajfel, 1959, 1969b), and on cognitive and social belief aspects of racism, prejudice, and discrimination (e.g., Tajfel, 1963, 1969a, 1970), but was really formulated and developed in collaboration with John Turner and others in the mid- to late-1970s at the University of Bristol (e.g., Tajfel, 1974, 1978, 1982; Tajfel & Turner, 1979; Turner, 1982). Tajfel despised prejudice and discrimination with a passion, both for personal and social reasons, and Turner was fascinated by the role of social conflict in social change. These passions tended to mark the theory from the outset as primarily a theory of intergroup relations between large-scale social categories (e.g., races, nations, ethnic groups, socioeconomic classes).

Another factor that may have contributed to this perception is the way in which the development of social identity theory was, particularly in the early days, intertwined with the burgeoning and sometimes polemical development of a distinct post-World War II European social psychology. Since the mid-1960s many European social psychologists have considered themselves to have a different social and theoretical agenda to North American social psychologists (e.g., Jaspars, 1980, 1986; Tajfel, 1972)--one that recognizes metatheoretical and conceptual limitations of theoretical reductionism and instead seeks theories that articulate individual psychological processes and wider social forces (cf. Doise, 1986; Lorenzi-Cioldi & Doise, 1990). These goals also framed and continue to frame social identity theory (e.g., Turner & Oakes, 1986) and its more recent extension into self-categorization theory; however, the geographical distinction between Europe and North America has now become blurred (Manstead, 1990; Moreland, Hogg, & Hains, 1994). Nevertheless, despite this blurring, the theory remains, for many people, primarily a theory about intergroup relations between large-scale social categories.

The Theory

Social identity theory is a social-psychological theory of intergroup relations and group processes (e.g., Hogg, 1996; Hogg & Abrams, 1988; Tajfel, 1978, 1982; Tajfel & Turner, 1979; Turner, 1982; Turner & Giles, 1981). The basic idea is that a self-inclusive social category (e.g., nationality, political affiliation, sports team) provides a category-congruent self-definition that constitutes an element of the self-concept. People have a repertoire of such discrete category memberships that vary in relative overall importance in the self-concept. The category is represented in the individual member's mind as a social identity that both describes and prescribes one's attributes as a group member. That is, when a specific social identity is the salient basis for self-regulation, self-perception and conduct become ingroup stereotypical and normative, perceptions of relevant outgroup members become outgroup stereotypical, and intergroup behavior acquires, to varying degrees depending on the history of relations between the groups, competitive and discriminatory properties. Social identities are not only descriptive and prescriptive, but also evaluative. They furnish a relatively consensual evaluation of a social category, and thus its members, relative to other relevant social categories. Because social identities have important self-evaluative consequences, groups and their members are motivated to adopt strategies for achieving or maintaining intergroup comparisons that favor the ingroup, and thus the self.

To account for social identity phenomena, social identity theory invokes the operation of two underlying processes:

1. *Categorization* clarifies intergroup boundaries by producing group stereotypical and normative perceptions and actions, and assigns people, including self, to the contextually relevant category. It is a basic cognitive process that operates on social and nonsocial stimuli alike, to highlight and bring into focus those aspects of experience that are subjectively meaningful in a particular context.

2. *Self-enhancement* guides the social categorization process such that ingroup norms and stereotypes are largely ingroup favoring. It is assumed that people have a very basic need to see themselves in a relatively positive light in relation to relevant others (i.e., have an evaluatively positive self-concept), and that in group contexts self-enhancement can be achieved through evaluatively positive social identity in relation to relevant outgroups (but see Hogg & Abrams, 1993).

An important feature of social identity theory is that in order to explain the behavior of group members, it formally articulates categorization and self-enhancement processes with *subjective belief structures*. The latter refer to people's beliefs about the nature of relations between their own group and relevant outgroups. These beliefs (which are not necessarily accurate reflections of reality) concern the stability and legitimacy of intergroup status relations, and the possibility of social mobility or social change. They influence the specific behaviors that group members adopt in the pursuit of self-enhancement through evaluatively positive social identity.

Social Identity Research

Although many social identity researchers consider the theory to be a general framework for the analysis of the social group (e.g., Hogg & Abrams, 1988), much of the research has actually focused on intergroup behavior rather than what goes on among individuals within a small group. This can easily be evinced from the pervasive presence of the word *intergroup* in articles and books adopting a social identity perspective (e.g., Hogg & Abrams, 1988; Tajfel, 1978, 1982; Tajfel & Turner, 1979; Turner & Giles, 1981). Research has tended to dwell on crowd behavior (e.g., Reicher, 1987), stereotyping (e.g., Oakes, Haslam, & Turner, 1994; Tajfel, 1981), the way in which subjective belief structures influence intergroup behavior (e.g., Brown, 1978; Sachdev & Bourhis, 1991; Taylor & McKirnan, 1984; van Knippenberg & Ellemers, 1993), the role of ethnolinguistic vitality perceptions in interethnic relations and language behavior (e.g., Giles & P. Johnson, 1987; Sachdev & Bourhis, 1993), and so forth. Even the minimal group studies, which are often invoked as critical evidence for social identity, are studies of intergroup behavior between social categories (e.g., Diehl, 1990; Tajfel, Billig, Bundy, & Flament, 1971).

Recent critical remarks about social identity theory often tend to focus on whether or not it is a good intergroup theory rather than whether it is a good social-psychological theory of the group as a whole (e.g., Condor, 1990; Wetherell & Potter, 1992; cf. Harrington & Miller, 1993).

SELF-CATEGORIZATION THEORY

Origins

During the early to mid-1980s an important theoretical development of social identity theory was initiated by John Turner. This new theory, self-categorization theory (Turner, 1985; Turner, Hogg, Oakes, Reicher, & Wetherell, 1987), reflected a shift in emphasis from intergroup relations, social change, and so forth, to fundamental group processes and the psychological nature of group membership. There was now a stronger emphasis on intragroup processes (e.g., conformity, cohesiveness), but also upon the social-cognitive basis of group membership and group phenomena. Although quite distinct from social identity theory in some respects, self-categorization theory is closely related in others—both theories come from the same stable and are part of the same broader theoretical and metatheoretical enterprise (cf. Hogg & McGarty, 1990).

Because it focuses upon the individual cognitive process of categorization, because it mainly talks about categories rather than groups, and because much of its research base is noninteractive individuals, there has been a general tendency for people to treat self-categorization theory as a part of social cognition rather than as a theory that is relevant to small interactive groups.

The Theory

Self-categorization theory elaborates the operation of the categorization process as the cognitive basis of group behavior. Categorization accentuates both similarities among stimuli (physical, social, or aspects of the self) belonging to the same category and differences among stimuli belonging to different categories on dimensions believed to be correlated with the categorization. This process clarifies intergroup discontinuities, and ultimately serves the function of rendering experience of the world subjectively meaningful, and identifies those aspects relevant to action in a particular context.

People can categorize themselves and others at a number of different levels of abstraction, of which the most relevant here is the level of ingroup–outgroup (defining one's social identity). Categorization of self and others at this level accentuates the group prototypicality, stereotypicality, or normativeness of people. The individual is perceptually and behaviorally depersonalized in terms of the relevant ingroup prototype. For self-categorization theory, "the depersonalization of self-perception is the basic process underlying group phenomena (social stereotyping, group cohesion and ethnocentrism, cooperation and altruism, emotional contagion and empathy, collective behaviour, shared norms and mutual influence process, etc.)" (Turner, 1985, pp. 99–100). Nothing negative is implied by the term *depersonalization*. It contains none of the implications of "dehumanization" or "deindividuation," but simply refers to a contextual *change* in the level of identity, not to a loss of identity.

For self-categorization theory, people cognitively represent social groups in terms of prototypes. A prototype is a subjective representation of the defining attributes (beliefs, attitudes, behaviors, etc.) of a social category, which is actively constructed and is context dependent. Because common group members generally find themselves relatively similarly placed within the same social field, their prototypes will usually be very similar—that is, shared. Prototypes are ordinarily unlikely to be checklists of attributes (though they can of course be elicited in this form by probing), rather they are fuzzy sets that capture the context-dependent features of group membership often in the form of exemplary members (actual group members who best embody the group) or ideal types (an abstraction of group features). People are able to assess the prototypicality of real group members, including self—that is, the extent to which a member is perceived to be close or similar to the group prototype.

The social self-concept is context dependent insofar as specific social self-categorizations are brought into play (i.e., become the basis of perception and conduct) by the social field. The cognitive system, in seeking to maximize meaning in a specific context, engages whatever categorization best accounts for the similarities and differences among stimuli. This categorization simultaneously minimizes perceived *intra*category differences and maximizes perceived *inter*category differences, with respect to relevant prototypes, within the social frame of reference. Once formed on the basis of perceived similarities and differences among stimuli, categories are consequently used as a basis for the perceptual accentuation of these similarities and differences, thereby maximizing separateness and clarity. The subjective salience of social categories is not only governed by the mechanics of stimulus-category fit, but also by the motivated availability of social categories. By this I mean that people actively engage in more or less competitive (and more or less successful) renegotiation of the frame of reference in order to achieve a self-categorization that is relatively more favorable for conceptualization of self in that context.

Self-Categorization Research

To date, self-categorization research has been most evident in perhaps three areas: (a) social influence, including the study of conformity and group polarization (e.g., Abrams & Hogg, 1990; Turner, 1991; Turner & Oakes, 1989), (b) social perception, including the study of stereotyping, relative homogeneity effects, and illusory correlation (e.g., Haslam, Oakes, Turner, & McGarty, in press; Oakes, Haslam, & Turner, 1994), and (c) group solidarity and cohesiveness (e.g., Hogg, 1992, 1993). Critics of self-categorization theory are generally concerned that the theory is overly cognitive and that it has lost its commitment to the intergroup perspective that originally framed it.

THE SMALL GROUP

Taken together, social identity theory and self-categorization theory should provide analyses of small-group phenomena that rest on the notion of depersonalization, and that treat the intergroup context as an essential component of intragroup behavior. People in small groups categorize themselves as members of that group, construct a contextually appropriate ingroup prototype from salient ingroup–outgroup comparative information, perceive themselves and others in terms of this prototype, and conform, attitudinally, behaviorally, and emotionally, to the prescriptions of the prototype.

This straightforward application of the theories to small groups is, on the one hand, unproblematic because the theories are intended to apply to all groups. However, on the other hand, perhaps there are features of small groups that may raise problems for the theories—perhaps the theories do not account well for small-group phenomena.

What is a small group, and how may it differ from other sorts of groups? Social psychology has no single accepted definition of the social group. Definitions tend, instead, to reflect different emphases. D. W. Johnson and F. P. Johnson (1987) listed seven separate emphases (interaction, interdependence, mutual influence, perception of belonging to a group, mutual goal achievement, mutual need satisfaction, and structure in terms of roles and norms), and proposed that "A group is two or more individuals in face-to-face interaction, each aware of his or her membership in the group, each aware of the others who belong to the group, and each aware of their positive interdependence as they strive to achieve mutual goals" (p. 8). I would like to propose that this is actually a useful definition of the *small group,* but is too restrictive to deal with the social group as a whole (e.g., large-scale social categories such as ethnic groups, nations, religions, political factions, trade unions, the sexes). The feature that seems to distinguish the small group from other groups is not size per se, but the possibility of simultaneous face-to-face interaction among most or all members of the group.

It was the small group, in this sense, that was the focus of traditional social-psychological research into group dynamics and group processes: for example, classic studies such as M. Sherif's (1966) boys' camp studies, Sherif and Sherif's (1964) and Whyte's (1943) studies of adolescent gangs, Coch and French's (1948) study of an assembly line, Festinger, Schachter, and Back's (1950) investigation of a housing project, and Lippitt and White's (1943) study of after-school activities clubs. Small groups, then, are human aggregates such as gangs, juries, committees, bands, work groups, sports teams, therapy groups, small organizations, small departments, flight crews, and so forth. Small groups have all the properties of other groups but with the additional factor that simultaneous face-to-face interaction among most or all members is possible.

This may not be a trivial additional factor. For instance, face-to-face groups may construct ingroup norms and prototypes in different ways than larger noninteractive groups—the information base may be different. Face-to-face groups may also be characterized by much stronger interpersonal relationships than larger groups in which interpersonal relationships among all members are hardly possible—interpersonal and group-membership-based relationships may coexist in complex ways not originally envisaged by self-categorization theory. Although small and quite possibly distinctive in an intergroup sense, face-to-face groups may well embody increased pressure for intragroup differentiation among group members (i.e., uniqueness—cf. Brewer, 1991, 1993). I return to these issues later. In the meantime it should be noted that for social identity and self-categorization theories to be useful explanations of small groups, they must address the special features of such groups.

INTERGROUP ASPECTS OF SMALL GROUPS

One of the most distinctive aspects of a social identity/self-categorization analysis of small groups is the importance placed on the intergroup context. Processes within small groups are explicated with reference to intergroup relations. Specifically, intergroup, or ingroup–non-ingroup, relations may influence solidarity, conformity, and group identification via subjective belief structures, and ingroup standards (norms, stereotypes, prototypes) are constructed from intragroup and intergroup social comparisons governed by the principle of metacontrast.

Research on small groups has often recognized that groups do not exist in isolation, and that what happens between groups may have an important influence on what happens within the small group. For instance, in his theory of groupthink, Janis (1972, 1982) included insulation of the group from other groups, high stress from external threats, and stereotypic views of outgroups, as antecedents and symptoms of deficient group decision-making processes. There is also a literature on the relationship between intergroup conflict and intragroup cohesion (e.g., Fisher, 1990), much of which deals primarily with large-scale social categories (e.g., Brewer & Campbell, 1976; LeVine & Campbell, 1972), but some of which deals with small groups (e.g., Deutsch, 1949; Dion, 1979; Julian, Bishop, & Fiedler, 1966; M. Sherif, 1966; Stagner & Eflal, 1982). For example, intergroup conflict can lead to scapegoating and exclusion of less central group members (e.g., Lauderdale, Smith-Cunnien, Parker, & Inverarity, 1984; Marques, 1990; Marques & Paez, 1994). The role of intergroup factors is also explicitly recognized in research on bargaining and negotiation (e.g., Morley, Webb, & Stephenson, 1988; Pruitt, 1981).

The strength of a social identity analysis is that intergroup factors are an *intrinsic* feature of the analysis of group behavior, not merely an additional factor that may sometimes be important. Let us now describe some of the ways in which social identity and self-categorization theories can address some small-group phenomena.

CONFORMITY AND GROUP POLARIZATION

One of the chief applications of social identity/self-categorization theory to small-group phenomena has been in the area of conformity and group polarization (e.g., Abrams & Hogg, 1990; Hogg & Turner, 1987; Turner, 1982, 1985, 1991; Turner & Oakes, 1989; Wetherell, 1987). Traditionally, theories of conformity have distinguished between two basic processes of social influence in groups: (a) *normative influence* in which people publicly comply with group norms in order to avoid social disapproval or to gain social approval, and (b) *informational influence* in which people publicly and privately change their perceptions in line with the behavior of others in order to disambiguate physical reality (e.g., Deutsch & Gerard, 1955; Kelley, 1952). Relatedly, traditional explanations of group polarization fall into two broad categories: (a) those that emphasize compliance, for self-presentational motives, with the culturally valued position as it is represented by the distribution of ingroup positions, and (b) those that emphasize the intrinsic persuasiveness of novel arguments brought up in discussion that support one's original position (e.g., Burnstein & Vinokur, 1977; Sanders & Baron, 1977; cf. Isenberg, 1986).

Social identity theorists have felt that the distinction between the phenomena of conformity and polarization may not reflect any real difference in underlying processes, and that the distinction between normative and informational types of influence may be misleading because it distracts theoretical attention from the possible operation of a single process of social influence that is mediated by group identification or self-categorization. Instead it is suggested that the local social comparative context (ingroup–outgroup or ingroup–non-ingroup) determines the degree and direction of polarization, if any, of the ingroup prototype, or subjective norm, and that the process of self-categorization that underlies group identification produces individual conformity to that norm. Other individuals are the sources of context-specific social comparative information from which local group norms are constructed—rather than sources of social approval, intrinsically persuasive arguments, or information about physical reality or culturally valued norms.

Experiments have used both interactive and noninteractive small groups to provide support for these ideas (e.g., Abrams, Wetherell, Cochrane, Hogg, & Turner, 1990; Hogg & Turner, 1987; Hogg, Turner, & Davidson, 1990; Mackie, 1986; Mackie & Cooper, 1984; McGarty, Turner, Hogg, David, & Wetherell, 1990; Wetherell, 1987). However, this research tends, though not always, to use noninteractive groups, and tends almost always to use unidimensional prototypes. Perhaps more complex effects might emerge with more interactive groups in which interpersonal relationships play a role, and with more complex multidimensional prototypes.

GROUP COHESIVENESS

Since the study of group dynamics in the 1940s, small-group researchers have described psychological group membership and solidarity in terms of group cohesiveness. Although originally a complex concept referring to the cognitively represented field of forces acting on a member to remain in a group (e.g., Festinger et al., 1950), it was quite quickly simplified, both operationally and conceptually, to refer in most cases to the attractiveness of the group or ultimately interpersonal attraction (e.g., B. E. Lott, 1961; A. J. Lott & B. E. Lott, 1965). Although small groups may well be characterized by interpersonal attraction and friendship, a number of critics have felt that something is being missed if *group* cohesiveness is no more than aggregated *interpersonal* attraction (e.g., Evans & Jarvis, 1980; Hogg, 1992; Mudrack, 1989; Turner, 1984).

Social identity theory offers an alternative conceptualization of cohesiveness that is based on a separation of *personal attraction,* grounded in specific interpersonal relationships and idiosyncratic preferences, from *social attraction,* group-membership-based regard grounded in depersonalized prototype-based perception of self and others—positive regard for ingroup members and negative regard for outgroup members (Hogg, 1992, 1993). Social attraction describes the positive interindividual attitude usually found in salient ingroups—but explains it not in terms of interpersonal relations, but in terms of the genuinely group process of self-categorization and depersonalization. The most important prediction to be made from this perspective is that in salient groups, ingroup liking is depersonalized in terms of the ingroup prototype, and is independent from interpersonal attraction.

In addition to indirect evidence, and earlier studies that contrast attraction and categorization (for overviews, see Hogg, 1987; J. C. Turner, 1984), there are now some direct tests of the depersonalized attraction hypothesis. These studies all use small groups to try to demonstrate that ingroup liking is depersonalized in terms of the ingroup prototype, and is separate from interpersonal attraction. Hogg and Hardie (1992) conducted an experiment in which four-person single-gender groups made estimates of autokinetic movement under conditions accentuating individuality, or accentuating gender-category membership. The degree of convergence of estimates within the group across trials (i.e., conformity) was an index of group behavior and identification with the group. Dependent measures monitored liking and perceptions of prototypicality within the group, so that it was possible to compute the amount of intermember agreement on who was liked most and who was most prototypical. As predicted (see Table 9.1), female groups in the high-salience condition converged more sharply and had a more consensual pattern of liking and perceived prototypicality than those in the low-salience condition. The results for men were less consistent. However, most important, across all subjects we found that groups that converged most sharply had the most consensual patterns of liking and perceived prototypicality, and were least likely to use interpersonal similarity as a basis for liking. This suggests that in psychologically salient groups, liking is related to prototypicality.

To complement this laboratory experiment we conducted a field study of an Australian football team (Hogg & Hardie, 1991). A questionnaire was adminis-tered at a team practice session to elicit subjective perceptions of prototypical features of the team, and a rating of self-prototypicality. Respondents then rank

TABLE 9.1
Selected Means From Hogg and Hardie's (1992) Autokinetic Study

Dependent Measures	Cell Means			
	Female Groups		Male Groups	
	Low $n = 13$	High $n = 13$	Low $n = 7$	High $n = 6$
Convergence	-0.25	-0.44	-0.30	-0.54
	0.44	0.54	0.68	0.38
	0.55	0.65	0.64	0.49

Note. "Low" and "high" indicate the low- and high-salience conditions. Convergence can range from -1 (complete convergence) to +1 (complete divergence). For the consensual liking and prototypicality measures, more positive scores indicate greater consensuality. From Hogg (1993). Copyright 1993 by Wiley. Adapted by permission.

ordered fellow members in terms of prototypicality, social attraction, and personal attraction. These last two were elicited by special instructions making the team or interpersonal friendships, respectively, salient. As predicted, we found a significantly stronger relationship between social attraction and target prototypicality than personal attraction and prototypicality. We also found that this effect was strongest for those subjects who identified most strongly with the team, and saw themselves as highly prototypical. In addition, there was a stronger relationship between being socially popular (i.e., consensually liked as a team member) and prototypically popular (i.e., consensually rated as highly prototypical) than personally popular (i.e., consensually liked as a personal friend) and prototypically popular. Members who were most socially and prototypically popular were also those who themselves identified most strongly with the team, and defined themselves as most prototypical. These data again point to the depersonalized nature of intragroup attraction.

Using a similar methodology, we conducted two studies to address the same general hypothesis that self-categorization depersonalizes the basis of attraction so that it becomes based on group prototypicality (Hogg, Cooper-Shaw, & Holzworth, 1993). We sought to replicate findings from the earlier study (which was essentially a single-case study of a specific type of all-male group), but also to test a wider range of specific hypotheses derived from self-categorization theory (including ones concerning interpersonal similarity, perceived self-prototypicality, and prototype clarity).

In the first study 61 members of six small, well-established, mixed-gender interactive organizational groups in a large tertiary educational institution completed a questionnaire measuring perceptions of the cohesiveness/solidarity of the group, the nature and clarity of the group prototype, membership and involvement in the group, prototypicality of self and fellow members, and friendship-based and group-membership-based sociometric choice. The salience of the group was manipulated as a within-subjects variable by focusing subjects' attention on group membership and group activities during one phase of the study, and then on interpersonal relations and activities unrelated to group membership during another phase. The second study was very similar but used 112 student subjects in 15 small, ad hoc, mixed-gender, 1-hour interactive groups. There were also some different dependent measures.

The results replicated Hogg and Hardie's (1991) findings, and revealed a number of other predicted effects: (a) Subjects who considered the group to be relatively important and homogenous, and to contain members who were generally prototypical, were not popular on an interpersonal liking basis, (b) group-based liking for fellow members was more strongly associated with perceived prototypicality than with interpersonal liking, (c) prototypical and group-liking popularity were enhanced among members who had a positive attitude toward the group, and who felt the group had a clear prototype, (d) prototypicality was a stronger basis for group liking among members who reported greater clarity,

(e) perceived interpersonal similarity was a stronger basis than prototypicality for interpersonal liking, (f) interpersonally popular members were more popular on the basis of similarity than prototypicality, and (g) the relationship between interpersonal liking and similarity was unrelated to group variables such as cohesiveness, prototype clarity, positive group attitude, and self-prototypicality. Once again, and consistent with the self-categorization analysis presented in this chapter, these data indicate that attraction among members of a salient social group is quite separate from interpersonal attraction, and is based on perceptions of self and others that are depersonalized in terms of the ingroup prototype.

Because self-categorization accentuates perceived prototypical similarity within the group, perhaps one way in which social attraction is produced is via a similarity-attraction process (cf. Byrne, 1971). However, it is important to stress that it is not interpersonal similarity, but similarity on group prototypical dimensions (i.e., depersonalized similarity) that is related to social attraction and group cohesiveness. To test this idea, we conducted a rather complicated experiment in which subjects evaluated another individual who was either a member of an ingroup with whom they were about to take part in an interactive task, or was merely an individual who would be their partner for the upcoming task (Hogg, Hardie, & Reynolds, 1995). Subjects learned that the other person was similar or dissimilar to self on each of two dimensions relating to the task at hand—however, one dimension was prototypical of group membership and the other was not. Effectively (though in reality more complicated), the design was a 2 (interpersonal vs. group) × 2 (similar vs. dissimilar on the prototypical dimension) × 2 (similar vs. dissimilar on the nonprototypical dimension). The general finding was that in groups attitude toward the target person was more strongly related to similarity on the prototypical than nonprototypical dimension, and that this effect was more pronounced for subjects who identified more strongly with the group. In contrast, in the interpersonal condition attitude was related to overall similarity. It would appear that self-categorization depersonalized perception so that subjects focused only on prototypicality as a basis for their feelings about fellow group members.

One of the strengths of the social identity perspective on cohesiveness is that it incorporates an analysis of intergroup relations. In a final study, we investigated the effects of intergroup relations on depersonalized attraction as a function of subjective belief structures and social identification (Hogg & Hains, 1996). Members of 11 female netball teams playing in a local amateur league were administered a questionnaire measuring identification, interpersonal relations, depersonalized social attraction, true personal attraction, and social beliefs concerning team status and the stability, legitimacy, and permeability of that status. Position in the league was a measure of objective status. Using a linear structural equation modeling technique (EQS method) we found that social attraction was directly influenced by identification; indirectly influenced, via identification, by status and stability beliefs; and uninfluenced by interpersonal relations. Social attraction and personal attraction were, once again, relatively independent.

Taken together, these studies suggest how an intergroup perspective embodied by social identity and self-categorization theories can make quite distinct predictions about small groups. Although the studies generally support the depersonalized social attraction hypothesis, it is worth noting that the empirical independence of social and personal attraction is not always complete. This is not wholly surprising—indeed, Mullen and Copper (1994) performed a meta-analysis of research on the cohesiveness-performance relationships and found that although social and interpersonal aspects of cohesiveness were relatively separate factors, they tended to co-occur in cohesive groups. Although personal and social attraction may be generated in different ways, both processes may occur to some extent particularly in small groups: Friends develop a sense of being a group and thus social attraction arises, and individuals who interact within a group may become friends. It remains a challenge for social identity theory to be able to distinguish more clearly between social and personal attraction at the operational level.

GROUPTHINK

This problem also arises in trying to distinguish between social attraction- and personal attraction-based cohesiveness in groupthink. In his theory of groupthink, Janis (1972, 1982) assigned cohesiveness an important role—it is the main cause of excessive concurrence seeking that characterizes suboptimal small-group decision making that can produce poor decisions with disastrous consequences. By cohesiveness Janis appeared to mean a mixture of, among other things, group solidarity, close friendship, loyalty, and interpersonal attraction (cf. Hogg, 1992; Hogg & Hains, 1994).

Investigations of the role of cohesiveness in groupthink are inconclusive. Descriptive tests of the groupthink hypothesis provide some support for the general model but the data do not permit conclusive examination of the role of group cohesiveness (e.g., Esser & Lindoerfer, 1989; Hensley & Griffin, 1986; Huseman & Driver, 1979; Janis, 1972; Manz & Sims, 1982; Raven, 1974; Smith, 1984; Tetlock, 1979). In fact, Moorhead and Montanari (1986) found on some measures a negative relationship between cohesiveness and groupthink, and Tetlock, Peterson, McGuire, Chang, and Feld (1992) found no evidence for cohesiveness as a predictor of symptoms of groupthink.

Experimental studies are less plentiful, but more useful for examining the causal role of cohesiveness. Studies that have manipulated cohesiveness in terms of friendship (i.e., by having groups of strangers or groups of acquaintances) found either no relationship between cohesiveness and groupthink (Flowers, 1977) or a negative relationship (Leana, 1985). Fodor and Smith (1982) manipulated cohesiveness by creating an intergroup competition for a scarce reward, and found no significant relationship between cohesiveness and groupthink. The manipulation of cohesiveness in terms of "alleged" compatibility and similarity that engenders liking reveals that high cohesiveness produces groupthink only where no directions for effective group decision making are given (Callaway & Esser, 1984) or where rapid concurrence is an explicit group objective (Courtright, 1978). Finally, M. E. Turner, Pratkanis, Probasco, and Leve (1992) found limited support for a positive relationship between cohesiveness, manipulated by explicitly labeling three-person groups (cf. minimal group techniques— e.g., Billig & Tajfel, 1973), and symptoms of groupthink.

The conclusion to be drawn from these experimental findings is that the effect of group cohesiveness on groupthink may depend on how groupthink is operationalized and hence conceptualized. Indeed, a number of critics have now noted the need for a more detailed specification of cohesiveness and its role in groupthink (e.g., Hogg, 1992; Hogg & Hains, 1994; Longley & Pruitt, 1980; McCauley, 1989).

Adopting a social identity/self-categorization analysis, we pursued this idea by conducting two very similar experiments that distinguished between cohesiveness based on friendship and cohesiveness based on social attraction (Hogg & Hains, 1994). Against background conditions that would be conducive to groupthink we crossed friendship and social attraction and had small four-person groups engage in decision-making discussions that were tape recorded. There was also a wide range of subjective measures of friendship, identification/social attraction, and the decision-making process. The results of the two experiments were remarkably consistent:

1. Friendship (thus cohesiveness defined in interpersonal terms) tended to be associated with *improved* subjective and objective group decision-making procedures: less striving for uniformity, less deference to the leader, less desire to reach consensus, greater assessment of risks, more requests for information, and introduction of more facts into the discussion. The effect, which is consistent with findings reported by Leana (1985), was relatively weak.

2. Identification, solidarity, and social attraction (thus cohesiveness defined in group terms) was much more strongly associated with subjective and objective group decision-making procedures, and was equally strong in both experiments. Cohesiveness generally impoverished decision making (greater striving for uniformity, more effort to reach agreement, greater desire for consensus, greater deference to the leader, more rationalization, discussion of fewer risks, and introduction of fewer facts), but also improved decision making in some ways (better information handling, less self-censorship, greater endorsement of majority decision making, less verbal pressure on deviants to agree, and more discussion of alternative scenarios sooner).

Apart from helping to clarify the relationship between cohesiveness and groupthink, these experiments also show more generally how a social identity/self-categorization analysis can address issues in the study of small-group processes.

SOCIAL LOAFING

There is a long and noble tradition of small-group research that has investigated the way in which people may work less hard or perform less well when they are in groups than when they are alone. Recently this tradition has expressed itself in research into social loafing (e.g., Geen, 1991; Harkins & Szymanski, 1987; Williams, Karau, & Bourgeois, 1993), defined as "a reduction in individual effort when working on a collective task (in which one's outputs are pooled with those of other group members) compared to when working either alone or coactively" (Williams et al., 1993, p. 131).

Although a robust phenomenon that has been replicated across more than 80 studies, there are some conditions under which people may not loaf (see Stroebe et al., chap. 2, this volume). Of particular relevance here is conflicting, largely unpublished, evidence concerning the effect of cohesiveness on loafing—sometimes it increases loafing and at other times it diminishes it. From a social identity perspective we might argue that cohesiveness operationalized as social attraction might reduce loafing, whereas cohesiveness operationalized as interpersonal attraction would not affect it (Hogg, 1992). Research is currently underway to investigate this idea (Hogg, 1994).

INTRAGROUP DIFFERENTIATION

A notable difference between small-group research and intergroup research is that the former often focuses on, and theorizes about, intragroup differentiation (e.g., roles, communication networks, leadership—cf. Levine & Moreland, 1990), whereas the latter emphasizes, and theorizes about, intragroup homogeneity (e.g., stereotypes, conformity—cf. Messick & Mackie, 1989).

Clearly groups (of all sizes) are internally structured and embrace dynamic tensions between structural components. However, according to social identity/self-categorization theory the process of categorization associated with group membership produces an accentuation of perceived intragroup similarities on contextually relevant stereotypical dimension—there is evidence for this from Tajfel's accentuation principle (e.g., Doise, Deschamps, & Meyer, 1978; Eiser & Stroebe, 1972; Tajfel, 1959). Furthermore, there is behavioral homogenization due to conformity. Social identity and self-categorization theory have not been framed to deal theoretically with intragroup differentiation (but see Hogg, 1996).

Some perspectives on intergroup perceptions (i.e., stereotypes) do recognize the existence of greater *perceived* homogeneity of the outgroup relative to the ingroup (e.g., Mullen & Hu, 1989; Park & Rothbart, 1982; Quattrone & Jones, 1980). The effect has been explained in terms of relatively greater familiarity with ingroup members (e.g., Linville, Fischer, & Salovey, 1989) or relative familiarity in conjunction with knowledge of the group as a whole (e.g., Park, Ryan, & Judd, 1992). Under some circumstances, however, the ingroup can be perceived to be more homogeneous than the outgroup (e.g., Simon, 1993; Simon & Brown, 1987; Stephen, 1977; cf. Haslam et al., in press)—for example, some minorities can see themselves as being more homogeneous and thus having greater solidarity. Social identity theory is unproblematically able to explain this in terms of the specific nature of the relations between two groups, and group members' beliefs about those relations.

Optimal Distinctiveness

Perceived homogenization effects aside, we are still left with some need to explain intragroup differentiation—actual attitudinal, behavioral, or emotional differentiation between ingroup members, as opposed to subjectively perceived differences. One explicit attempt to address this issue from a broadly intergroup perspective is Brewer's optimal distinctiveness theory (Brewer, 1991, 1993; Brewer & Weber, 1994). Brewer argued that people are governed by two powerful social motives—for distinctiveness/uniqueness and for inclusion/sameness. These motives are dynamically balanced such that people strive for greater inclusion when they feel too distinctive, and for greater distinctiveness when they feel too included. They try to achieve an optimal balance. Roughly speaking, personal identity maximally satisfies the need for uniqueness, and social identity the need for inclusion. The implication is that people in groups are simultaneously trying to differentiate themselves as individuals from the group, and trying to "lose" themselves as members in the group.

This theory has an implication for small groups. Smaller groups are, by definition, less inclusive and more distinctive than larger groups. Therefore people in smaller groups feel less loss of individual distinctiveness, and are more likely to strive for greater inclusiveness. The paradox exists, then, that it is precisely in smaller groups, where people can interact closely and have interpersonal relations with all members, that people may strive to conform more and to be more like other members of the group.

Prototypical Consensuality

Optimal distinctiveness theory tends to equate uniqueness with personal identity and inclusion with social identity, and thus explains differentiation within groups in terms ultimately of competing interpersonal and group motives. An alternative perspective on intragroup differentiation can be proposed—it traces intragroup differentiation to certain consequences of the single group-level process of self-categorization. This analysis proceeds from Codol's (1975, 1984) early work on overconformity (called the PIP, *primus inter pares*, effect)—people in salient groups sometimes appear to strive to be different from one another, but not as individuals, rather in terms of being seen to conform more than others to the ingroup-defining norm.

This point can be extended on the basis of self-categorization theory. In groups people strive to conform to their representation of the group norm (i.e., the subjective prototype). Thus, if there is virtual consensus on the prototype self-categorization will produce homogeneity of attitudes, opinions, and behaviors. If there is a diversity of representations of the prototype then self-categorization will produce heterogenous behavior as individuals conform to their own subjective and different prototypes. Consensual prototypes are likely to arise under conditions in which all group members are exposed to the identical social comparative context—that is, they have identical information from which to construct the prototype. These are the sorts of conditions that might prevail in, for example, highly orthodox, rigid, ideologically controlled groups (e.g., religions, cults, military groups, adolescent gangs, totalitarian regimes), active sociopolitical minorities (e.g., environmental groups, ethnic minorities), ad hoc groups used in laboratory research into group processes (e.g., the polarization studies cited earlier), and, all things being equal, smaller groups where all members can communicate with one another. Nonconsensual prototypes are likely to arise under conditions in which group members are exposed to different social comparative contexts—that is, they have different information from which to construct the prototype. These are the sorts of conditions that might prevail in, for example, groups that contain factions (e.g., a social movement that is undergoing ideological change), democratic, laissez-faire societies or organizations, and, all things being equal, larger groups where all members cannot communicate with one another.

This model identifies a process of social differentiation within groups that is not produced by interpersonal processes, but rather by characteristics of intergroup relations and the immediate or larger scale social comparative context that influences the degree of intragroup consensuality of the subjective prototype. People differentiate because they are conforming to different representations of the group. From the perspective of self-categorization theory this is a relatively new idea that remains to be explored (but cf. Duck, Hogg, & Terry, 1995; Hogg, Cooper-Shaw, & Holzworth, 1993; Moreland, Levine, & Cini, 1993). The implication for small-group research is that salient small groups are likely to be prototypically homogeneous despite the prevalence of interpersonal relations. However, to the extent that close interpersonal relations are responsible for unshared social contextual information then the group will become less homogeneous.

Evaluative Intragroup Differentiation

Prototypical dissensuality is perhaps only one way in which intragroup differen-tiation may arise. Another potent mechanism rests on the self-evaluative conse-quences of group membership. Generally, people strive for group memberships that mediate positive self-evaluation—this is a basic tenet of social identity theory (but see Hogg & Abrams, 1993). One consequence is that when membership is a salient basis for self-perception less prototypical members will be liked less than more prototypical members (this is a direct implication of the depersonalized attraction hypothesis described in detail previously). In this way, self-categoriza-tion produces intragroup evaluative and affective structuring. Furthermore, in smaller groups where prototypes may be more consensual this structuring itself may be more consensual—some people may become socially unpopular or con-sensually disliked in group terms. This process may go so far as effectively to exclude the most unpopular members from membership at all. They become black sheep who are ostracized and rejected (cf. Marques, 1990; Marques & Paez, 1994; Marques & Yzerbyt, 1988; Marques, Yzerbyt, & Leyens, 1988).

ROLES AND GROUP SOCIALIZATION

These self-categorization implications for the study of intragroup differentiation tend to focus upon differences in degree—for instance, degree of liking, favorabil-ity of attitude, extent of prototypicality. Groups are also structured, however, in terms of content—specifically in terms of roles, with important evaluative connotations, that prescribe different types of behavior as group members.

In their diachronic model of group socialization in small groups, Moreland and Levine (e.g., Levine & Moreland, 1994; Moreland & Levine, 1982, 1984, 1989) identified a number of generic roles (i.e., prospective member, new member, full member, marginal member, exmember) that people can occupy at different stages of their passage through the group. At any given time, then, the group is differentiated into different roles, and members' commitment to the group is reflected in role-consistent behavior. Recently, Moreland et al. (1993) identified ways in which their notion of commitment may be approached from a self-cate-gorization perspective. Specifically, they suggested that the group's commitment to members may depend on the perceived prototypicality of members, and members' commitment to the group on their perceived self-prototypicality. The sort of behavior that commitment produces depends on how group membership is defined from the perspective of the member, and this in turn is influenced by the member's role in the group. In terms of the earlier discussion of prototypical consensuality, social comparative information influences the subjective, or self-relevant prototype of group membership, and self-categorization produces pro-totype consistent behavior.

An important feature of Moreland and Levine's work is the emphasis on the diachronic features of group life, which they feel are often neglected in group research. A similar concern can be expressed about social identity and self-categorization theory. In general these theories, although they have the potential to address temporal features of groups and intergroup relations, do not do so—one notable exception is Taylor and McKirnan's (1984) five-stage social identity model of intergroup relations.

LEADERSHIP

Leadership is one generic role that has been an important focus of small-group research (e.g., Bass, 1981), as well as wider social science perspectives (e.g., Graumann & Moscovici, 1986; Hunt, Baliga, Dachler, & Schriesheim, 1988; cf. Levine & Moreland, 1990; see also chaps. 3 and 4). Social identity/self-categorization theory has clear implications for the conceptualization of leadership.

Leaders are individuals who have disproportionate influence, often through possession of consensual prestige and/or the exercise of power, over the attitudes, behaviors, and destiny of group members. The group leader would thus be expected to be the individual who occupies the contextually most prototypical group position—as this is the position that embodies the behaviors to which most group members conform. If the comparative context remains relatively stable, so will the prototype and thus the same person will remain in the leadership (most influential) position. Thus far this is a relatively passive process, and the leader does not lead in an active sense but merely embodies the aspirations, attitudes, and behaviors of the group. Leadership is more than being prototypical—it also involves the active exercise of individual power.

People occupying prototypical positions may, however, acquire such power to influence in at least two ways: (a) They are socially attractive (cf. Hogg, 1992, 1993) and thus, because they are liked, people in the group are more likely to comply with their suggestions, requests, and orders; (b) they are perceived to have charismatic/leadership personalities, due to the operation of attribution processes that cause members to attribute the leader's apparent influence to the person rather than the prototypicality of the position they occupy (cf. the fundamental attribution error—Ross, 1977). The longer a specific individual remains in a leadership position the more that person will be socially "liked," the more consensual will social attraction be, and the more entrenched will the fundamental attribution effect be. Having acquired power in these ways, the person occupying the prototypical position will be able to adopt the more active aspects of being a leader, including the power to maintain his or her leadership position by influencing the social comparative context and thus his or her prototypicality. In addition, groups with consensual prototypes (see earlier discussion), and that may include small groups, are more likely to have entrenched leaders due to the consensuality of perceptions of and feelings for the leader by the group. In groups with less consensual prototypes, there will be greater dissensus of perceptions of and feelings for the leader and thus the leader may have less power and may occupy a less stable position.

We recently conducted a preliminary study of these ideas—specifically the role of prototypicality in leadership (Hains, Hogg, & Duck, 1994). Under conditions of high or low group salience (self-categorization), subjects anticipated joining a discussion group and were given information about the group leader that described him or her as being group prototypical or nonprototypical and as possessing commonly recognized, stereotypical leadership qualities or not. As we predicted, under high-salience conditions subjects responded to prototypicality, not stereotypicality, information—they rated the prototypical leader as more of a leader than the nonprototypical leader. Under low-salience conditions subjects responded to stereotypicality, not prototypicality, information—they felt the stereotypical leader was more of a leader than the nonstereotypical leader.

CONCLUSIONS

In this chapter I have tried to show how social identity theory and self-categorization theory have relevance for the study of processes that occur in small groups (see also chapter 10, this volume). Although these are intended to be general social-cognitive theories of the social group, their relevance to small groups is often not recognized. Social identity theory is treated as a theory of large-scale intergroup relations, and self-categorization theory a theory about the operation of the individual cognitive process of self-categorization. In fact, these theories have a great deal of potential for and intended relevance to small-group processes (see Hogg, 1996)—though to date the main focus of relevant research has been on social influence and cohesiveness, and much of this research has not employed interacting small groups. Nevertheless, social identity theory and self-categorization theory have been significant contributors to a recent revival, documented by Moreland et al. (1994), of social-psychological research on groups, and there are some good prospects for their contribution to the study of roles and role relations (Hogg, Terry, & White, 1995).

The small group raises a number of challenges for social identity theory and self-categorization theory, of which perhaps three can be summarized here:

1. Social identity research has often tended to use noninteractive minimal-type groups to test hypotheses. This raises a particular problem for the study of small groups, because in general small groups are ones in which all or most members interact with one another, and in which interpersonal relationships may thrive. Social identity and self-categorization research needs to investigate interactive groups more fully. Perhaps this would include an analysis of dia-

chronic aspects of group life, and a study of the more realistic multidimensional prototypes that underlie depersonalization in nonlaboratory settings.

2. The conceptual distinction of interpersonal from group processes that is a central feature of social identity theory can sometimes be difficult to measure or operationalize in small groups. In such groups, interpersonal relationships and group solidarity often co-occur. Better methods are needed to distinguish empirically between interpersonal and group processes in small groups.

3. Social identity perspectives focus on intergroup differentiation and intragroup homogenization, and do not fully address theoretically or empirically intragroup differentiation (e.g., into roles). Intragroup differentiation is a prevalent characteristic of groups, and one that has traditionally been a major focus of group research. For social identity theory to address small groups more fully, the study of intragroup differentiation (and intragroup structure) is an important direction.

ACKNOWLEDGMENT

I would like to thank Bridget Hogg for her help in preparing this chapter.

REFERENCES

Abrams, D., & Hogg, M. A. (1990). Social identification, self-categorization, and social influence. *European Review of Social Psychology, 1*, 195–228.

Abrams, D., Wetherell, M. S., Cochrane, S., Hogg, M. A., & Turner, J. C. (1990). Knowing what to think by knowing who you are: Self-categorization and the nature of norm formation, conformity and group polarization. *British Journal of Social Psychology, 29*, 97–119.

Bass, B. M. (1981). *Stogdill's handbook of leadership*. New York: The Free Press.

Billig, M., & Tajfel, H. (1973). Social categorization and similarity in intergroup behaviour. *European Journal of Social Psychology, 3*, 27–52.

Brewer, M. B. (1991). The social self: On being the same and different at the same time. *Personality and Social Psychology Bulletin, 17*, 475–482.

Brewer, M. B. (1993). The role of distinctiveness in social identity and group behaviour. In M. A. Hogg & D. Abrams (Eds.), *Group motivation: Social psychological perspectives* (pp. 1–16). London: Harvester Wheatsheaf.

Brewer, M. B., & Campbell, D. T. (1976). *Ethnocentrism and intergroup attitudes: East African evidence*. New York: Sage.

Brewer, M. B., & Weber, J. G. (1994). Self-evaluation effects of interpersonal versus intergroup social comparison. *Journal of Personality and Social Psychology, 66*, 268–275.

Brown, R. J. (1978). Divided we fall: An analysis of relations between sections of a factory workforce. In H. Tajfel (Ed.), *Differentiation between social groups* (pp. 395–429). London: Academic Press.

Burnstein, E., & Vinokur, A. (1977). Persuasive argumentation and social comparison as determinants of attitude polarization. *Journal of Experimental Social Psychology, 13*, 315–332.

Byrne, D. (1971). *The attraction paradigm*. New York: Academic Press.

Callaway, M. R., & Esser, J. K. (1984). Groupthink: Effects of cohesiveness and problem solving procedures on group decision making. *Social Behavior and Personality, 12*, 157–164.

Coch, L., & French, J. R. P., Jr. (1948). Overcoming resistance to change. *Human Relations, 1,* 512–532.

Codol, J.-P. (1975). On the so-called "superior conformity of the self" behaviour. *European Journal of Social Psychology, 5,* 457–501.

Codol, J.-P. (1984). Social differentiation and non-differentiation. In H. Tajfel (Ed.), *The social dimension: European developments in social psychology* (Vol. 1, pp. 314–337). Cambridge, England: Cambridge University Press.

Condor, S. (1990). Social stereotypes and social identity. In D. Abrams & M. A. Hogg (Eds.), *Social identity theory: Constructive and critical advances* (pp. 230–249). London: Harvester Wheatsheaf, and New York: Springer-Verlag.

Courtright, J. A. (1978). A laboratory investigation of groupthink. *Communication Monographs, 45,* 229–246.

Deutsch, M. (1949). An experimental study of the effects of co-operation and competition upon group processes. *Human Relations, 2,* 199–232.

Deutsch, M., & Gerard, H. B. (1955). A study of normative and informational influence upon individual judgement. *Journal of Abnormal and Social Psychology, 51,* 629–636.

Diehl, M. (1990). The minimal group paradigm: Theoretical explanations and empirical findings. *European Review of Social Psychology, 1,* 263–292.

Dion, K. (1979). Intergroup conflict and intragroup cohesiveness. In W. G. Austin & S. Worchel (Eds.), *The social psychology of intergroup relations* (pp. 211–224). Monterey, CA: Brooks-Cole.

Doise, W. (1986). *Levels of explanation in social psychology.* Cambridge, England: Cambridge University Press.

Doise, W., Deschamps, J.-C., & Meyer, G. (1978). The accentuation of intra-category similarities. In H. Tajfel (Ed.), *Differentiation between social groups* (pp. 159–170). London: Academic Press.

Duck, J. M., Hogg, M. A., & Terry, D. J. (1995). Me, us and them: Political identification and the third-person effect in the 1993 Australian federal election. *European Journal of Social Psychology, 25,* 195–215.

Eiser, J. R., & Stroebe, W. (1972). *Categorization and social judgment.* London: Academic Press.

Esser, J. K., & Lindoerfer, J. S. (1989). Groupthink and the space shuttle "Challenger" accident: Towards a quantitative case analysis. *Journal of Behavioral Decision Making, 2,* 167–177.

Evans, N. J., & Jarvis, P. A. (1980). Group cohesion: A review and re-evaluation. *Small Group Behavior, 11,* 359–370.

Festinger, L., Schachter, S., & Back, K. (1950). *Social pressures in informal groups.* New York: Harper & Row.

Fisher, R. J. (1990). *The social psychology of intergroup and international conflict resolution.* New York: Springer-Verlag.

Flowers, M. L. (1977). A laboratory test of some implications of Janis's groupthink hypothesis. *Journal of Personality and Social Psychology, 35,* 888–896.

Fodor, E. M., & Smith, T. (1982). The power motive as an influence on group decision making. *Journal of Personality and Social Psychology, 42,* 178–185.

Geen, R. G. (1991). Social motivation. *Annual Review of Psychology, 42,* 377–399.

Giles, H., & Johnson, P. (1987). Ethnolinguistic identity theory: A social psychological approach to language maintenance. *International Journal of the Sociology of Language, 68,* 256–269.

Graumann, C. F., & Moscovici, S. (Eds.). (1986). *Changing conceptions of leadership.* New York: Springer-Verlag.

Hains, S. C., Hogg, M. A., & Duck, J. M. (1994). *Self-categorization theory and leadership: Effects of group prototypicality and leader stereotypes.* Unpublished manuscript, University of Queensland, Brisbane, Australia.

Harkins, S. G., & Szymanski, K. (1987). Social loafing and social facilitation: New wine in old bottles. In C. Hendrick (Ed.), *Review of personality and social psychology: Group processes and intergroup relations* (Vol. 9, pp. 167–188). Newbury Park, CA: Sage.

Harrington, H., & Miller, N. (1993). Do group motives differ from individual motives? Considerations regarding process distinctiveness. In M. A. Hogg & D. Abrams (Eds.), *Group motivation: Social psychological perspectives* (pp. 149–172). London: Harvester Wheatsheaf.

Haslam, S. A., Oakes, P. J., Turner, J. C., & McGarty, C. (in press). Social identity, self-categorization and the perceived homogeneity of ingroups and outgroups: The interaction between social motivation and cognition. In R. M. Sorrentino & E. T. Higgins (Eds.), *Handbook of motivation and cognition* (Vol. 3). New York: Guilford.

Hensley, T. R., & Griffin, G. W. (1986). Victims of groupthink: The Kent State University Board of Trustees and the 1977 gymnasium controversy. *Journal of Conflict Resolution, 30*, 497–531.

Hogg, M. A. (1987). Social identity and group cohesiveness. In J. C. Turner, M. A. Hogg, P. J. Oakes, S. D. Reicher, & M. S. Wetherell, *Rediscovering the social group: A self-categorization theory* (pp. 89–116). Oxford, England, & New York: Blackwell.

Hogg, M. A. (1992). *The social psychology of group cohesiveness: From attraction to social identity.* London: Harvester, Wheatsheaf, and New York: New York University Press.

Hogg, M. A. (1993). Group cohesiveness: A critical review and some new directions. *European Review of Social Psychology, 4*, 85–111.

Hogg, M. A. (1994). *The influence of friendship and group solidarity on individual effort on group tasks: Social loafing revisited.* Unpublished grant proposal to the Australian Research Council, University of Queensland, Brisbane, Australia.

Hogg, M. A. (1996). Intragroup processes, group structure and social identity. In W. P. Robinson (Ed.), *Social groups and identity: Developing the legacy of Henri Tajfel.* Oxford: Butterworth-Heinemann.

Hogg, M. A., & Abrams, D. (1988). *Social identifications: A social psychology of intergroup relations and group processes.* London & New York: Routledge.

Hogg, M. A., & Abrams, D. (1993). Towards a single-process uncertainty-reduction model of social motivation in groups. In M. A. Hogg & D. Abrams (Eds.), *Group motivation: Social psychological perspectives* (pp. 173–190). London: Harvester Wheatsheaf.

Hogg, M. A., Cooper-Shaw, L., & Holzworth, D. W. (1993). Studies of group prototypicality and depersonalized attraction in small interactive groups. *Personality and Social Psychology Bulletin, 17*, 175–180.

Hogg, M. A., & Hains, S. C. (1994). *Friendship and group identification: A new look at the role of cohesiveness in groupthink.* Unpublished manuscript, University of Queensland, Brisbane, Australia.

Hogg, M. A., & Hains, S. C. (1996). Intergroup relations and group solidarity: Effects of group identification and social beliefs on depersonalized attraction. *Journal of Personality and Social Psychology, 70*.

Hogg, M. A., & Hardie, E. A. (1991). Social attraction, personal attraction, and self-categorization: A field study. *Personality and Social Psychology Bulletin, 17*, 175–180.

Hogg, M. A., & Hardie, E. A. (1992). Prototypicality, conformity and depersonalized attraction: A self-categorization analysis of group cohesiveness. *British Journal of Social Psychology, 31*, 41–56.

Hogg, M. A., Hardie, E. A., & Reynolds, K. J. (1995). Prototypical similarity, self-categorization, and depersonalized attraction: A perspective on group cohesiveness. *European Journal of Social Psychology, 25*, 159–177.

Hogg, M. A., & McGarty, C. (1990). Self-categorization and social identity. In D. Abrams & M. A. Hogg (Eds.), *Social identity theory: Constructive and critical advances* (pp. 10–27). London: Harvester Wheatsheaf, and New York: Springer-Verlag.

Hogg, M. A., Terry, D. J., & White, K. M. (1995). A tale of two theories: A critical comparison of identity theory with social identity theory. *Social Psychology Quarterly, 58*, 255–269.

Hogg, M. A., & Turner, J. C. (1987). Social identity and conformity: A theory of referent informational influence. In W. Doise & S. Moscovici (Eds.), *Current issues in European social psychology* (Vol. 2, pp. 139–182). Cambridge, England: Cambridge University Press.

Hogg, M. A., Turner, J. C., & Davidson, B. (1990). Polarized norms and social frames of reference: A test of the self-categorization theory of group polarization. *Basic and Applied Social Psychology, 11*, 77–100.

Hunt, J. G., Baliga, B. R., Dachler, H. P., & Schriesheim, C. A. (Eds.). (1988). *Emerging leadership vistas.* Lexington, MA: Heath.

Huseman, R. C., & Driver, R. W. (1979). Groupthink: Implications for small group decision making in business. In R. Huseman & A. Carroll (Eds.), *Readings in organizational behavior* (pp. 100–110). Boston: Allyn & Bacon.

Isenberg, D. J. (1986). Group polarization: A critical review and meta-analysis. *Journal of Personality and Social Psychology, 50*, 1141–1151.

Janis, I. L. (1972). *Victims of groupthink.* Boston: Houghton Mifflin.

Janis, I. L. (1982). *Groupthink: Psychological studies of policy decisions and fiascoes.* Boston: Houghton Mifflin.

Jaspars, J. M. F. (1980). The coming of age of social psychology in Europe. *European Journal of Social Psychology, 10*, 421–429.

Jaspars, J. M. F. (1986). Forum and focus: A personal view of European social psychology. *European Journal of Social Psychology, 16*, 3–15.

Johnson, D. W., & Johnson, F. P. (1987). *Joining together: Group theory and group skills* (3rd ed.). Englewood Cliffs, NJ: Prentice-Hall.

Julian, J. W., Bishop, D. W., & Fiedler, F. E. (1966). Quasi-therapeutic effects of intergroup competition. *Journal of Personality and Social Psychology, 3*, 321–327.

Kelley, H. H. (1952). Two functions of reference groups. In G. E. Swanson, T. M. Newcomb, & E. L. Hartley (Eds.), *Readings in social psychology* (2nd ed., pp. 410–414). New York: Holt, Rinehart & Winston.

Lauderdale, P., Smith-Cunnien, P., Parker, J., & Inverarity, J. (1984). External threat and the definition of deviance. *Journal of Personality and Social Psychology, 46*, 1058–1068.

Leana, C. R. (1985). A partial test of Janis's groupthink model: Effects of group cohesiveness and leader behavior on defective decision making. *Journal of Management, 11*, 5–17.

Levine, J. M., & Moreland, R. L. (1990). Progress in small group research. *Annual Review of Psychology, 41*, 585–634.

Levine, J. M., & Moreland, R. L. (1994). Group socialization: Theory and research. *European Review of Social Psychology, 5*, 305–336.

LeVine, R. A., & Campbell, D. T. (1972). *Ethnocentrism: Theories of conflict, ethnic attitudes and group behavior.* New York: Wiley.

Linville, P. W., Fischer, G. W., & Salovey, P. (1989). Perceived distributions of the characteristics of in-group members: Empirical evidence and a computer simulation. *Journal of Personality and Social Psychology, 57*, 165–188.

Lippitt, R., & White, R. (1943). The "social climate" of children's groups. In R. G. Barker, J. Kounin, & H. Wright (Eds.), *Child behavior and development* (pp. 485–508). New York: McGraw-Hill.

Longley, J., & Pruitt, D. G. (1980). Groupthink: A critique of Janis's theory. In L. Wheeler (Ed.), *Review of personality and social psychology* (Vol. 1, pp. 74–93). Beverly Hills, CA: Sage.

Lorenzi-Cioldi, F., & Doise, W. (1990). Levels of analysis and social identity. In D. Abrams & M. A. Hogg (Eds.), *Social identity theory: Constructive and critical advances* (pp. 71–88). London, Harvester Wheatsheaf, and New York: Springer-Verlag.

Lott, A. J., & Lott, B. E. (1965). Group cohesiveness as interpersonal attraction. *Psychological Bulletin, 64*, 259–309.

Lott, B. E. (1961). Group cohesiveness: A learning phenomenon. *Journal of Social Psychology, 55*, 275–286.

Mackie, D. M. (1986). Social identification effects in group polarization. *Journal of Personality and Social Psychology, 50*, 720–728.

Mackie, D. M., & Cooper, J. (1984). Attitude polarization: Effects of group membership. *Journal of Personality and Social Psychology, 46*, 575–586.

Manstead, A. S. R. (1990). Developments to be expected in European social psychology in the 1990s. In P. J. D. Drenth, J. A. Sergeant, & R. J. Takens (Eds.), *European perspectives in psychology* (Vol. 3, pp. 183–203). Chichester, England: Wiley.

Manz, C. C., & Sims, H. P. (1982). The potential for groupthink in autonomous work groups. *Human Relations, 35,* 773–784.

Marques, J. M. (1990). The black-sheep effect: Out-group homogeneity in social comparison settings. In D. Abrams & M. A. Hogg (Eds.), *Social identity theory: Constructive and critical advances* (pp. 131–151). London: Harvester Wheatsheaf, and New York: Springer-Verlag.

Marques, J. M., & Paez, D. (1994). The "black sheep effect": Social categorization, rejection of ingroup deviates and perception of group variability. *European Review of Social Psychology, 5,* 37–68.

Marques, J. M., & Yzerbyt, V. Y. (1988). The black sheep effect: Judgmental extremity towards ingroup members in inter- and intra-group situations. *European Journal of Social Psychology, 18,* 287–292.

Marques, J. M., Yzerbyt, V. Y., & Leyens, J.-P. (1988). The black sheep effect: Extremity of judgements towards in-group members as a function of group identification. *European Journal of Social Psychology, 18,* 1–16.

McCauley, C. (1989). The nature of social influence in groupthink: Compliance and internalization. *Journal of Personality and Social Psychology, 57,* 250–260.

McGarty, C., Turner, J. C., Hogg, M. A., David, B., & Wetherell, M. S. (1990). Group polarization as conformity to the prototypical group member. *British Journal of Social Psychology, 31,* 1–20.

Messick, D. M., & Mackie, D. M. (1989). Intergroup relations. *Annual Review of Psychology, 40,* 45–81.

Moorhead, G., & Montanari, J. R. (1986). An empirical investigation of the groupthink phenomenon. *Human Relations, 39,* 399–410.

Moreland, R. L., Hogg, M. A., & Hains, S. C. (1994). Back to the future: Social psychological research on groups. *Journal of Experimental Social Psychology, 30,* 527–555.

Moreland, R. L., & Levine, J. M. (1982). Socialization in small groups: Temporal changes in individual-group relations. *Advances in Experimental Social Psychology, 15,* 137–192.

Moreland, R. L., & Levine, J. M. (1984). Role transitions in small groups. In V. Allen & E. van de Vliert (Eds.), *Role transitions: Explorations and explanations* (pp. 181–195). New York: Plenum.

Moreland, R. L., & Levine, J. M. (1989). Newcomers and oldtimers in small groups. In P. B. Paulus (Ed.), *Psychology of group influence* (2nd ed., pp. 143–186). Hillsdale, NJ: Lawrence Erlbaum Associates.

Moreland, R. L., Levine, J. M., & Cini, M. (1993). Group socialization: The role of commitment. In M. A. Hogg & D. Abrams (Eds.), *Group motivation: Social psychological perspectives* (pp. 105–129). London: Harvester Wheatsheaf.

Morley, I. E., Webb, J., & Stephenson, G. M. (1988). Bargaining and arbitration in the resolution of conflict. In W. Stroebe, A. W. Kruglanski, D. Bar-Tal, & M. Hewstone (Eds.), *The social psychology of intergroup conflict: Theory, research and applications* (pp. 117–134). New York: Springer-Verlag.

Mudrack, P. E. (1989). Defining group cohesiveness: A legacy of confusion. *Small Group Behavior, 20,* 37–49.

Mullen, B., & Copper, C. (1994). The relation between group cohesiveness and performance: An integration. *Psychological Bulletin, 115,* 210–227.

Mullen, B., & Hu, L.-t. (1989). Perceptions of ingroup and outgroup variability: A meta-analytic integration. *Basic and Applied Social Psychology, 10,* 233–252.

Oakes, P. J., Haslam, S. A., & Turner, J. C. (1994). *Stereotyping and social reality.* Oxford, England: Blackwell.

Park, B., & Rothbart, M. (1982). Perception of outgroup homogeneity and levels of social categorization. Memory for the subordinate attributes of in-group and out-group members. *Journal of Personality and Social Psychology, 42,* 1051–1068.

Park, B., Ryan, C. S., & Judd, C. M. (1992). Role of meaningful subgroups in explaining differences in perceived variability for ingroups and outgroups. *Journal of Personality and Social Psychology, 63*, 553–567.

Pruitt, D. G. (1981). *Negotiation behavior.* New York: Academic Press.

Quattrone, G. A., & Jones, E. E. (1980). The perception of variability within ingroups and outgroups: Implications for the law of small numbers. *Journal of Personality and Social Psychology, 38*, 141–152.

Raven, B. H. (1974). The comparative analysis of power and power preference. In J. T. Tedeschi (Ed.), *Perspectives on social power* (pp. 172–198). Chicago: Aldine.

Reicher, S. D. (1987). Crowd behaviour as social action. In J. C. Turner, M. A. Hogg, P. J. Oakes, S. D. Reicher, & M. S. Wetherell, *Rediscovering the social group: A self-categorization theory* (pp. 171–202). Oxford, England, & New York: Blackwell.

Ross, L. (1977). The intuitive psychologist and his shortcomings. *Advances in Experimental Social Psychology, 10*, 174–220.

Sachdev, I., & Bourhis, R. Y. (1991). Power and status differentials in minority and majority group relations. *European Journal of Social Psychology, 21*, 1–24.

Sachdev, I., & Bourhis, R. Y. (1993). Ethnolinguistic vitality: Some motivational and cognitive considerations. In M. A. Hogg & D. Abrams (Eds.), *Group motivation: Social psychological perspectives* (pp. 33–51). London: Harvester Wheatsheaf.

Sanders, G. S., & Baron, R. S. (1977). Is social comparison irrelevant for producing choice shifts? *Journal of Experimental Social Psychology, 13*, 303–314.

Sherif, M. (1966). *In common predicament: Social psychology of intergroup conflict and cooperation.* Boston: Houghton Mifflin.

Sherif, M., & Sherif, C. W. (1964). *Reference groups.* New York: Harper & Row.

Simon, B. (1993). On the asymmetry in the cognitive construal of ingroup and outgroup: A model of egocentric social categorization. *European Journal of Social Psychology, 23*, 131–147.

Simon, B., & Brown, R. J. (1987). Perceived intragroup homogeneity in minority-majority contexts. *Journal of Personality and Social Psychology, 53*, 703–711.

Smith, S. (1984). Groupthink and the hostage rescue mission. *British Journal of Political Science, 15*, 117–126.

Stagner, R., & Eflal, B. (1982). Internal union dynamics during a strike: A quasi-experimental study. *Journal of Applied Psychology, 67*, 37–44.

Stephen, W. G. (1977). Cognitive differentiation in intergroup perception. *Sociometry, 40*, 50–58.

Tajfel, H. (1959). Quantitative judgment in social perception. *British Journal of Psychology, 50*, 16–29.

Tajfel, H. (1963). Stereotypes. *Race, 5*, 3–14.

Tajfel, H. (1969a). Cognitive aspects of prejudice. *Journal of Social Issues, 25*, 79–97.

Tajfel, H. (1969b). Social and cultural factors in perception. In G. Lindzey & E. Aronson (Eds.), *Handbook of social psychology* (Vol. 3, pp. 315–394). Reading, MA: Addison-Wesley.

Tajfel, H. (1970). Experiments in intergroup discrimination. *Scientific American, 223*, 96–102.

Tajfel, H. (1972). Some developments in European social psychology. *European Journal of Social Psychology, 2*, 307–322.

Tajfel, H. (1974). *Intergroup behaviour, social comparison and social change.* Unpublished Katz–Newcomb lectures, University of Michigan at Ann Arbor.

Tajfel, H. (Ed.). (1978). *Differentiation between social groups.* London: Academic Press.

Tajfel, H. (1981). Social stereotypes and social groups. In J. C. Turner & H. Giles (Eds.), *Intergroup behaviour* (pp. 144–167). Oxford, England: Blackwell.

Tajfel, H. (Ed.). (1982). *Social identity and intergroup relations.* Cambridge, England: Cambridge University Press.

Tajfel, H., Billig, M., Bundy, R. P., & Flament, C. (1971). Social categorization and intergroup behavior. *European Journal of Social Psychology, 1*, 149–177.

Tajfel, H., & Turner, J. C. (1979). An integrative theory of intergroup conflict. In W. G. Austin & S. Worchel (Eds.), *The social psychology of intergroup relations* (pp. 33–47). Monterey, CA: Brooks Cole.

Taylor, D. M., & McKirnan, D. J. (1984). A five-stage model of intergroup relations. *British Journal of Social Psychology, 23*, 291–300.

Tetlock, P. E. (1979). Identifying victims of groupthink from public statements of decision makers. *Journal of Personality and Social Psychology, 37*, 1314–1324.

Tetlock, P. E., Peterson, R. S., McGuire, C., Chang, S., & Feld, P. (1992). Assessing political group dynamics: A test of the groupthink model. *Journal of Personality and Social Psychology, 63*, 403–425.

Turner, J. C. (1982). Towards a cognitive redefinition of the social group. In H. Tajfel (Ed.), *Social identity and intergroup relations* (pp. 15–40). Cambridge, England: Cambridge University Press.

Turner, J. C. (1984). Social identification and psychological group formation. In H. Tajfel (Ed.), *The social dimension: European developments in social psychology* (Vol. 2, pp. 518–538). Cambridge, England: Cambridge University Press.

Turner, J. C. (1985). Social categorization and the self-concept: A social cognitive theory of group behaviour. In E. J. Lawler (Ed.), *Advances in group processes: Theory and research* (Vol. 2, pp. 77–122). Greenwich, CT: JAI.

Turner, J. C. (1991). *Social influence.* Milton Keynes: Open University Press.

Turner, J. C., & Giles, H. (Eds.). (1981). *Intergroup behaviour.* Oxford, England: Blackwell.

Turner, J. C., Hogg, M. A., Oakes, P. J., Reicher, S. D., & Wetherell, M. S. (1987). *Rediscovering the social group: A self-categorization theory.* Oxford, England, and New York: Blackwell.

Turner, J. C., & Oakes, P. J. (1986). The significance of the social identity concept for social psychology with reference to individualism, interactionism and social influence. *British Journal of Social Psychology, 25*, 237–252.

Turner, J. C., & Oakes, P. J. (1989). Self-categorization theory and social influence. In P. B. Paulus (Ed.), *The psychology of group influence* (2nd ed., pp. 233–275). Hillsdale, NJ: Lawrence Erlbaum Associates.

Turner, M. E., Pratkanis, A. R., Probasco, P., & Leve, C. (1992). Threat, cohesion, and group effectiveness: Testing a social identity maintenance perspective on groupthink. *Journal of Personality and Social Psychology, 63*, 781–796.

van Knippenberg, A., & Ellemers, N. (1993). Strategies in intergroup relations. In M. A. Hogg & D. Abrams (Eds.), *Group motivation: Social psychological perspectives* (pp. 17–32). London: Harvester Wheatsheaf.

Wetherell, M. S. (1987). Social identity and group polarization. In J. C. Turner, M. A. Hogg, P. J. Oakes, S. D. Reicher, & M. S. Wetherell, *Rediscovering the social group: A self-categorization theory* (pp. 142–170). Oxford, England, & New York: Blackwell.

Wetherell, M. S., & Potter, J. (1992). *Mapping the language of racism: Discourse and the legitimation of exploitation.* London: Harvester Wheatsheaf.

Whyte, W. H. (1943). *Street corner society* (2nd ed.). Chicago: University of Chicago Press.

Williams, K., Karau, S., & Bourgeois, M. (1993). Working on collective tasks: Social loafing and social compensation. In M. A. Hogg & D. Abrams (Eds.), *Group motivation: Social psychological perspectives* (pp. 130–148). London: Harvester Wheatsheaf.

10

A Behavioral Interaction Model: Toward an Integrative Theoretical Framework for Studying Intra- and Intergroup Dynamics

Jacob M. Rabbie
Hein F. M. Lodewijkx
University of Utrecht

Generally, in research and in daily life, there is a tendency for people to favor ingroups over outgroups. This ingroup–outgroup differentiation may be reflected in favorable attitudes, intentions, and behavior toward the ingroup and its members and in negative attitudes, intentions, and behavior to the outgroup and its members. However, ingroup favoritism is not a universal phenomenon (Hinkle & Brown, 1990). Lewin (1948) argued that sometimes members of psychological minority groups, who feel discriminated against by the more powerful, privileged majority in our society, may try to leave their own group because membership in it has become nothing but a burden to them. They may attempt to pass the intergroup boundaries that divide them in an effort to gain more social status, self-worth, and security. Particularly, when they are rejected by the privileged outgroup and despised by members of their own minority group for trying to leave them, these people may end up in a marginal no-man's land in which they belong to neither group. In this marginal situation such people may use the unfavorable attitudes the privileged outgroup has about them as a frame of reference or schema to evaluate themselves. This process may lead to low self-esteem, a shattered social identity, or even feelings of self-hatred. These kinds of intra- and intergroup dynamics have motivated our research program on intra- and intergroup relations.

In this chapter, a behavioral interaction model (BIM) is presented in which an attempt is made to integrate a variety of theories in this area. These theories have been developed to explain the origins of these various forms of intergroup differentiation. We are particularly interested in integrating two seemingly conflicting approaches to intergroup relations: the *interdependence perspective* (IP) and the *social identity* (SI) approach. The IP tradition includes a variety of theories that have the following in common: their emphasis on the importance of perceived outcome, means, task, and resource interdependence of people within and between groups, and how their behavior is affected by the anticipated or actual behavior of others. The IP was initiated by Lewin (e.g., 1947, 1948, 1951), Sherif (1936, 1966), Asch (1952), Deutsch, (1949, 1973, 1982), Cartwright and Zander (1968), Festinger, Schachter, and Back (1950), Kelley and Thibaut (1978), Horwitz (1953), Rabbie and Horwitz (1969, 1988), Horwitz and Rabbie (1982, 1989), Pruitt and Kimmel (1977), and many other interdependence theorists.

The SI approach includes the social identity theory (SIT) of Tajfel and Turner (1979, 1986), and the social identification model of Turner (1982), or the self-categorization theory (SCT), a cognitive elaboration of SIT developed by Turner, Hogg, Oakes, Reicher, and Wetherell (1987), Hogg and Abrams (1988), Hogg (1992), and other researchers working in this cognitive, self-centered, individualistic tradition. Generally, these authors reject the IP in favor of their own approach (e.g. Turner, 1982; Turner et al., 1987; see Hogg, chapter 9, this volume).

In contrast to Turner et al. (1987), we have argued that the IP and SI approaches are not incompatible with each other but should instead complement one another. As we wrote earlier: "Our basic assumption is that at least both perspectives are needed to explain and predict the psychological orientations and behavior within and between groups (and other social systems). The question has become under what kind of conditions one perspective seem more plausible than another" (Rabbie, Schot, & Visser, 1989, p. 198). In our behavioral interaction model, which can be considered as our own version of the interdependence perspective, we have tried to specify some of the conditions under which the two approaches may lead to similar or different predictions.

In many ways the SI approach can be seen as a critical reaction to the research and theories developed in the IP tradition, for example, to the realistic conflict theory (RCT) of LeVine and Campbell (1972), which was based on the research of Sherif (1951, 1966), to the research on group cohesion of Festinger, Schachter, and Back, (1950), which was stimulated by Lewin's ideas, and to our own research on minimal groups. In the first section of this chapter we discuss our minimal group experiments because they furnished the basis for our own research program on intra- and intergroup relations, and as we show, they furthered the development of the minimal group paradigm (MGP) by Tajfel, Billig, Bundy, and Flament, (1971). The surprising results of the standard MGP of Tajfel et al. provided the main impetus for the development of the SI position. In the second section the results of our research program are briefly summarized. In the third section we discuss some of the basic assumptions in which the IP and SI seem to differ from one another. In the fourth section the behavioral interaction model is described, and in the fifth and last section three studies are summarized that demonstrate the validity of our model. In our conclusion we argue that the SIT and IP approaches should be integrated in one theoretical framework.

MINIMAL GROUPS

The research on intergroup relations among minimal groups was initiated by Rabbie (1965), Rabbie and Horwitz (1969), and Rabbie and Wilkens (1971). The point of departure of our minimal group experiments was the deep concern expressed by Lewin (1948) about the effects of the persecution of Jews in Nazi Germany on the Jewish identity and feelings of belongingness of young people to the Jewish minority group in the United States. Addressing himself to their parents he wrote: "... belonging or not belonging to the Jewish group is not a matter mainly of similarity or dissimilarity, *nor even one of like or dislike* (emphasis added). He will understand that regardless of whether the Jewish group is a racial, religious, national or cultural one, the fact that it is classified by the majority as a distinct group is what counts ... He will see that the main criterion of belongingness is an *interdependence of fate*" (Lewin, 1948, p. 184, emphasis in the original). Lewin (1951) made a clear distinction between groups and categories. He argued that "it may be wrong to state that the blond women living in a town 'exist as a group,' in the sense of being a dynamic whole characterized by a close interdependence among its members. They are merely a number of individuals who are 'classified under one concept' according to the similarity of one of their properties. If, however, the blond members of a workshop are made an 'artificial' minority and are discriminated against by their colleagues they may well become a group with specific structural properties" (p. 192). In his view "structural properties are characterized by *relations* between parts rather than by the parts or elements themselves" (p. 192).

In the Rabbie and Horwitz (1969) experiment, an attempt was made to create "artificial minorities" in the laboratory that shared a positive interdependence of fate with the ingroup and a negative interdependence of fate with the out-group as a means of finding out what kind of conditions are sufficient or necessary to form (minimal) social groups. As noted by Horwitz and Rabbie (1989), our research on the minimal intergroup situation can be traced back to the well-known boys' camp studies by Sherif, Harvey, White, Hood, and Sherif (1961). Based on this work, Sherif extended Lewin's ideas (1948) about a dynamic interdependence within a group system to perceived interdependence within an "intergroup system." Sherif believed that given two organized groups, the existence of competing group goals (negative goal interdependence) will lead to intergroup hostility and discrimination whereas a common superordinate goal (positive goal interdependence) would lead to intergroup cooperation and harmony. In his research Sherif worked with young boys' groups that had developed "structural properties" such as interdependent roles, a hierarchical leadership structure, and common norms and values. Placing these organized groups in competition with each other produced severe intergroup antagonism and discrimination.

In the Rabbie and Horwitz (1969) experiment we had no doubts that a perceived positive interdependence with members of one's own group would lead to intragroup cooperation and ingroup cohesiveness (Deutsch, 1949), whereas a perceived negative interdependence with members of the outgroup would lead to intergroup competition, mutual frustration, and consequent outgroup hostility. However, we wondered whether this intergroup differentiation would only occur among organized groups. Therefore, we tried to "isolate the minimal conditions that are sufficient to generate discriminatory ingroup–outgroup attitudes" (Rabbie & Horwitz, 1969, p. 270).

The Rabbie and Horwitz (1969) experiment employed several treatments that varied the perceived interdependence of fate within and between two groups. Cartwright and Zander (1968), following Lewin (1948), suggested that the "external designation" of members into a "socially defined category" imposes a "common fate" upon them in the sense that opportunities are given or denied to them "simply because of their membership in the category." They argued that "interdependence among members develops because society gives them a 'common fate' " (Cartwright & Zander, 1968, pp. 56–57). Following this suggestion and the ideas of Lewin, an experiment was designed in which strangers, males and females, were classified at random into two "distinct" Blue or Green groups for alleged "administrative reasons." They had no opportunity to interact with each other, either within or between the groups involved. Thus, they had no history nor any future together. In the experimental "common fate" conditions, group members perceived themselves as "being in the same boat." They were either privileged or deprived relative to a (minimal) outgroup solely as a function of their membership in the Blue or Green group (negative intergroup interdependence). These members were rewarded or not on the basis of chance (a flip of a coin), an authority figure (the experimenter), or, allegedly, by the actions of one of the two groups. Presenting the experiment as a study of first impressions, we asked subjects to stand up in turn, introduce themselves, and rate each other on a variety of personality and group traits scaled along a favorable–unfavorable dimension. Thus, the ingroup–outgroup bias was measured by individual traits as well as by "structural group properties," which cannot be reduced to the attributes of single individuals. Following Sherif et al. (1961), we used also the ratio of sociometric ingroup choices to outgroup choices to measure the degree of intergroup differentiation or the experience of the we–they distinction.

As expected, in the experimental privileged and deprived common fate conditions, a significantly greater ingroup–outgroup bias was found in favor of the own group and its members, particularly under the chance condition, than was found under a control condition in which an attempt was made to create minimal or near-zero interdependence within and between the groups. In the latter condition, the subjects were only classified as members of Blue or Green groups and were neither privileged nor deprived as a function of their membership in these groups. Our 1969 experiment failed to detect an ingroup bias in the control condition, but with an increased N in follow-up experiments, subjects were found to give more favorable ratings to the ingroup and its members than to the outgroup and its members, especially on social-emotional or relational traits (Horwitz & Rabbie, 1982). Apparently, the experimenter's interest in dividing subjects into two groups could have suggested to them that differential consequences might befall each group as a whole, which would lead to (a weak) intergroup differentiation (Rabbie & Horwitz, 1988).

A preliminary version of our study was reported in a conference in which Henry Tajfel was also present (Rabbie, 1965). He reacted enthusiastically to the method we had used to study the effects of social categorization on intergroup differentiation, but he disagreed strongly with our interpretation of the results (Rabbie, 1982a). This debate about the differences in interpretation has lasted for about 30 years. So the time has come to emphasize the "potential complementarity" of our perspectives as proposed by Tajfel (1982) in his thoughtful comments on our chapter in a book he edited. (See also Rabbie & Horwitz, 1988, for our reaction to these comments.)

Our minimal group experiments stimulated the development of the MGP experiments by Tajfel et al. (1971), which later inaugurated the SI approach. As Turner (1988) commented on these early MGP experiments: "The results of these studies were unexpected and in terms of conventional theories unexplainable." As Tajfel put it, they were "data in search of a theory" (cited in Hogg & Abrams, 1988). In this chapter we try to show that their data are perfectly explainable by the "conventional" interdependence theories.

Willem Doise (1988), who worked closely with Tajfel and his associates at the University of Bristol, suggested that the MGP was modeled with some modifications on the control condition of our experiment. In the initial modification by Tajfel et al. (1971), subjects were again classified into groups for administrative reasons. However, this time they were led to believe that they were divided according to similarities or differences in their individual characteristics, purportedly measured by tests of aesthetic preference (pro-Kandinski vs. pro-Klee) or by estimation tendencies (overestimators vs. underestimators). The dependent measures of ingroup and outgroup bias were a series of distribution matrices by means of which subjects could allocate money to and receive money from anonymous members of each group. We call these matrices "Tajfel's matrices." Tajfel's modifications had the effect, first, of transforming the experiment from one that manipulated perceived intergroup interdependence as the sole independent variable to one that simultaneously manipulated two independent variables: intergroup interdependence and categorization. A second effect, as we show later, was to make explicit and strengthen subjects' perceptions of their differential interdependence with ingroup and outgroup members with respect to their own monetary outcomes. The results of the experiment by Tajfel et al. revealed that subjects tended to allocate more money to ingroup members than to outgroup members, but they also found that they did not depart too far from fairness, that is, from equal allocations to anonymous members of both minimal groups.

Referring to our work, Tajfel et al. (1971) were considering "Rabbie's studies against the background of social norms and expectations that his Ss may have found pertinent as a guide to their behavior in the social situations in which they found themselves" (p. 153). Therefore, initially, they interpreted their results as a compromise solution between two conflicting social norms guiding subjects' behavior, a "generic outgroup attitude" (p. 151), according to which it seems "appropriate" to favor ingroup members and discriminate against outgroup members and a norm of fairness: to give each group an equal share. They wrote: ". . . another social norm, that of fairness, is also a powerful strategy in guiding their choices . . . and the pattern of data can be best understood as showing a strategy in which a compromise between these two norms is achieved (pp. 173–174). In the same article, Tajfel et al. (1971) added a point that probably accounts for their later abandonment of the generic "groupness" norm explanation. They asserted (gratuitously we believe) that the norm induces bias "even when such behavior has no 'utilitarian' value to the individual or to his group" (p. 151). The statement seems to deny that subjects in the MGP perceived any interdependence among their outcomes.

The assumption that there is no (perceived) interdependence of interest among groups and their members in the MGP has been a central tenet in the development of social identity theory (Horwitz & Rabbie, 1989). The claim is repeatedly made that in the allocation task there is "neither . . . a conflict of interests between the 'groups' nor there is any rational link between economic self interest and the strategy of in-group favoritism" (Tajfel & Turner, 1979, pp. 38–39). Again insisting on the absence of goal interdependence, Turner (1982) asserted that ". . . subjects discriminated against anonymous outgroup members under conditions that they could not benefit from this strategy" (p. 20; see also Turner et al., 1987). It follows that if the cause of behavior cannot be found in the person's perception of the situation, it must be located within the person. The intrapersonal cause or motive proposed in the theory is the "need to maintain or enhance . . . self esteem" (Tajfel & Turner, 1979, p. 40). They assumed that individual members in social categories or social groups—they used these terms interchangeably—strive to maintain or to achieve superiority or a positive distinctiveness over an outgroup on some relevant dimension as a means of achieving self-esteem or to attain a positive social identity, that is, "those aspects of an individual's self-image that derive from the social categories to which he perceives himself as belonging" (p. 40). When their social identity becomes unsatisfactory individuals will either try to leave their social category or group or they strive to create new dimensions in which the ingroup is seen as superior over an relevant outgroup (Lemaine, 1966). In this sense intergroup relations are always discriminatory and "essentially competitive" (Tajfel & Turner, 1979, p. 41). Thus, in their view intergroup comparisons are made to satisfy an intraindividual need or motive: the tendency to achieve or maintain a positive social identity or self-esteem. This motive is supposed to produce "essentially" competitive intergroup relations.

It should be noted that the belief that people are motivated to maintain or enhance self-esteem through their group membership is very similar to the ideas of Lewin (1948). He thought that people may derive social status, and feelings of self-worth and other symbolic outcomes from the groups to which they perceive themselves as belonging. However, Tajfel and Turner (1979, 1986), in their main formulation of SIT, did not refer to his work. In our research we have argued that allocations in the MGP may serve various needs, including economically tangible self-interests or more symbolically intangible outcomes such as prestige or self-esteem. What kind of allocation behavior will be obtained in the MGP will partly depend on these kinds of material or symbolic resources or incentives (Rabbie & Schot, 1989; Schot, Rabbie, Visser, & Lodewijkx, 1994). In the Rabbie et al. (1989) experiment we showed that in the standard MGP, there *is* a rational, instrumental link between economic self-interests and the two major allocation strategies that are often found in the MGP experiments: ingroup favoritism and fairness. The erroneous assumption that the ingroup–outgroup allocations in the standard MGP of Tajfel et al. (1971) had no instrumental, "utilitarian" value to the individual or his or her group is probably based on the idea that subjects in the standard MGP could only allocate monetary points by means of the Tajfel matrices to anonymous ingroup members or anonymous outgroup members but never directly to themselves.

In line with our model we have a different view. In the standard instructions of the Tajfel et al. (1971) experiment subjects were told that "They would always allot money to others" (p. 156; i.e., always members of the ingroup or outgroup). "At the end of the task ... each would receive the amount of money that the others had rewarded him" (p. 156). These instructions imply that subjects are dependent for maximizing their own outcomes on the allocation decisions of anonymous ingroup members and anonymous outgroup members.

Thus their (perceived) "outcome dependence" (Kelley & Thibaut, 1978) is two-sided: on the ingroup and on the outgroup. Although subjects in the usual MGP cannot directly allocate money to themselves, they can do it *indirectly* on the reasonable assumption that the other ingroup members would do the same for them (Hornstein, 1976), just as outgroup members will be perceived as showing a preference for members of their own social category. By giving more to their ingroup members than to the outgroup members, in the expectation that the other ingroup members will reciprocate this cooperative action, they stand to increase the chances of maximizing their own (monetary) outcomes. Thus, although subjects in the standard MGP may be seen by an "objective" outside observer as acting independently from one another, the subjects *perceive* themselves to be interdependent on one another with respect to reaching their individualistic goal of maximizing their monetary outcomes. When the subjects act on these reciprocal expectations and perceptions, a "tacit coordination" (Schelling, 1963) is achieved, which helps them to gain as much as they can.

In the MGP, subjects received no immediate feedback in the standard MGP about the consequences of their allocation decisions. Thus, they react to a perceived or "constructed" reality based on their reciprocal expectations of how other anonymous members, particularly in their own social category would probably react to them (Berger & Luckmann, 1967). This reasoning illustrates the importance of what Ross and Nisbett (1991) called "the principle of construal," the idea that ". . . the impact of any 'objective' stimulus situation depends upon the personal and subjective meaning that the actor attaches to that situation" (p. 11).

In Rabbie et al. (1989), we tested our reciprocal interdependence hypothesis by using the standard MGP of Tajfel et al. (1971) as a control condition in which it was found, consistent with our expectations, that subjects perceived themselves to be dependent on individuals in their own category (or ingroup I) *and* on the other social category (or outgroup O). This 'two-sided' IOD control condition was compared with two other 'one-sided' conditions in which subjects perceived themselves to be solely dependent (a) on anonymous members of their own social category (ID) and (b) on anonymous members of the other social category (OD). The results in the control condition replicated the findings of Tajfel et al.: Where subjects viewed their outcomes as dependent on the actions of members in both social categories (IOD) they allocated slightly (but significantly) more money to members in their own category than to members in the other category. This ingroup favoritism can be attributed to a "normative ingroup schema" or a learned belief that more can generally be expected from ingroup members than from outgroup members (Rabbie, 1993b). This notion is consistent with Tajfel's "generic groupness norm" and our own hypothesis that people tend to give more weight to the desires of ingroup members than of outgroup members (Horwitz & Rabbie, 1982; Rabbie & Lodewijkx, 1994). Moreover, subjects showed also a relatively strong tendency of fairness: the tendency to allocate about as much to the ingroup as to the outgroup, because they perceived themselves to be (instrumentally) dependent on members of both minimal groups. Where they viewed their outcomes as solely dependent on the actions of the ingroup member (ID), they showed a strong ingroup favoritism or intragroup cooperation; that is, they allocated much more money to members of the own social category than to members of the other social category. They also showed significantly less fairness than subjects in the control condition. However, in the conditions in which they viewed their outcomes as solely dependent on the action of subjects in the other category or minimal group (OD) they showed a strong outgroup favoritism; that is, they allocated much more money to the members of the other social category than to members of their own social category (Rabbie et al., 1989). Apparently, a perceived positive goal interdependence on the minimal outgroup leads to the reciprocal expectations that one's economic outcomes can be best served if one "cooperates" or achieves a "tacit coordination" with members of the other social category rather than with members of one's own category. In real life, most of the time people perceive themselves to be dependent on members of their own "natural" group or category to which they belong. However, when categorization and interdependence are experimentally separated from each other, perceived instrumental (outgroup) interdependence appears to be a more important determinant of a subject's allocation behavior than mere categorization. Thus, contrary to the SI interpretation of the standard MGP experiments, there appears to be an indirect, rational, instrumental link between economic self-interests and the allocation behavior in the standard MGP. Thus, the realistic conflict theory advanced by LeVine and Campbell (1972) and Sherif (1966) cannot be excluded as a viable explanation of the usual MGP results.

Tajfel and Turner (1979) focused their attention almost exclusively on the strategy of ingroup favoritism, but neglected the "powerful strategy" of fairness in guiding subjects' choices in the MGP (see also Branthwaite et al., 1979). In fact, this "influential strategy of fairness" (Tajfel & Turner, 1979, p. 39) is difficult to reconcile with SIT, which assumes that people in the MGP are only interested in achieving a positive distinctiveness on some valued dimension in an attempt to achieve or maintain self-esteem or a positive social identity. In this sense, our reciprocal interdependence hypothesis provides a more parsimonious explanation of *all* significant findings obtained by the standard MGP experiments. In our view, the influential strategy of fairness, is not only a reflection of a "norm of fairness" as Tajfel et al. suggested, but it has also an instrumental or utilitarian value to the subjects, particularly when monetary incentives are involved (Rabbie et al., 1989; Schot et al., 1994).

The results of the Rabbie et al. (1989) experiment are rather convincing: "The clear-cut evidence is that by altering the perceived interdependence of subject's outcomes, one can obtain either ingroup or outgroup favoritism, holding category differentiation constant" (Horwitz & Rabbie, 1989, p. 111). We have replicated these findings in several other studies (e.g., Lodewijkx, Syroit, & Rabbie, 1994; Mlicki, 1993; Rabbie & Schot, 1990; Schot, 1992; Schot et al., 1994). Our conclusion from this research has been that in the standard MGP there are mainly self-centered individuals in social categories, who tacitly coordinate their choices with anonymous members of their own and other social categories in an effort to maximize their individual economic self-interests at least when monetary incentives are involved (Rabbie & Schot, 1989). They tend to use the category labels not so much as a means for "self-categorization" or "self-identification," as Turner et al. (1987) in their SCT asserted, nor are they primarily used as an effort to enhance their self-esteem as Tajfel and Turner (1986) argued, but in our view these social categories serve mainly as means or instruments to attain their selfish instrumental monetary interests (Rabbie, 1993a).

OVERVIEW OF RESEARCH PROGRAM

The results of our early studies on minimal groups led to the development of a research program on intra- and intergroup relations that was intended to replicate Sherifs' research findings under more controlled laboratory conditions (Rabbie, 1993b). In this program we have tried to study both the effects of intragroup cooperation on ingroup favoritism and cohesiveness and the effects of intergroup competition on intergroup hostility and aggression (Rabbie, 1992; 1993b; Rabbie & Lodewijkx, 1994). In our view, Sherifs' findings on the development of ingroup cohesion and outgroup hostility among organized groups can be attributed to a variety of factors, which we have presented in Table 10.1. In our research program we have tried to study the effects of each of these factors separately and in combination with one another.

The conditions summarized in Table 10.1 can be considered as steps in the development of intra- and intergroup relations from the coexistence of individuals in social categories or members of minimal groups to the aggression among organized groups that was observed by Sherif and Sherif (1979) in their summer

TABLE 10.1
Factors in the Development of Ingroup-Outgroup Differentiation

1. The mere *classification of people* into social categories. Lewin (1951); Rabbie (1965). (cf. control condition in Rabbie and Horwitz, 1969).

2. The experience of a perceived positive *interdependence of fate* with the ingroup relative to a negative interdependence of fate with an outgroup, which were either privileged or discriminated relative to each other (Lewin, 1948; Mlicki, 1993; Rabbie & Horwitz, 1969; Rabbie & Schot, 1990; Schot, 1992).

3. *Intra-group coaction* (Rabbie & Lodewijkx, 1992), tacit coordination (Rabbie et al., 1989), or intragroup cooperation based on unit-forming factors, for example, shared territory, goal-, means-, and task-interdependence (Rabbie & Wilkens, 1971; Rabbie, 1991a).

4. Variations in intergroup goal incompatibility per se (Sherif, 1966), for example, the *expectation* to cooperate or to compete with another group (Rabbie & Wilkens, 1971; Rabbie & de Brey, 1971; Rabbie & Huygen, 1972; Rabbie, Benoist, Oosterbaan & Visser, 1974).

5. Actual intergroup competition or cooperation (Rabbie et al., 1982). The mutual frustration and consequent aggression during the intergroup competition (Lodewijkx, 1989; Rabbie & Lodewijkx, 1987, 1995; Goldenbeld, 1992; Rabbie et al., 1992).

6. The realization of group members that one has lost or won from the other group (Sherif, 1967; Rabbie & Lodewijkx, 1995).

7. Whether one group lost from another group either by legitimate or by illegitimate means (Sherif, 1966; Lodewijkx, 1989).

camp studies. These conditions may correspond to the different phases of group formation and the types of groups that can be associated with each of these phases.

Although there is no agreement in the literature as to how groups should be defined, several defining characteristics have been mentioned by Deutsch (1973), Johnson and Johnson (1992), Shaw (1971), and others (e.g., Rabbie, 1993a, 1993b).

The Individual–Group Continuum

The different types of groups presented in Table 10.2 can be ordered along a individual-centered/group-centered continuum that varies along a perceived (positive) interdependence dimension. At the individualistic pole of this continuum "self-centered individuals in social categories" can be located who perceive themselves to be minimally interdependent on each other for attaining their outcomes and are mainly interested in maximizing their selfish, individualistic outcomes. Near the group or collective pole of the continuum, "group-centered members of social or organized groups" can be situated who perceive themselves as maximally interdependent on each other for attaining their group and individual outcomes. They not only are willing to maximize their individual interests but are also motivated to maximize the interest of the group as a whole, sometimes at some costs to themselves (Rabbie & Schot, 1990).

It has been found that the greater the perceived positive goal interdependence between members of social groups, as compared to the minimal interdependence perceived between individuals of social categories, the greater the sense of group belongingness and cohesiveness, and the more members feel motivated to enhance or maintain their individual self-esteem as well as the social identity of their group as a whole (Mlicki, 1993; Rabbie & Lodewijkx, 1994; Rabbie & Schot, 1990; Rabbie, Schot, Visser, & Lodewijkx, 1995).

BASIC ASSUMPTIONS

Before giving a full description of our model it appears worthwhile to bring our own position into focus by comparing the IP and SI approaches on those points at which they seem to differ from each other. These differences require a discussion (a) of how social groups are defined, (b) of whether a conceptual distinction should be made between social groups and social categories, and (c) at what levels of analyses should intra- and intergroup relations be studied. The individual-centered/group-centered continuum, as just described, forms another basic assumption of our model that is quite different from the interpersonal-intergroup continuum advanced by SIT (for a critique of their conception, see Rabbie, 1993a).

TABLE 10.2

A Taxonomy of Groups

From Social Categories to Social Organizations

---

1. From the perspective of an outside observer, a group has been defined as a *social category:* a collection of two or more individuals who have at least one attribute in common that distinguishes them from members in other social categories (Deutsch, 1973; Horwitz & Rabbie, 1982).

2. From an internal perspective, members of a social category may become a *psychological group* or a "perceptual category" (Turner et al., 1987) when they perceive themselves (and are often perceived by outsiders) as belonging to the same social category, forming a distinctive, bounded social unit, differentiated from other psychological groups (Deutsch, 1973; Turner, 1982).

3. When individuals are classified on the basis of a similar sociological characteristic such as age, gender, occupation, education, color of their skin, profession, etc., they are socially defined as members of a *sociological category* (Merton, 1957).

4. Coacting individuals in social categories become members of *minimal groups* when they are randomly classified as members of a Blue group relative to another Green group (Rabbie & Horwitz, 1969) or are categorized on the basis of their preferences for paintings of Klee or Kandinski (Tajfel et al., 1971). As a consequence they perceive themselves as members belonging to one social or sociological category (e.g., "a loose mass, " Lewin, 1948) rather than to another social or sociological category.

5. Members of minimal groups become a *social group* when they perceive an "interdependence of fate" (Lewin, 1948) or a "common predicament" (Sherif, 1966) when they experience positive or negative outcomes solely as a consequence of their membership in one social group relative to another social group.

6. A social group becomes an interacting *compact group* (Lewin, 1948) when some or all of its members cooperate face-to-face with each other, sometimes on behalf of the whole group, in an effort to achieve the interdependent goals, and the instrumental and relational interests and outcomes of individual members as well of the group as a whole (Deutsch, 1973; Johnson & Johnson, 1992; Horwitz & Rabbie, 1989).

7. Over time, a compact group may develop into an *organized group,* which is characterized by a hierarchical structure of power, status, and role relationships among its members, by a set of explicit or implicit norms and values that regulate member interaction, with respect to specific activities, obligations, rights, and entitlements of each of its members and eventually to members of other organized groups in the physical and social environment (Sherif, 1966; Deutsch, 1982; Rabbie & Lodewijkx, 1994).

8. A *social organization* can be defined as a hierarchical, interdependent social system of organized groups that are often engaged in a power struggle with each other to determine the dominant operational goals of the organization. According to the resource--dependency model of Pfeffer and Salansic (1978), groups or departments acquire power when they control critical resources needed by other subunits, and when these subunits, groups, or departments help to reduce the levels of uncertainty experienced by other departments (Rabbie & van Oostrum, 1984).

Note. From Rabbie and Lodewijkx (1994). Copyright 1994 by JAI Press. Adapted by permission.

Groups as Dynamic Tension Systems. In his discussion of the reality of social groups Lewin (1948), has noted that the group has been considered as something more or higher than the sum of individuals composing it. This wholeness or unity has been attributed to a "group mind." Rejecting this doctrine, he wrote:

> Groups are sociological wholes; the unity of these sociological wholes can be defined in the same way as the unity of any other dynamic whole, namely, by the interdependence of its parts. Such a definition takes mysticism out of the group and brings the problem down to a thoroughly empirical and testable basis. At the same time it means a full recognition of the fact that properties of a social group, such as its organization, its stability, are something different from the organization, the stability and the goals of the individuals in it. (p. 73)

It is interesting to realize that these words were written at a time when it was common for psychologists to deny the existence or reality of social groups (cf. Allport, 1924). Only individuals were real, and it was considered as nonscientific and mystical to refer to group characteristics as "leadership climates," "group processes," "group action," and "group goals" (Deutsch, 1954).

As an example of an empirical study of a social group as "a sociological, dynamic whole," studied at a group level of analysis, Lewin (1948) referred to his famous experiment on the effects of democratic, laissez-faire, and autocratic leadership climates in small groups. In his view the purpose of this experiment was not to duplicate any given democracy but to create set-ups or a model "which would give insight into the underlying group dynamics" (Lewin, 1948, pp. 74–75; emphasis added). This experiment had a major impact on social and organizational psychology (van Oostrum & Rabbie, 1995).

Ross and Nisbett (1991) pointed out that "individual psyches, as well as collectivities ranging from the informal social group to the nation, must be considered as systems in a state of tension" (p. 13). This concept of individuals and groups as dynamic tension systems is based on Lewin's (1947, 1951) force-field analysis. In his view, the status quo in a tension system is the result of a multitude of forces. Some forces support each other, some oppose each other. Some are driving forces, others are restraining forces. These conflicting forces result after a given period in "quasi-stationary equilibria," a term he borrowed from physics (Deutsch, 1954). In his summary of Lewin's group decision and change theory, Deutsch observed that a change from the status quo can be produced either by adding forces in the desired direction or by diminishing opposing factors. These two methods of producing change may have different consequences: Adding driving forces may increase the tension in the system because the strength of the opposing forces will become even stronger, whereas decreasing the opposing forces to the new level would be accompanied by lower tension. For example, if the level of productivity of a worker in a factory is determined by a group norm or standard, productivity may be increased by offering him or her higher wages but this higher level of productivity will result in stronger counteracting forces, induced upon the worker by his or her coworkers to push the worker back into line. Thus, efforts to change the level of production of individual workers will be counteracted by the norms or standards of their groups. The same will happen when the level of prejudice and discrimination of the individual is rooted in his or her group. It will be difficult to change these discriminatory attitudes and behavior at the level of the individual when these change efforts are directed only to the individual but not to the group as a whole. Thus changing individual attitudes and behavior requires a system approach (see v. Cranach, chapter 6, this volume).

Consistent with the view that groups can be considered as dynamic tension systems, Lewin (1948) defined a social group in the following way: "The essence of a group is not similarity or dissimilarity of its members, but their interdependence. A group can be characterized as a 'dynamic whole,' this means that a change in the state of any subpart changes the state of any other subpart. The degree of interdependence varies all the way from a loose 'mass' to a compact unit. It depends, among other factors, upon the size, organization, and intimacy of the group" (p. 84).

Following Lewin (1948), we have defined a social group as a dynamic whole or bounded social system, ranging from a compact unit, which may differ in the degree of intimacy and organization, to a loose mass or large-scale social grouping, whose individual members and other subparts are defined, not so much by their similarities with another, but by the shared experience of a common fate among its members and within the group as a whole (Deutsch, 1973; Horwitz & Rabbie, 1989; Rabbie & Horwitz, 1988). The perception of an "interdependence of fate" of being in the same boat, as it is colloquially known, comes about when people perceive a "common fate" (Lewin, 1948), a "common predicament" (Sherif, 1966), or realize "that they share a common identical plight" (Leyens, Yzerbyt, & Schadron, 1994 p. 58) that causes them to experience shared positive or negative consequences solely as a function of their membership in a social category or group relative to another group or social category.

In contrast to Turner et al. (1987) who have asserted that (interpersonal) interdependence for need satisfaction should be rejected as the basis for group formation, we assume that the perceived positive goal interdependence of a number of individuals is a prime precondition for group formation. The stronger the perceived goal, means, task, and resource interdependence among members in social categories or groups, particularly when their members can directly interact with each other, the greater the degree of organization, intimacy, and sense of group belongingness and group cohesion will be obtained (Johnson & Johnson, 1992). Groups are considered as distinctive social units with boundaries that differentiate them from other groups. These boundaries may differ in permeability: the degree to which an individual member can easily "pass" from one group to another (Lewin, 1948; Rabbie et al., 1989; Tajfel & Turner, 1979).

Members of compact social groups are psychologically bound together by mutually linked instrumental and socioemotional or relational interests as they make collective decisions in trying to achieve individualistic as well as collective group goals or outcomes. It is in the process of collective decision making by face-to-face interacting group members (who may act on behalf of large-scale groupings, e.g., a cabinet of a nation-state, the board of directors of a multinational organization, or the Security Council of the United Nations) where the dynamic, empirical reality of the group is best revealed. That is why in our research we have studied groups qua groups as socio-structural entities "to create set-ups" or models in the laboratory that would offer insights into the intra- and intergroup dynamics of large-scale groups in our daily lives (Kroon, van Kreveld, & Rabbie, 1991a, 1991b, 1992; Rabbie & van Oostrum, 1984; van Oostrum & Rabbie, 1995).

Social Groups and Social Categories

In line with Lewin's (1948) conception of categories and groups, we have made a distinction between social groups and social categories (Horwitz & Rabbie, 1982; Rabbie et al., 1989). As we have indicated a social group is defined as a dynamic whole or social system, characterized by the perceived interdependence among its members, whereas a social category is viewed as a collection of individuals who share at least one attribute in common. This distinction is crucial for the understanding of *outgroup* favoritism in the MGP (Rabbie et al., 1989), the basic conceptual similarity between large-scale groupings and compact face-to-face groups (Rabbie & Horwitz, 1988), and the issue of categorization versus attribution in intergroup conflict (Horwitz & Rabbie, 1989).

In his article "The Cognitive Redefinition of a Social Group," Turner (1982) presented a different view. He proposed that: "a social group can be defined as two or more individuals who share a common social identification of themselves or, which is nearly [sic] the same thing, perceive themselves to be members of the same social category" (p. 15). Thus, in his opinion, a social group is no longer considered as a distinctive dynamic social system, acting and studied at a group level of analysis (as we have defined it), but instead it is "redefined cognitively" in terms of a common social identification, a psychological property of an individual, which he or she is supposed to share with another individual. The obvious problem with this cognitive, individualistic position is that these "common identifications" as intraindividual psychological properties in the human mind, cannot be directly assessed but can only be inferred from overt behavior with all the difficulties involved in such inferences (Rabbie, 1993a). In fact, a student of Turner, Hogg (1992) argued that in minimal groups, created in the standard MGP, "social identity" or "social identifications" cannot be measured directly but only indirectly. He asserted "that the distribution matrices used to measure social identifications in minimal groups are only designed for such groups" (p. 98). If social identifications can indeed not be measured directly, as Hogg maintained, it raises serious questions whether the SI theories can ever be falsified by the MGP experiments. As we have indicated earlier, in the Rabbie et al. (1989) study we used the Tajfel matrices to measure the degree to which subjects in the MGP are motivated to maximize their individual (monetary) interests. In our case these matrices were *not* used to measure social identifications as Hogg proposed but were used to test the RCT of LeVine and Campbell (1972).

Levels of Analysis

Since the work of Lewin (1948) and Sherif (1966), there has been a distinct shift away from studying compact groups qua groups at the group level of analysis, and a shift toward focusing on intraindividual mental representations, cognitive schemata, and personal motives (like the enhancement of self-esteem) to account for intergroup phenomena (see Brewer & Kramer, 1985; Messick & Mackie, 1989). The SI approach is consistent with the individualistic dominant cognitive, information-processing approach in contemporary social psychology of intergroup relations for the last two decades. This individualistic cognitive approach has been very important in generating new research and ideas, although it has its own shortcomings as well (Schruijer, 1990). Our main objection to this exclusive cognitive approach has been that internal cognitive structures within individuals, but not social groups as dynamic, socio-structural tension systems are used as the main units of analysis to study intergroup behavior. This approach implies that we cannot study the effects of structural intragroup variables on intergroup relations and vice versa.

This cognitive, individualistic approach is exemplified by a review of Stephan (1985) on intergroup relations over the last 20 years in the recent *Handbook of Social Psychology.* He claimed that "the level of analysis of a social psychological inquiry into intergroup relations is the individual and his or her relationships with social groups ... Relations between groups *qua* groups (nations, social class, ethnic groups, etc.) will not be of prime interest, not because they are unimportant to an understanding of intergroup cognitions and behavior, but because they belong to a different level of analysis" (pp. 599–600; see also Brewer & Kramer, 1985). Similarly, Hogg and Abrams (1988), representing the SI position, equated interindividual behavior with intergroup behavior. They characterized the SI approach as one that "focuses on the *group in the individual*" (p. 3, emphasis added). Consequently, they defined intergroup behavior as "the manner in which *individuals* relate to one another as members of different groups" (p. 4, emphasis added).

In our model we have argued for a multilevel, multimethod approach to interpersonal and intergroup relations between and within individuals, groups, organizations, nation-states, and other large-scale social systems in the laboratory as well as in field research on natural groups. If we are interested in studying the effects of intragroup relations on relations between groups, and vice versa, we should use both individual- and group-level approaches to see how they relate to each other (Rabbie, 1982a; Rabbie & Lodewijkx, 1994, 1995; see also Doise, 1986). Our behavioral interaction model can be viewed as a reaction to this one-sided, individualistic, and cognitive approach to the study of intra- and intergroup relations.

A BEHAVIORAL INTERACTION MODEL

In our behavioral interaction model (BIM) it is assumed, consistent with the interactionistic position of Lewin (1948), that goal-directed behavior of individuals, groups, organizations, nation-states, or any other large-scale social system is a function of the perceived external environment and of the shared cognitive, emotional, motivational, and normative orientations of members of these social systems. These psychological orientations are in part elicited by the external environment and in part acquired by individuals, groups, organizations, and other human social actors in the course of their development (see Fig. 10.1). The main function of these psychological orientations is to reduce the uncertainty in the external environment to such a level as to enable individuals, groups, and other actors to cope effectively with the environment in an effort to achieve desirable and to avoid undesirable goals or outcomes. The goal-directed behavior of these actors or social systems may include the allocation behavior of individuals in the MGP (Rabbie et al., 1989), or the cooperative or

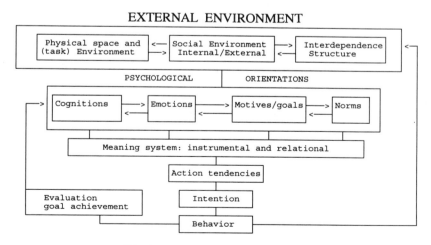

FIG. 10.1. Behavioral interaction model.

competitive choices of individuals and groups in experimental games like the prisoners' dilemma game (PDG) (e.g., Lodewijkx, 1989; Rabbie & Lodewijkx, 1992; Rabbie, Visser, & van Oostrum, 1982) and the power allocation game or PAG (Rabbie & Lodewijkx, 1987, 1991a, 1995). The PDG and PAG were also used to study the aggressive behavior of individual and groups in their reaction to the norm violation of their opponents, that is, other individuals or groups (e.g., Rabbie & Horwitz, 1982; Rabbie & Lodewijkx, 1987, 1991a, 1994, 1995). In our organizational research we examined the effects of manipulated uncertainty in the external environment on the intra- and intergroup behavior of members in simulated organizations (Rabbie & van Oostrum, 1984; van Oostrum & Rabbie, 1988, 1991, 1995). The goal-directed behavior of people in all of these studies share the characteristic that the outcomes of their actions have positive or negative consequences for the actors themselves, for the individuals or groups with whom they are interacting, and often for all the actors and parties involved.

The External Environment

The external environment consists of three components: (a) a physical (task) environment, (b) an internal and external social environment (i.e., the behavior of other people within and external to the group or social system), and (c) the nature of the interdependence structure between the parties with respect to their goals, means, resources and tasks (Harrington & Miller, 1993; Johnson & Johnson, 1992; Rabbie, 1987; Raven & Rubin, 1983).

Task Environment

A task is that part of the physical environment that poses a problem for an individual or group to be solved. It presupposes a system of goal-directed acts that have to be performed in order to attain a certain product or project. A task can be performed by single individuals or by groups. In a cooperative group task (McGrath, 1984), group members have a shared interest in working together toward a group goal that provides some standard for performance from the perspective of the group members themselves or from the perspective of outside observers (Baron, Kerr, & Miller, 1992). Asch (1952) argued that these cooperative group actions are possible only when each participant has a representation that includes the actions of others and their relations. He wrote:

> The respective actions converge relevantly, assist and supplement each other only when the joint situation is represented in each and when the representations are structurally similar. Only when these conditions are given can individuals subordinate themselves to the requirements of joint action from whom ... we have a social system or a process of definite form that embraces the action of a number of individuals. Such a system does not reside in individuals taken separately, though

each individual contributes to it; nor does it reside outside them; it is present in the interrelations between the activities of individuals. (p. 252)

In most cases group action requires face-to-face cooperative interaction. However, as we have shown in the Rabbie et al. (1989) experiment, the "internal representations of joint action" of individuals in the same social category enabled them to tacitly coordinate their actions with one another, which led to the attainment of their individual goals to maximize their monetary outcomes. We see later that members in the MGP will behave differently when group goals rather than individual goals are involved (Rabbie & Schot, 1990).

The Internal and External Social Environment

When dealing with groups or organizations, we have distinguished between two types of environments: (a) the internal social environment, which refers to the social interaction processes within the group or organization that may lead to the development of organized groups (Sherif, 1966), and (b) the external environment, which consists of the transactions of these social systems with the external social world. One of the major concerns in our intra- and intergroup research has been how changes in the internal environment of the group affect the relations between the groups and vice versa. In our research we have examined the effects of intergroup cooperation and competition on intragroup relations such as cohesion, leadership structure, conformity processes, task performance, and socioemotional (relational) or task and (instrumental) relations in the group (Deutsch, 1973, 1982). Conversely, we have tried to find out how these intragroup variables affect intergroup conflict: for example, the effects of intragroup conflict on intergroup competition, or the willingness of leaders to engage in competition or cooperation in intergroup negotiations when they feel threatened in their leadership position in their own group (Bekkers, 1977; Rabbie & Bekkers, 1976).

The external social environment involves perceptions of changes in the behavior of other people or groups, organizations, nation-states, and other social systems with which an actor must deal, for example, how organizations react to the policies of the government, the consequences of collective actions (e.g., market fluctuations), and so on. In our organizational studies we have been interested in testing the contingency theories of Lawrence and Lorsch (1969) and the control graph theory of Tannenbaum (1968). In an effort to test their theories experimentally, laboratory organizations were confronted with either highly uncertain or rather stable market conditions in order to find out how these differences would affect social interaction processes within the internal social environment: for example, the hierarchization of leadership, the degree of participation in the decision-making process, task satisfaction, and productivity (Rabbie & van Oostrum, 1984; van Oostrum & Rabbie, 1988, 1991, 1995).

In line with our contention that multilevel and multimethod approaches should be used to test our theories, similar field studies were conducted in research laboratories (van Looy, 1982), schools of social work (Knip, 1981), university departments (Rabbie, Visser, & Vernooy, 1976), and the postal services (van Haren, 1984). Despite the differences in levels of analysis, the kind of organizations that were studied, and the research methods that were employed, very similar results were obtained. These results suggests that the study of small, compact groups in the laboratory may have some relevance for the understanding of similar processes in large-scale complex organizations, examined at an organizational level of analysis.

Interdependence Structure

Another important aspect of the external environment is the nature of the interdependence structure between the parties. Parties may be dependent on each other for their outcomes with respect to their goals, means, resources, and tasks (Rabbie et al., 1994). Following Raven and Rubin (1983), positive interdependence is defined as the degree to which the action of one party improves the outcomes of one or more other parties, whereas negative interdependence refers to a situation in which the outcome of one party is made worse by the action of other parties. Positive or negative means interdependence exists when one party is either positively or negatively affected in reaching its goal by the means employed by the other party or parties to reach their own goals. Cooperative or competitive *goal* interdependence occurs when the movement of one party toward its goal increases (cooperation) or decreases (competition) the likelihood that the other party or parties will reach their own goals. There is a continuum between a zero-sum or pure win-lose competition in which one party can only win at the costs of the other, and a pure win-win coordination, in which there is little or no conflict of interest between the parties as they try to coordinate their own behavior with those of others, for example, in a traffic situation. Because pure conflict or pure coordination do not occur very often in real life, most interdependence relationships contain a mixture of both cooperative and competitive motives as exists in mixed-motive games like the PDG (Deutsch, 1973). The interdependence between the parties may be either loosely or tightly coupled or they may act independently from each other (Weick, 1979). When one party is more dependent on the actions of the other party than vice versa for its outcomes, we are dealing with an asymmetric power relationship in which one party has more power than the other. Besides cooperation and competition, or equal versus unequal power distributions between the parties, several other types of interdependence relationships can be discerned, such as instrumental or task-oriented versus social-emotional or relation-oriented relationships, formal or informal relationships, and the intensity or superficiality of the relationship between the parties (Deutsch, 1982). In our research with the

PDG and PAG we have mainly focused on the differences in instrumental and relational orientations between individuals and groups (and between men and women; Goldenbeld & Rabbie, 1995; Rabbie, Goldenbeld, & Lodewijkx, 1992).

Psychological Orientations

The assumption of our model is that the three components of the external environment, listed in Fig. 10.1., elicit specific cognitive, emotional, motivational, and normative orientations. These orientations give meaning to the situation and serve to guide one's intentions, behavior, or responses to that environment (Ajzen & Fishbein, 1980; Deutsch, 1982). These meaning systems might be relatively stable, as in certain personality dispositions (e.g., Kelley & Stahelski, 1970) or in the cultures of groups, organizations, or nations (e.g., Markus & Kitayama, 1991; Triandis, 1989), or they might be much more tentative like hypotheses about the relationships between different features of the external environment that may be confirmed or disconfirmed as a function of the kind of information the parties receive from the environment with which they are trying to cope. Whether relatively stable or tentative, the main function of these meaning systems is to reduce the uncertainty and unpredictability of the external environment to such a level that the parties involved feel able to cope with it. The degree of the uncertainty of the physical task environment for the parties is determined by the simplicity or complexity of the task or technological environment, the stability or dynamic character of the situation, and the homogeneity or heterogeneity of the external environment with which the individual, group, or organization must deal (Lawrence & Lorsch, 1969; Mintzberg, 1979; Rabbie & van Oostrum, 1984; van Oostrum & Rabbie, 1988, 1991, 1995). The uncertainties of the social environment, that is, the behavior of others within and external to the social system, are often aroused by the unpredictability and capriciousness of the behavior of others and by the difficulty of attributing stable internal or external causality to intentions of other parties (Katz & Kahn, 1978; Kelley & Michela, 1980).

Earlier we defined the evaluative ingroup–outgroup differentiation in terms of positive or negative attitudes, intentions and behavior. In line with the cognitive, affective, and behavioral analysis of attitudes (Eagly & Chaiken, 1993) and the theory of reasoned action of Ajzen and Fishbein (1980), we have made a distinction in our model between cognitive, emotional, motivational, and normative orientations and how these psychological orientations relate to our intentions and behavior toward ingroups and outgroups. In this way we have tried to relate the insights gained in the attitude-change literature to the study of intra- and intergroup dynamics, which up until now have been considered as relatively unrelated research areas in contemporary social psychology. It is difficult to make sharp, empirical and conceptual distinctions between the cognitive, emotional, and behavioral components of attitudes, although Eagly and Chaiken concluded that "evidence supports the empirical separability of three classes of evaluative responses under some but certainly not all circumstances" (p. 13).

Cognitive Orientations

These are defined by Deutsch (1982) as a "structure of expectations that help the individual cognitively to the situation confronting him" (p. 24). These cognitive orientations may imply both "primary" and "secondary" appraisal processes (Lazarus, 1966). Primary appraisal processes refer to the expectations about the risks and opportunities or potential benefits and harms (which are provided by the external environment), whereas secondary appraisal processes involve the expectations held by individuals or groups of their resources and abilities to cope with the uncertain contingencies in the environment. Primary appraisals, for example, may include costs and benefit analyses, which include beliefs about the likelihood that a given behavior leads to a positive or negative outcome (Ajzen & Fishbein, 1980). Secondary cognitive appraisal processes refer to the coping capability (Lazarus, 1966) self-efficacy (Bandura, 1986), or the perceived behavioral control (Ajzen, 1988) over the attainment of individual or group goals (Rabbie, 1987). In their coping theory, Lazarus and Folkman (1984) distinguished four components of secondary appraisal processes: accountability, problem-focused potential, emotion-focused coping potential, and future expectancy. The accountability evaluation provides information about who is to be blamed or to receive credit for the encounter. Problem-focused coping reflects evaluation of the actor's ability to manage the demands of the encounter, whereas emotion-focused coping refers to the regulation of the emotional state to the harmful or threatening consequences that may be generated. Future expectancies refer to the perceived possibilities for changes in the actual or psychological situation that would make the encounter more or less motivationally congruent (Smith, 1991).

In this literature, the focus of the coping capability or perceived behavior control is on the individual rather than on the group as the main unit of analysis. In our research we have found that interacting group members faced with a stable, predictable physical task environment attributed more influence to each other and hence experienced a greater sense of behavioral control or coping capability over their physical environment than did interacting group members faced with a highly complex, unstable, and unpredictable environment (Rabbie & van Oostrum, 1984; van Oostrum & Rabbie, 1988, 1991). Thus, these "coping potentials" may apply to individuals as well as to groups as they have to react individually or collectively to their perceived environments.

In their motivation to predict and control the external environment, individuals and groups will use schemata (Fiske & Taylor, 1984), scripts (Schank & Abelson, 1977), causal attributions (Heider, 1958; Kelley & Michela, 1980), and social categorizations (Tajfel & Turner, 1979) in trying to reduce the uncertainty in their environment, not only as passive recipients of environmental stimuli and influences but also as active agents who negotiate and construct their environments (Berger & Luckmann, 1967; Rabbie, 1993a; Ross & Nisbett, 1991).

It should be noted that the development of cognitive orientations about ingroups or outgroups does not only depend on intraindividual information-processing capabilities (Stephan, 1985), but also on the collective processing of information among members of organized groups. In this context, Wegner (1987) studied transactive memory of groups, which he defined as a shared system for the encoding, storage, and retrieval of information. (For a review of the development of shared cognitions, norms, and interpretation of events in groups, see Levine, Resnick, & Higgins, 1993).

Emotional Orientations

These refer to subjective experiences and perceptions of relative sudden changes (emotions) or the more slowly evolving fluctuations (moods) related to physiological arousal in the autonomic nervous system. Emotional orientations have cognitive as well as motivational functions: They alert people to threatening or pleasing events in the environment, which further motivates them to avoid or approach them (Frijda, 1986). Smith (1991) made a distinction between (a) harm-related or "negative" emotions (such as anger, guilt, anxiety, sadness, etc.), which are often equated with stressful experiences, and (b) benefit-related or "positive" emotions, such as hope, challenge, happiness, pride, and gratitude, which are often experienced after the successful achievement of individual (and group) goals. Coping with negative emotional experiences often involves social or emotional comparison processes with people who are similar to, worse off than, or better off than oneself (Gerard & Rabbie, 1961; Rabbie, 1963; Taylor & Brown, 1988; Taylor & Lobel, 1989; Wills, 1991).

In our aggression research we have been interested in the question of whether individuals and groups differ from each other in the arousal of those negative emotions, such as anger and indignation, which motivate them to punish other individuals and groups for the violation of important procedural and distributive social justice norms (Rabbie & Lodewijkx, 1987, 1991a, 1995). Also in this research we have found that emotional experiences such as anger, guilt, sadness, and elation are not only intraindividual phenomena but are communicated and enhanced by other group members leading to emotional contagion, which can be studied at an interindividual or at a group level of analysis (Hatfield, Cacioppo, & Rapson, 1994; Rabbie & Lodewijkx, 1985).

Motivational Orientations

These orient people to the possibilities of gratification or frustration of certain kinds of drives, needs, urges, and concerns that change over time as they interact with the environment (Deutsch, 1982). In our research we have used the desirability and attainability of individual and group goals as our main motivational constructs (Kruglanski, 1991). In the context of the experimental games that we have employed in our conflict research, including PDG, MGP, or PAG, several motivational orientations have been discerned: for example, individualism (maximizing one's own gain), cooperation (maximizing joint gain), competition: (maximizing relative gain), equality (minimizing differences), minimizing a maximal possible loss (or defensive motives), altruism (maximizing other's gain), and so on (Kelley & Thibaut, 1978).

There is some evidence that the cooperative, individualistic, and competitive orientations reflect rather stable personality dispositions for particular outcome distributions to self and other interdependent people (Chin & McClintock, 1993; Grzelak, 1982; Kelley & Stahelski, 1970; McClintock & Liebrand, 1988). In a recent study we used a measure of "outcome preferences" developed by Grzelak of these stable motivational orientations of subjects participating in a MGP (Lodewijkx, Syroit, & Rabbie, 1994). Consistent with our expectations, we found that a great deal of the variance in their allocation behavior in the MGP could be attributed to the individual motive to maximize one's own economic outcomes. Other research also indicates that allocations in the MGP are affected by individual differences in outcome preferences and cannot be exclusively ascribed to social identity pressures as SIT has assumed (Chin & McClintock, 1993; Platov, McClintock, & Liebrand, 1990). Again, these different motivational orientations are characteristic not only of individuals but of groups as well. When groups have to make collective decisions in a PDG, very similar motives or reasons are given for their choices by group members as well as by single individuals (Rabbie et al., 1982; Visser, 1995).

Normative Orientations

Norms are rules and regulations in groups that govern the behavior of their members (Pruitt & Rubin, 1986). Norms have a moral, prescriptive quality: They refer to obligations, rights, and entitlements people may have in particular relations (Deutsch, 1982). People tend to behave in accordance with these perceived normative prescriptions or "subjective norms" when they evaluate the behavior positively, and when they believe that important others think that they should perform it (Ajzen, 1988).

When these moral norms or prescriptions are violated, individuals and groups are likely to react with anger and aggression in an effort to rectify the injustice (Lodewijkx, 1989; Rabbie & Lodewijkx, 1987, 1991a, 1995). It has been proposed that people's eagerness to see transgressions adequately punished derives mainly from the need to create stable and predictable environmental conditions in order to assure that every member of a group or community can operate effectively (Zillmann, 1979).

Norms may have also a descriptive, informational function: They provide group members with evidence about social reality (Deutsch & Gerard, 1955; R. M.

Turner & Killian, 1972). Social norms differ among various dimensions from each other. This may depend upon various circumstances: whether they specify the latitudes of acceptance and latitudes of rejection of attitudes and behavior (Sherif & Sherif, 1969), whether they are central or peripheral to the vital concerns of the group or individual, whether they are explicitly verbalized or implicitly understood, whether they are sanctioned by unspecified expectations or by well-defined rewards and punishments, whether they provide general direction or specific guidance, and whether they imply a broad consensus or are accepted by only a few members of the group. Explicitly verbalized norms that are sanctioned by well defined rewards and punishments may provide specific guidance. They are central to the vital concerns of the group and are based on a broad consensus in one's community. In this way they become part and parcel of the external social environment. Through socialization practices norms may become internalized as normative orientations that guide one's attitude and behavior in specific interaction situations (Rabbie, 1987). In our earlier discussion of quasi-stationary equilibria, we have indicated that groups may provide specific standards or norms of performance for their members or can set standards of prejudice and discrimination of other groups.

Meaning Structure, Intentions, and Behavior

These different psychological orientations produce a meaning structure or interpretative system about the situation, which in turn generates various action tendencies in the actor or party. Although many types of meaning systems may exist, we have focused our attention on instrumental and relational orientations that combine with the different cognitive, emotional, motivational, and normative orientations that have been distinguished in the literature (Deutsch, 1982). In this context we have made a distinction between instrumental and relational cooperation, competition, fairness, and altruism.

Consistent with various value-expectancy models (e.g., Ajzen & Fishbein, 1980; Lewin, 1951; Porter & Lawler, 1960), it is assumed that among competing action tendencies and available strategies, those actions and alternatives will be selected that promise, with a high probability of success, to attain the most valued goals or profitable outcomes, whereby the gains seem to exceed the costs of achieving them. Thus, in an effort to maximize their individual (as well as their collective outcomes), it can be expected that people will choose to cooperate rather than compete with each other when mutual instrumental cooperation seems to be more profitable to them than mutual (instrumental) competition (Pruitt & Kimmel, 1977). In the strategic, instrumental, and rational task environments of experimental games, individuals (and groups in particular) come more often to their decisions by a careful and thoughtful consideration of all the alternative choices. Thus they are more likely to follow the "central route" of information processing than using the more "peripheral route" to arrive at their decisions (Goldenbeld &

Rabbie, 1995; Petty & Cacioppo, 1986). It should be recognized, however, that due to the complexities of the environment and the severe limits to cognitive rationality to process information, people will strive for "satisficing" rather than for "optimizing" solutions for their problems (March & Simon, 1958).

The action tendencies, depicted in Fig. 10.1, result in an intention: The commitment to perform or not to perform a certain action. According to the theory of reasoned action (Ajzen & Fishbein, 1980) or planned behavior (Ajzen, 1988), the intention is the best predictor for the behavior. The action or the behavior may lead to outcomes or to a present state that has to be evaluated against a desired future state: the goal or standard the party desires to achieve. When no discrepancy is observed between the intended and the desired state, the action sequence is terminated or "exited" as can be seen in Fig. 10.1. When a discrepancy is observed between the present and desired state, the actor has to revise or reconsider the psychological orientations that led to the behavior that appeared to be not successful in reaching the earlier standards or goals the actor tried to realize. The mismatch between the behavioral outcomes and goals may induce a change in the psychological orientations, symbolized by an arrow from the "evaluation of goal achievement" box to the situational meaning system in Fig. 10.1. This may initiate a new action sequence that will be terminated when the goal is achieved or when different or more attainable goals are substituted for the original objectives.

The direct arrow at the right-hand side of the figure, which extends from the behavior to the external environment at the top of Fig. 10.1, reflects the notion that acting on the external environment may have the effect of changing it, leading to different psychological orientations and meaning structures of the situation, which in turn may induce different action tendencies, intentions, and behaviors, initiating a new cycle in the action sequence until the standards or goals (either original or modified) are achieved. Just like other cybernetic action models (e.g., the control model of Carver & Scheier, 1981, or the TOTE concept of Miller, Galanter, & Pribram, 1960), our model can be considered as a self-regulating, negative feedback system. The model is particularly useful in tracing the development of the conflict over time, within and between groups and individuals, for example by examining the changes in psychological orientations and behavior during the different trials of a PDG (Rabbie et al., 1982; Visser, 1995).

EMPIRICAL EVIDENCE

Our model has been used to analyze armed conflicts between nations (Rabbie, 1987), aggressive reactions to social injustice (Rabbie & Lodewijkx, 1987, 1991a, 1994, 1995), instrumental intragroup cooperation (Rabbie, 1991a), terrorism (Rabbie, 1991b), intra- and intergroup conflict (Rabbie, 1992), gender differences in conflict and aggression (Goldenbeld, 1992; Lodewijkx, 1989; Rabbie et al. 1992), the allocation behavior of individuals in social categories in the MGP (e.g., Mlicki,

1993; Rabbie et al., 1989; Rabbie & Schot, 1989; Schot, 1992; Schot et al., 1994) and intra- and intergroup behavior in large-scale organizations and in laboratory groups (e.g., Rabbie, Visser, & Vernooy, 1976; Rabbie & van Oostrum, 1984; van Oostrum & Rabbie, 1988, 1991, 1995).

In this section we confine ourselves to a summary of three experiments in the area of intra- and intergroup dynamics that seem to provide support for some of the basic assumptions of our model in accounting for intergroup cooperation and competition in the MGP.

Common Fate in Categories and Groups

On the basis of their MGP experiments, Tajfel and Turner (1979) asserted "that the mere perception of belonging to two distinct groups—that is social categorization per se—is sufficient to trigger intergroup discrimination favoring the in-group" (p. 38). According to our model, explicit social categorization is only one of the many factors that may contribute to the perception of a bounded social group or system that is characterized by perceived interdependence among its members. Other *unit-forming factors* may include common fate and perceived interdependence, proximity, a shared territory, similar preferences and shared labels, shared threat, the anticipation or actual intragroup interaction, intergroup competition, and so on (cf. Dion, 1979; Rabbie & Wilkens, 1971). According to our unit formation hypothesis, the greater the salience, importance, and number of these unit-forming factors within the group, the greater will be the ingroup favoritism between groups (Rabbie et al., 1989).

In her review of research on ingroup bias in the minimal intergroup situation, Brewer (1979) suggested that the ingroup–outgroup differentiation can be more attributed to ingroup favoritism than to outgroup discrimination. Referring to her work, Horwitz and Rabbie (1982) proposed that the stronger the perceived "entitativity" (Campbell, 1958), "groupness" (Insko & Schopler, 1987), or "unity" (Rabbie & Wilkens, 1971) of the group the stronger the extent to which members would favor their own group over the outgroup. This would mean that the greater the number and importance of unit-forming factors the greater the intergroup differentiation. In line with Brewer and Horwitz and Rabbie, but in contrast to SIT, it is to be expected that the ingroup–outgroup differentiation can be more attributed to ingroup favoritism (due to intragroup cooperation) than to outgroup discrimination (due to intergroup competition).

These hypotheses were tested in a recent study reported in a dissertation of Mlicki (1993), supervised by Rabbie and Lodewijkx. The study employed a one-way factorial design with four conditions:

1. In a common fate (CF) condition, *all* subjects in a classroom received a ticket worth 10 guilders (about $6.00 U.S.) for their participation in the experiment. Afterward individuals were randomly assigned to one of two subcategories (Alpha and Omega).

2. In the mere categorization (MC) condition (modeled after the control condition of Rabbie & Horwitz, 1969), individuals were randomly assigned to the two subgroups, Alpha and Omega, that were not physically separated from each other.

3. In a visual separation (VS) condition, individuals were randomly assigned to the Alpha and Omega categories but were physically separated from each other: Members belonging to the Alpha category were seated on the left side of the room whereas the members belonging to the Omega category were seated on the right side of the room.

4. In the relative common fate (RCF) condition, individuals were randomly classified into the Alpha and Omega categories, but this time each of the individuals in the two categories were either privileged or deprived relative to individuals in the other category.

The allocation of the reward: 10 guilders for each individual in one social category was determined by chance. In the presence of all subjects, one representative of each category drew lots. All the winning members of the privileged Alpha group received the 10-guilder tickets, whereas members of the deprived or losing Omega group received nothing. The RCF condition corresponds (conceptually) to the experimental chance condition in the Rabbie and Horwitz (1969) study, in which the greatest ingroup–outgroup differentiation was obtained.

Four Tajfel matrices (the same as used by Rabbie et al., 1989) were employed to assess behavioral allocation strategies of distributing points to anonymous members in one's own category, and to anonymous members in the other category. In the instructions, the points to be allocated were defined as "tokens for one's appreciation for the others and for oneself": The more points allocated the more one could show his or her appreciation for individuals in each of the two categories.

We had expected that the experience of a common fate for *all* individuals in the CF condition would have a unifying effect for the whole group and would consequently diminish the intergroup differentiation between the minimal Alpha and Omega subgroups, in comparison to the differentiation between these minimal groups in the MC, VS, and RCF conditions. This expectation was not confirmed. Only the RCF condition in which the categorization completely coincides or overlaps with the experience of a relative common fate (i.e., of being privileged or deprived from the reward relative to another group) produced a significant ingroup differentiation. Thus it appears, consistent with BIM, that a perceived interdependence of fate relative to another group is the most important unit-forming factor that leads to intergroup differentiation. Moreover, in line with our second hypothesis, the greater ingroup–outgroup differentiation in the RCF condition is mainly due to ingroup favoritism (due to intragroup cooperation) rather than to the outgroup discrimination (or intergroup competition) as Tajfel and Turner (1979) would claim. These findings provide strong support for our model, in which it is assumed that "the more a collection of people begin to share the features of a compact group ... the more mutual *intragroup cooperation* will occur (Rabbie, 1991b, p. 240, emphasis added).

Additional questionnaire data also provide support for our normative ingroup schema (Rabbie, 1993a, 1993b). Subjects, in all conditions, perceived themselves to be more dependent on ingroup members than on outgroup members and consequently expected more from ingroup members than from outgroup members. (For a more complete review of these and other findings, see Mlicki, 1993.)

The Individual–Group Continuum

As we indicated earlier, we propose in our model an individual-centered/group-centered continuum that varies along a perceived (positive) interdependence dimension. At the individual pole of this continuum there are self-centered individuals in social categories who perceive themselves to be minimally interdependent on each other for attaining their outcomes and are mainly interested in maximizing their individualistic, personal outcomes. At the group or collective pole of the continuum, there are group-centered individuals in social or organized groups who perceive themselves to be maximally interdependent on each other for attaining their outcomes. They are not only willing to maximize their individual interests but are also motivated to maximize the interest of the group as a whole, sometimes at some costs to themselves. In a recent experiment we tested the validity of this continuum (Rabbie & Schot, 1990; Rabbie et al., 1995).

At the individual pole of the continuum, individuals in social categories were urged to maximize their instrumental, monetary interests as well as they could. This individual goal condition was compared with a control condition in which the standard instructions of Tajfel et al. (1971) were given. These instructions do not ask subjects to maximize either their individual or their group interests. Because we have argued that the subjects in the standard MGP are mainly interested in maximizing their individual monetary interests (Rabbie et al., 1989), we expected that there would be no significant differences in allocation behavior between the social categories in the individual goal and control conditions. At the group-centered pole of the continuum, in a group goal condition, subjects were urged to maximize their instrumental, monetary group interests as well as they could. We expected that in the group goal condition more intragroup cooperation and intergroup competition would occur than in the two individualistic category conditions.

This hypothesis is based on a long research tradition. In his ethnocentrism theory, Sumner (1906) argued that ingroup cohesion and outgroup hostility are always related to each other. He wrote: "the relation of comradeship and peace in the we-group and that of hostility and war toward others-groups are correlative to each other" (p. 12). In our research we have found that intragroup cohesion and outgroup hostility are not invariably correlated between each other, as Sumner believed, but should be viewed as a consequence of two independent processes: intragroup cooperation and intergroup competition (Rabbie, 1982a, 1982b, 1992, 1993a). Intragroup cooperation will lead to ingroup cohesiveness or ingroup favoritism, whereas intergroup competition will lead to mutual frustration, hostility, and outgroup discrimination. This means that the mere categorization of individuals into groups does not invariably lead to intergroup competitiveness and outgroup discrimination as Tajfel and Turner (1986) asserted. Whether intragroup cooperation or intergroup competition will occur depends on the perceived positive or negative interdependence within and between groups (Deutsch, 1973, 1982).

These hypotheses received strong support. As expected, no difference in allocation behavior was found between the individual and the control condition in the MGP. These results suggest, contrary to the claims by Turner (1982), that in the standard MGP of Tajfel et al. (1971) we are dealing more with interindividual (or interpersonal) behavior, designed to maximize monetary outcomes, than with intergroup behavior. Moreover, more intragroup cooperation and more intergroup competition occurred in the group goal than in the individualistic category conditions. Consistent with our expectations, intergroup orientations in the group goal condition led to less fairness, and more discrimination in favor of the own group than interindividual orientations in the category conditions. When subjects could directly allocate monetary points to themselves or to the other group members, it was shown that in intergroup relations members in the group goal condition, in comparison with the self-centered individuals in the social category conditions, appeared to be more willing to sacrifice a direct economic gain for themselves in favor of their own preference group as a whole.

Consistent with our model, questionnaire results indicated that subjects in the individualistic category conditions perceived a greater sense of "independence than of interdependence," and perceived themselves as "acting more as individuals than as group members" in comparison to subjects in the group goal condition. Consistent with our hypotheses more social identity pressures occurred in the group goal that in the social category conditions: Subjects reported that they were more motivated "to be better than the other group" and were "trying to enhance their self-esteem" to a greater extent in the group goal than in the individualistic category conditions. These results provide more support for our version of the IP than for the SI position, represented by the work of Tajfel and Turner (1986) and Turner et al. (1987). These findings also appear to be consistent with recent hypotheses developed by Hinkle, Brown, and Ely (1992).

Symbolic and Economic Rewards

In our model it is assumed that the degree of instrumental cooperation and competition will depend on the kind of incentives or resources that are at stake in the MGP. When economic or instrumental incentives are involved, mainly instrumental cooperation and competition will occur. When symbolic incentives are at stake (e.g., points), people will be more motivated to engage in social or relational competition (i.e., to strive more for prestige, recognition, or a "positive social identity" as is assumed by SIT). To obtain information on this issue, the Rabbie et al. (1989) experiment was replicated, but this time symbolic points instead of monetary points had to be allocated (Rabbie & Schot, 1989; Schot, 1992; Schot et al., 1994). As expected, more ingroup favoritism was obtained in the points than in the money condition. Moreover, in the symbolic points condition there was a greater tendency to differentiate oneself from the others and less willingness to cooperate with others. Thus, when money was at stake, subjects were more interested in maximizing their own tangible economic outcomes than when symbolic points were involved. Consistent with our model, a significant interaction between the money and point conditions was obtained. In the money condition there was strong support for our reciprocal interdependence hypothesis: Subjects allocate the most money to those group members on whom they perceived themselves to be the most instrumentally dependent. For example, in the outgroup dependence (OD) money condition, a strong expected outgroup favoritism was obtained. When symbolic points had to be allocated, the outgroup favoritism in the OD condition disappeared. In fact, when points were allocated in the OD condition a significant ingroup favoritism was obtained, although this ingroup favoritism is smaller in the OD condition than in the IOD control condition of Tajfel et al. (1971) and the ingroup dependence (ID) conditions. Thus, as expected, dependent on the nature of the incentives or resources being allocated, support was found for our reciprocal interdependence hypothesis as well as for SIT. This finding suggests, in accordance with our model, that the two perspectives are not incompatible with each other, as Turner et al. (1987) asserted. Both hypotheses may explain the allocation behavior in the MGP, dependent on the incentive conditions that stimulate instrumental cooperation or relational competition. These results have been replicated by Mlicki (1993).

CONCLUSION

In his comparison of his own social identification model with the cohesion model (his way of characterizing the interdependence perspective), Turner (1982) stressed the value of polemics: ". . . [T]here is some polemical value in stressing single-mindedly the virtues of a new idea and playing down those of the old. It might well be, indeed it is almost certain, that at some stage a theoretical conception of the social group will emerge which integrates the truth contained in both definitions" (p. 17). In our model we have tried to make a beginning in developing such an integrative theoretical conception of the social group.

We agree with Turner that pushing a single-minded idea to its limits might be very fruitful indeed. It must be acknowledged that the SI approach has become one of the most influential and productive theories in the social psychology of intergroup relations for the last two decades. In their recent review on intergroup relations, Messick and Mackie (1989) gave due credit to the theory. They wrote that "SIT has been responsible for almost single-handedly reviving intergroup research" (p. 61). However, Messick and Mackie are not without criticisms about the empirical validity of SIT. They concluded: "In summary, nearly 20 years after the discovery that mere categorization produced intergroup bias, an adequate theory of the phenomenon has yet to be developed. Both perceptual accentuation effects and self-esteem maintenance seem likely to be part of the story, but empirical findings have not definitely clarified their necessary or sufficient roles" (p. 62). Other reviewers have come to very similar conclusions. With regard to the central self-esteem hypothesis of SIT, Hogg and Abrams (1990) concluded: "The evidence for the self-esteem hypothesis is mixed and much derives from minimal group situations which may overimplicate intergroup discrimination" (p. 47). In their critique of SIT, Schiffmann and Wicklund (1992) asserted that the SIT "is little more than its own minimal paradigm, and is superfluous as an account of systematic social psychological phenomena" (p. 29). Hinkle et al. (1992) referred to the "narrow range of applicability" of SIT (p. 108). In his comments on the research of Hinkle et al., Triandis (1992) maintained "that SIT may only apply to individualistic cultures . . . and have even more serious limitations when social psychologists try to apply it to collective cultures" (p. 113). From a methodological point of view, Bornstein et al. (1983) concluded that the "Tajfel matrices yield minimal information and that further use of them would be heedless and indeed reckless" (p. 380).

Despite these possible flaws, or perhaps because of them, we believe that the time has come to work on a broader theoretical framework that allows us to integrate "the truth" contained in both perspectives. Henry Tajfel (1982), in his comments on our work, has already tried to unearth the "potential complementarity" of these perspectives. We think that our behavioral interaction model, which is still at the preliminary stage of its development, may provide another route to an integrative theory that does not just restrict itself to the research of intergroup relations from a relatively narrow intraindividual, cognitive perspective, but also takes the emotional, motivational, and normative intergroup processes into account as they change over time. Most important of all, it would stimulate research on dynamic tension systems within and between individuals, groups, and organizations, and how the behavior of these systems are affected by the changes in the wider cultural context in which they are embedded (Markus & Kitayama, 1991; Triandis, 1989).

In their work on intergroup relations, after the ravages of World War II, Lewin (1948, 1951) and Sherif had the vision that social psychology should have a bridging function between two social disciplines: sociology and psychology. They studied the collective behavior of groups qua groups to create setups or models that would give insight into the underlying dynamics within and between groups in an effort to understand the burning issues of their times. We have to return to the wider view of intergroup relations they envisaged, instead of limiting ourselves only to the narrow contemporary cognitive approaches as espoused by Stephan (1985) and other individualistic cognitive theorists. Intergroup conflict and aggression have become one of the most urgent problems of our time. We need the contribution of a broader "social" social psychology to cope with the daunting task of understanding why individuals and groups can do such gruesome things to one another.

ACKNOWLEDGMENTS

This chapter is dedicated to the memories of Murray Horwitz and Henry Tajfel. Both colleagues have enriched our thinking about intra- and intergroup relations. The research reported in this chapter has been funded by the Netherlands Organization for the Advancement of Research (NWO): Grants 57-07, 57-97, and 560-270-012.

REFERENCES

Allport, F. H. (1924). *Social psychology*. New York: Houghton Mifflin.

Asch, S. E. (1952). *Social psychology*. Englewood Cliffs, NJ: Prentice-Hall.

Ajzen, I. (1988). *Attitudes, personality and behavior*. Milton Keynes: Open University Press.

Ajzen, I., & Fishbein, M. (1980). *Understanding attitudes and predicting social behavior*. Englewood Cliffs, NJ: Prentice-Hall.

Bandura, A. (1986). *Social foundations of thought and action: A social cognitive theory*. Englewood Cliffs, NJ: Prentice-Hall.

Baron, R. S., Kerr, N., & Miller, N. (1992). *Group process, group decision, group action*. Buckingham: Open University Press.

Bekkers, F. (1977). Threatened leadership and intergroup conflicts. *Journal of Peace Research, 3*(14), 223–237.

Berger, P. L., & Luckmann, T. (1967). *The social construction of reality*. London: Allen Lane.

Bornstein, G., Crum, L., Wittenbraker, J., Harring, K., Insko, C. A., & Thibaut, J. (1983). Reply to Turner's comments. *European Journal of Social Psychology, 13*, 369–382.

Branthwaite, A., Doyle, S., & Lightbown, N. (1979). The balance between fairness and discrimination. *European Journal of Social Psychology, 9*, 149–163.

Brewer, M. B. (1979). Ingroup bias in the minimal intergroup situation: A cognitive-motivational analysis. *Psychological Bulletin, 86*, 307–324.

Brewer, M. B., & Kramer, R. M. (1985). The psychology of intergroup attitudes and behavior. *Annual Review of Psychology, 36*, 219–243.

Brown, R. (1986). *Social psychology* (2nd ed.). New York: The Free Press.

Campbell, D. T. (1958). Common fate, similarity, and other indices of the status of aggregates of persons as social entities. *Behavioral Science, 3*, 14–25.

Cartwright, D. S., & Zander, A. (1968). *Group dynamics* (3rd ed.). London: Tavistock.

Carver, C. S., & Scheier, M. (1981). *Attention and self regulation: A control theory approach to human behavior*. New York: Springer.

Chin, M. G., & McClintock, C. G. (1993). The effects of intergroup discrimination and social values on level of self-esteem in the MGP. *European Journal of Social Psychology, 23*, 63–75.

Deutsch, M. (1949). A theory of co-operation and competition. *Human Relations, 2*, 129–152.

Deutsch, M. (1954). Field theory in social psychology. In G. Lindzey (Ed.), *Handbook of social psychology* (pp. 181–222). Cambridge, MA: Addison-Wesley.

Deutsch, M. (1973). *The resolution of conflict: Constructive and destructive processes.* New Haven, CT: Yale University Press.

Deutsch, M. (1982). Interdependence and psychological orientation. In V. J. Derlega & J. Grzelak (Eds.), *Cooperation and helping behavior* (pp. 15–42). New York: Academic Press.

Deutsch, M., & Gerard, H. B. (1955). A study of normative and informational influence upon individual judgement. *Journal of Abnormal and Social Psychology, 51*, 629–636.

Dion, K. L. (1979). Intergroup conflict and intragroup cohesiveness. In W. G. Austin & S. Worchel (Eds.), *The social psychology of intergroup relations* (pp. 211–224). Monterey, CA: Brooks-Cole.

Doise, W. (1986). *Levels of explanation in social psychology.* Cambridge, England: Cambridge University Press.

Doise, W. (1988). Individual and social identities in intergroup relations. *European Journal of Social Psychology, 18*, 99–111.

Eagly, A. H., & Chaiken, S. (1993). *The psychology of attitudes.* Orlando, FL: Harcourt Brace.

Festinger, L., Schachter, S., & Back, K. (1950). *Social pressures in informal social groups.* New York: Harper & Row.

Fiske, S. T., & Taylor, S. E. (1984). *Social cognition.* New York: Random House.

Frijda, N. H. (1986). *The emotions.* New York: Cambridge University Press.

Gerard, H. B., & Rabbie, J. M. (1961). Fear and social comparison. *Journal of Abnormal and Social Psychology, 62*, 586–592.

Goldenbeld, C. (1992). *Aggression after provocation.* Unpublished doctoral dissertation, University of Utrecht, Utrecht, The Netherlands.

Goldenbeld, C., & Rabbie, J. M. (1995). *Effects of norm setting and modelling on retaliatory aggression of males and females in an intergroup context.* Manuscript submitted for publication.

Grzelak, J. L. (1982). Preferences and cognitive processes in interdependence situations: A theoretical analysis of cooperation. In V. J. Derlega & J. Grzelak (Eds.), *Cooperation and helping behavior* (pp. 95–122). New York: Academic Press.

Harrington, H., & Miller, N. (1993). Do group motives differ from individual motives? Considerations regarding process distinctiveness. In D. Abrams & M. A. Hogg (Eds.), *Social identity theory: Constructive and critical advances* (pp. 149–172). Hemel Hemstead: Harvester Wheatsheaf.

Hatfield, E., Cacioppo, J. T., & Rapson, R. L. (1994). *Emotional contagion.* Cambridge, England: Cambridge University Press.

Heider, F. (1958). *The psychological interpersonal relations.* New York: Wiley.

Hinkle, S., & Brown, R. J. (1990). Intergroup comparisons and social identity: Some links and lacunae. In D. Abrams & M. A. Hogg (Eds.), *Social identity theory: Constructive and critical advances* (pp. 48–70). Hemel Hemstead: Harvester Wheatsheaf.

Hinkle, S., Brown, R. J., & Ely, P. G. (1992). Social identity theory processes: Some limitations and limiting conditions. *Revista de Psicología Social, Monográfico*, 99–111.

Hogg, M. A. (1992). *The social psychology of group cohesiveness: From attraction to social identity.* New York: Harvester Wheatsheaf.

Hogg, M. A., & Abrams, D. (1990). Social motivation, self-esteem and social identity. In D. Abrams & M. A. Hogg (Eds.), *Social identity theory: Constructive and critical advances* (pp. 48–70). Hemel Hemstead: Harvester Wheatsheaf.

Hogg, M. A., & Abrams, D. (1988). *Social identifications: A social psychology of intergroup relations and group processes.* London and New York: Routledge.

Hornstein, H. A. (1976). *Cruelty and kindness: A new look at aggression and altruism.* Englewood Cliffs, NJ: Prentice-Hall.

Horwitz, M. (1953). The recall on interrupted group tasks: An experimental study of individual motivation in relation to group goals. In D. Cartwright & A. Zander (Eds.), *Group dynamics: Research and theory* (1st ed., pp. 370–394). Evanston, IL: Row, Peterson.

Horwitz, M., & Rabbie, J. M. (1982). Individuality and membership in the intergroup system. In H. Tajfel (Ed.), *Social identity and intergroup relations* (pp. 241–274). Cambridge, England: Cambridge University Press.

Horwitz, M., & Rabbie, J. M. (1989). Stereotypes of groups, group members and individuals in categories: A differential analysis of different phenomena. In D. Bar-Tal et al. (Eds.), *Stereotyping and prejudice: Changing conceptions* (pp. 105–129). New York: Springer-Verlag.

Insko, C. A., & Schopler, J. (1987). Categorization, competition and collectivity. In C. Hendrick (Ed.), *Group processes: Review of personality and social psychology* (Vol. 8, pp. 213–251). New York: Sage.

Johnson, D. W., & Johnson, R. T. (1992). Positive interdependence: Key to effective cooperation. In R. Hertz-Lazarowitz & N. Miller (Eds.), *Interaction in cooperative groups: The theoretical anatomy of group learning* (pp. 174–199). New York: Cambridge University Press.

Katz, D., & Kahn, R. L. (1978). *The social psychology of organizations* (2nd ed.). New York: Wiley.

Kelley, H. H., & Michela, S. C. (1980). Attribution theory and research. *Annual Review of Psychology, 31,* 457–502.

Kelley, H. H., & Stahelski, A. (1970). The social interaction basis of cooperators' and competitors' beliefs about others. *Journal of Personality and Social Psychology, 16,* 66–91.

Kelley, H. H., & Thibaut, J. W. (1978). *Interpersonal relations: A theory of interdependence.* New York: Wiley.

Knip, J. L. (1981). *Organizational studies in education.* Unpublished doctoral dissertation, University of Utrecht, Utrecht, The Netherlands.

Kroon, B. R., van Kreveld, D., & Rabbie, J. M. (1991a). Managing group decision making processes: Individual versus collective accountability. *The International Journal of Conflict Management, 2,* 91–216.

Kroon, B. R., van Kreveld, D., & Rabbie, J. M. (1991b). Police intervention in riots: The role of accountability and group norms: A field experiment. *Journal of Community and Applied Social Psychology, 1,* 249–267.

Kroon, B. R., van Kreveld, D., & Rabbie, J. M. (1992). Group versus individual decision making: Effects of accountability and gender on groupthink. *Small Group Research, 23*(4), 427–458.

Kruglanski, A. W. (1991, August). *Motivation and social cognition: Enemies or a love story?* Paper presented at the meeting of Division 8 of the American Psychological Association, San Francisco.

Lawrence, P. R., & Lorsch, J. W. (1969). *Organization and environment.* Cambridge, MA: Harvard University Press.

Lazarus, R. S. (1966). *Psychological stress and the coping process.* New York: McGraw-Hill.

Lazarus, R. S., & Folkman, S. (1984). *Stress, appraisal, and coping.* New York: Springer.

Lemaine, G. (1966). Inegalité, comparison, et incomparibilité: Esquisse d'une theorie de l'originalité socialite. *Bulletin de Psychologie, 252*(20), 1–9.

Levine, J. M., Resnick, L. B., & Higgins, E. T. (1993). Social foundations of cognition. *Annual Review of Psychology, 44,* 585–612.

LeVine, R. A., & Campbell, D. T. (1972). *Ethnocentrism: Theories of conflict, ethnic attitudes and group behavior.* New York: Wiley.

Lewin, K. (1936). *Principles of topological psychology.* New York: McGraw Hill.

Lewin, K. (1947). Group decision and social change. In T. Newcomb & E. Hartley (Eds.), *Readings in social psychology* (pp. 95–151). New York: Holt.

Lewin, K. (1948). *Resolving social conflicts.* New York: Harper & Row.

Lewin, K. (1951). *Field theory in social science.* New York: Harper & Row.

Leyens, J. P., Yzerbyt, V., & Schadron, G. (1994). *Stereotypes and social cognition.* London: Sage.

Lodewijkx, H. (1989). *Conflict and aggression between groups and individuals: Toward a behavioral interaction model.* Unpublished doctoral dissertation, University of Utrecht, Utrecht, The Netherlands.

Lodewijkx, H. F. M., & Rabbie, J. M. (1992). Group-centred and self-centred behavior in intergroup relations. *International Journal of Psychology, 27*(3–4), 267.

Lodewijkx, H. F. M., Syroit, J., & Rabbie, J. M. (1994, March). *Evocations of matrix-transformations by social orientations in the MGP.* Paper presented at a seminar on intergroup relations, Free University, Amsterdam.

March, J. G., & Simon, H. A. (1958). *Organizations.* New York: Wiley.

Markus, H., & Kitayama, S. (1991). Culture and the self: Implications for cognition, emotion and motivation. *Psychological Review, 98*, 224–253.

McClintock, C. G., & Liebrand, W. B. G. (1988). The role of interdependence structure, individual value orientation and other's strategy in social decision making: A transformational analysis. *Journal of Personality and Social Psychology, 55*, 396–409.

McGrath, J. E. (1984). *Groups: Interaction and performance.* Englewood Cliffs, NJ: Prentice-Hall.

Merton, R. K. (1957). *Social theory and social structure.* Glencoe, IL: The Free Press.

Messick, D. M., & Mackie, D. M. (1989). Intergroup relations. *Annual Review of Psychology, 40*, 45–81.

Miller, G. A., Galanter, E., & Pribram, K. H. (1960). *Plans and the structure of behavior.* New York: Holt, Rinehart & Winston.

Mintzburg, H. (1979). *The structure of organizations: A synthesis of the research.* Englewood Cliffs, NJ: Prentice-Hall.

Mlicki, P. P. (1993). *"Us and them": Effects of categorization and interdependence on differentiation between categories and groups.* Unpublished doctoral dissertation, University of Utrecht, Utrecht, The Netherlands.

Petty, R. E., & Cacioppo, J. T. (1986). *Communication and persuasion: Central and peripheral routes to attitude change.* New York: Springer-Verlag.

Pfeffer, J., & Salancik, G. R. (1978). *The external control of organizations: A resource dependence perspective.* New York: Harper & Row.

Platov, M. J., McClintock, C. G., & Liebrand, W. B. G. (1990). Predicting intergroup fairness and ingroup bias in the MGP. *European Journal of Social Psychology, 20*, 221–239.

Porter, L. W., & Lawler, E. (1968). *Managerial attitudes and performance.* Homewood, IL: Irwin.

Pruitt, D. G., & Kimmel, M. J. (1977). Twenty years of experimental gaming: Critique, synthesis, and suggestions for the future. *Annual Review of Psychology, 28*, 363–392.

Pruitt, D. G., & Rubin, J. C. (1986). *Social conflict: Escalation, stalemate and settlement.* New York: Random House.

Rabbie, J. M. (1963). Differential preference for companionship under threat. *Journal of Abnormal and Social Psychology, 67*, 586–592.

Rabbie, J. M. (1965, December). *Ingroup-outgroup differentiation under minimal social conditions.* Paper presented at the Second European Conference of Experimental Social Psychology, Frascati, Italy.

Rabbie, J. M. (1982a). The effects of intergroup competition on intragroup and intergroup relationships. In V. J. Derlega & J. Grzelak (Eds.), *Cooperation and helping behavior: Theories and research* (pp. 123–149). New York: Academic Press.

Rabbie, J. M. (1982b, September). *Are groups more aggressive than individuals?* Invited keynote address (The Henry Tajfel Lecture) presented at the annual conference of the Social Psychology Section of the British Psychological Society.

Rabbie, J. M. (1987). Armed conflicts: Toward a behavioral interaction model. In J. von Wright, K. Helkama, & A. M. Pirtilla-Backman (Eds.), *European psychologists for peace—Proceedings of the Congress in Helsinki, 1986.*

Rabbie, J. M. (1989). Group processes as stimulants of aggression. In J. Groebel & R. H. Hinde (Eds.), *Aggression and war: Their biological and social bases* (pp. 141–155). Cambridge, England: Cambridge University Press.

Rabbie, J. M. (1991a). A behavioral interaction model: A theoretical framework for studying terrorism. *Terrorism and Political Violence, 3*(4), 133–162.

Rabbie, J. M. (1991b). Instrumental intra-group cooperation. In J. Groebel & R. H. Hinde (Eds.), *Pro-social behavior, altruism and cooperation* (pp. 238–260). Cambridge, England: Cambridge University Press.

Rabbie, J. M. (1992). Effects of intra-group cooperation and intergroup competition on ingroup-outgroup differentiation. In A. Harcourt & F. de Waal (Eds.), *Cooperation in conflict: Coalitions and alliances in animals and humans* (pp. 175–205). Oxford, England: Oxford University Press.

Rabbie, J. M. (1993a). A behavioral interaction model: Towards an integrative framework for studying intra- and intergroup relations. In K. Larson (Ed.), *Conflict and social psychology* (pp. 86–108). Beverly Hills, CA: PRIO/Sage.

Rabbie, J. M. (1993b). Determinants of ingroup cohesion and outgroup hostility. *International Journal of Group Tensions, 23*(4), 309–328.

Rabbie, J. M., & Bekkers, F. (1976). Threatened leadership and intergroup competition. *European Journal of Social Psychology, 31*, 269–283.

Rabbie, J. M., Benoist, F., Oosterbaan, H., & Visser, L. (1974). Differential power and effects of expected competitive and cooperative intergroup interaction on intra-group and outgroup attitudes. *Journal of Personality and Social Psychology, 30*, 46–56.

Rabbie, J. M., & de Brey, J. H. C. (1971). The anticipation of intergroup cooperation and competition under private and public conditions. *International Journal of Group Tensions, 1*, 230–252.

Rabbie, J. M., Goldenbeld, C., & Lodewijkx, H. F. M. (1992). Sex differences in conflict and aggression in individual and group settings. In K. Björquist & P. Niemellä (Eds.), *Of mice and women: Aspects of female aggression* (pp. 217–228). New York: Academic Press.

Rabbie, J. M., & Horwitz, M. (1969). The arousal of ingroup-outgroup bias by a chance win or loss. *Journal of Personality and Social Psychology, 13*, 269–277.

Rabbie, J. M., & Horwitz, M. (1982). Conflicts and aggression among individuals and groups. In H. Hiebsch, H. Brandstätter, & H. Kelley (Eds.), *Proceedings of the Twenty-second International Congress of Psychology, Leipzig, Germany* (pp. 99–106).

Rabbie, J. M., & Horwitz, M. (1988). Categories versus groups as explanatory concepts in inter-group relations. *European Journal of Social Psychology, 18*, 117–123.

Rabbie, J. M., & Huygen, K. (1974). Internal disagreements and their effects on attitudes towards in- and outgroup. *International Journal of Group Tensions, 4*, 222–246.

Rabbie, J. M., & Lodewijkx, H. (1985). The enhancement of competition and aggression in individuals and groups. In F. L. Denmark (Ed.), *Social/ecological psychology and the psychology of women* (pp. 177–187). Amsterdam: North-Holland.

Rabbie, J. M., & Lodewijkx, H. (1987). Individual and group aggression. *Current Research on Peace and Violence, 2–3*, 91–101.

Rabbie, J. M., & Lodewijkx, H. F. M. (1991a). Aggressive reactions to social injustice by individuals and groups: Toward a behavioral interaction model. In R. Vermunt & H. Steensma (Eds.), *Social justice in human relations* (Vol. 1, pp. 279–309). New York: Plenum.

Rabbie, J. M., & Lodewijkx, H. F. M. (1991b, September). *Self-centered and group-centered behaviour of males and females in symmetric and asymmetric relationships.* Paper presented at the meeting of the Third International Conference on Social Value Orientations in Interpersonal and Intergroup Relations, Leuven, Belgium.

Rabbie, J. M., & Lodewijkx, H. F. M. (1992). *Instrumental and relational cooperation and competition along an individual-group continuum.* Unpublished manuscript.

Rabbie, J. M., & Lodewijkx, H. F. M. (1994). Conflict and aggression: An individual-group continuum. In B. Markovski, K. Heimer, & J. O'Brien (Eds.), *Advances in group processes* (Vol. 11, pp. 139–174). Greenwich, CT: JAI.

Rabbie, J. M., & Lodewijkx, H. F. M. (1995). Aggressive reactions to social injustice by individuals and groups as a function of social norms, gender and anonymity. *Social Justice Research,* *8*(1), 7–40.

Rabbie, J. M., Schot, J. C., & Visser, L. (1989). Social identity theory: A conceptual and empirical critique from the perspective of a behavioural interaction model. *European Journal of Social Psychology, 19,* 171–202.

Rabbie, J. M., & van Oostrum, J. (1984). Environmental uncertainty, power and effectiveness in laboratory organizations. In C. M. Stephenson & J. H. Davis (Eds.), *Progress in applied social psychology* (pp. 207–261). London: Wiley.

Rabbie, J. M., & Visser, L. (1972). Bargaining strength and group polarization in intergroup relations. *European Journal of Social Psychology, 4,* 401–416.

Rabbie, J. M., Visser, L., & van Oostrum, J. (1982). Conflict behaviour of individuals, dyads and triads in mixed-motive games. In H. Brandstätter, J. H. Davis, & G. Stocker-Kreichgauer (Eds.), *Group decision-making* (pp. 315–343). London: Academic Press.

Rabbie, J. M., Visser, L., & Vernooy, L. (1976). Uncertainty of the environment, differentiation and influence distribution in university departments. *Nederlands Tijdschrift voor de Psychologie, 31,* 285–303.

Rabbie, J. M., Schot, J. C., & Visser, L. (1987, July). *Instrumental intragroup cooperation and intergroup competition in the minimal group paradigm.* Paper presented at the Social Identity Conference, University of Exeter, Great Britain.

Rabbie, J. M., & Schot, J. C. (1989, July). *Instrumental and relational behavior in the minimal group paradigm.* Paper presented at the First European Congress of Psychology, Amsterdam.

Rabbie, J. M., & Schot, J. C. (1990). Group behaviour in the minimal group paradigm: Fact or fiction? In P. J. D. Drenth, J. A. Sergeant, & R. J. Takens (Eds.), *European perspectives in psychology* (Vol. 3, pp. 251–263). Chichester, England: Wiley.

Rabbie, J. M., Schot, J. C., Visser, L., & Lodewijkx, H. F. M. (1995). *The effects of goal and means interdependence on allocation behavior in the minimal group paradigm.* Manuscript submitted for publication.

Rabbie, J. M., & Wilkens, G. (1971). Intergroup competition and its effect on intragroup and intergroup relations. *European Journal of Social Psychology, 1,* 215–234.

Raven, B. H., & Rubin, J. Z. (1983). *Social psychology.* New York: Wiley.

Ross, L., & Nisbett, R. E. (1991). *The person and the situation: Perspectives of social psychology.* New York: McGraw-Hill.

Schank, R. C., & Abelson, R. P. (1977). *Scripts, plans, goals and understanding.* Hillsdale, NJ: Lawrence Erlbaum Associates.

Schelling, T. C. (1963). *The strategy of conflict.* Cambridge, MA: Harvard University Press.

Schiffmann, R., & Wicklund, R. A. (1992). The minimal group paradigm and its minimal psychology: On equating social identity with arbitrary group membership. *Theory and Psychology, 2,* 29–50.

Schot, J. C. (1992). *Allocations in the minimal group paradigm: Consequences of social identity pressures and perceived interdependence.* Unpublished doctoral dissertation, University of Utrecht, Utrecht, The Netherlands.

Schot, J. C., Rabbie, J. M., Visser, L., Lodewijkx, H. (1994). *Instrumental and relational conflicts in the minimal group paradigm.* Manuscript submitted for publication.

Schruijer, S. G. L. (1990). *Norm Violation, attribution and attitudes in intergroup relations.* Tilburg, The Netherlands: Tilburg University Press.

Shaw, M. E. (1971). *Group dynamics: The psychology of small group behavior* (3rd ed.). New York: McGraw-Hill.

Sherif, M. (1936). *The psychology of social norms.* New York: Harper.

Sherif, M. (1966). *Group conflict and cooperation.* London: Routledge & Kegan Paul.

Sherif, M. (1967). *In common predicament.* Boston: Houghton Mifflin.

Sherif, M., Harvey, O. J., White, B. J., Hood, W. R., & Sherif, C. (1961). *Intergroup conflict and co-operation: The Robbers Cave experiment.* Norman: University of Oklahoma, Institute of Intergroup Relations.

Sherif, M., & Sherif, C. W. (1969). *Social psychology.* New York: Harper & Row.

Sherif, M., & Sherif, C. W. (1979). Research on intergroup relations. In W. G. Austin & S. Worchel (Eds.), *The social psychology of intergroup relations* (pp. 7–18). Monterey, CA: Brooks-Cole.

Smith, C. A. (1991). The self, appraisal, and coping. In C. R. Snyder & D. R. Forsyth (Eds.), *Handbook of social and clinical psychology* (pp. 116–137). New York: Pergamon.

Stephan, W. G. (1985). Intergroup relations. In G. Lindzey & E. Aronson (Eds.), *Handbook of social psychology* (3rd ed., pp. 599–650). New York: Random House.

Sumner, W. G. (1906). *Folkways.* New York: Ginn.

Tajfel, H. (1982). Instrumentality, identity and social comparison. In H. Tajfel (Ed.), *Social identity and intergroup relations* (pp. 483–507). Cambridge, England: Cambridge University Press.

Tajfel, H., Billig, M. G., Bundy, H. P., & Flament, C. I. (1971). Social categorization and intergroup behavior. *European Journal of Social Psychology, 1,* 149–178.

Tajfel, H., & Turner, J. C. (1979). An integrative theory of intergroup conflict. In W. G. Austin & S. Worchel (Eds.), *The social psychology of intergroup relations* (pp. 33–47). Monterey, CA: Brooks-Cole.

Tajfel, H., & Turner, J. C. (1986). The social identity theory of intergroup behavior. In S. Worchel & W. G. Austin (Eds.), *Psychology of intergroup relations* (pp. 7–24). Chicago: Nelson-Hall.

Tannenbaum, A. S. (1968). *Control in organization.* New York: McGraw-Hill.

Taylor, S. E., & Brown, J. D. (1988). Illusion and well-being: A social psychological perspective on mental health. *Psychological Bulletin, 103,* 193–210.

Taylor, S. E., & Lobel, M. (1989). Social comparison activity under threat: Downward evaluation and upward contacts. *Psychological Review, 96,* 569–575.

Triandis, H. C. (1989). The self and social behavior in different cultural contexts. *Psychological Review, 96,* 506–520.

Triandis, H. C. (1992). Comments [on a paper by Hinkle et al., 1992]. *Revista de Psicología Social, Monográfico,* 113–115.

Turner, J. C. (1981). The experimental social psychology of intergroup behavior. In J. C. Turner & H. Giles (Eds.), *Intergroup behaviour* (pp. 66–101). Oxford, England: Blackwell.

Turner, J. C. (1982). Towards a cognitive redefinition of the social group. In H. Tajfel (Ed.), *Social identity and intergroup relations* (pp. 15–40). Cambridge, England: Cambridge University Press.

Turner, J. C. (1988). Foreword. In M. A. Hogg & D. Abrams (Eds.), *Social identifications: A social psychology of intergroup relations and group processes* (pp. xi–xv). London and New York: Routledge.

Turner, J. C., Hogg, M. A., Oakes, P. J., Reicher, S. D., & Wetherell, M. S. (1987). *Rediscovering the social group: Self-categorization theory.* Oxford, England: Blackwell.

Turner, R. M., & Killian, L. W. (1972). *Collective behavior* (2nd ed.). Englewood Cliffs, NJ: Prentice-Hall.

van Haren, T. (1984). *Power in organizations.* Unpublished doctoral dissertation, University of Utrecht, Utrecht, The Netherlands.

van Looy, L. (1982). *Participation in decision-making and centralization of influence processes in research organizations.* Unpublished doctoral dissertation, University of Utrecht, Utrecht, The Netherlands.

van Oostrum, J., & Rabbie, J. M. (1988). Participation in decision making: A contingency approach. *Gedrag en Organisatie, 1*(2), 55–70.

van Oostrum, J., & Rabbie, J. M. (1991). Environmental uncertainty, influence structures and effectiveness of laboratory organization: An experimental approach. *Gedrag en Organisatie, 6,* 411–428.

van Oostrum, J., & Rabbie, J. M. (1995). Intergroup competition and cooperation within autocratic and democratic management regimes. *Small Group Research, 2,* 269–295.

Visser, L. (1995). *Cooperation and competition between groups and individuals.* Unpublished doctoral dissertation, University of Utrecht, Utrecht, The Netherlands.

Wegner, D. M. (1987). Transactive memory: A contemporary analysis of the group mind. In B. Mullen & G. R. Goethals (Eds.), *Theories of group behavior* (pp. 185–208). New York: Springer-Verlag.

Weick, K. E. (1979). *The social psychology of organizing.* Reading, MA: Addison-Wesley.

Wills, T. A. (1991). Social comparison processes in coping and health. In C. R. Snyder & D. R. Forsyth (Eds.), *Handbook of social and clinical psychology* (pp. 376–394). New York: Pergamon.

Zillmann, D. (1979). *Hostility and aggression.* Hillsdale, NJ: Lawrence Erlbaum Associates.

11

SIMILARITIES AMONG VARIOUS CONCEPTUAL POSITIONS AND THEORETICAL POINTS OF VIEW

Erich H. Witte
University of Hamburg, Hamburg

Of course, it is not my intention to find a theoretical integration of the various conceptual approaches into one general theory. My aim is much more modest. I would like to show the similarities and dissimilarities among the different viewpoints as a first step to a more general theory of small-group behavior.

WHAT IS A SMALL GROUP?

This is an easy question but with a difficult answer. Most of the authors seem to prefer a systems-theoretical approach with some qualities of the small group not being reducible to individual behavior. Sometimes this is called the chemistry of the group. Such a theoretical viewpoint has some simple consequences: If it is acceptable to view a small group as a system, then there is a *structure*, a *process*, a *goal*, a *boundary*, and a *surrounding*. These are the constituent elements of a system, in general. Thus, if a small group is a microsystem, we should talk about these elements. Furthermore, a systems-theoretical approach also looks for the system-building and temporal developments of these processes. However, from these basic assumptions it does not follow that all systems-theoretical discussion should be based on chaos or catastrophe theory, as these are very special models of system behavior (see, e.g., Vallacher & Nowak, 1994). There is also the classical approach of system theory used for small groups by Simon (1952) almost totally ignored in small-group research (Witte, 1990). The most rudimentary systems-theoretical approach uses compound parameters of the group as a whole. Such parameters (e.g., the mean of the individual reactions) are not reducible to a single member. This rudimentary approach takes into account only one step of a dynamic process in which group influence occurs, and it leaves out the interaction between steps.

It is true that our research does not often explicitly need the metaphysical assumption of small groups as social systems. However, this background knowledge leads us to questions and problems that follow from such basic assumptions. The theory of social systems is a sort of framework theory posing questions and to some extent showing ways in which solutions may later be found (see chapter 6 of this volume). It is a heuristic, though almost never methodological device for generating and examining the data in group research (but see, Vol. 1). There is an increasing level of complexity of the research due to the need to integrate different approaches with their specific partial methodology (see introductory chapter of this volume). Because of this and of the increasing knowledge gained in this area, there is a necessity to differentiate between processes and outcomes that at first glance look similar. The consequent models of higher complexity need a more sophisticated data analysis to formalize the heuristic of a social system. Until now the idea of a social system has been thought of in a metaphorical sense. However, this is nothing less than the broadening of simple causal relations, which are simply very restricted systems-theoretical processes (Aulin, 1989). The discussion of the content in the chapters of this volume should be organized around the main elements of a social system given earlier.

WHAT IS SAID ABOUT THE STRUCTURE
OF A SMALL GROUP?

This is a very intensively discussed theme in this volume. The processes observed in groups can be seen as a reflection of their existing structure. If the conditions remain stable, then the structure will become more differentiated with time because the behavior of the individuals is guided by rules that stabilize the existing structure (see chapter 3 of this volume). This is, on one hand, a kind of stabilizing of the microsystem by role differentiation and, on the other hand, an integration of the individual behavior into a group pattern. This, consequently, leads to the discussion of the leadership role in small groups (see chapter 4 of this volume). Leadership is exerted by power and influence in order to control the group behavior, which is the systematically organized behavior of the group members to reach a goal. Such a role helps the individual member invest some of his or her resources because he or she expects comparable investments, which are controlled by the leader, from the other group members. Often he or she is also seen as the most capable member of the group to reach the goal and, as a consequence, other group members are extremely influenced by his or her view. Both aspects of leadership—power and influence—usually converge in group settings. This principle of stabilizing the microsystem has also the consequence of reducing the effectiveness of teams working on complex problems (see chapter 5 of this volume).

But this is only one side of such a role. Sometimes a compensation effect is observed to be produced by the more capable member of the group (see chapter 2 of this volume). If the structure, however, is not cleared up and stabilized, a production increase of the group might be observed, should the member with the lower ability tries to invert the given structure by a motivation gain. Contrary to this effect there is a motivation loss if there is a group product without structure (social loafing). Thus, as an isolated phenomenon, group structure might be positive or negative for the production process. Because of this, a more complex theoretical perspective is necessary.

WHAT IS SAID ABOUT THE PROCESSES IN SMALL GROUPS?

If the processes are the dependent variables and the structural components the independent variables, then linear positive and negative relationships are assumed along with curvilinear relationships containing a maximum in the middle (see chapter 5 of this volume). In addition to the shapes of the relationships being different, there is also a qualitative difference between these processes, which depend on the tasks' properties. Thus the processes have to be differentiated according to the goals to be reached. This goal dependency of the processes mediated by properties of tasks is called a teleological explanation. This kind of explanation has been introduced by Perez and Mugny (see chapter 7 of this volume) in their conflict elaboration theory. Different tasks elicit different conflicts between group members. Furthermore, a differentiating structural component is introduced causing conflict with a majority or minority. These two kinds of variables together determine the influence process of the group members as targets. There is another process enhanced by a group condition called confirmation bias (see chapter 8 of this volume). This is something like a collective strategy avoiding cognitive dissonance. This process also depends on such structural variables as the homogeneity of the group and the formal leadership. Thus, both structural characteristics help to stabilize the group as a microsystem as it is understood from the earlier discussion of its structure.

Now it should be described how this tendency can be reached. It can be reached through information selection, which is also a kind of conflict resolution. Thus, the observed confirmation bias should be dependent on the kind of goal to be reached and, consequently, on the properties of the task. For example, the confirmation bias could be reduced by an influence of a minority working on a problem of divergent thinking. Obviously, there is an interdependence between structure, goal, and process that has to be explained more specifically by a more complex theory.

WHAT HAS BEEN SAID ABOUT THE GOALS
OF THE SMALL GROUP?

There has been almost nothing said about goals of small groups. Sometimes the discussion of information pathologies, confirmation biases, motivation gains or losses, conformity effects, and so forth, gives us the impression that there is a goal that has not yet been reached. It is not only the question of how to create the ideal group, but also the question of what an ideal group is and who sets the standard for such a group. In our experimental research the standard is often implicitly introduced by means of the task chosen, by the experimenter, and by means of his or her expectation and evaluation. Sometimes social decision schemes or other models are used to find a reference standard for the evaluation of the group product.

This view, however, is a very restricted evaluation standard, taking only the experimenter's point of view into consideration. Does this view coincide with the views of the group members? What do we know about the intended goals of the group members? In general, only a combination of the two perspectives—the goal mediated by the task and the goal mediated by the needs of the group members—can be accepted as the goal of the microsystem in the sense used here. For example, the confirmation bias or the information pathologies are evaluations only from the perspective of viewing the task. If the need of the group members is selected, then these effects might be called social support or a positive social relationship. Usually, in small-group research there exists social standards that function as an evaluation of the observed processes or results. But what is the difference between conformity and solidarity? Obviously, it is neither the result nor the process but the evaluation. The evaluation, however, might diverge between experimenter and group member. Is a reduction in effort a free-riding effect or a motivation loss called social loafing? Perhaps, it is only the solution of two divergent tasks (Witte, 1994), namely the given task and the group-functioning task. The last one is introduced implicitly by the social condition and works in the following manner: The subjects feel as members of a microsystem, which may be established under minimal social conditions (see chapter 10 of this volume); they then want to be integrated into the group; furthermore, they assume that they are better than the average member and, as a consequence, feel they have to reduce their efforts to get the group functioning. The reason for the reduction of effort is cooperation and not free-riding or social loafing. On the level of viewing the group as a microsystem with a more complex task, the same empirical effect can be explained as illustrating a contrary social value. If the goal of the microsystem is defined as being more complex, then by taking both perspectives together, the evaluation of the observed results should become more cautious and accurate. Perhaps, the difficulties found to explain the empirical results of the Köhler effect depend on these different goal settings of the subjects (see chapter 2 of this volume). The interpretation of the experimental condition, the social representation of the group functioning, and the interpretation of the task have to be combined into a single complex explanation.

WHAT IS SAID ABOUT THE BOUNDARY OF A SMALL GROUP?

There are two lines of research that discuss this phenomenon. The first is the research on the minimal group paradigm, which focuses on finding out the sufficient conditions that establish a group feeling (see chapter 10 of this volume). The results are that a common fate together with a categorization are sufficient to distinguish a boundary with which a clear ingroup–outgroup bias can be observed. The second line starts with the categorization of the small-group members into different reference groups as boundaries and then tries to apply this theoretical conception on the small group (see chapter 9 of this volume). One result is that the understanding of group cohesiveness cannot be reduced to interpersonal attraction but rather is a phenomenon that has to be studied on the group level. Such a position implies a boundary that generally differentiates ingroup from outgroup. Furthermore, the process of distinguishing boundaries has to be implemented into this theoretical position, which is the central question of the first line of research. Thus, both approaches are more or less complementary and should be integrated. This is the intention of chapters 9 and 10. The boundary is both a dependent and an independent variable in small-group research.

WHAT HAS BEEN SAID ABOUT THE SURROUNDINGS OF SMALL GROUPS?

Mostly, the idea of the surrounding of a small group has been reduced to that of a competitive outgroup, as in the tradition of the classical research of Sherif's summer camps. However, the introduction of such a variable has been discussed more broadly (e.g., chapters 5, 6, and 10 of this volume).

There still exists a main problem: How do we characterize this more or less diffuse environment of a small group? In organizational psychology there is the idea of a corporate identity or of an organizational culture or climate as a surrounding of the work groups. In our experimental research with ad hoc groups the surrounding might be irrelevant, because the surrounding influences the processes in all experimental conditions. Often the surrounding plays an important role if natural groups are studied, because there is an interdependence effect between the surrounding and the internal processes, for example, the general climate for or against innovations in an organization and the intensity of the discussion in working teams about possible improvements. Sometimes sport teams create or change a surrounding for better results. This is, of course, with the idea that the surrounding helps. This is also true for scientific teams who need a stimulation from outside. This influence from the surrounding on the internal processes is neglected if we exclude the competition effect between groups or, to some extent, the effect of crowding conditions, from which a reduction of the problem-solving capacity or an increase of aggressiveness in a small group follows. Or if divorce is a socially acceptable behavior and one knows other couples well who are divorced, then it is easier to separate from one's own partner. That which has been called zeitgeist effects or the influence of a social value (see Witte, Vol. 1) can be subsumed under the influence of the surrounding in a more cognitive sense than that in which the more physically based crowding effects are understood. If these phenomena are to be interpreted as depending on the surrounding, then there will be many more effects labeled under this heading, for example, that which has been called "shared knowledge" (Tindale, Vol. 1) and the macrosystem's influence on leadership characteristics used in the small group (see chapter 4 of this volume). With this kind of reinterpretation of social phenomena, the systems-theoretical concept of a surrounding plays a more important role than before expected.

CONCLUSION

This preliminary discussion of the different conceptual viewpoints in this volume under elementary systems-theoretical conceptions can give some guidelines for theoretical integration. A small group as a microsystem has to be interpreted under all of the various aspects together, because these various aspects are the constituent elements of the system if such an elaborate view can be reduced to such basic assumptions (see chapter 6 of this volume). This systems-theoretical perspective not only tries to hint at what is not integrated into a theoretical approach but also at how research can be brought together under a more abstract viewpoint. To some extent, such a viewpoint might help to differentiate and integrate at the same time. Both are necessary for small-group research because both of these aspects open up more alternatives. The other demand has been given in the introductory chapter where the methodological necessity for a paradigm enrichment was discussed. Both demands together, in my view, will help to improve small-group research if we do not forget to formalize the theoretical concepts as was illustrated—though mostly without a systems-theoretical perspective—in several of the chapters in Volume 1.

Because our lives often depend on small-group decisions (a surgical team, a crew in the cockpit, jury decisions, etc.), it is a fundamental task for us to get a deeper understanding of small-group behavior, and finally, to create an "ideal group." This deeper understanding by means of theoretical discussions was the intention of the two volumes.

REFERENCES

Aulin, A. (1989). *Foundations of mathematical system dynamics.* Oxford, England: Pergamon.

Simon, H. A. (1952). A formal theory of interaction in social groups. *American Sociological Review, 17*, 202–211.

Vallacher, R. R., & Nowak, A. (Eds.). (1994). *Dynamical systems in social psychology.* San Diego: Academic Press.

Witte, E. H. (1990). Zur Theorie sozialer Systeme und ihre Verwendung in Soziologie und Sozialpsychologie: Ein klassisches Beispiel, moderne Begriffsbildungen und abzuleitende Konsequenzen. In E. H. Witte (Ed.), *Sozialpsychologie und Systemtheorie* (pp. 145–166). Braunschweig, Germany: Braunschweiger Studien.

Witte, E. H. (1994, June). *Group performance—The solution of two divergent tasks.* Handout presented at the Groups, Networks, and Organizations Conference, Nags Head, NC.

AUTHOR INDEX

A

Abakoumkin, G., 51, 65
Abelson, R. P., 103, 122, 276, 292
Abrams, D., 204, 206, 228, 229, 230, 232, 234, 235, 244, 247, 249, 256, 259, 270, 286, 288
Ajzen, I., 132, 145, 275, 276, 278, 279, 280, 287
Albanese, R., 14, 28
Albert, S., 120, 122
Alexander, D., 14, 34
Allen, V. L., 191, 195, 206
Allison, S. T., 79, 87
Allport, F. H., 267, 287
Ames, M., 79, 89
Ammann, R., 161, 164, 186
Ancona, D. G., 17, 19, 27, 28
Anderson, L. R., 14, 30
Anderson, R. E., 83, 87
Aranda, E., 16, 33
Argyle, M., 130, 133, 144, 150, 184
Arkoff, A., 82, 90
Arnscheid, R., 51, 57, 63, 64, 65
Arrowood, A. J., 82, 84, 89
Asch, S. E., 194, 200, 206, 218, 224, 256, 272, 287
Ashbrook, R. M., 20, 32
Ashby, W. R., 95, 122
Asuncion, A. G., 204, 208
Atkin, R. S., 13, 28
Aulin, A., 296, 301
Austin, J. L., 94, 122

B

Bacherach, S. B., 71, 87
Back, K., 233, 235, 248, 256, 288
Bakeman, R., 13, 28
Bales, R. F., 14, 28, 67, 68, 70, 87, 96, 97, 112, 122
Baliga, B. R., 245, 250
Bamberger, P., 71, 87

Bandura, A., 276, 287
Bantel, K. A., 16, 28, 34
Barnard, C., 93, 108, 122
Barnett, L. L., 83, 88
Barnett, W. P., 17, 33
Baron, R. S., 38, 64, 234, 252, 272, 287
Bar-Tal, D., 164, 179, 184
Bass, B. M., 12, 14, 21, 22, 28, 96, 118, 119, 122, 245, 247
Baumgartel, H., 14, 28
Bavelas, A., 169, 184
Beaman, A. L., 14, 29
Beck, D., 1, 8, 129, 145
Beck, S., 13, 28
Beckmann, J., 132, 144, 221, 224
Bekkers, F., 273, 287, 291
Belbin, R. M., 12, 28
Bell, D. V. J., 117, 122
Bennis, W. G., 118, 122
Benoist, F., 264, 291
Berg, D., 153, 186
Berger, J., 70, 71, 73, 74, 76, 87, 88, 89, 90
Berger, P. L., 131, 144, 262, 277, 287
Berkowitz, L., 23, 33
Berry, P. C., 37, 65
Berscheid, E., 77, 90
Billig, M. G., 230, 240, 247, 252, 256, 259, 260, 261, 262, 266, 283, 284, 285, 293
Birbaumer, N., 130, 144
Birnbach, G., 138, 145
Bishop, D. W., 234, 250
Black, R. H., 22, 24, 32
Blackstone, T., 191, 210
Blackwell, J. W., 74, 87
Blatter, Th., 156, 184
Block, C. H., 37, 65
Block, C. J., 18, 30
Bond, M. A., 13, 28
Bornstein, G., 287, 287
Bottger, P., 14, 34
Bourgeois, M., 241, 253
Bourhis, R. Y., 230, 252
Boyd, S. D., 19, 29

Braden, J. L., 83, 88
Brandstätter, V., 200, 206
Branthwaite, A., 263, 287
Braver, S. R., 78, 79, 90
Brawley, L. R., 13, 29
Bray, R. M., 13, 22, 28
Brehm, J. W., 139, 144
Bresnitz, H., 212, 224
Brett, J. F., 17, 19, 20, 31
Brewer, M. B., 14, 15, 29, 32, 78, 89, 233, 234, 242, 247, 270, 281, 287
Brickner, M. A., 14, 29
Brockner, J., 138, 145, 222, 224
Broverman, D. M., 73, 88
Broverman, J. K., 73, 88
Brown, J. D., 277, 293
Brown, R. J., 230, 242, 247, 252, 255, 284, 286, 288
Bruins, J., 71, 83, 88, 91
Bruun, S. E., 42, 64
Bryman, A., 118, 119, 122
Buchanan, J. M., 40, 64
Bühler, K., 6, 8
Bundy, H. P., 256, 259, 260, 261, 262, 266, 283, 284, 285, 293
Bundy, R. P., 230, 252
Burgess, J. W., 13, 29
Burns, J. M., 118, 119, 120, 122
Burnstein, E., 101, 122, 234, 247
Burt, C., 130, 145
Busceme, M. S., 191, 210
Buschmeier, U., 133, 144, 145
Butera, F., 191, 194, 198, 200, 203, 206, 207, 208, 209
Butler, R., 71, 88
Buys, C. J., 13, 29
Byrne, D., 238, 247

C

Cacioppo, J. T., 101, 124, 195, 196, 209, 277, 280, 288, 290
Caldwell, D. F., 17, 19, 27, 28, 33
Caldwell, M., 82, 88
Callaway, M. R., 240, 247
Callon, M., 107, 108, 122
Campbell, D. T., 234, 247, 250, 256, 263, 270, 281, 287, 289
Caplow, T., 82, 88
Carron, A. V., 13, 14, 29
Carter, L., 17, 30

Cartwright, D., 102, 111, 122, 133, 145, 256, 258, 287
Carver, C. S., 159, 184, 280, 287
Castagne, T., 217, 225
Castore, C. H., 17, 34
Caudron, S., 16, 29
Chaiken, D., 219, 225
Chaiken, S., 191, 196, 206, 207, 275, 288
Chang, S., 214, 218, 225, 239, 253
Cheney, D. L., 130, 145
Chertkoff, J. M., 83, 88
Chin, M. G., 278, 287
Christensen, C., 157, 185
Cialdini, R. B., 191, 206, 208
Cini, M.A., 13, 29, 243, 244, 251
Clark, R. D., 4, 8, 180, 181, 182, 183, 185, 191, 198, 204, 207
Clarkson, F. E., 73, 88
Coch, L., 233, 248
Cochrane, S., 235, 247
Codol, J. -P., 243, 248
Cohen, A., 18, 31
Cohen, E. G., 74, 88
Cohen, M. D., 116, 122
Cohen, S. P., 112, 122
Cole, S. G., 83, 88
Collins, B. E., 67, 88
Comrey, A. L., 22, 24, 29
Condor, S., 230, 248
Conger, J. A., 119, 122
Cooper, D. M., 17, 19, 20, 31
Cooper, J., 235, 250
Cooper-Shaw, L., 237, 243, 249
Copper, C., 239, 251
Cosier, R. A., 19, 29
Costanzo, Ph. R., 165, 186
Couch, A., 17, 30
Coulon, D. A., 153, 186
Courtright, J. A., 240, 248
Cranach, M. von, 114, 122, 151, 152, 154, 156, 157, 161,162, 164, 166, 176, 179, 183, 184, 185, 186, 187
Crano, W., 202, 207
Crozier, M., 108, 110, 123
Crum, L., 286, 287

D

Dachler, H. P., 245, 250
Dalton, D. F., 19, 29
Daniel, H. -D., 1, 8, 129, 145
David, B., 235, 251

Davidson, B., 235, 249
Davidson-Podgorny, G., 13, 32
Davis, J. H., 22, 34, 134, 145
Dawes, R. M., 37, 64, 78, 79, 88, 90
Day, N. E., 19, 30
de Brey, J. H. C., 264, 291
De Gilder, D., 72, 73, 74, 88
De Soto, C. B., 68, 88
De Swaan, A., 82, 88
De Waal, F. B. M., 82, 88
DeBiasio, A. R., 18, 29
Deitcher, J., 138, 145
DeNinno, J. A., 17, 34
Dennis, A. R., 13, 29
Deschamps, J. -C., 241, 248
Desportes, J. P., 13, 29
Deutsch, M., 76, 88, 101, 123, 200, 201,
    207, 234, 248, 256, 258, 265, 266, 267,
    273, 274, 275, 276, 277, 278, 279, 284,
    288
Devanna, M. A., 118, 125
Diehl, M., 13, 29, 43, 51, 57, 63, 64, 65,
    230, 248
Diener, E., 14, 29
Dion, K. L., 281, 288
Doise, W., 103, 105, 114, 116, 123, 124,
    194, 200, 207, 208, 228, 234, 241, 248,
    250, 259, 271, 288
Doms, M., 191, 207
Dörner, D., 161, 185
Dovidio, J. F., 205, 207
Doyle, S., 263, 287
Driskell, J. E., 12, 21, 22, 29, 30, 74, 90
Driver, M. J., 137, 145
Driver, R. W., 239, 250
Duchon, D., 24, 29
Duck, J. M., 243, 246, 248
Duffy, T., 12, 29
Dukerich, J. M., 118, 124
Dumaine, B., 12, 29
Durand, V. M., 14, 29

E

Eagly, A. H., 191, 196, 207, 275, 288
Eden, D., 22, 24, 34
Edwards, J. E., 15, 33
Eflal, B., 234, 252
Egan, T. D., 17, 34
Ehrlich, S. B., 118, 124
Eiser, J. R., 241, 248
Elejabarrieta, F., 204, 208

Ellemers, N., 200, 206, 230, 253
Ely, P. G., 286, 288
Emshoff, J. R., 222, 225
Epting, L. A., 19, 29
Erffmeyer, E. S., 14, 29
Erlick, D. E., 23, 33
Esser, J. K., 220, 224, 239, 247, 248
Etzioni, A., 131, 133, 136, 145
Evans, N. J., 239, 248
Evans, R. I., 194, 209

F

Falomir, J. M., 205, 209
Farr, R. M., 131, 145, 164, 185
Federico, R. F., 16, 29
Feld, P., 214, 218, 225, 239, 253
Feld, S. L., 13, 30
Ference, R., 220, 225
Fernandez, J. C., 22, 29
Fernandez, J. P., 16, 29
Ferrini-Mundy, J., 21, 29
Festinger, L., 57, 63, 64, 71, 88, 102, 103,
    104, 123, 130, 132, 137, 145, 194, 201,
    207, 211, 212, 219, 224, 233, 235, 248,
    256, 288
Fiedler, F. E., 234, 250
Fierres, R., 205, 209
Fimrite, R., 21, 29
Fink, C. F., 13, 34
Finkelstein, S., 13, 30
Fisch, R., 1, 8, 129, 145
Fischer, G. W., 242, 250
Fisek, M. H., 74, 76, 87
Fishbein, M., 132, 145, 275, 276, 279,
    280, 287
Fisher, R. J., 234, 248
Fiske, S. T., 68, 69, 88, 276, 288
Flament, C. I., 230, 252, 256, 259, 260,
    261, 262, 266, 283, 284, 285, 293
Flowers, M. L., 239, 240, 249
Foa, U. G., 130, 145
Fodor, E. M., 138, 145, 240, 248
Folkman, S., 276, 289
Ford, R. S., 74, 90
Ford, T. W., 74, 90
Foti, R. J., 23, 35
Fox, J., 14, 30
Frank, F., 14, 30
Fraser, S. C., 14, 29
French, J. R. P., 68, 88, 97, 110, 123, 167,
    185, 233, 248

Frey, B. S., 40, 41, 42, 65
Frey, D., 212, 214, 216, 217, 221, 224, 225
Fries, A., 212, 224
Frijda, N. H., 277, 288
Fry, L. W., 15, 30

G

Gaertner, S. L., 205, 207
Galanter, E., 147, 150, 159, 185, 280, 290
Galen, M., 18, 30
Gallistel, C. R., 159, 185
Gamson, W. A., 83, 85, 88
Gaudard, M., 21, 29
Gaviria, E., 200, 206
Geen, R. G., 241, 248
George, J. M., 19, 30
Gerard, H. B., 101, 123, 200, 201, 207, 207, 234, 248, 278, 288
Gerber, P., 156, 184
Gerhard, H. B., 277, 288
Gersick, C. J. G., 97, 123
Gianinazzi, M., 198, 208
Gierschner, H. C., 131, 133, 139, 146
Giles, H., 228, 230, 253, 230, 248
Gill, D. L., 22, 30
Giosue, F., 200, 206
Glover, S. H., 19, 29
Goldenbeld, C., 264, 275, 279, 280, 288, 291
Graumann, C. F., 99, 123, 245, 248
Graves, J., 39, 64
Green, S. G., 24, 29
Greenstein, T. N., 74, 89
Griffin, G. W., 239, 249
Griffith, S. J., 15, 34
Grofman, B., 13, 30
Grzelak, J. L., 278, 288
Gugler, B., 154, 184
Guyer, M., 14, 30
Guzzo, R. A., 14, 30

H

Haberkorn, G., 191, 204, 207
Habermas, J., 2, 8, 94, 123
Hacker, W., 159, 161, 173, 185
Hackman, J. R., 97, 123, 135, 145
Haefner, D., 17, 30
Hains, S. C., 1, 7, 8, 11, 32, 228, 238, 239, 240, 246, 248, 249, 251
Haleblian, J., 13, 30

Hall, J., 129, 145
Hallmark, B. W., 23, 31
Hamberger, H., 14, 30
Hanson, L., 14, 34
Harbour, J. L., 15, 30
Hardie, E. A., 236, 237, 249
Hardin, G., 78, 88
Hardy, C. J., 14, 30
Hare, A. P., 13, 30
Harkins, S. G., 13, 14, 15, 29, 31, 34, 40, 42, 64, 65, 241, 248
Harré, R., 4, 8, 156, 185
Harring, K., 286, 287
Harrington, H., 230, 249, 272, 288
Hart, P.'t., 220, 224
Harvey, O. J., 257, 258, 293
Haslam, S. A., 230, 232, 242, 249, 251
Hatfield, E., 277, 288
Haythorn, W. W., 16, 17, 27, 30
Heckhausen, H., 158, 185
Heide, H., 130, 146
Heider, F., 71, 88, 132, 145, 276, 288
Heilman, M. E., 18, 30, 199, 207
Heller, T., 67, 90
Hembroff, L. A. 75, 89
Hensley, T. R., 239, 249
Herman, C. P., 191, 210
Herzog, W., 2, 8
Heslin, R., 12, 30
Higgins, E. T., 138, 145, 277, 289
Hill, G. W., 13, 22, 30, 213, 225
Hinkle, S., 255, 284, 286, 288
Hodson, D., 19, 30
Hoffman, L. R., 16, 30
Hoffmann, L., 131, 133, 139, 146
Hogan, R., 12, 21, 22, 29, 30
Hogg, M. A., 1, 7, 8, 11, 32, 101, 105, 106, 111, 125, 175, 176, 177, 178, 179, 187, 203, 204, 206, 207, 210, 228, 229, 230, 232, 234, 235, 236, 237, 238, 239, 240, 241, 243, 244, 245, 246, 247, 248, 249, 251, 253, 256, 259, 260, 263, 266, 269, 270, 284, 285, 286, 288, 293
Hollander, E. P., 106, 108, 123
Hollingshead, A. B., 170, 171, 172, 173, 174, 185
Hollister, L. A., 19, 30
Holmes, J. G., 77, 89
Holzworth, D. W., 237, 243, 249
Homans, G. C., 76, 77, 80, 86, 89
Hood, W. R., 257, 258, 293
Hornstein, H. A., 261, 288

Horwitz, M., 256, 257, 258, 259, 260, 262, 263, 264, 266, 268, 269, 272, 281, 282, 289, 291
House, J. S., 2, 8
House, R. J., 117, 123
Houser, R., 138, 145
Hu, L. -T., 14, 15, 33, 242, 251
Huguet, P., 200, 202, 206, 207, 208
Hunt, J. G., 245, 250
Huseman, R. C., 239, 250
Huygen, 264, 291

I-J

Ibánez, T., 204, 208
Indermühle, K., 154, 184
Ingham, A. G., 39, 64
Iniguez, L., 204, 208
Insko, C. A., 132, 145, 281, 286, 287, 289
Inverarity, J., 234, 250
Irle, M., 132, 144, 211, 221, 224, 225
Isenberg, D. J., 234, 250
Jackson, S. E., 12, 16, 17, 19, 20, 28, 30, 31
Jacques, E., 104, 120, 123
James, J., 13, 31
Janis, I. L., 119, 123, 136, 137, 145, 211, 213, 220, 225, 234, 239, 250
Jantsch, E., 149, 185
Jarvis, P.A., 23, 248
Jaspars, J. M. F., 165, 185, 228, 250
Jehn, K. A., 18, 31
Jesaitis, P. T., 19, 30
Jette, R. D., 14, 30
Johnson, D. W., 135, 137, 138, 145, 146, 232, 250, 265, 266, 268, 272, 289
Johnson, F. P., 232, 250
Johnson, P., 230, 248
Johnson, R. T., 135, 137, 138, 145, 146, 265, 266, 268, 272, 289
Jones, E. E., 199, 207, 242, 252
Jones, M. B., 19, 21, 24, 31
Jones, R. G., 199, 207
Jovanovic, J., 204, 209, 210
Judd, C. M., 242, 251
Julian, J. W., 234, 250
Julin, J. A., 17, 19, 20, 31

K

Kahn, R. L., 85, 89, 108, 111, 115, 116, 117, 119, 123, 166, 185, 275, 289
Kaiser, C., 197, 200, 208, 209

Kanter, R. M., 12, 18, 26, 31, 100, 123
Kanungo, R. N., 119, 122
Karau, S. J., 14, 31, 44, 62, 65, 241, 253
Kashy, D. A., 23, 31
Kasterstein, J., 73, 89
Katz, A. H., 19, 20, 31
Katz, D., 85, 89, 108, 111, 115, 116, 117, 118, 119, 123, 166, 185, 275, 289
Katzell, R. A., 14, 30
Katzenbach, J. R., 12, 31
Kelem, R. T., 14, 29
Kelley, H. H., 82, 84, 89, 106, 123, 234, 250, 256, 261, 275, 276, 278, 289
Kelman, H. C., 199, 207
Kenny, D. A., 23, 31, 35
Kerr, H. L., 42, 64
Kerr, N. L., 13, 15, 22, 31, 34, 28, 38, 64, 272, 287
Keys, C. B., 13, 28
Kiessler, K., 138, 145
Killian, L. W., 279, 293
Kimmel, M. J., 256, 279, 290
Kipnis, D., 138, 139, 146
Kirchmeyer, C., 18, 31
Kirmeyer, S. L., 14, 34
Kirsch, W., 131, 146
Kitayama, S., 275, 286, 290
Klabermatten, U., 154, 184
Knottnerus, J. D., 74, 89
Koenigs, R. J., 112, 122
Kohlberg, L., 120, 123
Kohler, H., 157, 185
Köhler, O., 38, 44, 45, 46, 47, 48, 49, 50, 51, 52, 53, 59, 64
Komorita, S. S., 82, 89
Kotter, J. P., 110, 118, 123
Kramer, R. M., 14, 29, 270, 287
Kravitz, D. A., 39, 64
Kroon, B. R., 269, 289
Kroon, M., 200, 206
Kruglanski, A. W., 191, 192, 197, 201, 207, 278, 289
Kuhn, T. S., 2, 6, 8
Kumar, K., 20, 34

L

LaFasto, F. M. J., 12, 31
Lage, E., 179, 186
Lamb, R., 165, 185
Langham, P., 17, 30
Larson, C. E., 12, 31

Larson, J. R., 22, 34, 157, 185
Larson, K. L., 13, 29
Lasch, E., 198, 207
Lassiter, D. L., 12, 32
Latané, B., 14, 15, 30, 31, 34, 40, 42,
    64, 65, 101, 123, 191, 195, 207
Latour, B., 107, 108, 122, 123
Lauderdale, P., 234, 250
Laughlin, P. R., 18, 22, 31, 170, 171, 172,
    173, 174, 185, 193, 207
Lawler, E. E., 117, 124, 279, 290
Lawrence, P. R., 107, 123, 273, 275, 289
Lazarus, R. S., 276, 289
Legrenzi, P., 194, 201, 203, 206
Lemaine, G., 73, 89, 198, 204, 207, 261, 289
Lemaine, J. M., 13, 29
Leoni, C., 198, 208
Lerner, J., 77, 89
Leve, C., 240, 253
Leventhal, G. S., 77, 89
Levi, A., 103, 122
Levine, J. M., 11, 13, 20, 24, 27, 29, 31, 32,
    191, 196, 207, 244, 245, 250, 251, 277, 289
LeVine, R. A., 234, 250, 256, 263, 270, 289
Levinger, G., 39, 64
Lewin, K., 98, 99, 100, 123, 255, 256,
    257, 258, 261, 264, 266, 267, 268, 269,
    271, 279, 286, 289
Leyens, J. -P., 244, 251, 268, 289
Libby, R., 27, 31
Lieberson, S., 118, 123
Liebrand, W. B. G., 278, 290
Lightbown, N., 263, 287
Likert, R., 111, 123
Lindoerfer, J. S., 220, 224, 239, 248
Linville, P. W., 242, 250
Lippit, R., 98, 99, 100, 123, 233, 250
Little, B. R., 155, 185
Llavata, E., 205, 209
Lloyd, K., 138, 145
Lobel, M., 277, 293
Lockheed, M. E., 26, 31
Lodewijkx, H. F. M., 263, 264, 265, 266,
    271, 272, 274, 275, 277, 278, 280, 289,
    290, 291, 292
Longley, J., 240, 250
Lonner, W. J., 130, 146
Lord, R. G., 117, 118, 123, 124
Lorenzi-Cioldi, F., 228, 250
Lorge, I., 37, 64
Lorsch, J. W., 107, 123, 273, 275, 289
Lott, A. J., 235, 250

Lott, B. E., 235, 250
Lucas, J. A., 18, 30
Luckmann, T., 131, 144, 262, 277, 287
Lumsden, C. J., 13, 33
Lundgren, S., 191, 210
Lundy, J. L., 19, 31
Lüthgens, C., 212, 214, 215, 224

M

Maass, A., 4, 8, 180, 181, 182, 183, 185,
    191, 198, 204, 207, 208, 210
Maccoby, E. E., 20, 31
Mackie, D. M., 191, 204, 207, 208, 235,
    250, 251, 270, 280, 286, 290
Magaro, P. A., 20, 32
Maggi, J., 193, 198, 208
Maher, K. J., 117, 118, 123, 124
Maheswaran, D., 219, 225
Maier, J. R. F., 16, 30
Maier, N. R. F., 138, 146
Mann, L., 14, 32, 219, 225
Manstead, A. S. R., 228, 250
Manz, C. C., 239, 251
March, J. G., 116, 122, 280, 290
Markus, H., 67, 68, 89, 275, 286, 290
Marquart, D. I., 37, 64
Marques, J. M., 234, 234, 244, 251
Martens, T., 212, 224
Martin, B., 39, 64
Martin, M. W., 75, 89
Martin, R., 204, 208
Maruyama, G., 135, 137, 138, 145
Marwell, G., 27, 32, 79, 89
Mason, R. O., 222, 225
Matern, B., 173, 185
May, W. H., 130, 146
Maznevski, M. L., 16, 19, 32
McAdams, J., 12, 29
McCain, B. R., 17, 32
McCauley, C., 214, 225, 240, 251
McClintock, C. G., 278, 287, 290
McGarty, C., 230, 232, 235, 242, 249, 251
McGrath, J. E., 13, 32, 97, 124, 149,
    152, 158, 185, 272, 290
McGuire, C. V., 26, 32, 214, 218, 225,
    239, 253
McGuire, W. J., 26, 32
McKirnan, D. J., 230, 245, 253
McPherson, J. M., 13, 20, 32
Meertens, R., 82, 91
Meindl, J. R., 118, 124

Merton, R. K., 266, 290
Messé, L. A., 80, 83, 89
Messick, D. M., 15, 32, 78, 79, 87,
  89, 90, 241, 251, 270, 280, 286, 290
Meyer, G., 241, 248
Michaelsen, L. K., 20, 22, 24, 32, 34
Miller, C. E., 19, 32
Miller, D. T., 77, 89
Miller, G. A., 147, 159, 185, 280, 290
Miller, J. G., 149, 185
Miller, K. I., 138, 146
Miller, N., 13, 32, 38, 54, 230, 249, 272,
  287, 288
Mills, T. M., 14, 28
Mintzberg, H., 108, 110, 124, 275, 290
Miron, M. S., 130, 146
Mitroff, I. I., 222, 225
Mlicki, P. P., 263, 264, 265, 280, 282,
  282, 285, 290
Moede, W., 38, 64
Mokken, R. J., 82, 89
Monge, P. R., 138, 146
Montanari, J. R., 239, 251
Montgomery, H., 219, 225
Moorhead, G., 220, 225, 239, 251
Morchain, P., 200, 206
Moreland, R. L., 1, 7, 8, 11, 13, 20, 27, 29
  31, 32, 228, 243, 244, 245, 246, 250, 251
Moreno, J. L., 167, 186
Morgan, B. B., 12, 32
Morgan, G., 108, 124
Morley, I. E., 234, 251
Morris, C. G., 135, 145
Moscovici, S., 4, 8, 67, 89, 94, 101, 102, 103,
  105, 106, 110, 113, 114, 116, 124, 131, 145,
  164, 174, 179, 180, 181, 182, 185, 186,
  191, 200, 202, 195, 198, 205, 208, 209,
  212, 214, 216, 218, 224, 225, 245, 248
Mucchi-Faina, A., 198, 204, 208, 210
Mudrack, P. E., 235, 251
Mugny, G., 101, 113, 124, 191, 192, 193,
  194, 197, 198, 199, 200, 201, 202, 203, 204,
  205, 206, 207, 208, 209, 210
Mulder, M., 84, 91
Mullen, B.,14, 15, 26, 32, 33, 239, 242, 251
Mundell, B., 71, 87
Murnigham, J. K., 83, 89, 153, 186

N

Nadler, D. A., 119, 124
Naffrechoux, M., 179,186

Nahavandi, A., 16, 33
Nanus, B., 118, 122
Nasser, D. L., 12, 33
Nathanson, S., 138, 145
Navarro, E., 204, 209, 210
Neck, C. P., 220, 25
Nehnevajsa, J., 167, 186
Nelson, D., 135, 137, 138, 145
Nemeth, C. J., 16, 18, 33, 116, 117, 124,
  194, 198, 201, 202, 209
Newman, G. A., 15, 33
Nida, S., 14, 31
Nisbett, R. E., 262, 267, 277, 292
Noble, A. M., 22, 28
Norman, R. Z., 74, 76, 87
Norton, F. T. M., 14, 28
Nowak, A., 295, 301

O-P

O'Brien, G. E., 24, 33
O'Connor, J. F., 118, 123
O'Dell, J. W., 13, 14, 33
O'Reilly, C. A., 17, 32, 34
Oakes, P. J., 26, 33, 101, 105, 106,
  111, 125, 175, 176, 177, 178, 179,
  187, 203, 204, 210, 230, 232, 234,
  242, 249, 251, 253, 256, 260, 263,
  266, 268, 284, 285, 293
Ochsenbein, G., 157, 161, 162, 176,
  184, 185, 186
Olson, J. M., 191, 210
Olson, M., 79, 89
Oosterbaan, H., 264, 291
Oppewal, H., 79, 91
Orbell, J. M., 37, 64, 78, 79, 90
Osborn, A. F., 37, 64
Osgood, C. E., 130, 146
Ostrom, T. M., 14, 29
Ouellette, J. A., 191, 210
Owen, G., 13, 30
Owens, A. G., 24, 33
Paez, D., 234, 244, 251
Paicheler, G., 182, 186, 191, 209
Papastamou, S., 197, 204, 208, 209
Park, B., 242, 251
Park, W. -W., 214, 225
Parker, G. M., 12, 33
Parker, J., 234, 250
Parsons, T., 93, 94, 108, 124, 152, 186
Partridge, P., 133, 146
Patterson, M. L., 14, 33

Peckham, V., 39, 64
Pelz, D. C., 100, 124
Pelz, J., 133, 146
Penrod, S., 191, 195, 210
Peregoy, P. L., 121, 125
Pérez, J. A., 101, 124, 191, 192, 194, 198,
    199, 200, 201, 202, 203, 204, 205, 206,
    207, 208, 209, 210
Personnaz, B., 73, 89, 197, 198, 199, 200,
    202, 208, 209
Peters, J., 118, 124
Petersen, R. P., 138, 146
Peterson, R. S., 214, 218, 225, 239, 253
Petty, R. E., 40, 64, 101, 14, 195, 196,
    209, 280, 290
Peyronnin, K., 17, 19, 20, 31
Pfeffer, J., 17, 32, 108, 118, 124, 266,
    290
Phillips, J. C., 80, 83, 89
Piaget, J., 120, 124, 136, 137, 146
Platov, M. J., 278, 290
Plutchik, R., 130, 146
Porter, L. W., 117, 124, 279, 290
Potter, J., 230, 253
Powers, W., 159, 186
Pratkanis, A. R., 240, 253
Pribram, K. H., 147, 150, 159, 185, 280,
    290
Probasco, P., 240, 253
Pruitt, D. G., 234, 240, 250, 252, 256,
    278, 279, 290
Pruyn, J., 83, 84, 91
Pugh, D., 108, 124
Pugh, M. D., 74, 89
Pujol, M., 200, 206
Pulver, U., 155, 186

Q-R

Quattrone, G. A., 242, 252
Rabbie, J. M., 256, 257, 258, 259, 260,
    261, 262, 263, 264, 265, 266, 267, 268,
    269, 270, 271, 272, 273, 274, 275, 276,
    277, 278, 279, 280, 281, 282, 283, 284,
    285, 288, 289, 290, 291, 292, 293, 294
Raisinghani, D., 110, 124
Raju, N. S., 15, 33
Rapson, R. L., 277, 288
Raven, B. H., 67, 68, 88, 97, 110, 123,
    167, 185, 239, 252, 272, 274, 292
Raza, S., 21, 30

Reicher, S. D., 101, 105, 106, 111, 125,
    175, 125, 175, 176, 177, 178, 179, 187,
    203, 204, 210, 230, 252, 253, 256, 260,
    263, 266, 268, 284, 285, 293
Rescher, N., 6, 8
Resnick, L. B., 277, 289
Reynolds, K. J., 238, 249
Ricateau, P., 198, 207
Rice, F., 19, 33
Ridgeway, C. L., 26, 33, 71, 72, 89, 90
Rijsman, J. B., 6, 8, 57, 63, 64
Riker, W. H., 85, 90
Ringelmann, M., 39, 64
Riordan, C., 74, 90
Rokeach, M., 120, 124, 194, 209
Roper, S. S., 74, 88
Rosch, M., 212, 224
Roseborough, M. E., 14, 28
Rosenberg, S., 23, 33
Rosenholtz, S. J., 70, 71, 73, 88
Rosenkrantz, P. S., 73, 88
Ross, L., 235, 252, 262, 267, 277, 292
Rotchford, N., 13, 32
Rothbart, M., 242, 251
Roux, P., 200, 209
Rubin, J. C., 138, 145, 272, 274, 278,
    290, 292
Rubini, M., 200, 206
Ruck, H. W., 161, 186
Ruess, M., 59, 64
Ruggiero, J., 74, 90
Russo, E. M., 191, 207
Rutte, C. G., 79, 90
Ryan, C. S., 242, 251

S

Sachdev, I., 230, 252
Salancik, G. R., 266, 290
Salas, E., 12, 14, 15, 22, 29, 33, 34
Salovey, P., 242, 250
Sampson, E. E., 71, 76, 90
Samuelson, D., 78, 79, 90
Samuelson, P. A., 40, 65
Sanchez-Mazas, M., 191, 204, 208, 210
Sanders, G. S., 234, 252
Sapin, B., 161, 186
Schachter, S., 233, 235, 248, 256, 288
Schadron, G., 268, 289
Schaerer, M., 162, 186
Schaffer, R. E., 14, 33
Schank, R. C., 276, 292

Scharf, A., 12, 33
Scheier, M., 159, 184, 280, 287
Schein, E. H., 27, 33
Schelling, T. c., 262, 292
Schiffmann, R., 286, 292
Schneider, B., 20, 33
Schoggen, P., 14, 33
Scholl, W., 127, 129, 131, 133, 134, 138, 139, 144, 145, 146
Schopler, J., 132, 145, 281, 289
Schot, J. C., 261, 262, 263, 264, 265, 269, 269, 270, 271, 273, 281, 282, 283, 285, 292
Schriesheim, C. A., 245, 250
Schruijer, S. G. L., 270, 292
Schulz-Hardt, S., 212, 214, 216, 217, 224, 225
Schutz, W. C., 12, 18, 33
Schwartzkopf, A., 22, 32
Schwenk, C. R., 222, 225
Secord, P. F., 156, 185
Sell, J., 75, 89
Sessa, V. I., 17, 19, 20, 31
Sev'er, A., 74, 90
Seyfarth, R. M., 130, 145
Sharp, W., 24, 34
Shaw, M. E., 13, 16, 22, 33, 37, 65, 165, 169, 186, 265, 292
Sheppard, J. A., 14, 33, 43, 65
Sherif, C. W., 233, 252, 257, 258, 264, 279, 293
Sherif, M., 111, 124, 218, 225, 234, 252, 256, 257, 258, 263, 264, 266, 268, 270, 273, 279, 292, 293
Shiflett, S., 21, 33
Shils, E. A., 152, 186
Shore, S. D., 21, 29
Simon, B., 242, 252
Simon, H. A., 107, 110, 124, 131, 146, 290, 295, 301
Sims, H. P., 239, 251
Singh, J. V., 13, 33
Skon, S., 135, 137, 138, 145
Slater, P. E., 13, 33
Slocum, J. W., 15, 30
Smith, C. A., 276, 277, 293
Smith, D. K., 12, 31

Smith, K. A., 138, 146, 153, 186
Smith, L., 71, 90
Smith, P. W., 194, 209
Smith, R. F., 74, 87
Smith, S., 239, 252
Smith, T., 138, 145, 240, 248
Smith-Cunnien, P., 234, 250
Smith-Lovin, L., 13, 20, 32
Snyder, R. C., 161, 186
Sobol, R., 14, 28
Solomon, H., 37, 64
Stagner, R., 234, 252
Stahelski, A., 275, 278, 289
Stahlberg, D., 212, 224
Stangor, C., 191, 206
Stasser, G., 13, 22, 34
Staw, B. M., 16, 33, 116, 117, 124
Stein, R. T., 67, 90
Steiner, I. D., 6, 8, 14, 18, 27, 34, 37, 38, 57, 65, 97, 124, 128, 134, 136, 140, 146, 158, 186
Stephan, W. G., 242, 252, 270, 277, 287, 293
Stephenson, G. M., 234, 251
Steur, Th., 82, 91
Stewart, I. N., 121, 125
Stogdill, R., 96, 125
Stokman, F. N., 82, 89
Streufert, S., 137, 145
Strodtbeck, F. L., 14, 28
Stroebe, W., 6, 8, 13, 29, 40, 41, 42, 43, 51, 64, 65, 241, 248
Sullivan, P., 23, 31
Sumner, W. G., 283, 293
Svenson, O., 219, 225
Swezey, R. W., 14, 34
Symonds, C., 14, 15, 33
Syroit, J., 263, 278, 290
Szymanski, K., 40, 42, 64, 65, 241, 248

T

Taber, T. D., 24, 29
Tajfel, H., 103, 104, 111, 125, 175, 177, 186, 205, 210, 228, 230, 240, 241, 247, 252, 256, 259, 260, 261, 262, 263, 266, 269, 276, 281, 282, 283, 284, 285, 286, 293
Tanford, S., 191, 195, 210
Tannenbaum, A. S., 273, 284, 293
Taylor, D. M., 230, 245, 253

Taylor, D. W., 37, 65
Taylor, L. A., 13, 19, 29, 34
Taylor, S. E., 68, 88, 276, 277, 288, 293
Terborg, J. R., 17, 34
Terry, D. J., 243, 246, 248, 249
Tetlock, P. E., 214, 218, 225, 239, 253
Théorêt, A., 110, 124
Thibaut, J. W., 106, 123, 256, 262, 278, 286, 287, 289
Thomas, E. J., 13, 34
Thommen, B., 161, 164, 186
Thompson, J. D., 107, 111, 125
Tichy, N. M., 118, 125
Tindale, R. S., 22, 34
Tomaszewski, T., 161, 186
Torrance, E. P., 138, 146
Traxel, W., 130, 146
Triandis, H. C., 275, 286, 293
Trotman, K. T., 27, 31
Tschan, F., 151, 157, 161, 176, 185, 186, 187
Tsui, A. S., 17,34
Tullock, G., 40, 64
Turner, J. C., 94, 95, 101, 102, 103, 104, 105, 106, 111, 125, 175, 176, 177, 178, 179, 187, 191, 203, 204, 210, 228, 230, 231, 232, 234, 235, 236, 240, 242, 247, 249, 251, 252, 253, 256, 259, 260, 261, 262, 263, 266, 268, 269, 276, 281, 282, 283, 284, 285, 286, 293
Turner, R. M., 279, 293
Tushman, M. L., 119, 124
Tziner, A., 22, 24, 34

U-V

Ulich, E., 173, 187
Valach, L., 157, 161, 185
Valacich, J. S., 13, 29
Vallacher, R. R., 80, 83, 89, 295, 301
Van Avermaet, E., 198, 208
Van de Kragt, A. J. C., 78, 79, 90
Van der Linden, W. J., 82, 90
Van Dijk, E., 80, 90
Van Fleet, D. D., 14, 28
van Haren, T., 274, 293
van Knippenberg, A., 83, 91, 230, 253
van Kreveld, D., 269, 289
van Looy, L., 274, 293
van Oostrum, J., 266, 267, 269, 272, 273, 275, 276, 278, 280, 281, 292, 193, 194

Van Osdol, D., 21, 29
Venderstoep, S. W., 170, 171, 172, 173, 174, 185
Verbeek, A., 82, 90
Vernooy, L., 274, 281, 292
Vinacke, W. E., 82, 90
Vinokur, A., 101, 122, 234, 247
Visser, L., 261, 262, 263, 264, 265, 269, 270, 271, 272, 273, 274, 278, 280, 281, 282, 283, 285, 291, 292, 294
Vogel, S. R., 73, 88
Vogt, J. F., 15, 34
Volpato, C., 204, 210
Volpert, W., 159, 187
von Wright, G. H., 3, 8
Vroom, V. H., 117, 125

W

Wagner, D. G., 74, 76, 87, 90
Wahrman, R., 74, 89
Walster, E., 77, 90
Walster, G. W., 77, 90
Waterman, R. H., 118, 124
Watson, W. E., 20, 2, 24, 32, 34
Webb, J., 234, 251
Weber, J. G., 242, 247
Weber, M., 93, 107, 108, 110, 125
Webster, M.A., Jr., 74, 75, 90
Wegner, D. M., 13, 34, 164, 187, 277, 294
Weick, K. E., 116, 125, 274, 294
Weingart, L. R., 15, 34
Wekselberg, V., 157, 187
Weldon, E., 15, 34
West, S. G., 191, 208
Wetherell, M. S., 101, 105, 106, 111, 125, 175, 176, 177, 178, 179, 187, 203, 203, 210, 230, 234, 235, 247, 251, 253, 256, 260, 263, 266, 268, 284, 285, 293
White, B. J., 257, 258, 293
White, K. M., 246, 249
White, R. K., 98, 99, 100, 123, 233, 250
Whyte, W. H., 233, 253
Wicker, A. W., 14, 34
Wicklund, R. A., 221, 225, 286, 292
Widemeyer, W. N., 13, 29
Wiersema, M. F., 16, 34
Wilder, D., 204, 210
Wilensky, H. L., 140, 146

Wilke, H. A. M., 71, 72, 73, 77, 79, 80, 82, 83, 84, 88, 90, 91
Wilkens, G., 257, 264, 281, 292
Williams, K. D., 13, 14, 15, 31, 34, 40, 42, 44, 62, 64, 65, 241, 253
Williamson, S. A., 112, 122
Willinghöfer, U., 144, 146
Wills, T. A., 277, 294
Wilson, L. A., II, 78, 79, 90
Winklund, R., 212, 224
Winton, W., 26, 32
Wit, A. P., 79, 91
Witte, E. H., 2, 3, 4, 8, 35, 50, 63, 65, 101, 125, 295, 298, 301
Wittenbraker, J., 286, 287
Wolf, S., 101, 123, 191, 195, 207, 210
Wood, W., 16, 34, 191, 210
Woolgar, S., 107, 123
Worth, L. T., 204, 208
Wright, R. A., 43, 65

Y-Z

Yamagishi, T., 15, 34
Yetton, P., 14, 34
Yukl, G. A., 116, 125
Yzerbyt, V. Y., 244, 251, 268, 289
Zaccaro, S. J., 14, 23, 31, 34, 35
Zajonc, R. B., 12, 35, 39, 65, 68, 89
Zander, A., 256, 258, 287
Zanna, M. P., 191, 210
Zelditch, M., Jr., 70, 71, 73, 88
Ziller, R. C., 16, 35
Zillmann, D., 278, 294
Zimmer, I., 27, 31

SUBJECT INDEX

A-D

Action theory, 147-184
Attitude change, 95, 96, 101, 176, 255, 275, 280
Brainstorming, 37, 43
Bureaucracy, 109-111
Coalition formation, 75, 81-85, 116, 223
Cohesion, 197, 204, 213, 232, 235-239, 246, 256, 258, 264, 265, 268, 273, 283-285, 299
Combinational rules
additive, 21, 24, 27, 44, 49, 52-54, 61-63
Combinatorial rules, 21
interactive, 21, 22, 24, 27, 44, 45, 61-63
Commitment, 15, 20, 95, 212
Communication acts, 94
Competition, 58, 62, 63, 95, 118, 119, 138, 258, 273, 274, 278, 281-285
Confirmation bias, 212-214, 218, 222, 297, 298
Conformity, 73, 74, 95, 100, 101, 104, 108, 110, 111, 115, 119, 136, 180, 191, 199-205, 214, 218, 219, 227, 232, 234, 235, 242, 243, 273, 298
Congruence, 127, 132-134, 140-144
Consensus, 19, 104, 194, 218
Coordination, 15, 24, 48, 135, 159, 160
Creativity, 24, 37, 99, 117, 202
Criterion of truth, 2-6
Culture, 3, 95, 103, 110, 131, 175, 205, 223, 270, 275, 286
Disciplinary matrices, 2-4, 6, 7
Dissonance, 127, 172, 183, 211-223, 297

E-G

Equality, 40, 75, 76, 85
Ethics, 120
Fairness, 75-77, 79-81, 85-87, 115, 260-264, 277, 279
Free riding, 14, 40-43, 61, 78
Group-natural, 13, 25, 28, 99, 127, 129, 140-144

Group laboratory, 20, 99, 129, 173
Group action, 148, 152-157, 158-162, 172-174, 273
Group chemistry, 12, 21-25, 132-134
Group composition, 11-28, 132-134
Group conflict, 11-13, 15-18, 20, 75-78, 84, 86, 97, 102, 118, 119, 191-206, 297
Group dynamics, 12, 13, 127, 128, 152, 167, 168, 177, 178, 227, 255-287, 298
Group member diversity, 12, 15-20, 214, 215, 218, 297
Group member characteristics, 11-13, 16, 25, 73-75, 258
Group moderation techniques, 131
Group norm, 20, 41, 80, 104, 168, 169, 223, 233
Group performance, 11-14, 16, 17, 23, 37-39, 45-47, 67, 134, 140-144, 170-175, 273
Group size, 11-15, 41-44, 127, 215, 268, 273
Group structure, 11-13, 18, 19, 68-70, 96, 97, 130-132, 148, 152, 158-160, 164, 165, 169, 174, 237, 241, 242, 258, 295
Group tasks, 14, 18, 27, 38, 39, 41-43, 55-58, 96, 134, 135, 157-160, 164, 165, 173, 174, 192-195, 272
Groupthink, 4, 5, 95, 119, 136-139, 211, 213, 214, 218, 220, 222, 234, 239-241

I-K

Ingroup-outgroup differentiation, 94, 95, 111, 114, 191, 195, 196, 198, 203-205, 229, 238, 255, 258-264, 273, 275, 281-287
Innovation, 16, 7, 95, 99, 100, 102, 104, 108, 111, 113, 116, 117, 121, 127, 139-143, 180, 221, 297, 299
Köhler effect, 37-63, 298

L

Lay epistemics, 127, 192, 196, 200-202
Leader, 15, 23, 27, 50, 67-87, 93-122, 131, 157, 159, 165, 167, 174, 214, 216-218, 221, 222, 245, 246, 258, 267, 296

M

Majority, 19, 108, 191, 196, 199, 200, 202, 214, 215, 219, 255, 257, 273
Methodological approaches, 2
Micro sociology, 128
Minimal group, 105, 108, 230, 240, 256, 257-264, 280-287, 208, 299
Minority influences, 4, 16, 113, 169, 179-183, 191, 196, 199, 200, 202, 205, 215, 216, 218, 243, 255, 257, 297
Motivation, 74, 114-121, 154, 157, 158, 163, 172, 218, 229, 234, 242, 261, 265, 270, 277
Motivation gain, 43-63, 298
Motivation loss, 13-15, 38-43, 298

N

Needs, 18, 86, 130, 134, 261, 277
Negotiation, 19, 81-85, 95, 102, 105, 116, 131, 180, 232, 234, 272-274, 277, 278
Nominal group, 23, 24, 27, 37

O-P

Opinion, 11, 193-195, 203-205, 218, 223
Paradigm, 2, 99, 101, 103
Paradigm change, 2, 3, 6
Paradigm enrichment, 2, 3, 6, 300
Partial methodology, 2, 98, 296
Partial methodology
  action research, 3, 25, 129
  hermeneutics, 3
  ideology critique, 3
  scientistic, 2, 4, 7
Persuasion, 93, 95, 195
Power, 71,93-122, 127, 129-133, 138, 139, 163, 167, 174, 245, 246, 274, 296
Problem solving, 127
Process loss, 14, 38, 39

R

Reactance, 127, 199
Research interest, 2, 3
Ringelmann effect, 38, 39
Role, 13, 165, 166, 232, 244, 245, 257, 286

S

Self-categorization, 94, 95, 101, 104, 111, 113, 115, 169, 175-179, 183, 203, 227-247, 255-287
Small-group, 1, 2-4, 7, 148-152, 227-247, 295, 296
Small-group research
  psychological, 2, 264-271
Small-group research
  sociological, 2, 127-144, 148-152, 295
Social cognition, 102, 276, 277, 279, 280
Social comparison, 51, 57, 61-63, 130, 131, 219, 277
Social compensation, 44, 52
Social decision schemes, 134, 170-175, 298
Social dilemma, 78-81, 271-280
Social identity, 227-247, 265, 269
Social influence, 70-75, 86, 93-122, 127, 163, 175, 191-206, 232, 234, 246
Social loafing, 14, 40, 61, 163, 227, 241, 297
Social psychology, 1
  faces, 1
  crisis, 1, 2
Social representation, 67, 69, 131, 151, 161, 164, 168, 179, 183, 299
Socialization process, 20, 227, 244, 245, 279
Status, 27, 50, 67-87, 166, 167, 174, 261
Symbolic interactionism, 3
Symlog, 112-114
Synergy, 13, 24, 149
System, 110, 111, 115, 128, 129, 147-184, 267-269, 271-273, 281, 295-300
System level, 26, 106, 127, 131, 147, 148, 150-155, 171, 174, 175, 181-183, 269-271
System theory, 148-164, 295

T

Team, 15, 17, 19, 21, 127-144, 220, 233, 281, 300
Trust, 19, 121